The BioPesticide Manual

First Edition

Editor: L G Copping

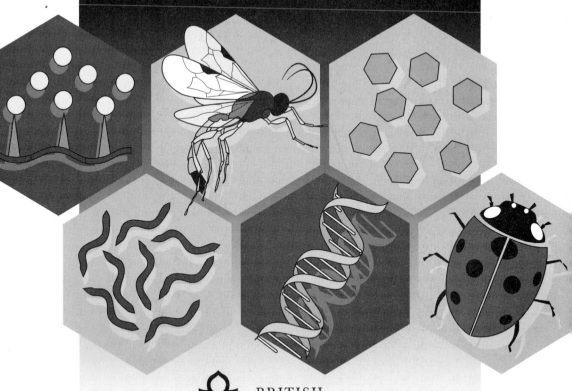

BRITISH
CROP
PROTECTION
COUNCIL

British Library Cataloguing in Publication Data.
A catalogue record of this book is available from the British Library.

ISBN 1 901396 26 6

Cover design by Major Design & Production, Nottingham
Typographic design by Alan Brannan Design, Stowmarket
Typeset and printed by Page Bros, Norwich

Published by:
British Crop Protection Council, 49 Downing Street, Farnham, Surrey GU9 7PH, UK
Tel: +44 (0)1252 733072   Fax: +44 (0)1252 727194
Email: md@bcpc.org   Internet: www.bcpc.org

All BCPC publications can be brought from:
BCPC Publications Sales, Bear Farm, Binfield, Bracknell, Berks RG42 5QE, UK
Tel: +44 (0)118 934 2727   Fax: +44 (0)118 934 1998
Email: publications@bcpc.org

Disclaimer
Every effort has been made to ensure that all information in this edition of *The BioPesticide Manual* is correct at the time of going to press. However, the editor and the publisher do not accept liability for any error or omission in the content, or for any loss, damage or any other accident arising from the use of the products listed therein.

Before handling, storing or using any crop protection product, it is essential to follow the manufacturer's instructions on the label.

Contents

1. Natural Products

2. Pheromones

3. Living Systems

4. Insect Predators

5. Genes

Reference

Foreword

For nearly 30 years, *The Pesticide Manual*, published by the British Crop Protection Council (BCPC), has been the standard reference work on pesticides. The great majority of active ingredients in the products listed in this established volume are synthetic chemicals, though progressively more and more natural products have been cited in recent editions.

Due to intense public pressure to exploit, wherever possible, environmentally benign agents for pest control, either alone or alongside synthetic compounds in integrated pest management programmes, the number of marketable natural agents, products and their derivatives has greatly increased. There are now enough in use to merit a separate publication devoted entirely to them. BCPC has, therefore, launched *The BioPesticide Manual* as an authoritative world compendium of the diverse range of natural compounds, living systems and genes now commercially available for pest, disease and weed control. It complements *The Pesticide Manual* in content and style, offering detailed information, in a readable form, on the sources, production, targets, biological activity, properties and tradenames of more than 170 "active ingredients" in over 500 biocontrol products.

The BioPesticide Manual is addressed to a wide international audience concerned with crop production, amenity uses, woodland planting and wildlife conservation. It will prove indispensable to the agrochemical industry, field advisors, private and government consultants, conventional and organic growers, nurseries, researchers in crop protection and molecular biology, seed companies, regulatory bodies, local authorities, reference libraries, indeed anyone with a professional interest in food and water quality, land use for farming or recreation and the conservation of terrestrial and aquatic flora and fauna.

I believe it is destined to enjoy the success and repeated up-dating of its already acclaimed companion publication. I strongly recommend this book to all concerned with new perspectives in crop protection.

Trevor Lewis
Lawes Trust Senior Fellow, Rothamsted
Formerly Director
Institute of Arable Crops Research, UK

The Publisher

This first edition of *The BioPesticide Manual* is published by the British Crop Protection Council (BCPC) – a registered charity. Formed in 1967, the principle objective of the BCPC is 'to promote and encourage the science and practice of crop protection for the benefit of all.'

BCPC brings together a wide range of organisations interested in the improvement of crop protection. The members of the Board represent the interests of government departments, the agrochemical industry, farmers' organisations, the advisory services and independent consultants, distributors, the research councils, agricultural engineers, environment interests, training and overseas development.

The corporate members, at 1 October 1998, of the BCPC are:

Agricultural Engineers Association
Association of Applied Biologists
Association of Independent Crop Consultants
Biotechnology and Biological Sciences Research Council
British Agrochemicals Association
British Institute of Agricultural Consultants
British Society for Plant Pathology
British Society of Plant Breeders
Campden & Chorleywood Food Research Association
Department for International Development
Department of Agriculture for Northern Ireland
Department of the Environment
Imperial College, London
Lantra
Ministry of Agriculture, Fisheries and Food represented by
    Pesticides Safety Directorate
National Association of Agricultural Contractors
National Farmers' Union
National Institute of Agricultural Botany
Natural Environment Research Council
Scottish Office Agriculture, Environment and Fisheries Department
Society of Chemical Industry – Crop Protection Group
United Kingdom Agricultural Supply Trade Association

To obtain further information about the BCPC, its activities, conferences or publications, please contact:

The General Secretary, British Crop Protection Council, 49 Downing Street, Farnham, Surrey GU9 7PH, UK

Tel: +44 (0)1252 733072   Fax: +44 (0)1252 727194
Email: gensec@bcpc.org   Internet: www.bcpc.org

Preface

The idea of producing a book dedicated to crop protection products derived from natural sources has been considered by BCPC for some time. It was important to ensure that such a book complemented *The Pesticide Manual* and included entries appropriate for a manual of biologically-based products but excluded from *The Pesticide Manual*. After two or more years of effort, the first edition of *The BioPesticide Manual* has been completed.

This publication is written in a different style to *The Pesticide Manual* in that it covers in detail the biological effects observed with all products listed and, wherever possible, gives information on the mode of action plus key references for readers to pursue if they wish. To ensure that no information is lost, the reader is referred to the appropriate entry number in *The Pesticide Manual* where details of chemistry, synthesis and physico-chemical data may be found.

The BioPesticide Manual is divided into five distinct sections:

1. Natural Products — containing 30 different naturally-occurring chemicals which have been commercialised for use in crop protection strategies.

2. Pheromones — containing 45 different pheromones used in mating disruption, lure and kill, or insect monitoring strategies. The 45 listed are amongst the most widely used products.

3. Living Systems — containing 60 entries of baculoviruses, protozoa, bacteria, fungi and nematodes used widely in crop protection.

4. Insect Predators — distinct from the Living Systems section, this comprises 40 insects that are sold commercially for use in the control of phytophagous insects and mites in glasshouses and in outdoor agriculture. It includes both predators and parasites.

5. Genes — containing information on the genes (and their gene products) that have been used to transform world crops to confer tolerance of herbicide application or resistance to attack by viruses or insects.

Most compounds mentioned in the book are highly compatible with organic farming practices and appropriate for use in environmentally sensitive situations. The few exceptions include transgenic crops.

Each individual entry lists a number of commercial products by tradename and company. All approved names, alternative names, common names, tradenames and code numbers are listed in Index 2 and relate to the entry number. Each entry number is preceded by the number (from 1 to 5) that represents the section into which it is placed. The Glossary contains the scientific names of all species and genera mentioned in the main text, classified into order and family. The English – Latin glossary is an attempt to make the finding of a species whose scientific name is not known as easy as possible.

Many people have contributed significantly to the production of *The BioPesticide Manual*. Colleagues at BCPC are mentioned because of their constant help, encouragement and enthusiasm. In particular, Trevor Lewis deserves special mention for overall guidance and support and Clive Tomlin's help was essential for the successful completion of a task that would have been impossible without his guidance, support and technical knowledge.

Section 1 is based on information received from Clive Tomlin (BCPC), Bhupinder Khambay (IACR-Rothamsted) and Gary Thompson (Dow AgroSciences); section 2 relied very heavily on help and advice from Cam Oehlschlager (ChemTica) and Nicky Agelopoulos (IACR-Rothamsted); section 3 was put together with the assistance of Helmut van Emden (University of Reading), Tariq Butt (IACR-Rothamsted) and Peter Smits (Wageningen); section 4 depended very heavily on guidance from Melvyn Fidgett (Novartis BCM), Wilf Powell (IACR-Rothamsted) and Helmut van Emden (University of Reading); and much advice was given by Ben Miflin (IACR-Rothamsted), Peter Shewry (IACR-Long Ashton) and Colin Merritt (Monsanto) in the production of section 5.

Others who have assisted in various ways include John Pickett (IACR-Rothamsted), Isamu Yamaguchi (Riken Institute) and Bernard Blum (IOBC). Paul Lister must be acknowledged for his imaginative computer programming and Denis Burges and Douglas Hartley are to be congratulated for the thoroughness of their proof reading.

Finally, I must thank all those individuals from companies around the world for responding to my enquiries and providing the data that you can read in the following pages. Any errors or omissions in the transcription or interpretation of this information gleaned from a variety of sources are my responsibility. I urge you to bring these errors to my attention as soon as possible so that they can be corrected in time for the second edition.

Leonard G Copping, *Editor*

Guide to using *The BioPesticide Manual*

The BioPesticide Manual is divided into five sections:

1. Natural Products;

2. Pheromones;

3. Living Systems;

4. Insect Predators; and

5. Genes.

The general layout of each section is similar and the main headings within each section are often the same. It is intended that *The BioPesticide Manual* will allow users to find information on the nature, origin, mode of action, use, commercial availability, mammalian toxicology and environmental impact of each entry. Those products that also appear in *The Pesticide Manual* - 11th edition are noted by entry number so more detailed information on their chemistry and physico-chemical properties can be found easily.

Sample Entries

The following are sample entries that illustrate how *The BioPesticide Manual* has been designed and to allow the reader to understand the topics that may be found under each heading. The five examples are as listed in the main volume.

Entry No:Approved name *Biological activity*

The Pesticide Manual - 11th edition: Entry number: *Entry number in* The Pesticide Manual *11th edition.*

STRUCTURE: *If a natural product or a pheromone.*

TAXONOMY: *If a living organism a description and classification of the organism by Order and Family.*

NOMENCLATURE: **Approved name:** *Approved common name of chemical plus approval authority, or scientific name plus authority if a living organism.*
Development code: *If the product had a development code.* **Other names:** *Any other names under which the entry may be known.* **Common name:** *Any other common name not necessarily approved by which the entry is known. Trivial or English name of organism.* **CAS RN:** *If a natural product or a pheromone.* **Name of promoter:** *If a gene.*

SOURCE: *If a natural product from where is it derived; if an organism, where is the organism found or from where was it isolated.*

SOURCE OF PROMOTER: *If a gene.*

TARGET PESTS: *Against which pest, disease or weed species is it recommended.*

TARGET CROPS: *In which crops is its use recommended.*

BIOLOGICAL ACTIVITY: **Biology:** *Details of the way the product controls its target pest; if a living organism by parasitism, competition, predation or production of toxic metabolites.*
Mode of action: *Biochemical mode of action for compounds and mechanism of action if living.*
Predation: Egg laying: and **Duration of development:** *Entries for insect predators and parasites.*
Efficacy: *Effectiveness of the product.* **Key references:** *The most relevant reference(s) giving more details about the entry.*

COMMERCIALISATION: **Formulation:** *How the entry is formulated or packaged.*
Tradename: *Name of product and manufacturers name.* **Patent:** *Patents covering the product.*

APPLICATION: *Rate of use, timing and frequency of application.*

PRODUCT SPECIFICATIONS: **Purity:** *Purity of the product. Acceptable contaminants. How the effectiveness is checked.* **Storage conditions:** *How should it be stored.* **Shelf-life:** *For how long will the stored product remain effective.*

COMPATIBILITY: *Any major incompatibilities or recommendations for combination products.*

MAMMALIAN TOXICITY: *As much information on the toxicity of the active ingredient and/or the formulated product as is available to include, where relevant or available:*
   Acute oral LD$_{50}$:
   Acute dermal LD$_{50}$:
   Inhalation:
   Skin and eye: ADI (JMPR):
   Toxicity class:
   Other:
   Reviews:

ENVIRONMENTAL IMPACT AND NON-TARGET TOXICITY: *As much information on the non-target toxicity and environmental impact of the active ingredient and/or the formulated product as is available to include effects on, where relevant and if known:*
   Birds:
   Fish:
   Other aquatic species:
   Beneficial insects:
   Metabolism:
   Behaviour in soil:
   Gene flow: *If a gene.*

Specific examples follow:

Section 1: Natural Products

1 Number representing the section into which the entry is placed e.g. 1 = Natural Products.

2 Sequential entry number.

3 Approved name.

4 Class of biological activity.

5 *The Pesticide Manual* - 11th edition: Entry no:

6 The approved name (with authorities), development code numbers and CAS RN.

7 As all compounds originate in Nature, the original source of every entry is included.

8 Some compounds are synthesised, some extracted from fermentation and some from the natural living organism. This section describes how the product is produced for commercialisation.

9 A list or description of the pest species against which the product is recommended.

10 A list of the crops in which the product is recommended.

11 A detailed list of the biological activity associated with the entry. This will include mode of action (where known) and a summary of the efficacy of the product.

1:27 spinosad
Microbial insecticide

❺ *The Pesticide Manual* - 11th edition: Entry number 754

spinosyn A, R = H-

spinosyn D, R = CH₃-

❻NOMENCLATURE: **Approved name:** spinosad (ANSI, ISO pending).
CAS RN: *[131929-60-7]* spinosyn A; *[131929-63-0]* spinosyn D.
Development codes: XDE-105; DE-105.

❼SOURCE: The commercial product is a mixture of spinosyn A and spinosyn D. Both compounds are secondary metabolites of the soil actinomycete, *Saccharopolyspora spinosa*. The organism is composed of long, yellowish-pink aerial chains of spores encased in distinctive, spiny spore sheaths. The bacterium is aerobic, gram-positive, non-acid fast, non-motile, filamentous and differentiated into substrate and aerial hyphae. The aerial mycelium is yellowish-pink and the vegetative mycelium is yellow to yellowish-brown. The parent strain was originally isolated from an abandoned rum still in the Caribbean.

❽PRODUCTION: Spinosad is obtained from a whole broth extraction following fermentation of the organism on a feedstock of water, vegetable flours, sugar and animal fat.

❾TARGET PESTS: Recommended for the control of caterpillars, leafminers, thrips and foliage-feeding beetles.

❿TARGET CROPS: May be used on row crops (including cotton), vegetables, fruit trees, turf, vines and ornamentals. No crop phytotoxicity has beeen observed.

⓫BIOLOGICAL ACTIVITY: **Mode of action:** Spinosad effects on target insects are consistent with the activation of the nicotinic acetylcholine receptor, but at a different site than for nicotine or imidacloprid. Spinosad also affects GABA receptors, but their role in the overall activity is unclear. There is currently no known cross-resistance to other insecticide classes. **Efficacy:** The mode of action causes a rapid death of target phytophagous insects. Its

12 A list of key references that describe the discovery, effectiveness and commercialisation of the product.

13 Details of the formulation type used commercially, the tradenames and the manufacturer and the patent number.

14 Details of frequency and methods of application and rate of use.

15 Information on the purity of the technical material, details of the recommended storage conditions and shelf-life.

16 Information on incompatibilities and other information on the possibility of interactions between the product and other crop protection products.

17 Toxicological data to include acute oral and dermal LD_{50}, skin and eye effects, no observeable effect level, EPA toxicity codes and any other information on adverse effects.

18 Effects on non-target organisms (birds, fish and other aquatic species), wild-life, persistence, degradation rates and pathways.

moderate residual activity reduces the possibility of the onset of resistance but it is strongly recommended that it be used within a strong, pro-active resistance management strategy. Spinosad is recommended as an Integrated Crop Management tool as it shows no effects on predatory insects such as ladybirds, lacewings, big-eyed bugs or minute pirate bugs. It has reduced activity against parasitic wasps and flies. It is toxic when sprayed directly onto honeybees and other pollinators, but, once dry, residues have little effect.

⓬**Key references:** 1) H A Kirst et al. 1992. In *Synthesis of Agrochemicals III*, D R Baker, J G Fenyes and J J Steffens (eds.), American Chemical Society, Washington DC, 214-25. 2) D J Porteus, J R Raines and R L Gantz. 1996. In *1996 Proceedings of Beltwide Cotton Conferences*, P Dugger and D Richter (eds.), National Cotton Council of America, Memphis, TN, 875-7. 3) T C Sparks et al. 1996. In *1996 Proceedings of Beltwide Cotton Conferences*, P Dugger and D Richter (eds.), National Cotton Council of America, Memphis, TN, 692-6. 4) V L Salgado. 1997. In *Down to Earth*, DowElanco, Indianapolis, IN, **52:1**, 35-44.

⓭COMMERCIALISATION: **Formulation:** Sold as an aqueous-based suspension concentrate (SC) formulation. **Tradenames:** Tracer – Dow AgroSciences, Conserve – Dow AgroSciences, Success – Dow AgroSciences, SpinTor – Dow AgroSciences. **Patents:** US: 5,202,242 (1993); EPO: 375316 (1990).

⓮APPLICATION: The compound is applied at rates of 12 to 150 g per hectare. Apply when pest pressure demands treatment. The active ingredient does not dissolve in water and continual agitation is required to prevent the active ingredient from settling out in the spray tank. The addition of adjuvants has not been shown to improve or reduce the performance of spinosad consistently, with the exception of leafminer control and the penetration of closed canopies, where emulsified vegetable oils have helped.

⓯PRODUCT SPECIFICATIONS: **Purity:** The commercial product is composed of spinosyn A and spinosyn D. Analysis is undertaken by hplc or immunoassay (details from Dow AgroSciences). **Storage conditions:** Spinosad is stable over a wide range of temperatures. Protect from freezing. Shake well before use. **Shelf-life:** The formulated product has a shelf-life of three years.

⓰COMPATIBILITY: No compatibility problems have been identified to date when tank mixing spinosad with other crop protection products, foliar fertilisers or adjuvants. A jar test for compatibility is recommended prior to use.

⓱MAMMALIAN TOXICITY: **Acute oral LD$_{50}$:** male rats 3,783 mg/kg; female rats >5,000 mg/kg. **Acute dermal LD$_{50}$:** rabbits >5,000 mg/kg. **Skin and eye:** Non-irritating to skin but slight irritation to eyes. **NOEL:** The no-observed effect level (NOEL) for dogs, mice and rats following 13 weeks of dietary exposure to spinosad was 5, 6 to 8 and 10 mg/kg/day, respectively. **Other toxicological effects:** In acute and sub-chronic tests, spinosad did not demonstrate any neurotoxic, reproductive or mutagenic effects on dogs, mice or rats.

⓲ENVIRONMENTAL IMPACT AND NON-TARGET TOXICITY: **Bird toxicity:** Spinosad is considered practically non-toxic to birds. The acute oral LD$_{50}$ for both bobwhite quail and mallard duck is 2,000 mg/kg. **Fish toxicity:** Spinosad is considered slightly to moderately toxic to fish. The LC$_{50}$ (96 hour) for rainbow trout, bluegill and carp was 30, 5.9 and 5 mg/litre,

respectively. **Effects on beneficial insects:** Spinosad is considered highly toxic to honeybees with less than 1 µg/bee of technical material applied topically resulting in mortality. Once residues are dry, they are non-toxic. **Metabolism:** Feeding studies produced no residues of spinosad in meat, milk or eggs. The half-life on plant surfaces ranged from 1.6 to 16 days, with photolysis as the main route of degradation. **Behaviour in soil:** Spinosad is rapidly degraded on soil surfaces by photolysis and below the soil surface by soil micro-organisms.

Key reference: D G Saunders and B L Bret. 1997. In *Down to Earth*, DowElanco, Indianapolis, IN, **52:1**, 14-21.

Section 2: Pheromones

1 Number representing the section into which the entry is placed e.g. 2 = Pheromones.

2 Sequential entry number.

3 Approved name.

4 Class of biological activity.

5 The approved name, other names by which it is known and CAS RN.

6 As all compounds originate in Nature, the original source of every entry is included. The authority for the insect's scientific name is given.

7 Most pheromones are synthesised rather than being extracted from the insect.

8 A list or description of the pest species against which the product is recommended (usually a single species).

9 A list of the crops in which the product is recommended.

10 A detailed list of the biological activity associated with the entry. This will include mode of action, behaviour of the insect when exposed to relatively high rates of the pheromone and a summary of the efficacy of the product.

11 A list of key references that describe the discovery, effectiveness and commercialisation of the product.

12 Details of the formulation type used commercially, the tradenames and the manufacturer and the patent number.

13 Details of frequency and methods of application, siting of the pheromone release system and rate of release.

14 Information on the purity of the technical material.

15 Information on incompatibilities and other information on the possibility of interactions between the product and other crop protection products.

16 Toxicological data as far as they are known.

17 Any information on the effects on non-target organisms and the environment.

❶ ❷ ❸

2:65 oryctalure

❹*Rhinoceros beetle aggregation pheromone*

$$CH_3(CH_2)_3CH(CH_3)(CH_2)_2COOCH_2CH_3$$

❺NOMENCLATURE: **Approved name:** oryctalure (ethyl 4-methyloctanoate).
Other names: rhinoceros beetle aggregation pheromone. **CAS RN:** [56196-53-3].

❻SOURCE: Male *Oryctes rhinoceros* (Linnaeus) volatile component that has been shown to attract both male and female adult beetles.

❼PRODUCTION: Manufactured for commercial use.

❽TARGET PESTS: Coconut rhinoceros beetle (*Oryctes rhinoceros*).

❾TARGET CROPS: Young oil palm plantations.

❿BIOLOGICAL ACTIVITY: **Mode of action:** Oryctalure is the aggregation pheromone of the coconut rhinoceros beetle. Males are located by following a plume of air rich in the odour of the pheromone. Evaporation of the pheromone vapours from traps attracts both male and female rhinoceros beetles to the traps. **Efficacy:** Use of pheromone-primed traps in young oil palm plantations reduces damage caused by rhinoceros beetle attack.
⓫Key reference: R H Hallett, A L Perez, G Gries, R Gries, H D Pierce Jr, J Yue, A C Oehlschlager, L M Gonzalez and J H Borden. 1995. Aggregation pheromone of coconut rhinoceros beetle, *Oryctes rhinoceros* (L.) (Coleoptera: Scarabaeidae), *J. Chem. Ecol.*, **21**, 1549-70.

⓬COMMERCIALISATION: **Formulation:** Sold as a slow-release formulation of the pheromone from plastic bags. **Tradenames:** Oryctalure – ChemTica International, Coconut Rhinoceros Beetle Attract and Kill Dispensers – SEDQ.

⓭APPLICATION: Pheromone dispensers are attached to vanes of a vaned bucket that is elevated two metres above ground at a density of one trap per two hectares.

⓮PRODUCT SPECIFICATIONS: The lures contain 95% chemically pure pheromone.

⓯COMPATIBILITY: The pheromone trap does not require insecticide applications but trapping can be used with the application of insecticides to any affected palms.

⓰MAMMALIAN TOXICITY: Oryctalure has shown no adverse toxicological effects on manufacturers, formulators or field workers.

⓱ENVIRONMENTAL IMPACT AND NON-TARGET TOXICITY: Oryctalure is a natural insect pheromone that is specific to the coconut rhinoceros beetle. There is no evidence that it has caused any adverse effects on any non-target organisms or had any adverse environmental impact.

Section 3: Living Systems

1 Number representing the section into which the entry is placed e.g. 3 = Living Systems.

2 Sequential entry number.

3 Approved name.

4 Class of biological activity.

5 *The Pesticide Manual* - 11th edition: Entry no:

6 Taxonomic classification by phylum, class and order.

7 The approved name (with authorities), common names, other names and development code numbers.

8 The history of the discovery of the biological activity and details of from where the organism was first isolated.

9 A summary of the method of production for commercial sale.

10 A detailed list or description of the pest species (with authorities) against which the product is recommended.

11 A list of the crops in which the product is recommended.

12 A full description of the biological activity associated with the entry, its mode of action and a summary of the efficacy of the product.

3:82   *Bacillus thuringiensis* subsp. *kurstaki*

❹*Biological insecticide*

❺ *The Pesticide Manual* - 11th edition: Entry number: 46

❻Bacterium: Schizomycetes: Eubacteriales

❼NOMENCLATURE: **Approved name:** *Bacillus thuringiensis* Berliner subsp. *kurstaki*. **Other names:** *Btk.* **Development code:** SAN 239 I; SAN 415 I; SAN 420 I (all originally Sandoz, subsequently Novartis and now Thermo Trilogy); CGA 237218 (conjugated strain of *Btk* and *Bta*, originally sold by Ciba, subsequently Novartis and now Thermo Trilogy).

❽SOURCE: *Bacillus thuringiensis* is common in soil, mills, warehouses and other insect-rich environments. Strains that are used in crop protection are selected from those isolated in Nature on the basis of their potency in test insect species, spectrum of host insects and the ease with which they can be grown in fermenters. The insecticidal activity of *Bt* was first observed in insects associated with man, such as Japanese silkworm rearings in 1901 and flour mill moths in a German mill in 1911.

❾PRODUCTION: Produced by accurately controlled fermentation in deep tanks of sterilised nutrient liquid medium. The endotoxins and living spores are harvested as water dispersible liquid concentrates for subsequent formulation.

❿TARGET PESTS: Lepidopteran larvae, particularly the diamond back moth (*Plutella xylostella* (Linnaeus)) and other vegetable pests and forest insects. Ecogen strain EG2424 (Raven and Jackpot) is used to control Colorado potato beetle (*Leptinotarsa decemlineata* (Say)) in addition to Lepidoptera.

⓫TARGET CROPS: Recommended for use in vegetables, fruit, maize, small grain cereals and in forests, orchards or for general tree care.

⓬BIOLOGICAL ACTIVITY: **Mode of action:** *Bacillus thuringiensis* produces parasporal, proteinaceous, crystal inclusion bodies during sporulation. Upon ingestion, these are insecticidal to larvae of the order Lepidoptera and to both larvae and adults of a few Coleoptera. Once in the insect, the crystal proteins are solubilised and the insect gut proteases convert the original pro-toxin into a combination of up to four smaller toxins. These hydrolysed toxins bind to the insect's midgut cells at high-affinity, specific receptor binding sites where they interfere with the potassium-ion dependent, active amino acid symport mechanism. This disruption causes the formation of large cation-selective pores that increase the water permeability of the cell membrane. A large uptake of water causes cell swelling and eventual rupture, disintegrating the midgut lining. Different toxins bind to different receptors in different insect species and with varying intensities: this explains species specificities. **Biology:** The crystal inclusions derived from *Btk* are generally lepidopteran specific. Because they have to be ingested and then processed within the insect's gut they are often slow acting (two to forty-eight hours) in comparison to conventional chemicals. The toxin stops feeding and young larvae may starve to death; insects not killed rapidly by direct

13 A list of key references that describe the discovery, effectiveness and commercialisation of the product.

14 Details of the formulation type used commercially, the tradenames and the manufacturer plus selected patent number.

15 Details of frequency and methods of application and rate of use.

16 Information on the purity and quality of the technical material, details of the recommended storage conditions and shelf-life.

action of the toxin may die from bacterial infection over a longer period. Different toxins have different spectra of activity. Different strains and serotypes have been developed by different companies. For example, Novartis (products now owned by Thermo Trilogy) developed serotypes 3a, 3b and strains Int. 15-313, SA-11, SA-12 and the conjugate of *Bacillus thuringiensis* subsp. *kurstaki* and *Bt* subsp. *aizawai* GC-91; Ecogen has developed strains EG2348, EG2349, EG2371 and EG2424. In addition to producing the endotoxins, many strains of *Bt* are potent insect pathogens. (Many *Bt* genes have been isolated and used to transform crops thereby rendering them insecticidal. These transgenic crops are included in Section 5 – Genes). **Efficacy:** Very effective when used against lepidopteran species where some damage to the crop is acceptable, such as in forestry. Light instability can cause problems if exposed to high light intensities. Rapidly hydrolysed under even mild alkaline conditions.

⓭Key references: 1) P Fast. 1981. The crystal toxin of *Bacillus thuringiensis*, in *Microbial Control of Pests and Plant Diseases 1970-1980*, H D Burges (ed.), Academic Press, New York. 2) L F Adams, C-L Liu, S C MacIntosh and R L Starnes. 1996. Diversity and biological activity of *Bacillus thuringiensis*. In *Crop Protection Agents from Nature: Natural Products and Analogues*, L G Copping (ed.), 360-88, Royal Society of Chemistry, Cambridge, UK. 3) P F Entwistle, J S Cory, M J Bailey and S Higgs (Eds.). 1993. Bacillus thuringiensis, *an Environmental Biopesticide: Theory and Practice*, Wiley, Chichester, UK, 311 pp. 4) H D Burges and K A Jones. 1989. Formulation of bacteria, viruses and protozoa to control insects. In *Formulation of Microbial Biopesticides: Beneficial Microorganisms, Nematodes and Seed Treatments*, H D Burges (ed.), 33-127, Kluwer Academic Publishers, Dordecht, the Netherlands.

⓮COMMERCIALISATION: Formulation: Sold as a combination of endotoxin crystals and living bacterial spores. Formulated as a suspension concentrate (SC), a granular bait (GB), a ready to use bait (RB), a suspo-emulsion (SE), a granule (GR), an oil miscible flowable concentrate (oil miscible suspension) (OF), a dispersible powder (DP) and a wettable powder (WP). **Tradenames:** Bactospeine – Abbott, Biobit – Abbott, Foray – Abbott , DiPel – Abbott, Cordalene – Agrichem, Bactucide – Caffaro, Baturad – Cequisa, Condor [EG2348] – Ecogen, Crymax [EG7841] – Ecogen, Cutlass [EG2371] – Ecogen, Lepinox [EG7826] – Ecogen, Raven [EG2424] – Ecogen, Ecotech Bio [EG2371] – Ecogen and AgrEvo, Ecotech Pro [EG2348] – Ecogen and AgrEvo, Jackpot [EG2424] - Ecogen and Intrachem, Rapax [EG2348] – Ecogen/Intrachem, Forwarbit – Forward International, Bactosid K – Sanex, Agrobac – Tecomag, Able – Thermo Trilogy, CoStar – Thermo Trilogy, Delfin – Thermo Trilogy, Javelin – Thermo Trilogy, Thuricide – Thermo Trilogy, Vault – Thermo Trilogy, Larvo-BT – Troy Biosciences, Troy-BT – Troy Biosciences, Biobest BT – Biobest, Collapse – Calliope, Bactospeine Koppert – Koppert, Insectobiol – Samabiol. **Patents:** Many worldwide including US 5080897; US 5024837 (both to Ecogen).

⓯APPLICATION: Use at rates of 100 – 300 g active ingredient per hectare ensuring that the crop is well covered with the spray suspension. Apply while insect larvae are small and repeat every five to seven days if infestations are high. *Bt*-based sprays can be applied up to the day of harvest.

⓰PRODUCT SPECIFICATIONS: Purity: All formulations are standardised at a toxin content expressed in terms of international units active against a target pest per mg of product. Guaranteed to be free of human and mammalian pathogenic contaminants.

17 Information on incompatibilities and other information on the possibility of interactions between the product and other crop protection products.

18 Toxicological data to include acute oral and dermal LD_{50}, skin and eye effects, no observeable effect level, EPA toxicity codes and any other information on adverse effects.

19 Effects on non-target organisms (birds, fish and other aquatic species), wild-life, persistence, degradation rates and pathways.

Storage conditions: Do not expose to direct sunlight. Keep cool but do not freeze.
Shelf-life: If stored under cool dark conditions, the products remain viable for two years or more.

⑰COMPATIBILITY: Do not use in combination with broad spectrum biocides such as chlorothalonil. Compatible with a wide range of acaricides, insecticides, fungicides, stickers, spreaders and wetters. Do not use water with a pH above 8.0.

⑱MAMMALIAN TOXICITY: Acute oral: No infectivity or toxicity observed in rats at 4.7×10^{11} spores/kg. No adverse effects at doses from 1×10^8 up to 7×10^{12} colony forming units (cfu) per rat. **Acute percutaneous LD$_{50}$:** rats >5,000 mg/kg; rabbits >10^9 cfu. **Skin and eye:** No infectivity or toxicity observed in rats at 3.4×10^{11} spores/kg. Some products can cause substantial, but temporary, eye injury. **Inhalation:** No infectivity or toxicity at 5.4 mg/litre (2.6×10^7 spores/litre). **NOEL:** (2 years) rats 8.4 g/kg body weight daily. **Other toxicological effects:** *Btk* has not shown evidence of toxicity, infectivity or hypersensitivity to mammals. No allergic reactions or other health problems have been shown by research workers, manufacturing staff or users. **Toxicity class:** EPA (formulation) III. Considered to be non-toxic. Tolerance exempt in the US on all raw agricultural commodities when applied to growing crops pre- or post-harvest.

⑲ENVIRONMENTAL IMPACT AND NON-TARGET TOXICITY: Birds: In 63 day feeding trials, chickens receiving 5.1×10^7 spores/g diet showed no ill-effects. **Fish:** LC$_{50}$ (96 hour) water gobies (*Pomatoschistus minutus*) >400 mg/litre (as Thuricide HP).
Beneficial insects: Non-toxic to honeybees, LD$_{50}$ (oral) >0.1 mg/honeybee. **General:** *Btk* has a short persistence owing to its sensitivity to ultra violet light. No adverse effects have been recorded in approved field use and none are anticipated. *Btk* should not be used near water-courses.

Section 4: Insect Predators

1   Number representing the section into which the entry is placed e.g. 4 = Insect Predators.

2   Sequential entry number.

3   Approved name.

4   Class of biological activity.

5   *The Pesticide Manual* - 11th edition: Entry no:

6   Taxonomic classification by order and family.

7   The approved name (with authorities), common names and other names.

8   The history of the discovery of the insect predator and details of from where the organism was first isolated.

9   A summary of the method used to produce the predator for commercial sale.

10 A detailed list or description of the pest species (with authorities) against which the predator is recommended.

11 A list of the crop situations in which the product is recommended.

12 A full description of the biological activity of the predator to include its development, egg laying, method of predation and longevity.

13 A list of key references that describe the discovery, effectiveness and commercialisation of the product.

❶ ❷   ❸
4:166 *Orius albidipennis*   ❹*Thrips predator*

❺ *The Pesticide Manual* - 11th edition: Entry number 535

❻ Predatory bug: Hemiptera: Anthocoridae

❼ NOMENCLATURE: **Approved name:** *Orius albidipennis* (Reuter).
Other names: minute pirate bug.

❽ SOURCE: Palaearctic species, found mainly in the Southern Mediterranean from North Africa to the Near East, Iran and Russian Asia Minor. It is also found in the Canary Islands, Cape Verde and Spain. *Orius* spp. were first reported as predators of thrips in 1914. Subsequent work in the USA in the late 1970s and early 1980s led to the introduction of *Orius* spp. as commercial products in Canada and Europe in the 1990s.

❾ PRODUCTION: Bred in insectaries on soft-bodied phytophagous adult, larval, nymphal and egg-stage insects. Lepidopteran eggs are a common food source.

❿ TARGET PESTS: Thrips are the main prey but it will also consume a wide range of arthropods including aphids, mites and the eggs of some lepidopteran species.

⓫ TARGET CROPS: Glasshouse-grown vegetables and ornamentals.

⓬ BIOLOGICAL ACTIVITY: **Biology:** There are seven development stages; egg, five nymphal stages and the adult. Eggs are laid within the plant tissue usually in the leaf stem or in the main vein on the underside of the leaf. Eggs are usually laid separately. All the nymphal stages have characteristic red eyes. Adults vary in size from 2 to 3 mm with the females being larger than the males. Males are clearly asymmetrical. **Predation:** All growth stages catch and kill small insects holding them motionless with their forelegs and sucking them dry. If insect numbers are high the bugs will kill more insects than they need to eat and they also kill other *Orius* species and other beneficial insects. Prey is located by touch rather than by sight. The larvae and adults are relatively fast-moving. **Egg laying:** Eggs are laid, usually singly with only their tops protruding above the plant surface, two to three days after mating. Temperature and food supply have a significant effect on the number of eggs laid by a female with the normal number being between 125 and 160 eggs in its lifetime.
Duration of development: Development is very dependent upon temperature and at 28 °C, total preimaginal development takes 14.5 days, whilst at 20 °C, it takes 23 days. A poor food supply slows this development timescale significantly. Females live for 20 to 23 days.
Efficacy: The adults can fly reasonably well and can locate new infested plants very easily. *Orius albidipennis* is able to survive in the absence of prey.
⓭ **Key references:** 1) R Chyzik, M Klein and Y Ben-Dov. 1995, Reproduction and survival of the predatory bug *Orius albidipennis* on various arthropod prey. *Entomologia Experimentalis et Applicata,* **75**, 27-31. 2) M Salim, S A Masud and H M Khan. 1987. *Orius albidipennis* (Reut.) (Hemiptera: Anthocoridae) - a predator of cotton pests. *Philippine Entomologist,* **7**, 37-42. 3) J Riudavets. 1995. Predators of *Frankliniella occidentalis* (Perg.) and *Thrips tabaci* Lind.: a review. *Wageningen Agric. Univ. Papers,* **95-1**, 43-87.

14 Details of the development stage and carrier materials used to sell the product together with the tradenames and the manufacturers.

15 Details of frequency and methods of application and rate of use.

16 Information on the purity and quality of the technical material, details of the recommended storage conditions and shelf-life.

17 Information on incompatibilities and other information on the possibility of interactions between the product and other crop protection products.

18 Toxicological data as far as they are known.

19 Details of effects on non-target organisms.

⑭COMMERCIALISATION: Formulation: Sold as adults in packaging material with a food supply. **Tradenames:** Minute Pirate Bug – Arbico (species not stated), Orius – Sautter & Stepper (species not stated), Orius-System – Biobest (species not stated), Ori-line a – Novartis BCM, Orius-Raubwanzen – Neudorff (species not stated).

⑮APPLICATION: Spread carrier material onto plants or place in release boxes. Apply at rate of one adult per two infested plants. Release close to site of infestation in early morning or late evening under low light conditions and when the glasshouse vents are closed.

⑯PRODUCT SPECIFICATIONS: Purity: Containers include adult bugs in a carrier plus a food source and no contaminants. **Storage conditions:** Store at 5 to 10 °C. Do not expose to direct sunlight. **Shelf-life:** Use as soon as possible.

⑰COMPATIBILITY: Do not use residual insecticides. Adults are easily disturbed. Egg laying is optimal in the presence of high-quality food source and at temperatures around 22 °C.

⑱MAMMALIAN TOXICITY: No allergic or other adverse reaction has been reported following its use under glasshouse conditions.

⑲ENVIRONMENTAL IMPACT AND NON-TARGET TOXICITY: *Orius albidipennis* occurs widely in Nature and has not shown any adverse effects on the environment but it will consume other insects.

Section 5: Genes

1 Number representing the section into which the entry is placed e.g. 5 = Genes.

2 Sequential entry number.

3 Approved name.

4 Class of biological activity.

5 List of approved names of the gene.

6 Name of promoter(s) used with the gene.

7 Source of gene and promoter - from where it was isolated.

8 Target pests.

9 Crops into which the gene has been introduced.

10 A description of the biological activity of the transgenic crops to include the biochemical basis of the tolerance (or resistance) to herbicides (or insects or viruses). This will include, as far as possible, a description of the properties of the gene product.

11 Key references describing the introduction of this trait into the target crops.

12 Details of the crops that are sold, the tradenames used and the companies selling the seed.

5:179 class II EPSP synthase gene

❹*Introduces tolerance to glyphosate*

❺NOMENCLATURE: **Approved name:** class II EPSP synthase gene; CP4-EPSPS gene; Roundup Ready gene.

❻PROMOTER: cauliflower mosaic virus (CaMV) 35S. Because EPSP synthase is located in the chloroplasts of plants, the CP4-EPSP gene has been linked to a promoter that operates within the chloroplast thereby ensuring that the gene is only functional where the enzyme is active.

❼SOURCE: The class II EPSP synthase gene was extracted from *Agrobacterium tumefaciens* strain CP4 isolated from the glyphosate production facilities and cloned into *E. coli*. The CaMV 35S promoter was isolated from the cauliflower mosaic virus and was found to be very effective at enhancing transcription levels of foreign genes in plants.

❽TARGET PESTS: A wide variety of weeds.

❾TARGET CROPS: The introduction of this glyphosate-insensitive gene into elite crop varieties allows the grower to apply glyphosate over-the-top of the crop for weed control. Major crops commercially available include soybeans, maize, cotton and canola.

❿BIOLOGICAL ACTIVITY: **Biology:** The transformed crops are tolerant of glyphosate application because the EPSP synthase gene expressed in the crop is not inhibited by the herbicide at the rates at which it is applied. **Mode of action:** The mutant EPSP synthase isolated from *Agrobacterium tumefaciens* has an affinity for glyphosate that is over 2,000 lower than natural plant EPSP synthase but with no adverse effects on the growth of transformed crop plants. Hence, transformed crops treated with rates of glyphosate of up to 1.68 kg acid equivalent/hectare show no visible signs of injury and no yield reduction. There are trials in progress with crops such as maize that contain both the class II EPSP synthase gene and the glyphosate oxidoreductase gene isolated from *Achromobacter* sp. strain LBAA. This enzyme catalyses the cleavage of the C-N bond in glyphosate to give aminomethylphosphonic acid (AMPA). **Efficacy:** The recommended use rate of glyphosate is 0.34 – 1.12 kg acid equivalent/hectare. At these application rates, all weeds infesting transformed crops are well controlled with no adverse effects on the crop. If the application is timed to coincide with small weed size and just prior to crop canopy cover, lower rates give excellent control.

⓫**Key reference:** G Kishore et al. 1988. EPSP synthase: from biochemistry to genetic engineering of glyphosate tolerance. In *Biotechnology for Crop Protection*, ACS Symp. Series No. 379, P A Hedin, J J Menn and R M Hollingsworth (Eds.), 37-48, American Chemical Society, Washington DC, USA.

⓬COMMERCIALISATION: Roundup Ready soybeans were first commercialised in the USA in 1996 and were followed by Roundup Ready canola in Canada, Roundup Ready cotton, Roundup Ready soybeans and Roundup Ready maize in the USA. Trials are in progress with Roundup Ready potatoes in the USA and Roundup Ready sugar beet, maize and oilseed rape

13 A description of the components of the product.

14 A list of compatible crop protection agents and those that should not be used.

15 Toxicological details on the transgenic crops as far as they are known.

16 Effects of the transgenic crops on the environment and non-target organisms.

in Europe. Cotton and maize crops containing the class II EPSP synthase and *Btk* genes have been commercialised in the USA. **Tradenames:** Roundup Ready Soybeans – AgraTech Seeds, AgriPro Seeds, AgVenture, Asgrow Seeds, Callahan Seeds, Campbell Seeds, Chemgro Seeds, Countrymark Cooperative, Croplan Genetics, Dairyland Seed Company, DEKALB Genetics, Deltapine Seed, Farmers Cooperative, Garst Seed, Golden Harvest Seeds, Gutwein Seeds, Hoegemeyer Hybrids, Hoffman Seeds, Interstate Seed, Merschman Seeds, Midwest Seeds, NC+ Hybrids, Novartis Seeds, Patriot Seeds, Sands of Iowa, Scott's Quality Seeds, Stine Seed, Terra Industries and Trisler Seed Farms.
Roundup Ready plus BollGard Cotton – Paymaster.
Roundup Ready Cotton – Paymaster.
Roundup Ready Canola – Monsanto.
Roundup Ready Corn – DEKALB Genetics.

⓭PRODUCT SPECIFICATIONS: Elite varieties of crop containing the strain CP4 class II EPSP synthase gene driven by CaMV 35S promoter.

⓮COMPATIBILITY: Roundup Ready crops are only guaranteed tolerant of glyphosate as Roundup. Other herbicides that are recognised as being selective in a particular crop can still be used.

⓯MAMMALIAN TOXICITY: There is no evidence that Roundup Ready crops have any unusual characteristics that will render them different from conventional crops. There have been no reports of allergic or other adverse effects from researchers, breeders or users of the products.

⓰ENVIRONMENTAL IMPACT AND NON-TARGET TOXICITY: There is no evidence that the use of Roundup Ready crops will have any deleterious effect on non-target organisms or the environment.

Resistance

The increased use of crop protection agents with single modes of action has resulted in the development of resistance to a wide range of chemicals in a large number of insects, mites, plant pathogens and weeds. The problem is so serious that the agrochemical industry has established a number of Resistance Action Committees as Specialist Technical Groups of the Global Crop Protection Federation. These Resistance Action Committees monitor the development of resistance and introduce industry-wide recommendations for the use of all crop protection agents in such a way as to reduce the possibility of resistance developing.

The Resistance Action Committees include the Insecticide Resistance Action Committee (IRAC), the Fungicide Resistance Action Committee (FRAC) and the Herbicide Resistance Action Committee (HRAC). Details of the recommendations and activities of these committees can be obtained from the following address:

Global Crop Protection Federation, Avenue Louise 143, 1050 Brussels, Belgium.

The use of natural products, pheromones, living systems, insect predators and parasites and the development of transgenic crops in Integrated Crop Management (ICM) systems is considered to be a valuable strategy to slow the development of resistance and, thereby, improve the value and life of many crop protection agents whilst maintaining a level of insect, disease and weed control that the grower demands. The reason for the success of this approach is the reduced ability of target pests to develop detoxification mechanisms or to avoid the attentions of a living control agent. It is probable that biological agents and products based on natural agents will find increasing use in future crop protection strategies.

1:01 abamectin *Microbial insecticide/acaricide*

The Pesticide Manual - 11th edition: Entry number 1

(i) R = CH$_3$

(ii) R = H

NOMENCLATURE: **Approved name:** abamectin (BSI, draft E-ISO, ANSI); abamectine ((f) draft F-ISO). **Other names:** avermectin B1. **CAS RN:** *[71751–41–2]* abamectin; *[65195–55–3]* (i); *[65195–56–4]* (ii). **Development codes:** MK-0936; C-076; L-676,863.

SOURCE: *Streptomyces avermitilis* is a naturally occurring soil actinomycete isolated from soil as part of a programme targeted at identifying new, biologically active secondary metabolites. Discovered in an *in vivo* screen when microbial fermentation broths were tested in mice against the nematode, *Nematospiroides dubious*, in a dual mice-nematode system.

PRODUCTION: Isolated following the fermentation of *Streptomyces avermitilis*. A mixture of two avermectins, avermectin B$_{1a}$ (i) and avermectin B$_{1b}$ (ii), was introduced as an insecticide/acaricide by Merck Sharp and Dohme Agvet. Now owned by Novartis.

TARGET PESTS: Recommended for the control of the motile stages of a wide range of mites, leafminers, suckers, beetles and other insects. Also used for control of fire ants (*Solenopsis* spp.).

TARGET CROPS: Recommended for use on ornamentals, cotton, citrus fruit, pome fruit, nut crops, vegetables, potatoes and many other crops.

BIOLOGICAL ACTIVITY: **Mode of action:** The target for abamectin is the γ-aminobutyric acid (GABA) receptor in the peripheral nervous system. The compound stimulates the release of GABA from nerve endings and enhances the binding of GABA to receptor sites on the post-synaptic membrane of inhibitory motor neurons of nematodes and on the post-junction membrane of muscle cells of insects and other arthropods. This enhanced GABA binding results in an increased flow of chloride ions into the cell, with consequent hyperpolarization and elimination of signal transduction resulting in an inhibition of neurotransmission. (See M J Turner and J M Schaeffer. 1989. In *Ivermectin and Abamectin*, W C Campbell (ed.), Springer-Verlag, New York, p. 73). Insecticide and acaricide with contact and stomach action. It has limited plant systemic activity, but exhibits translaminar movement.

Key references: 1) W C Campbell (ed.). 1989. *Ivermectin and Abamectin*, Springer-Verlag, New York. 2) M H Fisher and H Mrozik. 1984. *Macrolide antibiotics*, S Omura (ed.), Academic Press, New York.

COMMERCIALISATION: **Formulation:** Formulated as an emulsifiable concentrate (EC) and a ready for use bait (RB). **Tradenames:** Dynamec – Novartis, Avid – Novartis, Zephyr – Novartis, Agri-Mek – Novartis, Abacide – Mauget.

APPLICATION: Rates of use are 5.6 to 28 g active ingredient per hectare for mite control, 11 to 22 g active ingredient per hectare for control of leafminers. The effectiveness of the product is increased significantly by the addition of paraffinic oils to the spray tank.

PRODUCT SPECIFICATIONS: **Purity:** A mixture containing about 80% avermectin B_{1a} (i) and 20% avermectin B_{1b} (ii).

COMPATIBILITY: Can be used with other crop protection agents.

MAMMALIAN TOXICITY: **Acute oral LD$_{50}$:** rats 10, mice 13.6 mg/kg (in sesame oil). **Acute dermal LD$_{50}$:** rabbits >2,000 mg/kg. **Skin and eye:** Mild eye irritant; non-irritating to skin (rabbits). **ADI:** 0.0001 mg/kg b.w. [1992]; 0.0002 mg/kg b.w. [1994] (for mixture with Δ-8,9-isomer). **Toxicity class:** EPA (formulation) IV. **Toxicity review:** 1) *Pesticide residues in food – 1994*, FAO Plant Production and Protection Paper, 127, 1995. 2) *Pesticide residues in food – 1994 evaluations. Part II – Toxicology*. World Health Organisation, WHO/PCS/95.2, 1995. 3) *Pesticide residues in food – 1995*, FAO Plant Production and Protection Paper. 4) G Lankas and L R Gordon. 1989. In *Toxicology in Ivermectin and Abamectin*, W C Campbell (ed.), Springer-Verlag, pp. 89–112.

ENVIRONMENTAL IMPACT AND NON-TARGET TOXICITY: **Bird toxicity:** Acute oral LD$_{50}$: mallard ducks 84.6, bobwhite quail >2,000 mg/kg. **Fish toxicity:** LC$_{50}$ (96 hours): rainbow trout 3.2, bluegill sunfish 9.6 mg/litre. **Other aquatic toxicity:** EC$_{50}$ (48 hours): *Daphnia pulex* 0.34 ppb. LC$_{50}$ (96 hours): pink shrimp (*Panaeus duorarum*) 1.6, mysid shrimp (*Mysidopsis bahia*) 0.022 and blue crab (*Callinectes sapidus*) 153 ppb. **Effects on beneficial insects:** Toxic to bees. **Metabolism:** Metabolites found in animals include 3″-demethylavermectin B_1 and 24-hydroxymethylavermectin B_1. 8,9-(Z)-Avermectin B_1 has been identified as a metabolite in plants. The polar degradates are the largest fraction; these are unidentified, but are non-toxic. **Behaviour in soil:** Binds tightly to soil, with rapid degradation by soil micro-organisms. No bioaccumulation.

The Pesticide Manual - 11th edition: Entry number 36

NOMENCLATURE: **Approved name:** azadirachtin. **Other names:** azad, neem.
CAS RN: *[11141–17–6]*.

SOURCE: The neem tree (*Azadirachta indica* A Juss) has been known to resist insect attack and subsequently it was found that extracts, particularly of the seed, were insecticidal. It is an attractive broad-leaved evergreen tree which is thought to have originated in Burma. It is now grown in the more arid sub-tropical and tropical zones of South East Asia, Africa, the Americas, Australia and the South Pacific Islands.

PRODUCTION: Extracted from the neem tree (*Azadirachta indica* A Juss) and often sold as the crude extract, much of which is azadirachtin.

TARGET PESTS: A potent deterrent to many different genera of insects. Shown to be effective against whitefly, thrips, leafminers, caterpillars, aphids, jassids, San Jose scale, beetles and mealybugs. Some formulations claim effects against phytopathogenic fungi such as powdery mildews.

TARGET CROPS: Shows activity in a wide range of crops, including vegetables (such as tomatoes, cabbage, potatoes), cotton, tea, tobacco, coffee, protected crops and ornamentals.

BIOLOGICAL ACTIVITY: **Mode of action:** Azadirachtin has several effects on phytophagous insects. It has a dramatic antifeedant/repellent effect with many insects avoiding treated crops. It is thought to disrupt insect moulting by antagonising ecdysone and this leads to morphological defects in insects coming into contact with sprayed crops and, in some cases, the larval period is extended. This effect is independent of feeding inhibition. Azadirachtin is also believed to reduce the reproductive capabilities of phytophagous insects by disrupting normal mating behaviour and thereby reducing fecundity. The ecdysis inhibition also leads to effects on vitellogenesis leading to the re-absorption of vitellarium and oviducts. **Efficacy:** Most effective when used in spray programmes. Its mode of action means that it is slow to control insects, particularly when the populations are high. **Key references:** 1) H Schmutterer. 1995. *The Neem Tree; Source of Unique Natural Products for Integrated Pest Management, Medicine, Industry and Other Purposes.* VCH, Weinheim, Germany, 696 pp. 2) H Rembold. 1989. *Focus* on *Phytochemical Pesticides, Vol. 1, The Neem Tree*, M Jacobsen (ed.), CRC Press, Boca Raton, Florida.

COMMERCIALISATION: **Formulation:** Sold as an emulsifiable concentrate (EC) or as technical material (TC). **Tradenames:** Neemix 90EC (90 g/litre EC) – Thermo Trilogy, Neemazid – Thermo Trilogy, Trilogy 90 EC – Thermo Trilogy (neem oil for disease control), Triact 90 EC – Thermo Trilogy (neem oil for disease control), Bio-neem – Thermo Trilogy, Margosan-O – Thermo Trilogy, Azatin – Thermo Trilogy, Align – Thermo Trilogy, Turplex – Thermo Trilogy, Bollwhip – Thermo Trilogy, Fortune Aza – Fortune, Fortune Biotech – Fortune, Azatin – Agridyne, Neem Suraksha – Karapur Agro, Proneem – Karapur Agro, Neem Wave – Karapur Agro, Aza Technical – Karapur Agro, NeemAzal – Trifolio-M, Kayneem – Krishi Rasayan, Neemolin – Rallis, SureFire - Consep, Neemachtin – Consep, Nimbecidine – T Stanes.

APPLICATION: Apply at rates of 100 to 500 g active ingredient per hectare (0.15 to 0.65 oz active ingredient per acre). Frequent applications are more effective than single sprays.

PRODUCT SPECIFICATIONS: **Purity:** Azadirachtin-based products are produced from the extraction of the seeds of the neem tree. In all cases, there are other components in each formulation but the minimum claimed concentration of azadirachtin is guaranteed by the manufacturer.

COMPATIBILITY: No known incompatibilities with other crop protection agents.

MAMMALIAN TOXICITY: **Acute oral LD$_{50}$:** rats >5,000 mg/kg. Rats dosed once with Margosan-O and observed for 14 days showed no obvious effects with the oral toxicity being above 5 ml/kg. **Acute dermal LD$_{50}$:** rabbits >2,000 mg/kg. **Inhalation:** Albino rats exposed to 15.8 g of Margosan-O for four hours showed an LD_{50} above 43.9 mg/litre per hour (the limit of the test). **Skin and eye:** Not a skin or eye irritant. Not a skin sensitiser. **Toxicity class:** EPA (formulation) IV. **Other toxicological effects:** Neem seed oil and two components of neem oil, nimbolide and nimbic acid, showed no mutagenic effects in *Salmonella typhimurium* strains TA98 and TA100. **Toxicity review:** 1) M Jacobsen. 1986. Pharmacological and toxicological effects of neem and chinaberry on warm-blooded animals. *Neem Newsletter*, **3(4)**, 39–43. 2) M Jacobsen (ed.). 1989. Pharmacology and toxicology of neem. In *1988 Focus on Phytochemical Pesticides, Vol. 1, The Neem Tree*, 133–53, CRC Press, Boca Raton, Florida. 3) D Kanungo. 1993. In *Neem Research and Development*, N S Randhawa and B S Parmar (eds.), 250–62, Society of Pesticide Science, India.

ENVIRONMENTAL IMPACT AND NON-TARGET TOXICITY: **Bird toxicity:** mallard ducks – daily oral administration of Margosan-O at 1–16 mg/kg induced no negative effects over a 14-day test period. Bobwhite quail fed a daily basic diet with added Margosan-O at 1,000–7,000 ppm showed no negative effects over a five-day test period and a three day recovery phase. Ducks fed a basic diet plus Margosan-O at the same concentration for five days remained active and healthy throughout the test period. Dose levels of 1–16 ml of Margosan-O/kg body weight elicited no negative effects. **Fish toxicity:** LC_{50} to trout (96 hours) with Margosan-O – 8.8 ml/litre, to tilapia fingerlings (24 hours) with neem oil – 1,124.6 ppm, to carp (24 hours) with neem oil – 302.7 ppm.

1:03   6-benzylaminopurine

Plant growth regulator

The Pesticide Manual - 11th edition: Entry number 68

NOMENCLATURE: **Approved name:** 6-benzylaminopurine. **Other names:** 6-BAP, 6-BA, BAP, 6-benzyladenine. **CAS RN:** *[1214–39–7].* **EEC no:** 214–927–5.

SOURCE: Reported as a naturally occurring plant growth regulator in higher plants by Skinner *et al.* in 1958 and introduced as a plant growth regulator in Japan by Kumiai Chemical Industry Co. Ltd in 1975.

TARGET CROPS: Fruit trees, ornamentals and cereals.

BIOLOGICAL ACTIVITY: **Mode of action:** 6-Benzylaminopurine stimulates RNA and protein biosynthesis, producing a number of growth enhancing effects. These include a general increase in cell division, increased lateral bud formation in tree fruit, basal shoot formation in ornamentals, flowering in xerophytic species, fruit set in grapes, citrus and cucurbits and delayed senescence in rice. 6-Benzylaminopurine is used in combination with gibberellins A_4 and A_7 to thin apple trees in orchards and thereby increase the individual sizes of the fruit on each tree. **Key reference:** C G Skinner *et al.* 1958. *Plant Physiology,* **33**, 190–4.

COMMERCIALISATION: **Formulation:** Sold alone and as a combination product as a liquid concentrate (SL) and a paste (PA). **Tradenames:** Accel (mixture) – Abbott, Promalin (plus gibberellic acid) – Abbott and Point Enterprises, BA – Kumiai, Beanin – Riken Green, Paturyl – Reanal.

APPLICATION: Applied as a relatively high volume foliar spray to ensure good coverage as 6-benzylaminopurine is not well translocated in plants. Applied as a fruit thinning agent to apple trees from full blossom up to two weeks after petal fall.

PRODUCT SPECIFICATIONS: **Purity:** Contains only 6-benzylaminopurine.

COMPATIBILITY: Can be applied with other sprays.

MAMMALIAN TOXICITY: **Acute oral LD$_{50}$:** male rats 2,125, female rats 2,130 and mice 1,300 mg/kg. **Acute dermal LD$_{50}$:** rabbits 2,900 mg/kg. **Skin and eye:** Causes eye irritation. Not a skin sensitiser. **NOEL:** (2 years) male rats 5.2, female rats 6.5, male mice 11.6 and female mice 15.1 mg/kg body weight daily. **ADI:** 0.05 mg/kg.

Toxicity class: EPA (formulation) II; WHO (active ingredient) III (Table 5).
Other toxicological effects: Non-teratogenic in rats and rabbits and non-mutagenic in the Ames test.

ENVIRONMENTAL IMPACT AND NON-TARGET TOXICITY: The product does not accumulate in the environment and has no adverse effects on non-target organisms.
Fish toxicity: LC_{50} (48 hours) carp >40 mg/litre. Other aquatic toxicity: LC_{50} (24 hours) *Daphnia carinata* >40 mg/litre. Effects on beneficial insects: LD_{50} (oral) to honeybees 400 µg/bee. Metabolism: In ^{14}C-metabolism studies, almost all radio-activity was excreted in the urine and faeces of test animals with three metabolites being identified. In metabolism studies in plants, more than nine metabolites were found in studies on soybeans, grapes, maize and cocklebur (*Xanthium* sp.). Behaviour in soil: Sixteen days after application to soil at 22 °C, 6-benzylaminopurine had degraded to 5.3% (in a sandy loam soil) and 7.9% (in a clay loam soil) of the applied dose.

1:04   bilanafos   *Microbial herbicide*

The Pesticide Manual - 11th edition: Entry number 71

$$CH_3-\underset{\underset{OH}{|}}{\overset{\overset{O}{\|}}{P}}-CH_2 \quad \underset{\underset{NH_2}{\overset{|}{\vdots}}}{\overset{\overset{H}{\vdots}}{C}}-CONH-\underset{\underset{H}{\overset{\vdots}{}}}{\overset{\overset{CH_3}{\vdots}}{C}}-CONH-\underset{\underset{H}{\overset{\vdots}{}}}{\overset{\overset{CH_3}{\vdots}}{C}}-CO_2H$$

NOMENCLATURE: Approved name: bilanafos (BSI, draft E-ISO, (*m*) draft F-ISO); bialaphos (JMAF). Other names: phosphinothricylalanyl-alanine. CAS RN: [35597–43–4]; [71048–99–2] bilanafos-sodium. Development codes: MW-801; SF-1293.

SOURCE: Originally isolated from the soil inhabiting actinomycete *Streptomyces hygroscopicus* (Jensen) Waksman & Henrici, and introduced by Meiji Seika. It is also produced by *Streptomyces viridochromeogenes* (Krainsky) Waksman & Henrici.

PRODUCTION: Bilanafos-sodium is produced by *Streptomyces hygroscopicus* during fermentation.

TARGET PESTS: Post-emergence control of annual weeds in crop situations and control of annual and perennial weeds in uncultivated land.

TARGET CROPS: Used post-emergence in vines, apples, brassicas, cucurbits, mulberries, azaleas, rubber and many other crops and on uncultivated land.

BIOLOGICAL ACTIVITY: Mode of action: Bilanafos is the alanylalanine amide of the biologically active acid, phosphinothricin. Phosphinothricin is a potent, irreversible inhibitor of

glutamine synthetase, causing ammonia accumulation and inhibition of photophosphorylation in photosynthesis. The effects of bilanafos on plants is too rapid to be due to starvation of glutamine and other amino acids derived from glutamine and it was thought that the phytotoxic response was due to the high ammonium ion levels. However, the effects of the herbicide can be reversed by supplying the plant with glutamine and this does not reduce the levels of ammonium ions. Most of the phytotoxicity of inhibiting glutamine synthetase in C_3 plants is due to rapid cessation of photorespiration, resulting in accumulation of glyoxylate in the chloroplast and rapid inhibition of ribulose bisphosphate carboxylase. Inhibition of carbon fixation in the light leads to a series of events that end with severe photodynamic damage. Bilanafos has no *in vitro* activity on the enzyme but is converted to phosphinothricin within treated plants. Phosphinothricin is not metabolically degraded within higher plant tissue and is readily moved throughout treated plants in both the xylem and the phloem. The producing organism possesses an enzyme (phosphinothricin acetyl transferase (pat)) that acetylates the herbicide, rendering it non-inhibitory to glutamine synthetase and, hence, not phytotoxic. The gene that codes for this enzyme has been used to transform several crop plants to render them tolerant of over-the-top applications of bilanafos and its synthetic analogue, glufosinate (see section 5). **Efficacy:** Because bilanafos is converted into phosphinothricin that then interferes with glutamine synthetase, an essential enzyme of primary metabolism in higher plants, control of treated vegetation is total. However, effects often take several days to develop and death may take as long as 14 to 21 days. Regrowth of deep rooted perennials may occur and retreatment may be necessary. It has no effects pre-emergence.
Key references: 1) S Omura, M Murata, H Hanaki, K Hinotozawa, R Oiwa and H Tanaka. 1984. Phosalacine, a new herbicidal antibiotic containing phosphinothricin. Fermentation, isolation, biological activity and mechanism of action, *J. Antibiot.*, **37**, 829. 2) E Bayer, K K Gugel, K Kaegel, H Hagenmaier, S Jessipov, W A König and H Zähner. 1972. Stoffwechselprodukte von Mikroorganismen. Phosphinothricin und Phosphinothricinyl-alanyl-alanin, *Helv. Chim. Acta*, **55**, 224. 3) Y Ogawa, H Yoshida, S Inouye and T Niida. 1973. Studies on a new antibiotic SF-1293. III. Synthesis of a new phosphorus containing amino acid, a component of antibiotic SF-1293, *Meiji Seika Kenkyu Nempo*, **13**, 49.

COMMERCIALISATION: **Formulation:** Sold as soluble powder (SP) and liquid formulations. **Tradenames:** Meiji Herbiace (sodium salt) – Meiji Seika.

APPLICATION: Applied post-emergence at rates of 0.5–1.0 kg active ingredient per hectare for control of annual weeds and at higher rates for control of perennial weeds. Applied post-directed in crop situations.

PRODUCT SPECIFICATIONS: The product contains the sodium salt of bilanafos.
Purity: Purity of the product is determined by nmr.

COMPATIBILITY: Compatible with most crop protection agents.

MAMMALIAN TOXICITY: **Acute oral LD$_{50}$:** male rats 268, female rats 404 mg sodium salt/kg. **Acute dermal LD$_{50}$:** rats >5,000 mg/kg. Non-irritating to skin and eyes (rabbits). **Toxicity class:** WHO (active ingredient) II. **Other toxicological effects:** In sub-acute and chronic toxicity tests, no ill-effects were observed. Non-carcinogenic, non-mutagenic and non-teratogenic. Not mutagenic in Ames and Rec assays.

ENVIRONMENTAL IMPACT AND NON-TARGET TOXICITY: **Bird toxicity:** Acute oral LD_{50} chickens >5,000 mg/kg. **Fish toxicity:** LC_{50} (48 hours) carp 1,000 mg/litre. **Other aquatic toxicity:** LC_{50} (48 hours) *Daphnia pulex* 1,000 mg/litre. **Metabolism:** In the mouse, the main metabolite in the faeces following oral administration was 2-amino-4-[(hydroxy)(methyl)phosphinyl]butyric acid (A Suzuki *et al.* 1987. *J. Pestic. Sci*, **12**, 105). Metabolised in plants to the L-isomer of glufosinate, that has a similar activity. **Behaviour in soil:** Inactivated in soil.

1:05   blasticidin-S   *Microbial fungicide*

The Pesticide Manual - 11th edition: Entry number 78

NOMENCLATURE: **Approved name:** blasticidin-S (JMAF). **CAS RN:** *[2079–00–7]*; formerly *[11002–92–9]*, *[12767–55–4]*. **Development codes:** BcS-3; -BAB; -BABS.

SOURCE: Isolated from the soil actinomycete *Streptomyces griseochromogenes* in 1955 by K Fukunaga. Its fungicidal properties were first described by T Misato *et al.* in 1959.

PRODUCTION: By the fermentation of *Streptomyces griseochromogenes*. It is sold as the benzylaminobenzenesulfonate salt.

TARGET PESTS: Control of rice blast (*Pyricularia oryzae* Cavara; perfect stage *Magnaporthe grisea*) by foliar application.

TARGET CROPS: Rice.

BIOLOGICAL ACTIVITY: **Mode of action:** Blasticidin-S inhibits protein biosynthesis by binding to the 50S ribosome in prokaryotes (at the same site as gougerotin), leading to the inhibition of peptidyl transfer and protein chain elongation. It is a contact fungicide with protective and curative action. **Efficacy:** Blasticidin-S exhibits a wide range of inhibitory activity on the growth of bacterial and fungal cells. In addition, it has been shown to have antiviral and anti-tumour activity. It inhibits spore germination and mycelial growth of *Pyricularia oryzae* in the laboratory at rates below 1 µg per ml. **Key references:** 1) S Takeuchi, K Hirayama, K Ueda, H Sasaki and H Yonehara. 1958. Blasticidin S, a new antibiotic, *J. Antibiot.*

Ser. A, **11**, 1. 2) T Misato, I Ishii, M Asakawa, Y Okimoto and K Fukunaga. 1959. Antibiotics as protectant fungicides against rice blast. II. The therapeutic action of blasticidin S, *Ann. Phytopathol. Soc. Jpn.*, **24**, 302. 3) K T Huang, T Misato and H Suyama. 1964. Effect of blasticidin S on protein biosynthesis of *Pyricularia oryzae. J. Antibiot. Ser. A*, **17**, 65.

COMMERCIALISATION: **Formulation:** Sold as dispersible powder (DP), emulsifiable concentrate (EC) and wettable powder (WP) formulations. **Tradenames:** Bla-S – Kaken, Kumiai and Nihon Nohyaku.

APPLICATION: Applied at a rate of between 100 and 300 g active ingredient per hectare for the control of rice blast (*Pyricularia oryzae*) by foliar application. Damage can be caused to alfalfa, aubergines, clover, potatoes, soybean, tobacco, and tomatoes. Excessive application produces yellow spots on rice leaves.

PRODUCT SPECIFICATIONS: The efficacy of the product is checked by bioassay with *Bacillus cereus* strain IAM-1729. **Purity:** Sold as the benzylaminobenzenesulfonate to reduce the possibility of crop damage. Sometimes sold in admixture with calcium acetate to reduce the incidence of eye irritation.

COMPATIBILITY: Incompatible with alkaline materials.

MAMMALIAN TOXICITY: Blasticidin S is rather toxic to mammals. **Acute oral LD$_{50}$:** male rats 56.8, female rats 55.9, male mice 51.9, female mice 60.1 mg/kg. **Acute dermal LD$_{50}$:** rats >500 mg/kg. **Skin and eye:** Severe eye irritant. **NOEL:** (2 years) for rats 1 mg/kg diet. **Toxicity class:** WHO (active ingredient) 1b; EPA (formulation) II. **Other toxicological effects:** Non-mutagenic in bacterial reversion tests.

ENVIRONMENTAL IMPACT AND NON-TARGET TOXICITY: **Fish toxicity:** LC$_{50}$ (48 hours) carp >40 mg/litre. **Other aquatic toxicity:** LC$_{50}$ (3 hours) *Daphnia pulex* >40 mg/litre. **Metabolism:** Almost all of 3H-blasticidin-S administered to mice was excreted in the urine and faeces within 24 hours. In rice plants, cytomycin and deaminohydroxy blasticidin-S were identified as the main metabolites. **Behaviour in soil:** In soil, DT$_{50}$ <2 days (two soil types, o.c. 2.53%, 9.6%; moisture 42.6%, 87% respectively; pH 6.0, 25 °C).

1:06 fatty acids (oleic acid)

Herbicide, fungicide, insecticide

The Pesticide Manual - 11th edition: Entry number 532

$$CH_3(CH_2)_7CH{=}CH(CH_2)_7CO_2M$$

$$M = H, Na\ or\ K$$

NOMENCLATURE: **Approved name:** fatty acids, often oleic acid. **CAS RN:** *[112–80–1]* (Z)-isomer of oleic acid; *[112–79–1]* (E)-isomer of oleic acid; *[2027–47–6]* unspecified stereochemistry oleic acid.

SOURCE: Naturally occurring fatty acids extracted from plant and animal sources.

PRODUCTION: Extracted from plant and animal sources.

TARGET CROPS: Insecticide uses include vegetable, fruit and ornamentals, fungicide uses include grapes, roses and other crops and herbicide uses include total weed control and moss control in lawns.

BIOLOGICAL ACTIVITY: **Mode of action:** Fatty acid extracts interfere with the cell membrane constituents of the target organism leading to a breakdown of the integrity of the membrane and death. Different fatty acids are effective as insecticides, fungicides, total herbicides or as moss killers. **Efficacy:** M-Pede is effective at controlling soft-bodied insects such as aphids and gives curative control of powdery mildew pathogens. Scythe is an effective total, non-residual herbicide and DeMoss controls moss in lawns and moss and liverworts on fences, roofs and glasshouses.

COMMERCIALISATION: **Formulation:** Sold as a liquid concentrate (SL).
Tradenames: M-Pede – Mycogen, DeMoss – Mycogen, Scythe – Mycogen, Thinex – Mycogen, Neo-Fat – Akzo Nobel.

APPLICATION: Apply as a foliar spray to crops. Ensure good coverage of pest.

PRODUCT SPECIFICATIONS: Fatty acid components of the formulation differ according to the use recommendation.

COMPATIBILITY: It is unusual to apply fatty acids in combination with other crop protection products.

MAMMALIAN TOXICITY: Generally considered to be non-toxic. **Toxicity class:** EPA (formulation) II; Neo-Fat III.

ENVIRONMENTAL IMPACT AND NON-TARGET TOXICITY: Non-toxic to non-target organisms or to the environment. **Behaviour in soil:** Rapidly degraded in soil.

1:07 gibberellic acid   *Plant growth regulator*

The Pesticide Manual - 11th edition: Entry number 379

NOMENCLATURE: **Approved name:** gibberellic acid (BSI, draft E-ISO, accepted in lieu of a common name); acide gibbérellique (draft F-ISO). **Other names:** gibberellin A_3; GA_3 (ambiguous). **CAS RN:** [77-06-5].

SOURCE: Originally isolated from rice infected with *Gibberella fujikuroi* Wr. (*Fusarium moniliforme* Sheldon). Infected rice in Japan was a common sight and the seedlings grew well above the height of uninfected plants, leading to the name *bakanae* disease (foolish seedling). Discovered by E Kurosawa in 1926 who called it gibberellin A. Later ICI Plant Protection Ltd (now Zeneca Agrochemicals) isolated a compound with similar biological properties and chemical structure which was called gibberellic acid. It and over 70 other known members of the gibberellin group of plant growth regulators have been shown to occur naturally in a wide variety of plant species. It was introduced by ICI Plant Protection who no longer sell it.

PRODUCTION: Produced from the fermentation of *Gibberella fujikuroi*.

TARGET CROPS: Plant growth regulator, used in a variety of applications, e.g. to improve fruit setting of clementines and pears (especially William pears); to loosen and elongate clusters and increase berry size in grapes; to control fruit maturity by delaying development of the yellow colour in lemons; to reduce rind stain and retard rind ageing in navel oranges; to counteract the effects of cherry yellows virus diseases in sour cherries; to produce uniform seedling growth in rice; to promote elongation of winter celery crop; to induce uniform bolting and increase seed production in lettuce for seed; to break dormancy and stimulate sprouting in seed potatoes; to extend the picking season by hastening maturity in artichokes; to increase the yield in forced rhubarb; to increase the malting quality of barley; to produce brighter-coloured, firmer fruit, and to increase the size of sweet cherries; to increase yields and aid harvesting of hops; to reduce internal browning and increase yields of Italian prunes; to increase fruit set and yields of tangelos and tangerines; to improve fruit setting in blueberries; to advance flowering and increase the yield of strawberries; and also a variety of applications on ornamentals.

BIOLOGICAL ACTIVITY: **Mode of action:** A naturally occurring plant growth regulator that is part of the system that regulates plant growth and development. It acts as a plant growth regulator on account of its physiological and morphological effects in extremely low concentrations. Translocated. Generally affects only the plant parts above the soil surface. **Efficacy:** Gibberellic acid is very effective at low rates of use. It exerts a wide range of effects on many different plant processes. **Key references:** 1) E Kurosawa. 1926. *Trans. Nat. Hist. Soc. (Formosa)*, **16**, 213. 2) J F Grove. 1961. *Q. Rev. Chem. Soc.*, **15**, 56.

COMMERCIALISATION: **Formulation:** Sold as soluble powder (SP), crystal, water soluble granule (SG), emulsifiable concentrate (EC) and tablet (TB) formulations.
Tradenames: Ceku-Gib – Cequisa, GIB – Burlington, Gibbex – Griffin, Gibrel – Thermo Trilogy, Kri-Gibb – Krishi Rasayan, ProGibb – Abbott, Release - Abbott, RyzUp – Abbott, ProVide – Abbott, Ralex – Abbott, Regulex – Abbott, Strong – Sanonda, Uvex – Productos OSA, GibGro – Agtrol Chemical Products, Pol-Gibrescol – Ciech SA, Forgibbs – Forward International, Point Acigib – Point Enterprises, Ro-Gibb – Rotam Group, Strong – Sanonda Co, Tigibb – Tide International , Falgro – Fine Agrochemicals.

PRODUCT SPECIFICATIONS: **Purity:** The product quality is confirmed by hplc analysis.

COMPATIBILITY: Incompatible with alkaline materials and solutions containing chlorine.

MAMMALIAN TOXICITY: **Acute oral LD$_{50}$:** rats and mice >15,000 mg/kg.
Acute dermal LD$_{50}$: not available. **Inhalation:** No ill effect on rats subjected to 400 mg/litre for 2 hours per day for 21 days. **Skin and eye:** Non-irritating to skin and eyes. **NOEL:** (90 days) for rats and dogs >1000 mg/kg diet (6 days/week). **Toxicity class:** WHO (active ingredient) III (Table 5); EPA (formulation) III.

ENVIRONMENTAL IMPACT AND NON-TARGET TOXICITY: Gibberellic acid has no adverse effects on non-target organisms or on the environment.
Effects on beneficial insects: Not toxic to honeybees. **Behaviour in soil:** Rapidly degraded in soil.

1:08   gibberellin A$_4$ with gibberellin A$_7$

Plant growth regulator

The Pesticide Manual - 11th edition: Entry number 380

NOMENCLATURE: **Approved name:** gibberellin A$_4$ plus gibberellin A$_7$.
CAS RN: *[468–44–0]* gibberellin A$_4$ (i); *[510–75–8]* gibberellin A$_7$ (ii).

SOURCE: Produced from the fermentation of *Gibberella fujikuroi* Wr.

TARGET CROPS: Plant growth regulator used to reduce russetting in apples, increase fruit set in pears and seed germination and yield in celery.

BIOLOGICAL ACTIVITY: **Mode of action:** Naturally occurring plant growth regulators that are part of the system that regulates plant growth and development. The mixture acts as a plant growth regulator on account of its physiological and morphological effects in extremely low concentrations. Translocated. Generally affects only the plant parts above the soil surface.

COMMERCIALISATION: **Formulation:** Sold as a liquid concentrate (SL). **Tradenames:** ProVide – Abbott.

PRODUCT SPECIFICATIONS: Contains a mixture of gibberellins but predominately gibberellin A_4 and gibberellin A_7. **Purity:** The product quality is confirmed by hplc analysis.

COMPATIBILITY: Incompatible with alkaline materials and solutions containing chlorine.

MAMMALIAN TOXICITY: The combination of gibberellin A_4 and gibberellin A_7 is non-toxic to mammals.

ENVIRONMENTAL IMPACT AND NON-TARGET TOXICITY: Gibberellin A_4 and gibberellin A_7 occur naturally in plants and are not expected to cause any adverse effects on non-target organisms or the environment. **Effects on beneficial insects:** Not toxic to honeybees. **Behaviour in soil:** Rapidly degraded in soil.

1:09   indol-3-ylacetic acid

Plant growth regulator

The Pesticide Manual - 11th edition: Entry number 423

NOMENCLATURE: **Approved name:** indol-3-ylacetic acid. **Other names:** IAA, AIA (France). **CAS RN:** [87–51–4].

SOURCE: Naturally occurring plant growth regulator.

PRODUCTION: Indol-3-ylacetic acid is manufactured for use in agriculture rather than extracted from higher plants.

TARGET CROPS: Used on herbaceous and woody ornamentals to stimulate rooting of cuttings.

BIOLOGICAL ACTIVITY: **Mode of action:** Plant growth regulator which affects cell division and cell elongation. Indol-3-ylacetic acid is very effective at initiating the formation of roots in cuttings through causing cell division in the cambial tissue.

COMMERCIALISATION: **Formulation:** Sold as tablet (TB) and dispersible powder (DP) formulations. **Tradenames:** Rhizopon A – Fargro.

APPLICATION: Cuttings are dipped in the product prior to planting.

PRODUCT SPECIFICATIONS: Contains indol-3-ylacetic acid often with an added fungicide and inerts. **Purity:** Product quality is checked by u.v. spectrophotometry.

COMPATIBILITY: It is unlikely that indol-3-ylacetic acid would be used with any other crop protection chemical with the exception of broad-spectrum fungicides with which it is compatible.

MAMMALIAN TOXICITY: Indol-3-ylacetic acid occurs in all higher plants and has not shown any adverse effects on mammals. **Acute oral LD$_{50}$:** mice 1,000 mg/kg.

ENVIRONMENTAL IMPACT AND NON-TARGET TOXICITY: Indol-3-ylacetic acid occurs naturally in plants and is not expected to show any adverse effects on non-target organisms or on the environment. **Effects on beneficial insects:** Not toxic to honeybees. **Behaviour in soil:** Rapidly degraded in soil.

1:10   kasugamycin *Microbial fungicide/bactericide*

The Pesticide Manual - 11th edition: Entry number 438

NOMENCLATURE: **Approved name:** kasugamycin (JMAF). **CAS RN:** *[6980–18–3]*.

SOURCE: Isolated from the soil actinomycete *Streptomyces kasugaensis*. First described by H Umezawa *et al.* in 1965 and introduced by Hokko Chemical Industry Co. Ltd.

PRODUCTION: Produced by fermentation of *Streptomyces kasugaensis* and isolation of the secondary metabolite from the fermentation broth. Sold as the hydrochloride.

TARGET PESTS: Rice blast (*Pyricularia oryzae* Cavara), leaf spot in sugar beet and celery (*Cercospora* spp.), bacterial disease in rice and vegetables and scab (*Venturia* spp.) in apples and pears.

TARGET CROPS: Rice, top fruit and vegetables.

BIOLOGICAL ACTIVITY: **Mode of action:** Inhibition of protein biosynthesis by interfering with the binding of aminoacyl-tRNA to both the mRNA-30S and the mRNA-70S ribosomal subunit complexes, thereby preventing the incorporation of amino acids into proteins. Kasugamycin is a systemic fungicide and bactericide with both protectant and curative properties. **Efficacy:** Kasugamycin controls rice blast at concentrations as low as 20 mg per litre. Resistance to kasugamycin was detected within three years of its introduction in 1965 and by 1972 it had become a serious problem in Japanese rice fields. Today, mixtures of kasugamycin with other fungicides with different modes of action are used. Resistant strains of *Pyricularia oryzae* are less fit than susceptible strains and once applications of kasugamycin are discontinued in the field, the level of resistance declines very rapidly. Kasugamycin inhibits hyphal growth in *Pyricularia oryzae* on rice, preventing lesion development; it is a comparatively weak inhibitor of spore germination, appressorium formation and penetration into the epidermal cells. In contrast, against *Cladosporium fulvum* on tomatoes, inhibition of sporulation is high but its effects on hyphal growth are poor. Kasugamycin is taken up by plant tissue and is translocated. **Key references:** 1) H Umezawa, Y Okami, T Hashimoto, Y Suhara and N Otake. 1965. A new antibiotic, kasugamycin, *J. Antibiot. Ser. A*, **18**, 101. 2) M Hamada, T Hashimoto, S Takahashi, M Yoneyama, T Miyake, Y Takeuchi, Y Okami and H Umezawa. 1965. Antimicrobial activity of kasugamycin, *J. Antibiot. Ser. A*, **18**, 104. 3) N Tanaka, H Yamaguchi and H Umezawa. 1966. Mechanism of kasugamycin action on polypeptide synthesis, *J. Biochem.*, **60**, 429.

COMMERCIALISATION: **Formulation:** Sold as the hydrochloride as wettable powder (WP), dispersible powder (DP), ultra-low volume (UL), soluble concentrate (SL) and granule (GR) formulations. **Tradenames:** Kasugamin – Hokko, Kasumin – Hokko. **Patents:** JP 42006818; BE 657659; GB 1094566.

APPLICATION: Applied as a foliar spray, a dust or a seed treatment at rates from 20 g per litre.

PRODUCT SPECIFICATIONS: **Purity:** The product is analysed by cup assay with *Pseudomonas fluorescens* (NIHJ B-254).

COMPATIBILITY: Often sold or recommended for use in combination with other rice blast fungicides to counteract the onset of resistance. Incompatible with compounds that are strongly alkaline. There has been evidence of slight phytotoxicity on crops such as peas, beans, soybeans, grapes, citrus and apples. No injury has been found on rice, tomatoes, sugar beet, potatoes and many other vegetables.

MAMMALIAN TOXICITY: As with other aminoglycoside antibiotics, kasugamycin shows very low levels of mammalian toxicity. **Acute oral LD$_{50}$:** male rats >5,000 mg/kg. **Acute dermal LD$_{50}$:** rabbits >2,000 mg/kg. **Inhalation:** LC$_{50}$ (4 hours) rats >2.4 mg/litre. **Skin and eye:** Non-irritating to the eyes and skin (rabbits). **NOEL:** (2 years) rats 300 and dogs 800 mg/kg diet. Non-mutagenic and non-teratogenic in rats. No effects on reproduction. **Toxicity class:** WHO (active ingredient) III (Table 5); EPA (formulation) IV.

ENVIRONMENTAL IMPACT AND NON-TARGET TOXICITY: Kasugamycin is not expected to have any adverse effects on non-target organisms or on the environment. **Bird toxicity:** Acute oral LD_{50} male Japanese quail >4,000 mg/kg. **Fish toxicity:** LC_{50} (48 hours) carp and goldfish >40 mg/litre. **Other aquatic toxicity:** *Daphnia pulex* LC_{50} (6 hours) >40 mg/litre. **Metabolism:** Kasugamycin hydrochloride hydrate administered orally to rabbits was almost completely excreted in the urine within 24 hours. When injected intravenously to dogs, it was almost completely excreted within 8 hours. After oral administration to rats at 200 mg/kg, no residues were found in eleven organs or in the blood and 96% of the administered dose remained in the digestive tract one hour after administration. Plants metabolise kasugamycin to kasugamycinic acid and kasuganobiosamine and eventually to ammonia, oxalic acid, carbon dioxide and water. **Behaviour in soil:** Metabolism in soil is identical to that in plants with the final products being ammonia, water and carbon dioxide.

1:11   kasugamycin hydrochloride hydrate   *Microbial fungicide/bactericide*

The Pesticide Manual - 11th edition: Entry number 438

NOMENCLATURE: **Approved name:** kasugamycin hydrochloride hydrate. **CAS RN:** [19408–46–9].

SOURCE: Isolated from the soil actinomycete *Streptomyces kasugaensis*.

PRODUCTION: By fermentation of *Streptomyces kasugaensis*.

TARGET PESTS: Control of rice blast (*Pyricularia oryzae* Cavara) and some other diseases (particularly bacterial grain rot, bacterial seedling blight, and bacterial brown stripe caused by *Pseudomonas* spp.). Also used to control other plant diseases, e.g. leaf mould and bacterial canker, bean halo blight, scab, *Cercospora* leaf spot, bacterial soft rot, anthracnose and bacterial spot and other bacterial diseases (particularly *Pseudomonas* spp.).

TARGET CROPS: Recommended for use in rice, tomatoes, beans, apples and pears, sugar beet and celery, potatoes and carrots, cucumbers, citrus fruit and ornamentals.

BIOLOGICAL ACTIVITY: **Mode of action:** Protein synthesis inhibitor. Inhibits binding of aminoacyl-tRNA to the mRNA-30S complex, thereby preventing amino acid incorporation. Systemic fungicide and bactericide with protective and curative action. Inhibits hyphal growth of *Pyricularia oryzae* on rice, preventing lesion development; comparatively weak inhibitory action to spore germination, appressoria formation on the plant surface or penetration into the epidermal cell. Rapidly taken up into plant tissue and translocated. In contrast, against *Cladosporium fulvum* on tomato, inhibition of sporulation is strong, but inhibition of hyphal growth is weak. Non-phytotoxic to rice, tomatoes, sugar beet, potatoes and other vegetables, but slight injury has been noted to peas, beans, soybean, grapes, citrus, and apples. **Efficacy:** Kasugamycin hydrochloride hydrate controls rice blast at concentrations as low as 20 mg per litre. Resistance to kasugamycin was detected within three years of its introduction in 1965 and by 1972 it had become a serious problem in Japanese rice fields. Today, mixtures of kasugamycin hydrochloride hydrate with other fungicides with different modes of action are used. Resistant strains of *Pyricularia oryzae* are less fit than susceptible strains and, once applications of kasugamycin are discontinued in the field, the level of resistance declines very rapidly. Kasugamycin hydrochloride hydrate inhibits hyphal growth in *Pyricularia oryzae* on rice, preventing lesion development; it is a comparatively weak inhibitor of spore germination, appressorium formation and penetration into the epidermal cells. In contrast, against *Cladosporium fulvum* on tomatoes, inhibition of sporulation is high but its effects on hyphal growth are poor. Kasugamycin hydrochloride hydrate is taken up by plant tissue and is translocated. **Key references:** 1) H Umezawa, Y Okami, T Hashimoto, Y Suhara and N Otake. 1965. A new antibiotic, kasugamycin, *J. Antibiot. Ser. A*, **18**, 101. 2) M Hamada, T Hashimoto, S Takahashi, M Yoneyama, T Miyake, Y Takeuchi, Y Okami and H Umezawa. 1965. Antimicrobial activity of kasugamycin, *J. Antibiot. Ser. A*, **18**, 104. 3) N Tanaka, H Yamaguchi and H Umezawa. 1966. Mechanism of kasugamycin action on polypeptide synthesis, *J. Biochem.*, **60**, 429.

COMMERCIALISATION: **Formulation:** Sold as wettable powder (WP), dispersible powder (DP), granules (GR), ultra-low volume (UL) and soluble concentrate (SL) formulations. **Tradenames:** Kasugamin – Hokko, Kasumin – Hokko. **Patents:** JP 42006818; BE 657659; GB 1094566.

APPLICATION: Applied as a foliar spray, a dust or a seed treatment at rates from 20 g per litre.

PRODUCT SPECIFICATIONS: **Purity:** The product is analysed by cup assay with *Pseudomonas fluorescens* (NIHJ B-254).

COMPATIBILITY: Incompatible with pesticides which are strongly alkaline.

MAMMALIAN TOXICITY: **Acute oral LD$_{50}$:** male rats >5,000 mg/kg. **Acute dermal LD$_{50}$:** rabbits >2,000 mg/kg. **Inhalation:** LC$_{50}$ (4 hours) rats >2.4 mg/litre. **Skin and eye:** Non-irritating to eyes and skin (rabbits). **NOEL:** (2 years) rats 300, dogs 800 mg/kg diet. Non-mutagenic and non-teratogenic in rats and without effect on reproduction. **Toxicity class:** WHO active ingredient III (Table 5); EPA (formulation) IV.

ENVIRONMENTAL IMPACT AND NON-TARGET TOXICITY: **Bird toxicity:** Acute oral LD_{50} male Japanese quail >4,000 mg/kg. **Fish toxicity:** LC_{50} (48 hours) carp and goldfish >40 mg/litre. **Other aquatic toxicity:** LC_{50} (6 hours) *Daphnia pulex* >40 mg/litre. **Effects on beneficial insects:** LD_{50} to honeybees (contact) >40 μg per bee.
Metabolism: Kasugamycin hydrochloride hydrate orally administered to rabbits was mostly excreted in the urine within 24 hours. When injected intravenously to dogs, is was mostly excreted within 8 hours. After oral administration to rats at 200 mg/kg, no residues were detected in eleven organs or blood; 96% of the administered dose remained in the digestive tract 1 hour after administration. In plants, it is degraded to kasugamycinic acid and kasuganobiosamine and finally to ammonia, oxalic acid, carbon dioxide and water.
Behaviour in soil: Degradation proceeds as in plants.

1:12   milbemectin   *Microbial acaricide/insecticide*

The Pesticide Manual - 11th edition: Entry number 500

Milbemycin A_3 : R = CH_3
Milbemycin A_4 : R = CH_2CH_3

NOMENCLATURE: **Approved name:** milbemectin (BSI, pa E-ISO).
CAS RN: *[51596–10–2]* A_3; *[51596–11–3]* A_4. **Development codes:** B-41; E-187; SI-8601 (Sankyo).

SOURCE: Isolated from the soil actinomycete *Streptomyces hygroscopicus* subsp. *aureolacrimosus*.

PRODUCTION: Produced by the fermentation of *Streptomyces hygroscopicus* subsp. *aureolacrimosus* and isolation from the fermentation broth.

TARGET PESTS: Control of citrus red mites and pink citrus rust mites, Kanzawa spider mites and other spider mites.

TARGET CROPS: Recommended for use on citrus fruit, tea and aubergines.

BIOLOGICAL ACTIVITY: **Mode of action:** The target for milbemectin is the γ-aminobutyric acid (GABA) receptor in the peripheral nervous system. The compound stimulates the release of GABA from nerve endings and enhances the binding of GABA to receptor sites on the post-synaptic membrane of inhibitory motor neurons of mites and other arthropods. This enhanced GABA binding results in an increased flow of chloride ions into the cell, with consequent hyperpolarization and elimination of signal transduction resulting in an inhibition of neurotransmission. (See M J Turner and J M Schaeffer. 1989. In *Ivermectin and Abamectin*, W. C. Campbell (ed.), Springer-Verlag, New York, p. 73). Acaricide with contact and stomach action. It has limited plant systemic activity, but exhibits translaminar movement.
Efficacy: Milbemycin has been shown to have very high insecticidal and acaricidal activity but shows no antimicrobial effects. **Key references:** 1) Y Takiguchi, H Mishima, M Okuda, M Terao, A Aoki and R Fukuda. 1980. Milbemycins, a new family of macrolide antibiotics: Fermentation, isolation and physicochemical properties, *J. Antibiot.*, **33**, 1120. 2) M Mishima. 1983. Milbemycin: a family of macrolide antibiotics with insecticidal activity, In *IUPAC Pesticide Chemistry*, J Miyamoto and P C Kearney (eds.), Pergamon Press, Oxford, Vol. 2, 129.

COMMERCIALISATION: **Formulation:** Sold as an emulsifiable concentrate (EC) formulation.
Tradenames: Milbeknock – Sankyo.

APPLICATION: Rates of use are 5.6 to 28 g active ingredient per hectare for mite control. The effectiveness of the product is increased significantly by the addition of paraffinic oils to the spray tank.

PRODUCT SPECIFICATIONS: **Purity:** A mixture of the homologues milbemycin A_3 (methyl) and milbemycin A_4 (ethyl) in the ratio 3 to 7.

COMPATIBILITY: Compatible with most crop protection chemicals.

MAMMALIAN TOXICITY: **Acute oral LD_{50}:** male mice 324, female mice 313, male rats 762, female rats 456 mg/kg. **Acute dermal LD_{50}:** male and female rats >5,000 mg/kg.
Other toxicological effects: Not carcinogenic, not teratogenic, not mutagenic.

ENVIRONMENTAL IMPACT AND NON-TARGET TOXICITY: Milbemectin is not persistent in the environment and is not thought to pose any threat to non-target organisms.
Fish toxicity: LC_{50} carp 1.7 mg/litre.

NOMENCLATURE: **Approved name:** mildiomycin (JMAF). **Development codes:** Antibiotic B-98891 and TF-138.

SOURCE: Produced by the soil actinomycete *Streptoverticillium rimofaciens* strain B-98891.

PRODUCTION: Manufactured by fermentation of *Streptoverticillium rimofaciens* B-98891 and extraction from the culture medium.

TARGET PESTS: Powdery mildews (*Erysiphe* spp. *Uncinula necator* Burr., *Podosphaera* spp. *Sphaerotheca* spp.).

TARGET CROPS: Ornamentals.

BIOLOGICAL ACTIVITY: **Mode of action:** Mildiomycin is believed to inhibit protein biosynthesis in fungi by blocking peptidyl-transferase. It is effective as an eradicant with some systemic activity. **Efficacy:** Mildiomycin is specifically active against the pathogens that cause powdery mildew and is much less effective against bacteria. **Key references:** 1) S Harada and T Kishi. 1978. Isolation and characterisation of mildiomycin, a new nucleoside antibiotic, *J. Antibiot.*, **31**, 519. 2) Y Om, I Yamaguchi and T Misato. 1984. Inhibition of protein biosynthesis by mildiomycin, an anti-mildew substance, *J. Pestic. Sci.*, **9**, 317. 3) T Kusaka, K Suetomi, T Iwasa and S Harada. 1979. TF-138: a new fungicide, *Proc. 1979 Brit. Crop Prot. Conf. – Pests & Diseases*, **2**, 589–95.

COMMERCIALISATION: **Formulation:** Sold as a wettable powder (WP) formulation. **Tradenames:** Mildiomycin – Takeda.

APPLICATION: Used as a foliar spray to eradicate and subsequently protect crops from attack by powdery mildews at rates of 5 to 10 g per hectalitre.

PRODUCT SPECIFICATIONS: Product contains no other active metabolites.

MAMMALIAN TOXICITY: **Acute oral LD$_{50}$:** male rats 4,300, female rats 4,120, male mice 5,060 and female mice 5,250 mg/kg. **Acute dermal LD$_{50}$:** male and female rats and mice >5,000 mg/kg. **Skin and eye:** No irritation has been observed to the cornea and the skin of rabbits at 1,000 µg per ml over 10 days. **NOEL:** In 30-day feeding studies, there were no significant adverse effects to mice or rats fed 200 mg per kg daily. In a 3-month sub-acute feeding study in rats, the maximum no-effect level was 50 mg per kg daily.
Other toxicological effects: Negative results were obtained from the Ames test for mutagenicity conducted with or without rat liver homogenate.

ENVIRONMENTAL IMPACT AND NON-TARGET TOXICITY: Mildiomycin is not expected to have any adverse effects on non-target organisms or on the environment.
Fish toxicity: LC$_{50}$ (72 hours) carp >40 mg/litre, (168 hours) killifish >40 mg/litre.
Other aquatic toxicity: LC$_{50}$ (6 hours) *Daphnia pulex* >20 mg per litre.

1:14   natamycin   *Microbial fungicide*

The Pesticide Manual - 11th edition: Entry number 515

NOMENCLATURE: **Approved name:** natamycin (BAN), pimaricin and tennectin (traditional names). **Other names:** myprozine. **CAS RN:** *[7681–93–8]*.

SOURCE: Secondary metabolite of the actinomycetes *Streptomyces natalensis* and *S. chattanoogensis*.

PRODUCTION: Manufactured by fermentation.

TARGET PESTS: Fungal diseases, especially basal rots caused by *Fusarium oxysporum* Schlecht.

TARGET CROPS: Bulbs such as daffodils.

BIOLOGICAL ACTIVITY: **Efficacy:** Used as a dip, usually in combination with hot water treatment. Gives effective control of various fungal diseases of ornamental bulbs prior to planting.

COMMERCIALISATION: **Formulation:** Sold as a wettable powder (WP).
Tradenames: Delvolan – Gist-Brocades. **Patents:** GB 712547; GB 844289; US 3892850.

APPLICATION: Bulbs are dipped in a solution of the product. It is usual to accompany this treatment with a hot water treatment.

PRODUCT SPECIFICATIONS: **Purity:** Product purity is checked by bioassay with a suitable fungal pathogen such as *Fusarium oxysporum*.

COMPATIBILITY: It is unusual to apply natamycin in combination with any other crop protection agent.

MAMMALIAN TOXICITY: **Acute oral LD$_{50}$:** rats 2,730–4,670 mg/kg. **Skin and eye:** No acute toxicity, even at high doses. Not a skin sensitiser. Not a skin or eye irritant (rabbits). **Toxicity class:** WHO (active ingredient) III.

ENVIRONMENTAL IMPACT AND NON-TARGET TOXICITY: Natamycin is not toxic to fish and is readily biodegradable. No adverse effects have been observed on non-target organisms or on the environment.

1:15 nicotine *Plant derived insecticide*

The Pesticide Manual - 11th edition: Entry number 520

NOMENCLATURE: **Approved name:** nicotine (BSI, E-ISO, F-ISO, ESA, in lieu of a common name); nicotine sulfate (E-ISO (from 1984), JMAF, for sulfate salt); sulfate de nicotine (F-ISO). **CAS RN:** *[54–11–5]* (S)- isomer; *[22083–74–5]* (RS)- isomers; *[75202–10–7]* unstated stereochemistry. **EEC no.** 200–193–3.

SOURCE: A component of the genus *Nicotiana*, and particularly the species *Nicotiana rustica* L.

PRODUCTION: Once prepared from extracts of the tobacco plant but now manufactured and sold as either technical nicotine or nicotine sulfate.

TARGET PESTS: Used for the control of a wide range of insects including aphids, thrips and whitefly.

TARGET CROPS: Recommended for use on glasshouse ornamentals and field-grown crops including fruit, vines, vegetables and ornamentals.

BIOLOGICAL ACTIVITY: **Mode of action:** Non-systemic insecticide that binds to the cholinergic acetylcholine nicotinic receptor in the nerve cells of insects, leading to a continuous firing of this neuroreceptor. Active predominantly through the vapour phase, but also slight contact and stomach action. **Efficacy:** Nicotine has been used for many years as a fumigant for the control of many sucking insects. It can be used to give partial control of OP and pyrethroid resistant whitefly. **Key reference:** I Schmeltz. 1971. In *Naturally Occurring Insecticides*, M Jacobson and D G Crosby (eds.), Marcel Dekker, New York.

COMMERCIALISATION: **Formulation:** Sold as dispersible powder (DP), soluble concentrate (SL) or as fumigant formulations. **Tradenames:** Nico Soap – United Phosphorus Ltd, No-Fid – Hortichem, XL-All Nicotine – Vitax, Nicotine 40% Shreds – Dow AgroSciences.

APPLICATION: Applied as a foliar spray to cover the undersides of leaves, repeating as necessary. Best results are achieved when the temperature is above 16 °C. If used as a fumigant, the temperature must be above 16 °C. The maximum number of treatments in protected crops is three. Nicotine is subject to regulation under the Poisons Act.

PRODUCT SPECIFICATIONS: **Purity:** The predominant component of the crude alkaloid extract is (S)- (–)- nicotine; small amounts of related alkaloids may be present. Manufactured nicotine may be the racemic mixture.

COMPATIBILITY: May be used with most crop protection agents. Test for crop selectivity before treating large areas.

MAMMALIAN TOXICITY: **Acute oral LD$_{50}$:** rats 50–60 mg/kg. **Acute dermal LD$_{50}$:** rabbits 50 mg/kg. **Inhalation:** Toxic to man by inhalation. **Skin and eye:** Readily absorbed through the skin. Toxic to man by skin contact. **Toxicity class:** WHO (active ingredient) Ib; EPA (formulation) I. **Other toxicological effects:** Lethal oral dose for man is stated to be 40 to 60 mg.

ENVIRONMENTAL IMPACT AND NON-TARGET TOXICITY: **Bird toxicity:** Toxic to birds. **Fish toxicity:** LC$_{50}$ larval rainbow trout 4 mg/litre. **Other aquatic toxicity:** LC$_{50}$ *Daphnia pulex* 0.24 mg/litre. **Metabolism:** Nicotine decomposes relatively quickly under the influence of light and air.

$$\text{chemical structure}$$

OH OH N(CH₃)₂ ... (structure diagram)

NOMENCLATURE: **Approved name:** oxytetracycline (ISO, BSI, JMAF, BAN).
Other names: terramitsin (Russia). **CAS RN:** *[79–57–2]* oxytetracyline; *[2058–46–0]* oxytetracycline hydrochloride.

SOURCE: Oxytetracycline is produced by the fermentation of *Streptomyces rimosus*.

PRODUCTION: Produced by fermentation and usually sold as the hydrochloride.

TARGET PESTS: Bacterial diseases such as fireblight (*Erwinia amylovora* Winsl.) and diseases caused by *Pseudomonas* and *Xanthomonas* species. Also effective against diseases caused by mycoplasma-like organisms.

TARGET CROPS: Stone tree fruit, pome fruit and turf grass.

BIOLOGICAL ACTIVITY: **Mode of action:** Oxytetracycline is a potent inhibitor of protein biosynthesis in bacteria. It binds to the 30S and 50S bacterial ribosomal subunits and inhibits the binding of aminoacyl-tRNA and the termination factors RF1 and RF2 to the A site of the bacterial ribosome. It is much less active in mammalian systems. **Efficacy:** Oxytetracycline is rapidly taken up by plant leaves, particularly through stomata, and is subsequently readily translocated to other plant tissues. It is an effective antibacterial and is often mixed with streptomycin to prevent the development of streptomycin resistance.
Key references: 1) A C Finlay, G L Hobby, S Y Pan, P P Regna, J B Routier, D B Seeley, G M Shull, B A Sobin, I A Solomons, J W Vinson and J H Kane. 1950. Terramycin, a new antibiotic, *Science*, **111**, 519. 2) T Ishii, Y Doi, K Yora and H Asuyama. 1967. Suppressive effects of antibiotics of the tetracycline group on symptom development of mulberry dwarf disease, *Ann. Phytopathol. Soc. Jpn.*, **33**, 267. 3) C T Caskey. 1973. Inhibitors of protein biosynthesis. In *Metabolic Inhibitors*, R M Hochster, M Kates and J H Quastel (eds.), Academic Press, New York, Vol. IV, 131.

COMMERCIALISATION: **Formulation:** Sold as a water soluble powder (SP).
Tradenames: Mycoshield – Novartis, Terramycin – Novartis, Phytomycin (plus streptomycin sulfate) – Ladda.

APPLICATION: Applied as foliar spray to infected plants.

PRODUCT SPECIFICATIONS: **Purity:** Efficacy of the formulation can be checked by bioassay against a suitable bacterium.

COMPATIBILITY: Compatible with most crop protection agents. It is often applied in combination with streptomycin sulfate.

MAMMALIAN TOXICITY: Considered to be non-toxic to mammalian systems.

ENVIRONMENTAL IMPACT AND NON-TARGET TOXICITY: Oxytetracycline is not expected to show any adverse effects on non-target organisms or on the environment.

1:17   pelargonic acid   *Plant growth regulator*

The Pesticide Manual - 11th edition: Entry number 525

$$CH_3(CH_2)_7CO_2H$$

NOMENCLATURE: **Approved name:** pelargonic acid. **Other names:** nonoic acid, nonanoic acid, fatty acids. **CAS RN:** *[112–05–0]*. **Development codes:** JT-101.

SOURCE: Pelargonic acid occurs naturally in members of the family Geraniaceae.

PRODUCTION: May be extracted from plants but usually manufactured for use in crop protection.

TARGET CROPS: Apples and other tree fruit.

BIOLOGICAL ACTIVITY: **Mode of action:** Pelargonic acid is a mild phytotoxicant and, when applied to trees shortly after petal fall, causes the thinning of the fruit and thereby allowing larger, more regular shaped fruit to develop.

COMMERCIALISATION: **Formulation:** Sold as a liquid concentrate (SL). **Tradenames:** Thinex – Mycogen, Scythe – Mycogen, Grantico – Japan Tobacco.

APPLICATION: Apply to orchard trees at blossom or within two weeks of petal fall.

MAMMALIAN TOXICITY: **Acute oral LD$_{50}$:** rats and mice >5,000 mg/kg. **Acute dermal LD$_{50}$:** rats >2,000 mg/kg. **Inhalation:** LC$_{50}$: (4 hours) rats >5.3 mg/litre. **Toxicity class:** EPA (formulation) III.

ENVIRONMENTAL IMPACT AND NON-TARGET TOXICITY: Pelargonic acid occurs in Nature and is not expected to show any adverse effects on non-target organisms or on the environment. **Bird toxicity:** Dietary LC$_{50}$ mallard duck >5,620 ppm. **Fish toxicity:** LC$_{50}$ (48 hours) carp 59.2 ppm. **Other aquatic toxicity:** LC$_{50}$ (3 hours) *Daphnia similis* >100 ppm. **Effects on beneficial insects:** LC$_{50}$ (contact) to honeybees >25 μg/bee. **Behaviour in soil:** Rapidly degraded in soil.

1:18 plant-derived porphyrin-derivatives

Plant growth regulator

NOMENCLATURE: **Approved name:** porphyrin-derivatives.

SOURCE: Extracts of plant tissues and in particular of *Quercus falcata*, *Opuntia lindheimeri*, *Rhus aromatica* and *Rhizophoria mangle* L.

PRODUCTION: Prepared as crude extracts of the harvested plants.

TARGET CROPS: Recommended for use in a wide range of crops.

BIOLOGICAL ACTIVITY: **Mode of action:** It is claimed that the porphyrin-based plant extracts possess cytokinin-like activity and that their application to soil or growing plants promotes plant growth. This is claimed to happen either directly on the crop or indirectly by increasing the population of beneficial micro-organisms that raise the levels of soil nutrients.

COMMERCIALISATION: **Formulation:** Sold as liquid concentrate (SL).
Tradenames: Agrispon – Agricultural Sciences.

APPLICATION: Apply as a foliar spray or to the soil. Store away from direct sunlight.

PRODUCT SPECIFICATIONS: Products contain a variety of porphyrin derivatives.

MAMMALIAN TOXICITY: Plant-derived porphyrins are not considered to be toxic to mammals. **Acute oral LD$_{50}$:** rats >30,000 mg/kg. **Toxicity class:** EPA (formulation) IV.

ENVIRONMENTAL IMPACT AND NON-TARGET TOXICITY: Not considered to be hazardous to non-target organisms or to the environment. **Effects on beneficial insects:** Not toxic to honeybees. **Behaviour in soil:** Rapidly degraded in soil.

NOMENCLATURE: **Approved name:** polynactins. **CAS RN:** *[33596–61–5]* tetranactin; *[7561–71–9]* trinactin; *[20261–85–2]* dinactin.

SOURCE: Secondary metabolite from the actinomycete *Streptomyces aureus* strain S-3466.

PRODUCTION: Manufactured by fermentation.

TARGET PESTS: Spider mites such as carmine spider mite (*Tetranychus cinnabarinus* (Boisduval)), two spotted mite (*T. urticae* Koch) and European red mite (*Panonychus ulmi* Koch).

TARGET CROPS: Fruit trees.

BIOLOGICAL ACTIVITY: **Mode of action:** The polynactins are very effective at controlling spider mites under wet conditions. It is thought that the mode of action is through a leakage of basic cations (such as potassium ions) through the lipid layer of the membrane in the mitochondrion. Water is considered to be an essential component of this toxic effect by either assisting penetration or accelerating ion leakage. **Efficacy:** Following application of polynactins to apple trees, the proliferation of mites is stopped for a period of 32 days or more. The polynactins are usually sold as combination products to avoid the possibility of the development of resistance. **Key references:** 1) K Ando, H Oishi, S Hirano, T Okutomi, K Suzuki, H Okazaki. M Sawanda and T Sagawa. 1971. Tetranactin, a new miticidal antibiotoic. I. Isolation, characterization and properties of tetranactin, *J. Antibiot.*, **24**, 347. 2) K Ando, T Sagawa, H Oishi, K Suzuki and T Nawata. 1974. Tetranactin, a pesticidal antibiotic, *Proc. 1st Intersect. Congr. IAMS (Sci. Counc. Jpn.)*, **3**, 630.

COMMERCIALISATION: **Formulation:** Sold as emulsifiable concentrates (EC) mixed with other acaricides. **Tradenames:** Mitecidin (plus fenobucarb) – Eikou Kasei, Mitedown (plus fenbutatin oxide) – Eikou Kasei.

APPLICATION: Applied as a foliar spray when conditions are wet. Polynactins should not be used under very dry conditions.

PRODUCT SPECIFICATIONS: The product consists of a mixture of dinactin, trinactin and a major component of tetranactin.

COMPATIBILITY: Compatible with most other chemical acaricides. Ineffective under dry conditions.

MAMMALIAN TOXICITY: The polynactins are considered to be relatively non-toxic to mammals. **Acute oral LD$_{50}$:** mice >15,000 mg/kg. **Acute dermal LD$_{50}$:** mice >10,000 mg/kg. **Skin and eye:** Mild skin and eye irritant.
Toxicity class: EPA (formulation) IV.

ENVIRONMENTAL IMPACT AND NON-TARGET TOXICITY: Relatively non-toxic to beneficial insects. **Fish toxicity:** High toxicity to fish with a median tolerance limit to carp of 0.003 ppm.

1:20   polyoxin B   *Microbial fungicide*

The Pesticide Manual - 11th edition: Entry number 586

polyoxin B: R = − CH$_2$OH

polyoxorim: R = − CO$_2$H

NOMENCLATURE: **Approved name:** polyoxin B. **CAS RN:** *[19396–06–6]* polyoxin B; *[11113–80–7]* polyoxins.

SOURCE: Isolated from the soil actinomycete *Streptomyces cacaoi* var. *asoensis*. Polyoxin B was first isolated by K Isono *et al.* in 1965 and was introduced by Hokko Chemical Industry Company Ltd, Kaken Pharmaceutical Company Ltd, Kumiai Chemical Industry Company Ltd and by Nihon Noyaku Company Ltd.

PRODUCTION: The polyoxins are produced by fermentation of *Streptomyces cacaoi* var. *asoensis*.

TARGET PESTS: Various plant pathogenic fungi such as *Sphaerotheca* spp. and other powdery mildews, *Botrytis cinerea* Pers., *Sclerotinia sclerotiorum* De Bary, *Corynespora melonis* Lindau, *Cochliobolus miyabeanus* Drechs. and *Alternaria alternata*.

TARGET CROPS: Vines, apples, pears, vegetables and ornamentals.

BIOLOGICAL ACTIVITY: **Mode of action:** Polyoxins have been shown to cause a marked abnormal swelling on the germ tubes of spores and hyphal tips of the pathogen, rendering them non-pathogenic. In addition, the incorporation of $[^{14}C]$-glucosamine into cell-wall chitin of *Cochliobolus miyabeanus* was inhibited. It is suggested that polyoxins exert their effects through an inhibition of cell wall biosynthesis. They are systemic fungicides with protective action. **Efficacy:** Polyoxin B is effective at controlling a variety of fungal pathogens but is ineffective against bacteria and yeasts. It is particularly effective against pear black spot and apple cork spot (*Alternaria* spp.), grey moulds (*Botrytis cinerea*) and other sclerotia forming plant pathogens. Resistance to polyoxin B has been found in *Alternaria alternata* in some orchards in Japan following intensive treatment. This resistance has been shown to be due to lowered permeability of polyoxin B through the fungal cell membrane and, therefore, to the site of action. **Key references:** 1) S Suzuki, K Isono, J Nagatsu, T Mizutani, Y Kawashima and T Mizuno. 1965. A new antibiotic, polyoxin A, *J. Antibiot. Ser. A*, **20**, 109. 2) K Isono, J Nagatsu, Y Kawashima, and S Suzuki. 1965. Studies on polyoxins, antifungal antibiotics. Part 1. Isolation and characterisation of polyoxins A and B, *J. Antibiot. Ser. A*, **18**, 115. 3) J Eguchi, S Sasaki, N Ohta, T Akashiba, T Tsuchiyama and S Suzuki. 1968. Studies on polyoxins, antifungal antibiotics. Mechanism of action on the diseases caused by *Alternaria* spp., *Ann. Phytopathol. Soc. Jpn.*, **34**, 280.

COMMERCIALISATION: **Formulation:** Sold as wettable powder (WP), emulsifiable concentrate (EC) and soluble granule (SG) formulations. **Tradenames:** Polyoxin AL – Kaken, Kumiai, Nihon Nohyaku and Hokko. **Patents:** JP 577960.

APPLICATION: Applied as foliar sprays when disease becomes evident. Rates up to 200 g per hectalitre are recommended.

PRODUCT SPECIFICATIONS: The efficacy of the formulated product is determined by bioassay against *Alternaria mali* Roberts strain ACI-1157. **Purity:** Polyoxin complex consists of polyoxin B and several other polyoxins of lower potency.

COMPATIBILITY: Incompatible with alkaline products. May be mixed with various other fungicides with different modes of action to reduce or delay the onset of resistance.

MAMMALIAN TOXICITY: Polyoxin B shows very low levels of mammalian toxicity. Recognised as non-toxic. **Acute oral LD$_{50}$:** male rats 21,000, female rats 21,200, male mice 27,300 and female mice 22,500 mg/kg. **Acute dermal LD$_{50}$:** rats >2,000 mg/kg. **Inhalation:** LC$_{50}$ (6 hours) rats 10 mg/litre of air. **Skin and eye:** Non-irritant to mucous membranes and skin (rats). **NOEL:** (2 years) for rats and mice >48,000 mg/kg diet. **Toxicity class:** EPA (formulation) III (WP).

ENVIRONMENTAL IMPACT AND NON-TARGET TOXICITY: Polyoxin B is not expected to have any adverse effects on non-target organisms or on the environment because of the

specific mode of action against chitin biosynthesis. **Fish toxicity:** LC_{50} (48 hours) carp
>40 mg/litre. Japanese killifish were unaffected by 100 mg/litre for 72 hours.
Other aquatic toxicity: LC_{50} (3 hours) *Daphnia pulex* >40 mg/litre and *Moina macrocopa*
>40 mg/litre. **Behaviour in soil:** In upland soil at 25 °C, polyoxin B had a half-life of less than
two days.

1:21   polyoxorim   *Microbial fungicide*

The Pesticide Manual - 11th edition: Entry number 586

polyoxin B: R = − CH$_2$OH

polyoxorim: R = − CO$_2$H

NOMENCLATURE: **Approved name:** polyoxorim (BSI, pa ISO); polyoxin D (JMAF).
CAS RN: *[22976–86–9]* polyoxorim; *[146659–78–1]* zinc salt; *[11113–80–7]* polyoxins.

SOURCE: Polyoxorim (polyoxin D) was isolated by S Suzuki *et al.* in 1965. It is one of the
secondary metabolites produced by the fermentation of the soil actinomycete *Streptomyces
cacaoi* var. *asoensis*. The zinc salt was introduced as a fungicide by Kaken Pharmaceutical
Company Ltd, Kumiai Chemical Industry Company Ltd and Nihon Nohyaku Company Ltd.

PRODUCTION: Polyoxorim is produced from the fermentation of *Streptomyces cacaoi* var.
asoensis. It is isolated as the zinc salt.

TARGET PESTS: Used for the control of rice sheath blight (*Rhizoctonia solani* Kuehn
(*Pellicularia sasakii* Ito)). Also effective against apple and pear canker (*Nectria galligena* Bres.
(*Diplodia pseudodiplodia* Fckl.)) and *Drechslera* spp., *Bipolaris* spp., *Curvularia* spp. and
Helminthosporium spp.

TARGET CROPS: The major use is in rice but it also has applications in pome fruit and for
disease control in turf.

BIOLOGICAL ACTIVITY: **Mode of action:** Polyoxins have been shown to cause a marked abnormal swelling on the germ tubes of spores and hyphal tips of the pathogen, rendering them non-pathogenic. In addition, the incorporation of $[^{14}C]$-glucosamine into cell-wall chitin of *Cochliobolus miyabeanus* Drechs. was inhibited. This suggested that polyoxorim exerts its effect by disruption of cell wall biosynthesis by mimicking UDP-*N*-acetylglucosamine, the natural substrate for the enzyme chitin synthase. The polyoxins are systemic fungicides with protective action. **Efficacy:** Polyoxorim has good activity against rice sheath blight when applied as a foliar spray at rates of about 200 g per hectalitre. High volume sprays on turf are effective at controlling many fungal pathogens with the exception of members of the Phycomycetes (no chitin in the cell wall). Polyoxorim can be used to control apple and pear canker when applied as a paste. It is ineffective against bacteria and yeasts.
Key references: 1) K Isono and S Suzuki. 1979. The polyoxins: pyrimidine nucleoside peptide antibiotics inhibiting cell wall biosynthesis, *Heterocycles*, **13**, 333. 2) K Isono, J Nagatsu, K Kobinata, K Sasaki and S Suzuki. 1967. Studies on polyoxins, antifungal antibiotics. Part V. Isolation and characterisation of polyoxins, C, D, E, F, G, H and I, *Agric. Biol. Chem.*, **31**, 190.

COMMERCIALISATION: **Formulation:** Sold as wettable powder (WP) and paste (PA) formulations. **Tradenames:** Kakengel (zinc salt) – Kaken, Polyoxin Z (zinc salt) – Kaken, Stopit – Kaken. **Patents:** JP 577960.

APPLICATION: Applied as the zinc salt at rates of 200 g active ingredient per hectare for the control of sheath blight. Applications should be made when disease first appears or when conditions favour the onset of disease.

PRODUCT SPECIFICATIONS: The efficacy of the product is evaluated by bioassay against *Rhizoctonia solani* (*Pellicularia sasakii*) strain ACI-1134. **Purity:** The product contains a mixture of polyoxins of which polyoxorim is the main fraction.

COMPATIBILITY: Polyoxorim should not be used with alkaline materials. It is sold in admixture with other fungicides with different modes of action in order to delay the possibility of resistance developing. It has not shown any phytotoxicity to crops at rates above those recommended for use.

MAMMALIAN TOXICITY: The mode of action of polyoxorim means that it is unlikely to have any effects on mammals. **Acute dermal LD$_{50}$:** male and female rats >9,600 mg/kg. **Inhalation:** LC$_{50}$ (4 hours) for male rats 2.44 and for female rats 2.17 mg/litre of air. **Skin and eye:** Non-irritant to mucous membranes and skin (rats). **NOEL:** (2 years) for rats >50,000 and for mice >40,000 mg/kg diet. **Toxicity class:** EPA (formulation) III (WP).

ENVIRONMENTAL IMPACT AND NON-TARGET TOXICITY: The mode of action through the inhibition of chitin biosynthesis is unlikely to produce any adverse effects on non-target organisms and the environment. **Fish toxicity:** LC$_{50}$ (48 hours) carp >40 mg/litre. **Other aquatic toxicity:** LC$_{50}$ (3 hours) *Daphnia pulex* and *Moina macrocopa* >40 mg/litre. **Behaviour in soil:** In flooded soils at 25 °C, the half-life of polyoxorim is <10 days. In upland soils at 25 °C, the half-life is <7 days. In water at pH 5.5 at 24 °C, the half-life is 4 hours and at pH 5.8 at 26.5 °C, it is 8 hours.

1:22 pyrethrins (pyrethrum)

Plant derived insecticide/acaricide

The Pesticide Manual - 11th edition: Entry number 622

R   = - CH_3 or - CO_2CH_3

R_1 = - $CH=CH_2$ or - CH_3 or - CH_2CH_3

NOMENCLATURE: **Approved name:** pyrethrins (BSI, E-ISO, ESA, JMAF); pyrèthres (F-ISO). **CAS RN:** *[8003–34–7]*.

SOURCE: The dried, powdered flower of *Chrysanthemum cinerariaefolium* Vis. has been used as an insecticide from ancient times. Recent taxonomic revisions have transfered this species from the genus *Chrysanthemum* to the genus *Tanacetum*. In some circles, it is still recorded as *Pyrethrum*. The species was identified in antiquity in China. It spread West via Iran (Persia), probably via the Silk Routes in the Middle Ages. The dried, powdered flower heads were known as "Persian Insect Powder". Records of use date from the early 19th century when it was introduced to the Adriatic coastal regions of Yugoslavia (Dalmatia) and some parts of the Caucasus. Subsequently, it was grown in France, the United States of America and Japan. It is now widely grown in East African countries, especially Kenya (1930), Ecuador and Papua New Guinea (1950) and Australia (1980).

PRODUCTION: Pyrethrum is extracted from the flower of *Tanacetum cinerariaefolium*. The extract is refined using methanol (Pyrethrum Board of Kenya and MGK) or supercritical carbon dioxide (Agropharm).

TARGET PESTS: Control of a wide range of insects and mites.

TARGET CROPS: Recommended for use on fruit, vegetables, field crops, ornamentals, glasshouse crops and house plants as well as in public health, stored products, animal houses and on domestic and farm animals.

BIOLOGICAL ACTIVITY: **Mode of action:** Pyrethrums have been shown to bind to the sodium channels in insects, prolonging their opening and thereby causing knockdown and death. They are non-systemic insecticides with contact action. Initial effects include paralysis with death occurring later. They have some acaricidal activity. **Key references:** 1) J E Casida and G B Quistad (eds.). 1994. *Pyrethrum Flowers; Production, Chemistry, Toxicology and Uses*, Oxford University Press, Oxford. 2) J E Casida (ed.). 1973. *Pyrethrum, the Natural Insecticide,*

Academic Press, New York. 3) C B Gnadinger. 1936. *Pyrethrum Flowers*, 2nd edition, McLaughlin, Gormley King Co, Minneapolis, Minnesota.

COMMERCIALISATION: **Formulation:** Formulated as aerosol dispensers (AE), dispersible powders (DP), emulsifiable concentrates (EC), fogging concentrates, pressurised liquid CO_2, wettable powders (WP) and ultra-low volume liquids (UL). **Tradenames:** Alfadex – Novartis, Pyrocide – MGK, Evergreen – KGK, Pyronyl (mixture) – Prentiss, ExciteR – Prentiss, Milon – Delicia, Pycon (for concentrated mixture with piperonyl butoxide) – Agropharm, CheckOut – Consep, Prentox Pyrethrum Extract – Prentiss.

APPLICATION: Normally applied in combination with synergists, e.g. piperonyl butoxide, that inhibit detoxification. Good cover of crop foliage is essential for effective control. Many combination products with other insecticides are available.

PRODUCT SPECIFICATIONS: **Purity:** Pyrethrum extract is defined as three naturally occurring, closely related insecticidal esters of chrysanthemic acid, pyrethrins I, mixed with the three corresponding esters of pyrethrin acid, pyrethrins II. In the USA, it is standardised as 45 to 55% w/w total pyrethrins, but samples may be 20%; the ratio of pyrethrins I to II is typically 0.8–2.8; the ratio of individual esters (pyrethrins: cinerins: jasmolins) is 72:21:7. In Europe, pyrethrum extract is 25 to 55% pyrethrins. The three components of pyrethrins I are pyrethrin I ($R = CH_3$, $R_1 = CH:CH_2$); jasmolin I ($R = CH_3$, $R_1 = CH_2CH_3$); cinerin I ($R = CH_3$, $R_1 = CH_3$); the components of pyrethrins II correspond ($R = -CO_2CH_3$).

COMPATIBILITY: Incompatible with alkaline substances.

MAMMALIAN TOXICITY: **Acute oral LD50:** male rats 2,370, female rats 1,030 and mice 273–796 mg/kg. **Acute dermal LD50:** rats >1,500, rabbits 5,000 mg/kg. **Inhalation:** LC_{50} (4 hours) for rats 3.4 mg/litre. **Skin and eye:** Slightly irritating to skin and eyes. Constituents of the flowers may cause dermatitis to sensitised individuals, but are removed during the preparation of refined extracts. **NOEL:** for rats 100 ppm. **ADI:** 0.04 mg/kg body weight [1972]. **Toxicity class:** WHO (active ingredient) II; EPA (formulation) III.
Other toxicological effects: There is no evidence that synergists increase toxicity of pyrethrins to mammals. **Toxicity review:** 1) *Pesticide Residues in Food*. FAO Agricultural Studies, No. 90. 2) WHO Technical Report Series, No. 525. 1973. *1972 Evaluations of Some Pesticide Residues in Food*. AGP:1972/M/9/1. 3) WHO Pesticide Residue Series, No. 2. 1973.

ENVIRONMENTAL IMPACT AND NON-TARGET TOXICITY: **Bird toxicity:** Acute oral LD_{50} mallard ducks >10,000 mg/kg. **Fish toxicity:** Highly toxic to fish. LC_{50} (96 hours) (static tests) coho salmon 39, channel catfish 114 mg/litre. LC_{50} bluegill sunfish 10, rainbow trout 5.2 mg/litre. **Other aquatic toxicity:** LC_{50} *Daphnia pulex* 12 µg/litre.
Effects on beneficial insects: Highly toxic to honeybees but exhibits a repellent effect. LD_{50} (oral) 22 ng/bee, (contact) 130 to 290 ng/bee. **Metabolism:** In mammals, rapidly degraded in the stomach by hydrolysis of the ester bond to harmless metabolites. **Behaviour in soil:** In the environment, degradation, promoted by sunlight and u.v. light, begins at the alcohol group and involves the formation of numerous unknown cleavage products.

1:23   pyrethrins (chrysanthemates)

Plant derived insecticide/acaricide

The Pesticide Manual - 11th edition: Entry number 622

R = - CH$_3$
R$_1$ = - CH=CH$_2$ or - CH$_3$ or - CH$_2$CH$_3$

NOMENCLATURE: **Approved name:** pyrethrins (chrysanthemates). **CAS RN:** *[121–21–1]* pyrethrin I; *[2540–06–6]* cinerin I; *[4466–14–2]* jasmolin I.

BIOLOGICAL ACTIVITY: **Efficacy:** See entry 1.22 – pyrethrins (pyrethrum).

1:24   pyrethrins (pyrethrates)

Plant derived insecticide/acaricide

The Pesticide Manual - 11th edition: Entry number 622

R = - CO$_2$CH$_3$
R$_1$ = - CH=CH$_2$ or - CH$_3$ or - CH$_2$CH$_3$

NOMENCLATURE: **Approved name:** pyrethrins (pyrethrates). **CAS RN:** *[121–29–9]* pyrethrin II; *[1172–63–0]* cinerin II; *[121–20–0]* jasmolin II.

BIOLOGICAL ACTIVITY: **Efficacy:** See entry 1.22 – pyrethrins (pyrethrum).

1:25   rotenone   *Plant derived insecticide/acaricide*

The Pesticide Manual - 11th edition: Entry number 645

NOMENCLATURE: **Approved name:** rotenone (BSI, E-ISO, F-ISO, ESA, accepted in lieu of a common name); derris (JMAF). **Other names:** (for the plant extract) derris root; tuba-root; aker-tuba; (for the plants) barbasco; cubé; haiari; nekoe; timbo. **CAS RN:** *[83–79–4]*. **Development codes:** ENT 133. **EEC no.** 201–501–9.

SOURCE: Rotenone and related rotenoids were obtained from *Derris*, *Lonchocarpus* and *Tephrosia* species and were used originally in Asia and South America as fish poisons.

PRODUCTION: Produced by extraction of *Derris* roots and stabilised by phosphoric acid.

TARGET PESTS: Control of a wide range of arthropod pests including aphids, thrips, suckers, moths, beetles and spider mites. Also used for the control of fire ants and of mosquito larvae when applied to pond water. Recommended for the control of lice, ticks and warble flies on animals and for insect control in premises. Also used to control fish populations.

TARGET CROPS: Recommended for use in fruit and vegetable cultivation, in premises and for use on animals. Also used in fish management.

BIOLOGICAL ACTIVITY: **Mode of action:** Inhibitor of Site I respiration within the electron-transport chain. Selective non-systemic insecticide with contact and stomach action. Secondary acaricidal activity. **Key reference:** H Fukami and M Nakajima. 1971. *Naturally Occurring Insecticides*, M Jacobson and D G Crosby (eds.), Marcel Dekker, New York.

COMMERCIALISATION: **Formulation:** Sold as dispersible powder (DP), emulsifiable concentrate (EC) and wettable powder (WP) formulations. **Tradenames:** Chem Sect – Tifa, Cube Root – Tifa, Rotenone Extract – Tifa, Noxfire – AgrEvo Environmental Health, Rotenone FK-11 – AgrEvo Environmental Health, Prenfish (mixture) – Prentiss, Synpren Fish (mixture) – Prentiss, Prentox – Prentiss.

APPLICATION: Applied as an overall spray to give good cover of the foliage. Often used as a component of mixtures. Can be used in organic systems in extreme conditions of insect attack.

PRODUCT SPECIFICATIONS: **Purity:** Product purity is checked by i.r. spectrometry, by rplc or by solvent extraction and crystallisation.

COMPATIBILITY: Not compatible with alkaline substances.

MAMMALIAN TOXICITY: **Acute oral LD$_{50}$:** white rats 132–1,500, white mice 350 mg/kg. **Toxicity class:** WHO (active ingredient) II; EPA (formulation) III (EC formulation I). **EC risk** T (R25); Xi (R36/37/38). **Other toxicological effects:** Estimated lethal dose to humans is 300–500 mg/kg. Rotenone is more toxic when inhaled than when ingested. It is very toxic to pigs.

ENVIRONMENTAL IMPACT AND NON-TARGET TOXICITY: **Fish toxicity:** LC$_{50}$ (96 hours) rainbow trout 31, bluegill sunfish 23 µg/litre. **Effects on beneficial insects:** Rotenone is not toxic to bees, but combinations with pyrethrum are very toxic. **Metabolism:** In rat liver and in insects, the furan ring is enzymically opened and cleaved, leaving behind a methoxy group. The principal metabolite is rotenonone. An alcohol has been found as a further metabolite, this being formed via oxidation of a methyl group of the isopropenyl residue (I Yamamoto. 1969. *Residue Rev.,* **25**, 161).

1:26   ryania extracts *Botanical insecticide*

NOMENCLATURE: **Approved name:** ryania extract; ryanodine. **CAS RN:** *[15662–33–6].* **Development codes:** SHA 071502 (ryanodine).

SOURCE: Alkaloids from the stem of *Ryania* species, particularly *R. speciosa* Vahl, represent the first successful discovery of a natural insecticide. The collaboration between Rutgers University and Merck in the early 1940s followed the lead from the use of *Ryania* species in South America for euthanasia and as rat poisons. This collaborative work revealed that *Ryania* alkaloid extracts were insecticidal.

PRODUCTION: Ground stem wood of *Ryania speciosa*.

TARGET PESTS: Codling moth (*Cydia pomonella* Linnaeus), European corn borer (*Ostrinia nubilalis* (Hübner)) and citrus thrips.

TARGET CROPS: Maize, apples, pears and citrus.

BIOLOGICAL ACTIVITY: **Mode of action:** Ryanodine and related alkaloids affect muscles by binding to the calcium channels in the sarcoplastic reticulum. This causes calcium ion flow into the cells and death follows very rapidly. **Efficacy:** Ryania extracts have limited use as insecticides but do give effective control of selected species. The size and complexity of the natural product means that it can be used only to treat infested crops and it has no systemic activity. The rapidity of its effect is an advantage in the control of boring insects.
Key references: J E Casida, I N Pessah, J Seifert and A L Waterhouse. 1987. *Naturally Occurring Pesticides*, R Greenlaugh and T R Roberts (eds.), Blackwell Scientific Publishers, Oxford, p. 177.

COMMERCIALISATION: **Formulation:** Sold as a water dispersible powder.
Tradenames: Natur-Gro R-50 – AgriSystems International, Natur-Gro Triple Plus – AgriSystems International, Ryan 50 – Dunhill Chemical. **Patents:** US 2400295.

APPLICATION: Applied when insects are attacking the crop. Good coverage is essential. Avoid spraying near water courses.

PRODUCT SPECIFICATIONS: The product consists of the ground stem wood of *Ryania speciosa* and contains a number of alkaloids, the main component being ryanodine.

COMPATIBILITY: Compatible with most crop protection agents.

MAMMALIAN TOXICITY: **Acute oral LD$_{50}$:** rats 1,200 mg/kg. **Toxicity class:** EPA (formulation) III.

ENVIRONMENTAL IMPACT AND NON-TARGET TOXICITY: **Fish toxicity:** Ryania extracts are toxic to fish.

The Pesticide Manual - 11th edition: Entry number 754

spinosyn A, R = H-

spinosyn D, R = CH₃-

NOMENCLATURE: **Approved name:** spinosad (ANSI, ISO pending).
CAS RN: *[131929–60–7]* spinosyn A; *[131929–63–0]* spinosyn D.
Development codes: XDE-105; DE-105.

SOURCE: The commercial product is a mixture of spinosyn A and spinosyn D. Both compounds are secondary metabolites of the soil actinomycete, *Saccharopolyspora spinosa*. The organism is composed of long, yellowish-pink aerial chains of spores encased in distinctive, spiny spore sheaths. The bacterium is aerobic, gram-positive, non-acid fast, non-motile, filamentous and differentiated into substrate and aerial hyphae. The aerial mycelium is yellowish-pink and the vegetative mycelium is yellow to yellowish-brown. The parent strain was originally isolated from an abandoned rum still in the Caribbean.

PRODUCTION: Spinosad is obtained from a whole broth extraction following fermentation of the organism on a feedstock of water, vegetable flours, sugar and animal fat.

TARGET PESTS: Recommended for the control of caterpillars, leafminers, thrips and foliage feeding beetles.

TARGET CROPS: May be used on row crops (including cotton), vegetables, fruit trees, turf, vines and ornamentals. No crop phytotoxicity has beeen observed.

BIOLOGICAL ACTIVITY: **Mode of action:** Spinosad effects on target insects are consistent with the activation of the nicotinic acetylcholine receptor but at a different site than nicotine or imidacloprid. Spinosad also affects GABA receptors but their role in the overall activity is unclear. There is currently no known cross-resistance to other insecticide classes.
Efficacy: The mode of action causes a rapid death of target phytophagous insects. Its

moderate residual activity reduces the possibility of the onset of resistance but it is strongly recommended that it be used within a strong, pro-active resistance management strategy. Spinosad is recommended as an Integrated Crop Management tool as it shows no effects on predatory insects such as ladybirds, lacewings, big-eyed bugs or minute pirate bugs. It has reduced activity against parasitic wasps and flies. It is toxic when sprayed directly onto honeybees and other pollinators, but, once dry, residues have little effect.

Key references: 1) H A Kirst et al. 1992. In Synthesis of Agrochemicals III. D R Baker, J G Fenyes and J J Steffens (eds.), American Chemical Society, Washington DC, 214–25. 2) D J Porteus, J R Raines and R L Gantz. 1996. In 1996 Proceedings of Beltwide Cotton Conferences. P Dugger and D Richter (eds.), National Cotton Council of America, Memphis, TN, 875–7. 3) T C Sparks et al. 1996. In 1996 Proceedings of Beltwide Cotton Conferences. P Dugger and D Richter (eds.), National Cotton Council of America, Memphis, TN, 692–6. 4) V L Salgado. 1997. In Down to Earth, DowElanco, Indianapolis, IN, **52:1**, 35–44.

COMMERCIALISATION: **Formulation:** Sold as an aqueous based suspension concentrate (SC) formulation. **Tradenames:** Tracer – Dow AgroSciences, Conserve – Dow AgroSciences, Success – Dow AgroSciences, SpinTor – Dow AgroSciences. **Patents:** US Patent: 5,202,242 (1993); EPO: 375316 (1990).

APPLICATION: The compound is applied at rates of 12 to 150 g per hectare. Apply when pest pressure demands treatment. The active ingredient does not dissolve in water and continual agitation is required to prevent the active ingredient from settling out in the spray tank. The addition of adjuvants has not been shown to improve or reduce the performance of spinosad consistently, with the exception of leafminer control and the penetration of closed canopies, where emulsified vegetable oils have helped.

PRODUCT SPECIFICATIONS: **Purity:** The commercial product is composed of spinosyn A and spinosyn D. Analysis is undertaken by hplc or immunoassay (details from Dow AgroSciences). **Storage conditions:** Spinosad is stable over a wide range of temperatures. Protect from freezing. Shake well before use. **Shelf-life:** The formulated product has a shelf-life of three years.

COMPATIBILITY: No compatibility problems have been identified to date when tank mixing spinosad with other crop protection products, foliar fertilisers or adjuvants. A jar test for compatibility is recommended prior to use.

MAMMALIAN TOXICITY: **Acute oral LD$_{50}$:** male rats 3,783 mg/kg; female rats >5,000 mg/kg. **Acute dermal LD$_{50}$:** rabbits >5,000 mg/kg. **Skin and eye:** Non-irritating to skin but slight irritation to eyes. **NOEL:** The no-observed effect level (NOEL) for dogs, mice and rats following 13 weeks of dietary exposure to spinosad was 5, 6 to 8 and 10 mg/kg/day, respectively. **Other toxicological effects:** In acute and sub-chronic tests, spinosad did not demonstrate any neurotoxic, reproductive or mutagenic effects on dogs, mice or rats.

ENVIRONMENTAL IMPACT AND NON-TARGET TOXICITY: **Bird toxicity:** Spinosad is considered practically non-toxic to birds. The acute oral LD$_{50}$ for both bobwhite quail and mallard duck is 2,000 mg/kg **Fish toxicity:** Spinosad is considered slightly to moderately toxic to fish. The acute LC$_{50}$ (96 hours) for rainbow trout, bluegill and carp was 30, 5.9 and

5 mg/litre, respectively. **Effects on beneficial insects:** Spinosad is considered highly toxic to honeybees with less than 1 µg/bee of technical material applied topically resulting in mortality. Once residues are dry, they are non-toxic. **Metabolism:** Feeding studies produced no residues of spinosad in meat, milk or eggs. The half-life on plant surfaces ranged from 1.6 to 16 days, with photolysis as the main route of degradation. **Behaviour in soil:** Spinosad is rapidly degraded on soil surfaces by photolysis and below the soil surface by soil micro-organisms. **Key reference:** D G Saunders and B L Bret. 1997. In *Down to Earth*, DowElanco, Indianapolis, IN, **52:1**, 14–21.

1:28   streptomycin   *Microbial bactericide*

The Pesticide Manual - 11th edition: Entry number 661

NOMENCLATURE: **Approved name:** streptomycin (BSI, E-ISO, BAN, JMAF); streptomycine (F-ISO); no name (Denmark). **CAS RN:** *[57–92–1]*; streptomycin sesquisulfate *[3810–74–0]*.

SOURCE: Isolated from the soil actinomycete *Streptomyces griseus*. First reported by A Shatz (*Proc. Soc. Exp. Biol. Med.* **55**, 66) in 1944, its structure was elucidated in 1947 (F A Kuehl Jr, R L Peck, C E Hoffnine Jr, E W Peel and K Folkers, *J. Am. Chem. Soc.*, **69**, 1234). Discovered and first commercialised by Meiji Seika Kaisha Ltd.

PRODUCTION: Streptomycin is obtained by fermentation of *Streptomyces griseus*, and is isolated and sold as the sesquisulfate.

TARGET PESTS: Control of bacterial shot-hole, bacterial rots, bacterial canker, bacterial wilts, fire blight, and other bacterial diseases (especially those caused by gram-positive species of bacteria). Streptomycin is particularly effective against *Xanthomonas oryzae* Dows., *X. citri* Dows., *Pseudomonas tabaci* Stevens and *P. lachrymans* Carsner.

TARGET CROPS: Recommended for use in pome fruit, stone fruit, citrus fruit, olives, vegetables, potatoes, tobacco, cotton and ornamentals.

BIOLOGICAL ACTIVITY: **Mode of action:** Streptomycin inhibits protein biosynthesis by binding to the 30S ribosomal sub-unit and causing a mis-reading of the genetic code in protein biosynthesis. It is a bactericide with systemic action. **Efficacy:** Resistance to streptomycin has occurred and is wide-spread, reducing the value of the compound in crop protection. **Key references:** 1) A Schatz, E Bugie and S A Waksman. 1944. Streptomycin, a substance exhibiting antibiotic activity against Gram-positive and Gram-negative bacteria, *Proc. Soc. Exp. Biol. Med.*, **55**, 66. 2) T E Likover and C G Kurland. 1967. The contribution of DNA to translation errors induced by streptomycin *in vitro*, *Proc. Natl. Acad. Sci. USA*, **58**, 2385.

COMMERCIALISATION: **Formulation:** Sold as a wettable powder (WP) and liquid concentrate (SL). **Tradenames:** Agrimycin 17 – Novartis, AS-50 – Novartis, Plantomycin – Aries Agro-Vet Industries, Paushamycin – Paushak.

APPLICATION: Applied as a foliar spray at rates of 200 g active ingredient per hectalitre.

PRODUCT SPECIFICATIONS: **Purity:** Isolated and sold as the sesquisulfate. The product is analysed by bioassay against a suitable bacterium.

COMPATIBILITY: Can cause chlorosis to rice, grapes, pears, peaches and some ornamentals and these symptoms can be relieved by the addition of iron chloride or iron citrate to the spray tank. Incompatible with pyrethrins and other alkaline products. Often used in collaboration with a bactericide with a different mode of action (such as oxytetracycline) to reduce the onset of resistance.

MAMMALIAN TOXICITY: As with all aminoglycoside antibiotics, streptomycin has very low mammalian toxicity. **Acute oral LD$_{50}$:** mice >10,000 mg/kg. Streptomycin sesquisulfate – rats 9,000, mice 9,000 and hamsters 400 mg/kg. **Acute dermal LD$_{50}$:** male mice 400 and female mice 325 mg/kg. **Skin and eye:** May cause allergic skin reaction. **NOEL:** In chronic toxicity studies on rats, NOEL was 125 mg/kg. **Toxicity class:** EPA (formulation) IV.

ENVIRONMENTAL IMPACT AND NON-TARGET TOXICITY: Streptomycin is not considered to be hazardous to non-target organisms or to the environment.

The Pesticide Manual - 11th edition: Entry number 747

CH$_2$OH · · · OH · · · OH · HOH$_2$C · HO · HO · N H · CH$_2$OH · O · O · OH · HO · OH

NOMENCLATURE: **Approved name:** validamycin (JMAF); validamycin A (Japanese Antibiotics Research Association). **CAS RN:** *[37248–47–8]*.

SOURCE: Originally isolated from the soil actinomycete *Streptomyces hygroscopicus* var. *limoneus*.

PRODUCTION: By the fermentation of *Streptomyces hygroscopicus* var. *limoneus* nov. var. Validamycin A is the most active component of a mixture of seven closely related compounds known as validamycins A to G.

TARGET PESTS: Control of *Rhizoctonia solani* Kuehn and other *Rhizoctonia* species.

TARGET CROPS: Recommended for use in rice, potatoes, vegetables, strawberries, tobacco, ginger, cotton, rice, sugar beet and other crops.

BIOLOGICAL ACTIVITY: **Mode of action:** Non-systemic with fungistatic action. Validamycin shows no fungicidal action to *Rhizoctonia solani* but causes abnormal branching of the tips of the pathogen followed by a cessation of further development. It has been shown that validamycin has a potent inhibitory activity against trehalase in *Rhizoctonia solani* AG-1, without any significant effects on other glycohydrolytic enzymes tested. Trehalose is well known as a storage carbohydrate in the pathogen and trehalase is believed to play an essential role in the digestion of trehalose and transport of glucose to the hyphal tips. **Efficacy:** Low rates of use give excellent control of *Rhizoctonia solani* in various crops. Rates of 30 g per hectalitre gave effective control of rice sheath blight. **Key references:** 1) S Horii, Y Kameda and K Kawahara. 1972. Studies on validamycins, new antibiotics. VIII. Validamycins C, D, E and F, *J. Antibiot.*, **25**, 48. 2) K Matsuura. 1983. Characteristics of validamycin A in controlling *Rhizoctonia* diseases. In *IUPAC Pesticide Chemistry*, J Miyamoto and P C Kearney (eds.), Pergamon Press, Oxford, Vol. 2, 301. 3) R Shigemoto, T Okuno and K Matsuura. 1989. Effect of validamycin A on the activity of trehalase of *Rhizoctonia solani* and several sclerotial fungi, *Ann. Phytopathol. Soc. Jpn.*, **55**, 238.

COMMERCIALISATION: **Formulation:** Sold as dispersible powder (DP), soluble concentrate (SL), powder seed treatment (DS) and liquid formulations. **Tradenames:** Validacin – Takeda, Solacol – Takeda and AgrEvo, Valimun – Takeda, Mycin – Sanonda, Vivadamy – Vietnam Pesticide.

APPLICATION: Applied as a foliar spray, a soil drench, a seed teatment or by soil incorporation. Rates from 30 g per hectalitre give good control.

PRODUCT SPECIFICATIONS: Product specification can be checked by derivatisation and glc analysis (K Nishi and K Konishi. 1976. *Anal. Methods Pestic. Plant Growth Regul.*, **8**, 309).

COMPATIBILITY: Validamycin can be used in conjunction with many other agrochemicals. Concentrations as high as 1,000 mg per litre showed no phytotoxicity to over 150 different target crops.

MAMMALIAN TOXICITY: Validamycin, in common with other aminoglycoside antibiotics, shows very low mammalian toxicity. **Acute oral LD$_{50}$:** rats and mice >20,000 mg/kg. **Acute dermal LD$_{50}$:** rats >5,000 mg/kg. **Inhalation:** LC$_{50}$ (4 hours) rats >5 mg/litre air. **Skin and eye:** Non-irritating to skin (rabbits). Not a skin sensitiser (guinea pigs). **NOEL:** In 90-day feeding trials, rats receiving 1,000 mg/kg of diet and mice receiving 2,000 mg/kg of diet showed no ill-effects. In 2-year feeding trials, NOEL for rats was 40.4 mg/kg body weight daily. **Toxicity class:** WHO (active ingredient) III (Table 5); EPA (formulation) IV.

ENVIRONMENTAL IMPACT AND NON-TARGET TOXICITY: Validamycin has no adverse effects on non-target organisms or on the environment. **Fish toxicity:** LC$_{50}$ (72 hours) carp >40 mg/litre. **Other aquatic toxicity:** LC$_{50}$ (24 hours) *Daphnia pulex* >40 mg/litre. **Metabolism:** In animals, orally administered validamycin is readily decomposed to carbon dioxide and amine residues that are excreted. **Behaviour in soil:** Rapid microbial degradation in soil; DT$_{50}$ *ca.* 5 hours.

NOMENCLATURE: **Approved name:** zeatin. **CAS RN:** *[1637–39–4].*

SOURCE: Plant derived growth regulator. Involved in the initiation of plant cell division.

PRODUCTION: Extracted from plant tissue.

TARGET CROPS: Recommended for use on a wide range of crops including citrus, cucumber, stone fruit crops, pepper, pine, potato and tomato.

BIOLOGICAL ACTIVITY: **Mode of action:** Zeatin is a naturally occurring plant growth regulator from the cytokinin group. It is associated with cell division, and subsequently increased plant growth, and also delays senescence in treated organs.

COMMERCIALISATION: **Formulation:** Sold as a water soluble concentrate.
Tradenames: Cytex – Atlantic and Pacific Research.

APPLICATION: Apply as a foliar spray to growing crops. It can also be applied as a fluid-drilling gel at time of planting.

PRODUCT SPECIFICATIONS: Contains mixed cytokinins but predominantly zeatin.

MAMMALIAN TOXICITY: Naturally occurring plant growth regulator that has not shown any allergenic or other adverse effects on producers or users.

ENVIRONMENTAL IMPACT AND NON-TARGET TOXICITY: Cytokinins occur widely in Nature and are not expected to have any adverse effects on non-target organisms or the environment. **Effects on beneficial insects:** Not toxic to honeybees.
Behaviour in soil: Rapidly degraded in soil.

The Pesticide Manual - 11th edition: Entry number 157

$$
\begin{array}{c}
\text{H} \qquad \text{(CH}_2)_7\text{OH} \\
\text{H} \qquad \text{C}=\text{C} \\
\text{C}=\text{C} \qquad \text{H} \\
\text{CH}_3 \qquad \text{H}
\end{array}
$$

NOMENCLATURE: **Approved name:** codlemone ((*E,E*)-8,10-dodecadien-1-ol).
Other names: codling moth pheromone; *Cydia pomonella* pheromone; E8, 10–12OH (IOBC); EE8, 10–12OH. **CAS RN:** *[33956–49–9]*.

SOURCE: The sex pheromone of the codling moth (*Cydia pomonella* Linnaeus) was originally isolated from the terminal abdominal segments of virgin females.

PRODUCTION: Manufactured for use in crop protection.

TARGET PESTS: Codling moth (*Cydia pomonella*). Also effective against the hickory shuckworm (*C. caryana* (Fitch)).

TARGET CROPS: Recommended for use in pome fruit crops such as apples and pears and in walnut orchards.

BIOLOGICAL ACTIVITY: **Mode of action:** Codlemone is the sex pheromone of the codling moth. Male moths locate and subsequently mate with female moths by following the trail or pheromone plume emitted by virgin females. The application of codlemone applied indiscriminately interferes with this process as a constant exposure to high levels of pheromone makes trail following impossible (habituation/adaptation). Alternatively, the use of discrete sources of pheromone released over time presents the male with a false trail to follow (confusion). Control is subsequently achieved through the prevention of mating and the laying of fertile eggs. The natural female sex pheromone contains a number of components some of which enhance the attractiveness of (*E,E*)-8,10-dodecadien-1-ol to males (dodecan-1-ol) and others that reduce the attraction of males ((*E,E*)-8,10-dodecadien-1-ol acetate). **Efficacy:** Very low rates are required to cause mating disruption. Codlemone is volatile and distributes throughout the crop easily. Codlemone has been shown to maintain populations of codling moth effectively at economically tolerable levels between fruiting and harvest. The pheromone can also be used as a means of monitoring the incidence of the moths so that insecticidal sprays (such as *Cydia pomonella* granulosis virus) can be applied at the most susceptible stages of the insect larvae. The use of the pheromone to attract the moths to a contact insecticide (lure and kill) is also successful in controlling the moths.
Key reference: R J Bartell and T E Bellas. 1981. Evidence for naturally occurring, secondary compounds of the codling moth female sex pheromones, *J. Aust. Entomol. Soc.*, **20**, 197.

COMMERCIALISATION: **Formulation:** Sold as a coil or as polyethylene ampoules that release the pheromone slowly as a vapour. Codlemone is produced by Consep, Hercon and

2. Pheromones

Thermo Trilogy. **Tradenames:** Isomate-C (mixture) – Shin-Etsu and Biocontrol, NoMate CM – Scentry, RAK 3 – BASF, Sirene-CM (plus permethrin) – IPM Technologies, Hercon Disrupt CM (laminated plastic) – Hercon, Codlemone (plastic tubes) – Shin-Etsu, Codlemone (plastic barrier film) – Consep, CheckMate CM – Consep.

APPLICATION: Slow-release containers are placed at intervals within the crop from bud burst to small fruit stage and the pheromone is allowed to diffuse into the air and disperse throughout the orchard. The numbers of lures recommended to be used per hectare vary with release rates. Lures should be replaced every five weeks. Lure and kill strategies use codlemone together with a contact insecticide such as permethrin.

PRODUCT SPECIFICATIONS: **Purity:** The mating hormone of the codling moth (*Cydia pomonella*). Typical composition for mating disruption contains 62.5% codlemone, with 31% dodecan-1-ol and 6% tetradecanol.

COMPATIBILITY: Compatible with all crop protection agents that do not repel codling moth adults.

MAMMALIAN TOXICITY: Codlemone has no adverse toxicological effects on research or manufacturing workers or on users. Considered to be non-toxic.
Acute oral LD_{50}: rats >3,250 mg/kg.

ENVIRONMENTAL IMPACT AND NON-TARGET TOXICITY: Codlemone is a natural insect pheromone that is specific for the codling moth. There is no evidence that it has caused any adverse effects on non-target organisms or had any deleterious effect on the environment.

2:32 (*E*)-5-decenyl acetate plus (*E*)-5-decenol

Peach tree borer sex pheromone

$$R = \text{-H, -COCH}_3$$

NOMENCLATURE: **Approved name:** (*E*)-5-decenyl acetate plus (*E*)-5-decenol.
Other names: peach tree borer sex pheromone; (*E*)-5–10Ac and (*E*)-5–10OH.

SOURCE: The sex pheromone of the peach tree borer or peach twig borer (*Anarsia lineatella* Zeller) isolated from virgin female terminal segments.

PRODUCTION: Manufactured for use in crop protection.

TARGET PESTS: Peach tree borer (*Anarsia lineatella*).

TARGET CROPS: Peach tree orchards.

BIOLOGICAL ACTIVITY: **Mode of action:** The combination of (*E*)-5-decenyl acetate and (*E*)-5-decenol comprises the sex pheromone of the peach tree borer. Male moths locate and subsequently mate with female moths by following the pheromone trail or pheromone plume emitted by the virgin females. The application of inundative levels of this combination product makes the trail impossible for male *Anarsia lineatella* to follow (camouflage, competition between artificial and female plume, false trail following). Control is subsequently achieved through the prevention of mating and the laying of fertile eggs. **Efficacy:** Very low rates are required to cause mating disruption. (*E*)-5-Decenyl acetate and (*E*)-5-decenol are volatile and distribute throughout the crop very easily. **Key reference:** W Roelofs, J Kochansky, E Anthon, R Rice and R Cardé. 1975. Sex pheromone of the peach twigborer moth (*Anarsia lineatella*), *Environ. Entomol.*, **4**, 580.

COMMERCIALISATION: **Formulation:** Sold as a slow-release formulation of polyethylene ampoules. Consep also sells a sprayable flowable formulation. **Tradenames:** RAK 6 – BASF, CheckMate PTB-F – Consep, Hercon Disrupt PTB – Hercon.

APPLICATION: The slow-release dispensers are attached to individual trees in the orchard at a density of 500 per hectare.

PRODUCT SPECIFICATIONS: The product is composed of (*E*)-5-decenyl acetate and (*E*)-5-decenol in the ratio 6:1.

COMPATIBILITY: The pheromone is used alone without the addition of insecticides.

MAMMALIAN TOXICITY: (*E*)-5-Decenyl acetate and (*E*)-5-decenol combinations have not shown any allergic or other adverse toxicological effects on manufacturers, formulators, field workers or farmers.

ENVIRONMENTAL IMPACT AND NON-TARGET TOXICITY: The combination of (*E*)-5-decenyl acetate and (*E*)-5-decenol is a natural insect pheromone that is specific for the peach tree borer. There is no evidence that it has caused any adverse effects on any non-target organism or on the environment.

2:33 (R,Z)-5-(1-decenyl)dihydro-2(3H)-furanone

NOMENCLATURE: **Approved name:** (R,Z)-5-(1-decenyl)dihydro-2(3H)-furanone.
Other names: Japanese beetle sex pheromone.

SOURCE: Isolated from flasks that had contained female Japanese beetles (*Popillia japonica* Newman).

PRODUCTION: Manufactured for use in beetle control programmes.

TARGET PESTS: Japanese beetles (*Popillia japonica*).

TARGET CROPS: Ornamental turf and horticultural crops.

BIOLOGICAL ACTIVITY: **Mode of action:** The lures for the Japanese beetle are sold as a dual scented trap. One scent is a floral lure that attracts female beetles whilst the other is the sex pheromone that attracts the males. The strategy is a lure and trap or kill with the beetles trapped within bags and unable to move to the crops to be protected. **Efficacy:** The use of these baits in lure and trap or kill strategies has been shown to keep the beetle populations at a level that is acceptable. **Key reference:** J H Tumlinson, M G Klein, R F Doolittle, T L Ladd and A T Proveaux. 1977. Identification of the female Japanese beetle sex pheromone: inhibition of male response by an enantiomer, *Science (Washington)*, **197**, 798.

COMMERCIALISATION: **Formulation:** Sold as a combination dual lure trap containing food plant extracts attractive to females and (R,Z)-5-(1-decenyl)dihydro-2(3H)-furanone attractive to males. **Tradenames:** BioLure Japanese Beetle Trap – Arbico.

APPLICATION: The traps are hung in trees from a metal stand, ten to twenty metres downwind of the crops to be protected, before the adults migrate. The lures should be replaced after four to six weeks.

PRODUCT SPECIFICATIONS: **Purity:** (R,Z)-5-(1-Decenyl)dihydro-2(3H)-furanone is >95% chemically pure.

COMPATIBILITY: It is unusual to use the Japanese beetle lures in combination with other crop protection chemicals.

MAMMALIAN TOXICITY: There have been no reports of allergic or other adverse toxicological effects from (R,Z)-5-(1-decenyl)dihydro-2(3H)-furanone by researchers, manufacturers, formulators or field workers. It is considered to be non-toxic.

ENVIRONMENTAL IMPACT AND NON-TARGET TOXICITY: (R,Z)-5-(1-Decenyl)dihydro-2(3H)-furanone is the naturally occurring female sex pheromone of the Japanese beetle and is specific for this insect. Consequently, it is not expected to have any adverse effects on non-target organisms or on the environment.

2:34   1,7-dioxaspiro[5.5]undecane

Olive fly sex pheromone

NOMENCLATURE: **Approved name:** 1,7-dioxaspiro[5.5]undecane. **Other names:** olive fly sex pheromone.

SOURCE: Produced by virgin female olive flies (*Bactrocera oleae* Gmel.). The major component of pheromones isolated from the abdomen of virgin females.

PRODUCTION: Manufactured for use in control strategies.

TARGET PESTS: Olive flies (*Bactrocera oleae*).

TARGET CROPS: Olives.

BIOLOGICAL ACTIVITY: **Mode of action:** Male flies are attracted to females by following the pheromone trail released by virgin females. The use of the pheromone in slow-release devices will attract the flies to the traps where they can be collected as a means of monitoring the level of flies in the olive grove. Monitoring in this way ensures the application of insecticide to the trees at the best timing for fly control. In addition, the traps can be used as a lure and kill device in which an insecticide is incorporated so the attracted flies come into contact with the toxicant and, thereby, are eliminated from the olive grove. **Key references:** 1) R Baker, R H Herbert, P E Howse, O T Jones, W Franke and W Reith. 1980. Identification and synthesis of the major sex pheromone of the olive fruit fly (*Dacus oleae*), *J. Chem. Soc., Chem. Comm.*, 52–3. 2) O T Jones, J C Lisk, A W Mitchell, R Baker and P Ramos. 1985. A sex pheromone baited trap that catches the olive fruit fly (*Dacus oleae*) with a measurable degree of selectivity. In *Integrated Pest Control in Olive Groves*, R Cavalloro and A Crovetti (eds.), *Proc. CEC/IOBC Int. Joint Meet.*, Pisa, Italy, 3–6 April, 104–12.

COMMERCIALISATION: **Formulation:** Sold as technical material for use in lures for monitoring. Formulated as a sprayable formulation entrapped in polyurea microcapsules or polymer-entrapped micro-beads 5 to 10 μm in size and including an insecticide. Also sold as a lure and kill trap containing 1,7-dioxaspiro[5.5]undecane plus deltamethrin.
Tradenames: Polycore SKL – AgriSense.

APPLICATION: Slow-release lures containing either 1,7-dioxaspiro[5.5]undecane and insecticide or baited with ammonium salt dispensers as a food source, in the ratio 1:2 to 1:4 (sex pheromone:food source) are dispersed throughout the olive grove. The sprayable formulations are polymer entrapped beads that contain 20 g of pheromone per litre together with malathion or dimethoate. This mixed slow-release formulation is sprayed onto the olive trees either by air, treating 20 metre swathes every 100 metres of grove, or using ground equipment, treating only the south side of each row or tree. Organic farms can use these sprayable formulations if the insecticide used is natural pyrethrum or rotenone.

PRODUCT SPECIFICATIONS: **Purity:** The pheromone is >95% chemically pure.

COMPATIBILITY: Compatible with all compounds that are recommended for use in olive groves.

MAMMALIAN TOXICITY: There have been no reports of allergic or other adverse toxicological effects from reseachers, manufacturers, formulators or field workers from the pheromone. Considered to be non-toxic.

ENVIRONMENTAL IMPACT AND NON-TARGET TOXICITY: 1,7-Dioxaspiro[5.5]undecane is a naturally occurring pheromone that is specific for the olive fly. It is not expected to have any adverse effects on non-target organisms or on the environment.

2:35   disparlure   *Gypsy moth sex pheromone*

$$CH_3(CH_2)_9 \diagdown \quad \overset{O}{\triangle} \quad \diagup (CH_2)_4CH(CH_3)_2$$
$$H \qquad H$$

NOMENCLATURE: **Approved name:** disparlure ((7R,8S)-7,8-epoxy-2-methyloctadecane).
CAS RN: [29804–22–6].

SOURCE: Female *Lymantria dispar* Linnaeus emit a volatile component shown to be attractive to males. The main component was identified from extracts of the abdominal tips of virgin females.

PRODUCTION: Manufactured for use in protection of temperate fruit tree crops.

TARGET PESTS: Gypsy moth (*Lymantria dispar*).

TARGET CROPS: Temperate fruit tree crops such as apples, pears and peaches.

BIOLOGICAL ACTIVITY: **Mode of action:** (7R,8S)-Disparlure is the sex pheromone of the gypsy moth. Males locate females by following a plume of air rich in the odour of the pheromone. Evaporation of enantiomerically pure (7R,8S)-disparlure from traps attracts male moths to traps. Permeation of the canopy of an orchard with vapours of the racemic disparlure is used to disrupt location of females by males and decreases mating. It has been shown that the (+)-isomer is more effective at trapping and confusing males than the (−)-isomer. **Efficacy:** Several commercial formulations of racemic disparlure have been shown to maintain populations of gypsy moth effectively at economically tolerable levels during the time between fruiting and harvest. **Key references:** 1) J R Plimmer, C P Schwalbe, E C Paszek, B A Bierl, R E Webb, S Marumo and S Iwaki. 1977. Contrasting effectiveness of (+) and (−) enantiomers of disparlure for trapping native populations of the gypsy moth in Massachusetts, *Environ. Entomol.*, **6**, 518. 2) R T Cardé, C C Doane, T C Baker, S Iwaki and S Marumo. 1977. Attractancy of optically active pheromone for male gypsy moths, *Environ. Entomol.*, **6**, 768.

COMMERCIALISATION: **Formulation:** Slow-release formulations of pheromone from laminated plastics, plastic tubes or plastic barrier film. **Tradenames:** Disparlure (laminated plastic) – Hercon, Disparlure (plastic tubes) – Shin-Etsu, Disparlure (plastic barrier film) – Consep, Disparlure – Cyclo International, Disparlure – International Speciality Group, Disparlure – IPM Technologies, Luretape Disparlure – Hercon, Hercon Disrupt II – Hercon.

APPLICATION: Pheromone dispenser is attached to lower branches of trees at heights recommended by formulators. Numbers of lures recommended to be used per hectare vary with release rates. The lures are effective for about twelve weeks and should be applied before the adults fly.

PRODUCT SPECIFICATIONS: **Purity:** Pheromone that is >90% chemically pure is used in lures.

COMPATIBILITY: Pheromone disruption of mating does not require insecticide but can be used with application of insecticides.

MAMMALIAN TOXICITY: Disparlure has shown no adverse toxicological effects on manufacturers, formulators or field workers. Considered to be non-toxic.

ENVIRONMENTAL IMPACT AND NON-TARGET TOXICITY: Disparlure is a pheromone that is specific for the gypsy moth. There is no evidence that it has caused any adverse effect on non-target organisms or had an adverse environmental impact.

2:36 (E,E)-8,10-dodecadien-1-yl acetate

Pea moth sex pheromone

$$H_3C \quad H \quad C=C \quad C=C \quad (CH_2)_7OCOCH_3 \quad H \quad H$$

NOMENCLATURE: **Approved name:** (E,E)-8,10-dodecadien-1-yl acetate.
Other names: pea moth pheromone, Cydia [Laspeyresia] nigricana pheromone.

SOURCE: The sex pheromone of the pea moth (Cydia [Laspeyresia] nigricana (Fabricius)) extracted from the terminal segments of virgin females.

PRODUCTION: Manufactured for use in crop protection.

TARGET PESTS: Pea moth (Cydia [Laspeyresia] nigricana).

TARGET CROPS: Used in peas.

BIOLOGICAL ACTIVITY: **Mode of action:** (E,E)-8,10-Dodecadien-1-ol acetate is the major component of the sex pheromone of the pea moth. Male moths locate and subsequently mate with female moths by following the trail or pheromone plume emitted by the virgin females. The application of the product applied indiscriminately interfers with this process as a constant exposure to pheromone makes trail following impossible (habituation/adaptation). Alternatively, the use of discrete sources of pheromone released over time presents the male with a false trail to follow (confusion). The pea moth pheromone is of special interest as it has served as a model for a series of investigations on pheromone dispersal, orientation to a pheromone, trap design, trap interactions and population monitoring. The pea moth sex pheromone is usually used to monitor the presence of moths so that insecticide applications can be made at the time when the most vulnerable larval stages are present, shortly after egg lay. **Efficacy:** Very low rates are required to cause mating disruption. (8E,10E)-Dodecadien-1-ol acetate is volatile and distributes throughout the crop easily attracting male moths to traps. **Key references:** 1) A R Greenaway and C Wall. 1981. Attractant lures for males of the pea moth, Cydia nigricana (F.) containing (E)-10-dodecen-1-yl acetate and (E,E)-8,10-dodecadien-1-yl acetate, J. Chem. Ecol., **7**, 563. 2) J N Perry and C Wall. 1985. Orientation of male pea moth, Cydia nigricana, to pheromone traps in a wheat crop, Entomol. Exp. Appl., **37**, 161.

COMMERCIALISATION: **Formulation:** Sold in controlled release lures and traps. **Tradenames:** Pea Moth Pheromone – Agralan.

APPLICATION: The slow-release lures are distributed throughout the crop. The pheromone diffuses out of the dispenser and males follow the plume to the traps.

PRODUCT SPECIFICATIONS: **Purity:** (E,E)-8,10-Dodecadien-1-yl acetate is >95% chemically pure.

COMPATIBILITY: Can be used with all crop protection agents that do not repel the pea moth.

MAMMALIAN TOXICITY: The product has shown no adverse toxicological effects on research or manufacturing workers or on users.

ENVIRONMENTAL IMPACT AND NON-TARGET TOXICITY: The product is a natural insect pheromone that is specific for the pea moth. There is no evidence that it has caused any adverse effects on non-target organisms or had any deleterious effect on the environment.

2:37 (E,Z)-7,9-dodecadien-1-yl acetate
European grapevine moth sex pheromone

The Pesticide Manual - 11th edition: Entry number 263

$$CH_3CH_2 \quad \overset{H}{\underset{C=C}{\underset{H}{|}}} \quad \overset{(CH_2)_6OCOCH_3}{\underset{C=C}{\overset{|}{H}}}$$

NOMENCLATURE: **Approved name:** *(E,Z)*-7,9-dodecadien-1-yl acetate.
Other names: European grapevine moth pheromone; *Lobesia botrana* pheromone, E7Z9–12Ac (IOBC). **CAS RN:** *[54364–63–5]* (E,E)- isomer; *[55774–32–8]* (E,Z)- isomer.

SOURCE: The sex pheromone of the European grapevine moth (*Lobesia botrana* Denis and Schiffermüller). It was originally isolated from the female pheromone glands.

PRODUCTION: Manufactured for use in crop protection.

TARGET PESTS: European grapevine moth (*Lobesia botrana*).

TARGET CROPS: Recommended for use in vineyards.

BIOLOGICAL ACTIVITY: **Mode of action:** *(E,Z)*-7,9-Dodecadien-1-yl acetate is the sex pheromone of the European grapevine moth. Male moths locate and subsequently mate with female moths by following the trail or pheromone plume emitted by the virgin females. The application of the pheromone makes trail following impossible (camouflage, competition between artificial and female plume, false trail following). Control is subsequently achieved through the prevention of mating and the laying of fertile eggs.
Efficacy: Very low rates are required to cause mating disruption. *(E,Z)*-7,9-Dodecadien-1-yl acetate is volatile and distributes throughout the crop easily. Acts as an attractant and by disruption of mating in the disorientation mode. **Key reference:** R Roehrich, J-P Carles, Y Darrioumerie, P Pargade and B Lalanne-Cassou. 1976. Essais en vignoble de phéromones de

synthèse pour le capture des males de l'eudemis (*Lobesia botrana* Schiff.), *Ann. Zool. Ecol. Anim.*, **8**, 473.

COMMERCIALISATION: **Formulation:** Sold as a slow-release vapour-releasing dispenser. **Tradenames:** RAK 2 – BASF, Quant L.b. – BASF.

APPLICATION: Dispensers are distributed in the vineyard being attached to individual vines to give a density of 500 units per hectare. The pheromone diffuses out of the dispenser and is dispersed throughout the vineyard.

PRODUCT SPECIFICATIONS: Mating hormone of the European grapevine moth (*Lobesia botrana*). The main component of the natural pheromone is the (7E,9Z)- isomer; the (7E,9E)-isomer is a second component. **Purity:** The pheromone components in the product are >95% chemically pure.

COMPATIBILITY: Can be used with all crop protection agents that do not repel the European grapevine moth.

MAMMALIAN TOXICITY: The product has shown no adverse toxicological effects on research or manufacturing workers or on users.

ENVIRONMENTAL IMPACT AND NON-TARGET TOXICITY: The product is a natural insect pheromone that is specific for the European grapevine moth. There is no evidence that it has caused any adverse effects on non-target organisms or had any deleterious effect on the environment.

2:38   (*E*)-9-dodecen-1-yl acetate

European pine shoot moth sex pheromone

CH_3CH_2 ... H

H ... $(CH_2)_8OCOCH_3$

(*E*)- isomer

NOMENCLATURE: **Approved name:** (*E*)-9-dodecen-1-yl acetate. **Other names:** European pine shoot moth sex pheromone.

SOURCE: Originally isolated from the abdominal segments of virgin female European pine shoot moths (*Rhyacionia buoliana* (Denis and Schiffermüller)).

PRODUCTION: Manufactured for use in forestry management.

TARGET PESTS: European pine shoot moths (*Rhyacionia buoliana*).

TARGET CROPS: Pine forests.

BIOLOGICAL ACTIVITY: **Mode of action:** The male moths locate virgin females for mating by following a plume of volatile components emitted by the females. This location process can be disrupted by saturating the air surrounding the crop to be protected with synthetic pheromone. This confuses the males and means that the females cannot be found and mating does not take place. **Efficacy:** The use of the pheromone in Chile has been very effective in keeping the population of moths below the damage threshold. **Key reference:** R G Smith, G E Daterman, G D Daves Jr., K D McMurtrey and W L Roelofs. 1974. Sex pheromone of the European pine shoot moth: chemical identification and field tests, *J. Insect Physiol.*, **20**, 661.

COMMERCIALISATION: **Formulation:** Sold as a slow-release formulation.
Tradenames: CheckMate EPSM – Consep, Selibate EPSM – Thermo Trilogy.

APPLICATION: The slow-release devices are deployed throughout the pine forest at the time of flight of the moths.

PRODUCT SPECIFICATIONS: **Purity:** The product is >95% chemically pure.

COMPATIBILITY: It is unusual to use the product with other crop protection agents.

MAMMALIAN TOXICITY: There are no reports of allergic or other adverse toxicological effects from the use of (E)-9-dodecen-1-yl acetate by researchers, manufacturers, formulators or field workers. It is considered to be non-toxic. **Acute oral LD$_{50}$:** rats >15,000 mg/kg.
Acute dermal LD$_{50}$: rabbits >3,000 mg/kg.

ENVIRONMENTAL IMPACT AND NON-TARGET TOXICITY: (E)-9-Dodecen-1-yl acetate is the sex pheromone of the European pine shoot moth (*Rhyacionia buoliana*) and is specific for this species. It is not expected that its use will have any adverse effects on non-target organisms or on the environment.

2:39   (Z)-9-dodecen-1-yl acetate

Grape berry moth sex pheromone

CH_3CH_2 ___ $(CH_2)_8OCOCH_3$

H   H

(Z)- isomer

NOMENCLATURE: **Approved name:** (Z)-9-dodecen-1-yl acetate. **Other names:** grape berry moth sex pheromone; (Z)-9-12Ac.

SOURCE: The sex pheromone of the grape berry moth (*Eupoecilia ambiguella* (Hübner)) that was originally isolated from the terminal segments of virgin females.

PRODUCTION: Manufactured for use in crop protection.

TARGET PESTS: Grape berry moth (*Eupoecilia ambiguella*).

TARGET CROPS: Vineyards.

BIOLOGICAL ACTIVITY: **Mode of action:** (Z)-9-Dodecen-1-yl acetate is a component of the sex pheromone of the grape berry moth. Males locate and subsequently mate with female moths by following the pheromone trail or pheromone plume emitted by virgin females. The application of (Z)-9-dodecen-1-yl acetate makes trail following impossible (competition between applied and natural pheromone plume, false trail following). Control is eventually achieved by preventing the mating of the moths and the subsequent lack of fertile egg production. **Efficacy:** Very low rates are required to cause mating disruption. (Z)-9-Dodecenyl acetate is volatile and is rapidly dispersed throughout the crop. It has been shown that of the constituents of the female sex pheromone, (Z)-9-dodecen-1-yl acetate is the best male attractant. **Key references:** 1) H Arn, R Roehrich, C Descoins and S Rauscher. 1979. Performance of five sex attractant formulations for the grape moth, *Eupoecilia ambiguella* Hb. in European vineyards, *Mitt. Schweiz. Entomol. Ges.*, **52**, 45. 2) H Arn, S Rauscher and A Schmid. 1979. Sex attractant formulations and traps for the grape moth, *Eupoecilia ambiguella* Hb., *Mitt. Schweiz. Entomol. Ges.*, **52**, 49.

COMMERCIALISATION: **Formulation:** Sold as a slow-release formulation of polyethylene ampoules. **Tradenames:** RAK 1 Plus – BASF.

APPLICATION: The slow-release dispensers are attached to individual vines in the vineyard at a rate of 500 per hectare.

PRODUCT SPECIFICATIONS: RAK 1 Plus contains only (Z)-9-dodecen-1-yl acetate. **Purity:** The pheromone in the product is >95% chemically pure.

COMPATIBILITY: (Z)-9-Dodecen-1-yl acetate is used alone without the use of chemical insecticides.

MAMMALIAN TOXICITY: (Z)-9-Dodecen-1-yl acetate has shown no allergic or other adverse toxicological effects on manufacturers, formulators, research workers or farmers. **Acute oral LD$_{50}$:** rats >5,000 mg/kg. **Acute dermal LD$_{50}$:** rabbits >3,000 mg/kg.

ENVIRONMENTAL IMPACT AND NON-TARGET TOXICITY: (Z)-9-Dodecen-1-yl acetate is a natural insect pheromone that is specific for the grape berry moth. There is no evidence that it has had any adverse effects on non-target organisms or on the environment.

2:40 (Z)-dodec-8-en-1-yl acetate plus (E)-dodec-8-en-1-yl acetate plus (Z)-dodec-8-en-1-ol

Oriental fruit moth sex pheromone

The Pesticide Manual - 11th edition: Entry number 262

$$CH_3(CH_2)_2 \diagdown \quad \diagup (CH_2)_7OR$$
$$C=C$$
$$H \qquad H$$

$$H \diagdown \quad \diagup (CH_2)_7OCOCH_3$$
$$C=C$$
$$CH_3(CH_2)_2 \diagup \qquad H$$

(Z)-dodecenyl acetate (R = COCH$_3$)

(E)-dodecenyl acetate

(Z)-dodecenol (R = H)

2. Pheromones

NOMENCLATURE: **Approved name:** (Z)-dodec-8-en-1-yl acetate plus (E)-dodec-8-en-1-yl acetate plus (Z)-dodec-8-en-1-ol. **Other names:** Oriental fruit moth sex pheromone; *Grapholitha molesta* sex pheromone. **CAS RN:** *[28079–04–1]* (Z)-dodec-8-en-1-yl acetate; *[38363–29–0]* (E)-dodec-8-en-1-yl acetate; *[40642–40–8]* (Z)-dodec-8-en-1-ol.

SOURCE: Female *Grapholitha molesta* (Busck) emit several volatile components shown to be attractive to males. Originally extracted from the terminal segments of virgin females.

PRODUCTION: Manufactured for use in crop protection.

TARGET PESTS: Oriental fruit moth (*Grapholitha [Cydia] molesta*). Also effective against the macadamia nut borer (*Cryptophlebia ombrodelta* (Lower)) and the koa seedworm (*C. illepida* (Butler)).

TARGET CROPS: Orchard fruit such as apples, pears, peaches, nectarines and apricots.

BIOLOGICAL ACTIVITY: **Mode of action:** Males locate females by following a plume of air rich in the odour of a complete pheromone blend emitted by females. Evaporation of the pheromone blend given above from traps attracts male moths to traps. Permeation of the canopy of an orchard with vapours of the same pheromone is used to disrupt location of females by males and thus decrease mating. **Efficacy:** The combination of the three components has given more effective disruption than the use of the (Z)-dodec-8-en-1-yl acetate alone. Some products contain only one component. Very low rates are required to cause mating disruption. The pheromone blend is volatile and distributes throughout the crop easily. **Key reference:** T C Baker, W Meyer and W L Roelofs. 1981. Sex pheromone dosage and blend specificity of response by oriental fruit moth, *Environ. Entomol.*, **30**, 269.

COMMERCIALISATION: **Formulation:** Sold in slow-release devices. Commercialised by Consep, Hercon, Biosys and Scentry. Consep also sells a sprayable flowable formulation. **Tradenames:** Isomate-M – Shin-Etsu and Biocontrol, Confusalin – AgrEvo and Calliope, RAK 5 – BASF, Quant G.m. – BASF, Isomate OFM Plus (long life formulation) – Biocontrol, CheckMate OFM-F – Consep, Hercon Disrupt OFM – Hercon.

APPLICATION: The slow-release devices are placed within the orchard at a height specified by the manufacturer. It is usual to allow 500 dispensers per hectare. The pheromone diffuses out of the dispenser and disperses throughout the orchard.

PRODUCT SPECIFICATIONS: The pheromones are present in the ratio 90:6:4; (Z)-dodec-8-en-1-yl acetate:(E)-dodec-8-en-1-yl acetate:(Z)-dodec-8-en-1-ol. **Purity:** The pheromones are >90% chemically pure.

COMPATIBILITY: Can be used with all crop protection agents that do not repel the Oriental fruit moth.

MAMMALIAN TOXICITY: Oriental fruit moth pheromone blend has shown no adverse toxicological effects on manufacturers, formulators or field workers. Considered to be non-toxic. **Acute oral LD$_{50}$:** rats >15,000 mg/kg ((Z) and (E)-dodec-8-en-1-yl acetate). **Acute dermal LD$_{50}$:** rabbits >15,000 mg/kg ((Z) and (E)-dodec-8-en-1-yl acetate).

ENVIRONMENTAL IMPACT AND NON-TARGET TOXICITY: Oriental fruit moth pheromone blend is a natural insect pheromone that is specific for the Oriental fruit moth. There is no evidence that it has caused an adverse effect on non-target organisms or had an adverse environmental impact.

2:41 (2R',5R')-ethyl-1,6-dioxaspiro-[4.4]nonane plus (2R',5S')-ethyl-1,6-dioxaspiro[4.4]nonane

Six-toothed spruce bark beetle aggregation pheromone

NOMENCLATURE: **Approved name:** chalcogran ((2R',5R')-ethyl-1,6-dioxaspiro[4.4]nonane plus (2R',5S')-ethyl-1,6-dioxaspiro[4.4]nonane). **Other names:** six-toothed spruce bark beetle aggregation pheromone.

SOURCE: The volatiles were isolated from adult male beetles and were shown to be the aggregation pheromone of the six-toothed spruce bark beetle (*Pityogenes chalcographus* (Linnaeus)).

PRODUCTION: Manufactured for use in forestry management.

TARGET PESTS: The six-toothed spruce bark beetle (*Pityogenes chalcographus*).

TARGET CROPS: Spruce forests.

BIOLOGICAL ACTIVITY: **Mode of action:** (2R',5R')-Ethyl-1,6-dioxaspiro[4.4]nonane and (2R',5S')-ethyl-1,6-dioxaspiro[4.4]nonane are the components of the aggregation pheromone of the six-toothed spruce bark beetle. Males and females locate host trees by following a plume of air enriched with the odour of the host tree and the aggregation pheromone. Evaporation of pheromone vapours from lures attached to host trees attracts both male and female bark beetles to baited trees and establishes conditions for mass attack of baited trees. Also used for insect monitoring. **Efficacy:** The baiting of selected areas of the forest has reduced the number of attacks in the main forest area. The baited trees are felled before the brood emerges from the infested trees. **Key reference:** W Francke, V Heeman, B Gerken, J A A Renwick and J P Vité. 1977. 2-ethyl-1,6-dioxaspiro[4.4]nonane, principal aggregation pheromone of *Pityogenes chalcographus* (L.), *Naturwissenschaften*, **64**, 590.

COMMERCIALISATION: **Formulation:** Sold as a slow-release dispenser containing the pheromone. **Tradenames:** Linoprax – Cyanamid.

APPLICATION: The idea is to attract the bark beetle to specific areas where baited trees are attacked. These heavily-infested trees are then felled and the population of insects is destroyed before the brood emerges. To accomplish this the pheromone dispensers are attached to trees at chest height at a distance of 50 metres apart in the baiting area. Baiting four trees per hectare is usually sufficient to concentrate the beetles.

PRODUCT SPECIFICATIONS: The two components are present in the ratio 1:1. **Purity:** The pheromones are >95% chemically pure.

COMPATIBILITY: It is unusual to apply the pheromones with other crop protection agents although insecticides can be used to kill the insects in the baited trees.

MAMMALIAN TOXICITY: There are no reports of allergic or other adverse toxicological effects from the use, manufacture or formulation of (2R',5R')-ethyl-1,6-dioxaspiro[4.4]nonane plus (2R',5S')-ethyl-1,6-dioxaspiro[4.4]nonane. It is considered to be non-toxic.

ENVIRONMENTAL IMPACT AND NON-TARGET TOXICITY: (2R',5R')-Ethyl-1,6-dioxaspiro[4.4]nonane plus (2R',5S')-ethyl-1,6-dioxaspiro[4.4]nonane is the aggregation pheromone of the six-toothed spruce bark beetle and it is specific for this species. It is not expected that it will have any adverse effects on non-target organisms or on the environment.

2. Pheromones

2:42 exo-brevicomin plus endo-brevicomin

Western balsam bark beetle aggregation pheromone

exo-brevicomin

endo-brevicomin

NOMENCLATURE: **Approved name:** exo-brevicomin (exo-7-ethyl-5-methyl-6,8-dioxabicyclo[3.2.1]octane); endo-brevicomin (endo-7-ethyl-5-methyl-6,8-dioxabicyclo[3.2.1]octane). **Other names:** Western balsam bark beetle aggregation pheromone. **CAS RN:** [60018–04–4] exo-brevicomin; [62532–53–0] endo-brevicomin.

SOURCE: Male *Dryocoetes confusus* Swaine volatile components shown to attract adult beetles. Originally isolated from extracts of males.

PRODUCTION: Manufactured for use in crop protection.

TARGET PESTS: Western balsam bark beetle (*Dryocoetes confusus*).

TARGET CROPS: Fir forests.

BIOLOGICAL ACTIVITY: **Mode of action:** Western balsam bark beetle tree bait is the aggregation pheromone of the Western balsam bark beetle. Males and females locate host trees by following a plume of air enriched with the odour of the host tree and the aggregation pheromone. Evaporation of pheromone vapours from lures attached to host trees attracts both male and female Western balsam bark beetles to baited trees and establishes conditions for mass attack of baited trees. **Efficacy:** The baiting of selected areas of the forest has reduced the number of attacks in the main forest area. The baited trees are felled before the brood emerges from the infested trees. **Key reference:** J H Borden, A M Pierce Jr, L J Chong, A J Stock and A C Oehlschlager. 1987. Semiochemicals produced by Western balsam bark beetle, *Dryocoetes confusus* Swaine (Coleoptera: Scolytidae), *J. Chem. Ecol.*, **13**, 823.

COMMERCIALISATION: **Formulation:** Sold as a slow-release formulation of the mixed products from polymer plugs or plastic bags. Development work on the pheromone has been undertaken at the Chemical Ecology Research Group of Simon Fraser University, Canada. **Tradenames:** Western Balsam Bark Beetle Tree Bait – PheroTech, Western Balsam Bark Beetle Tree Bait – ChemTica.

APPLICATION: Pheromone dispensers are attached to trees at chest height at a distance of 50 metres apart in the baiting area where the beetle population is to be concentrated. Four baited trees per hectare are usually sufficient for effective concentration.

PRODUCT SPECIFICATIONS: The chemicals are 95% pure and are present in the product in the ratio 9:1 exo-brevicomin:endo-brevicomin.

COMPATIBILITY: Pheromone-baited trap trees do not require insecticide to kill the beetles as they arrive. Baited trees and surrounding trees are felled and removed before the brood emerges.

MAMMALIAN TOXICITY: Western balsam bark beetle tree bait has shown no allergic or other adverse toxicological effects on manufacturers, formulators and field workers.

ENVIRONMENTAL IMPACT AND NON-TARGET TOXICITY: Western balsam bark beetle tree bait contains only naturally occurring insect pheromones that are specific for the Western balsam bark beetle. There is no evidence that it has had any adverse effect on non-target organisms or on the environment.

2:43   exo-brevicomin plus trans-verbenol

Mountain pine beetle aggregation pheromone

exo-brevicomin

NOMENCLATURE: **Approved name:** exo-brevicomin (exo-7-ethyl-5-methyl-6,8-dioxabicyclo[3.2.1]octane); trans-verbenol (trans-4,6,6-trimethylbicyclo[3.3.1]hept-3-en-2-ol). **Other names:** mountain pine beetle aggregation pheromone. **CAS RN:** [60018–04–4] exo-brevicomin; [1845–30–3] trans-verbenol.

SOURCE: Male Dendroctonus ponderosae Hopkins volatile components that have been shown to attract adult beetles. Isolated from the extracts of the hindgut of emergent and feeding males and females.

PRODUCTION: Manufactured for use in crop protection.

TARGET PESTS: Mountain pine beetle (*Dendroctonus ponderosae*).

TARGET CROPS: Pine forests.

BIOLOGICAL ACTIVITY: **Mode of action:** Mountain pine beetle tree bait is the aggregation pheromone of the mountain pine beetle. Male and female adults locate host trees by following a plume of air enriched with the odour of the host pine tree and containing the pheromone. The attachment of lures to host trees attracts male and female mountain pine beetles to baited trees and establishes conditions that are appropriate for mass attack of the baited trees. **Efficacy:** The attraction of beetles to baited trees and the subsequent felling and destruction of these trees before the insect brood emerges has been very successful in reducing attack in non-baited areas and reducing the population of the mountain pine beetle. **Key reference:** J H Borden, L C Ryker, L J Chong, H D Pierce Jr, B D Johnston and A C Oehlschlager. 1983. Semiochemicals for the mountain pine beetle, *Dendroctonus ponderosae*, in British Columbia: baited tree studies, *Can. J. For. Res.*, **13**, 325.

COMMERCIALISATION: **Formulation:** The pheromones are formulated separately. *Exo*-brevicomin is produced as a slow-release formulation in a polymer plug or plastic bag and *trans*-verbenol is a slow-release formulation from plastic bags. Development work on the pheromone has been undertaken at the Chemical Ecology Research Group of Simon Fraser University, Canada. **Tradenames:** Mountain Pine Beetle Tree Bait – PheroTech, Mountain Pine Beetle Tree Bait – ChemTica.

APPLICATION: The idea is to attract the mountain pine beetle to specific areas where baited trees are attacked. These heavily-infested trees are then felled and the population of insects is destroyed before the brood emerges. To accomplish, this the pheromone dispensers are attached to trees at chest height at a distance of 50 metres apart in the baiting area. Baiting four trees per hectare is usually sufficient to concentrate the beetles.

PRODUCT SPECIFICATIONS: *Exo*-brevicomin is >95% chemically pure and *trans*-verbenol is >65% chemically pure.

COMPATIBILITY: Pheromone-baited trees do not require insecticide to kill the arriving beetles. Baited trees and surrounding trees are felled and removed before the brood emerges.

MAMMALIAN TOXICITY: Mountain pine beetle tree bait has shown no allergic or other adverse toxicological effects on manufacturers, formulators or field workers.

ENVIRONMENTAL IMPACT AND NON-TARGET TOXICITY: Mountain pine beetle tree bait contains only naturally occurring insect pheromones that are specific for the mountain pine beetle. There is no evidence that its use has had any adverse effects on non-target organisms or on the environment.

2:44   farnesol with nerolidol

Spider mite alarm pheromone

The Pesticide Manual - 11th edition: Entry number 298

CH$_3$ H

CH$_3$ (CH$_2$)$_2$ CH$_2$OH

(CH$_3$)$_2$C =CH(CH$_2$)$_2$ H

farnesol

NOMENCLATURE: **Approved name:** farnesol ((*Z,E*)-3,7,11-trimethyl-2,6,10-dodecatrien-1-ol); nerolidol (3,7,11-trimethyl-1,6,10-dodecatrien-3-ol). **Other names:** spider mite alarm pheromone. **CAS RN:** *[4602–84–0]* farnesol; *[7212–44–4]* nerolidol, *[3790–78–1]* cis-isomer, *[40716–66–3]* trans-isomer.

SOURCE: The alarm pheromone from the two-spotted spider mite (*Tetranychus urticae* Koch). Isolated from the crude extracts of homogenised female deutonymphs.

TARGET PESTS: Two-spotted spider mite (*Tetranychus urticae*).

TARGET CROPS: All crops infested with spider mites.

BIOLOGICAL ACTIVITY: **Mode of action:** The product is the alarm pheromone of *Tetranychus urticae*. It is released under natural conditions when the population is threatened or is being attacked by a mite predator. The result is an increase in the activity of the mites with consequent greater exposure to a co-applied miticide. **Efficacy:** *Tetranychus urticae* is very sensitive to the alarm pheromone and it has been shown that mixtures with conventional acaricides result in significant increases in mortality over those found with acaricides used alone. In addition, the alarmed spider mites feed less than undisturbed mites.
Key reference: S Regev and W W Cone. 1975. Evidence of farnesol as a male sex attractant for the two-spotted spider mite, *Tetranychus urticae* Koch, *Environ. Entomol.*, **4**, 307.

COMMERCIALISATION: **Formulation:** Formulated as a controlled release liquid concentrate. **Tradenames:** Stirrup M – Troy, Stirrup Mylox (plus sulfur) – Troy.

APPLICATION: Applied in combination with conventional acaricides. Used at a rate of 150 to 425 mls of product per hectare.

PRODUCT SPECIFICATIONS: Mixture of structural isomers.

COMPATIBILITY: Compatible with most crop protection agents particularly acaricides.

2. Pheromones

MAMMALIAN TOXICITY: The product has shown no adverse toxicological effects on research or manufacturing workers or on users. **Acute oral LD_{50}:** rats >5,000 mg/kg; rabbits >2,000 mg/kg.

ENVIRONMENTAL IMPACT AND NON-TARGET TOXICITY: The product is a natural insect pheromone that is specific for the two-spotted spider mite. There is no evidence that it has caused any adverse effects on non-target organisms or had any deleterious effect on the environment.

2:45   ferrolure+

Red palm weevil aggregation pheromone

$$CH_3(CH_2)_2CH(CH_3)CH(OH)(CH_2)_3CH_3$$
$$+$$
$$CH_3(CH_2)_2CH(CH_3)C(O)(CH_2)_3CH_3$$

NOMENCLATURE: **Approved name:** ferrolure+ (4-methyl-5-nonanol plus 4-methyl-5-nonanone). **Other names:** red palm weevil aggregation pheromone.
CAS RN: *[35900–26–6]* 4-methyl-5-nonanone.

SOURCE: Ferrolure+ is the male *Rhynchophorus ferrugineus* volatile component that has been shown to attract adult weevils.

TARGET PESTS: Red palm weevil (*Rhynchophorus ferrugineus*).

TARGET CROPS: Mature coconut and date palm plantations.

BIOLOGICAL ACTIVITY: **Mode of action:** Ferrolure+ is the aggregation pheromone of the red palm weevil. Adults locate males by following a plume of air enriched with the odour of the pheromone. Evaporation of pheromone vapours from traps containing palm, palm fruit, apples or sugarcane stalks attracts male and female weevils to the traps.

COMMERCIALISATION: **Formulation:** Sold as a slow-release formulation from plastic bags containing liquid pheromone. AgriSense and Calliope produce products.
Tradenames: Ferrolure+ – ChemTica, Red Date Palm Weevil Attract and Kill Dispensers – SEDQ.

APPLICATION: The pheromone dispenser is attached inside bucket traps containing food pieces. These traps are buried in the ground near palms in infested areas at a density of one trap per three hectares.

PRODUCT SPECIFICATIONS: The product is >95% chemically pure and contains the two components in the ratio 9:1, 4-methyl-5-nonanol:4-methyl-5-nonanone.

COMPATIBILITY: Pheromone use does not require the use of insecticides but trapping can be used in addition to the chemical treatment of infested palms.

MAMMALIAN TOXICITY: Ferrolure+ has shown no allergic or other adverse toxicological effects on manufacturers, formulators or field workers.

ENVIRONMENTAL IMPACT AND NON-TARGET TOXICITY: Ferrolure+ is a naturally occurring insect pheromone that is specific for the red palm weevil. There is no evidence that it has caused any adverse effects on any non-target organisms or had any adverse effects on the environment.

2:46 frontalin plus camphene
Douglas fir beetle aggregation pheromone

frontalin   camphene

NOMENCLATURE: **Approved name:** frontalin (1,5-dimethyl-6,8-dioxabicyclo[3.2.1]octane); with camphene. **Other names:** Douglas fir beetle aggregation pheromone.
CAS RN: *[60478-96-8]* frontalin.

SOURCE: Frontalin and camphene are two of several components isolated from adult females of the Douglas fir beetle (*Dendroctonus pseudotsuga* Hopkins). These compounds are key components of the aggregation response of male and female beetles.

PRODUCTION: The chemicals are manufactured for use in insect control.

TARGET PESTS: Douglas fir beetle (*Dendroctonus pseudotsuga*).

TARGET CROPS: Douglas fir (*Pseudotsuga menziesii* Franco).

BIOLOGICAL ACTIVITY: **Mode of action:** Douglas fir beetle tree bait is the aggregation pheromone of the Douglas fir beetle. Males and females locate host trees by following a plume of air enriched with the odour of the host tree and containing the aggregation pheromone. Evaporation of the pheromone from lures attached to host trees attracts both male and female beetles to the baited trees and establishes conditions for mass attack of baited trees. **Efficacy:** The use of four baited trees per hectare has been successful in concentrating the beetle population in the baited areas and reduces the population in non-baited areas. Baited trees and those close to baited trees are felled before the brood emerges. **Key reference:** G B Pitman and J P Vité. 1970. Field response of *Dendroctonus pseudotsugae* to synthetic frontalin, *Ann. Entomol. Soc. Am.*, **63**, 661.

COMMERCIALISATION: **Formulation:** Formulated as a slow-release product releasing frontalin and camphene. **Tradenames:** Douglas Fir Beetle Aggregation Pheromone – PheroTech.

APPLICATION: The pheromone dispenser is attached to trees at chest height 50 metres apart in the baiting area where the beetles are to be concentrated. Four baited trees per hectare have been used successfully to reduce populations in non-baited areas.

PRODUCT SPECIFICATIONS: **Purity:** The pheromones are >95% chemically pure.

COMPATIBILITY: Pheromone-baited trap trees do not require insecticide to kill arriving beetles. Baited trees and surrounding trees are felled and removed before the brood emerges.

MAMMALIAN TOXICITY: There are no reports of allergic or other adverse toxicological effects from the use of the aggregation pheromone of the Douglas fir beetle. Considered to be non-toxic.

ENVIRONMENTAL IMPACT AND NON-TARGET TOXICITY: The aggregation pheromone is specific for the Douglas fir beetle and is not expected to have any adverse effects on non-target organisms or on the environment.

2:47 frontalin plus *endo*-brevicomin plus 3-carene plus α-pinene

Southern pine beetle aggregation pheromone

endo-brevicomin   frontalin   α-pinene

NOMENCLATURE: **Approved name:** frontalin (1,5-dimethyl-6,8-dioxabicyclo[3.2.1]octane); with *endo*-brevicomin (*endo*-7-ethyl-5-methyl-6,8-dioxabicyclo[3.2.1]octane); with 3-carene; with α-pinene. **Other names:** Southern pine beetle aggregation pheromone.
CAS RN: [62532-53-01] endo-brevicomin; [60478-96-8] frontalin; [80-56-8] α-pinene.

SOURCE: Frontalin and *endo*-brevicomin are insect-produced aggregation pheromones. 3-Carene and α-pinene are host-produced synergists of the pheromones.

PRODUCTION: Manufactured for use in forest protection strategies.

TARGET PESTS: Southern pine beetle (*Dendroctonus frontalis* Zimmerman).

TARGET CROPS: Pine trees.

BIOLOGICAL ACTIVITY: **Mode of action:** Both male and female beetles are attracted by the aggregation pheromone and follow its trail in order to locate host trees. The attachment of lures to selected trees establishes conditions for mass insect attack of these baited trees. **Efficacy:** The use of four baited trees per hectare has been successful in concentrating the beetle population in the baited areas and reduces the population in non-baited areas. **Key reference:** T L Payne, J E Coster, J V Richerson, L J Edson and E R Hart. 1978. Field response of the Southern pine beetle to behavioral chemicals, *Environ. Entomol.*, **7**, 578.

COMMERCIALISATION: **Formulation:** Sold as slow-release formulations from devices such as polymer plugs or plastic bags.

APPLICATION: The slow-release devices are attached to the trees at chest height at a distance of fifty metres apart in the baiting area where the beetles are to be concentrated. The baited trees and those surrounding the baits are felled and removed before the brood emerges.

PRODUCT SPECIFICATIONS: **Purity:** All components are >95% chemically pure.

COMPATIBILITY: It is unusual to use these pheromone lures in conjunction with other crop protection agents.

MAMMALIAN TOXICITY: There are no records of allergic or other adverse toxicological effects from research staff, manufacturers, formulators or field workers from the product. It is considered to be non-toxic.

ENVIRONMENTAL IMPACT AND NON-TARGET TOXICITY: Southern pine beetle aggregation pheromone is composed of natural pheromones from *Dendroctonus frontalis* and host tree volatiles all of which occur widely in Nature. It is not expected that the product will have any adverse effects on non-target organisms or on the environment.

2:48　frontalin plus α-pinene

Spruce beetle aggregation pheromone and host kairomone

frontalin　　　　　　　α-pinene

NOMENCLATURE: **Approved name:** frontalin (1,5-dimethyl-6,8-dioxabicyclo[3.2.1]octane); α-pinene. **Other names:** spruce beetle aggregation pheromone and host kairomone. **CAS RN:** [60478-96-8] frontalin; [80-56-8] α-pinene.

SOURCE: Male *Dendroctonus rufipennis* (Kirby) volatile components and spruce-produced α-pinene have been shown to attract male and female adult beetles.

PRODUCTION: Manufactured for use in crop protection.

TARGET PESTS: Spruce beetle (*Dendroctonus rufipennis*).

TARGET CROPS: Spruce forests.

BIOLOGICAL ACTIVITY: **Mode of action:** Spruce beetle tree bait is the aggregation pheromone of the spruce beetle. Males and females locate host trees by following a plume of air enriched with the odour of the host tree and containing the aggregation pheromone. Evaporation of the pheromone from lures attached to host trees attracts both male and female spruce beetles to the baited trees and establishes conditions for mass attack of baited trees. **Efficacy:** The use of four baited trees per hectare has been successful in concentrating the beetle population in the baited areas and reduces the population in non-baited areas. **Key reference:** E D A Dyer and P M Hall. 1980. Effect of living host tree (*Picea*) on the responses of *Dendroctonus rufipennis* and a predator *Thanasimus undulatus* to frontalin and suedenol, *Can. Entomol.*, **107**, 979.

COMMERCIALISATION: **Formulation:** Formulated as a slow-release product releasing frontalin and α-pinene from a polymer plug or plastic bag. Development work on the pheromone has been undertaken at the Chemical Ecology Research Group of Simon Fraser University, Canada and by the British Columbia Forestry Service, Canada. **Tradenames:** Spruce Beetle Tree Bait – PheroTech, Spruce Beetle Tree Bait – ChemTica.

APPLICATION: The pheromone dispenser is attached to trees at chest height 50 metres apart in the baiting area where the beetles are to be concentrated. Four baited trees per hectare have been used successfully to reduce populations in non-baited areas.

PRODUCT SPECIFICATIONS: **Purity:** Frontalin is >95% chemically pure.

COMPATIBILITY: Pheromone-baited trap trees do not require insecticide to kill arriving beetles. Baited trees and surrounding trees are felled and removed before the brood emerges.

MAMMALIAN TOXICITY: Spruce beetle tree bait has not shown allergic or other adverse toxicological effects on manufacturers, formulators or field workers.

ENVIRONMENTAL IMPACT AND NON-TARGET TOXICITY: Spruce beetle tree bait contains only natural insect pheromones that are specific for the spruce beetle and host volatile components. There is no evidence of any adverse effects on non-target organisms or on the environment.

2:49 gossyplure

Pink bollworm sex pheromone

The Pesticide Manual - 11th edition: Entry number 384

$$CH_3(CH_2)_3 \quad (CH_2)_2 \quad (CH_2)_6OCOCH_3$$
$$C=C \qquad C=C$$
$$H \qquad H \ H \qquad H$$

(Z,Z)-

$$CH_3(CH_2)_3 \quad (CH_2)_2 \qquad H$$
$$C=C \qquad C=C$$
$$H \qquad H \ H \qquad (CH_2)_6OCOCH_3$$

(Z,E)-

NOMENCLATURE: **Approved name:** gossyplure (name in common use); ((Z,Z)- and (Z,E)-hexadeca-7,11-dien-1-yl acetate). **Other names:** pink bollworm sex pheromone.
CAS RN: [53042–79–8]; [51606–94–4] (Z,E)- isomer; [52207–99–5] (Z,Z)- isomer; [122616–64–2] (7-Z,11-unspecified stereochemistry)- isomer; [50933–33–0] unspecified stereochemistry.

SOURCE: The sex pheromone of the pink bollworm (Pectinophora gossypiella (Saunders)). Isolated from the abdominal tip of virgin females.

PRODUCTION: Manufactured for use in crop protection.

TARGET PESTS: Pink bollworm (Pectinophora gossypiella).

TARGET CROPS: Cotton.

BIOLOGICAL ACTIVITY: **Mode of action:** Gossyplure is the sex pheromone of the pink bollworm. Male moths locate and subsequently mate with female moths by following the trail or pheromone plume emitted by the virgin females. The application of gossyplure indiscriminately interferes with this process as a constant exposure to inundative levels of pheromone makes trail following impossible (habituation/adaptation). Alternatively, the use of discrete sources of pheromone released over time presents the male with a false trail to follow (confusion). Control is subsequently achieved through the prevention of mating and the laying of fertile eggs. **Efficacy:** Very low rates are required to cause mating disruption. Gossyplure is volatile and distributes throughout the crop easily. **Key reference:** J R Merkl and H M Flint. 1981. Responses of male pink bollworms to various mixtures of the (Z,Z-) and (Z,E-) isomers of gossyplure, *Environ. Entomol.*, **6**, 114.

COMMERCIALISATION: **Formulation:** Slow-release formulations of hollow fibres of polyacrylate resin containing gossyplure, laminated flakes covering a porous layer impregnated with gossyplure, polyamide micro-capsules containing gossyplure, twist tie dispensers and polymer bands are all commercially available. Consep has introduced a flowable formulation. **Tradenames:** Nomate PBW – Scentry, Pectone – Zeneca, PBW Rope-L – Shin-Etsu, PB Rope – Shin-Etsu, Frustrate PBW – Thermo Trilogy, DeCoy PBW band – Thermo Trilogy, Selibate PBW – Thermo Trilogy and Monterey, Last Flight – Troy, Lost Dream – Troy, CheckMate PBW – Consep, CheckMate PBW-F – Consep, Disrupt PBW – BASF and Hercon, Dismate – Russell, Pherocon – Trece, Sirene-PBW (plus permethrin) – IPM Technologies, Sirene PBW – Novartis.

APPLICATION: Many slow-release formulations are applied by aerial spraying with the slow-release plastic device adhering to the crop's foliage and the pheromone diffusing into the field. Other dispensers are attached to individual plants within the cotton field by hand. Apply at a rate of 50 to 60 grams active ingredient per hectare.

PRODUCT SPECIFICATIONS: The product is composed of the two isomers in the ratio 1:1. **Purity:** The isomers are >95% chemically pure.

COMPATIBILITY: Gossyplure can be used alone or in combination with insecticides as a lure and kill strategy.

MAMMALIAN TOXICITY: Gossyplure has shown no adverse toxicological effects on manufacturers, formulators, research workers or farmers. It is considered to be non-toxic. **Acute oral LD$_{50}$:** rats >5,000 mg/kg. **Acute dermal LD$_{50}$:** rabbits >2,000 mg/kg. **Inhalation:** LC$_{50}$ (4 hours) rats >2,000 mg/litre.

ENVIRONMENTAL IMPACT AND NON-TARGET TOXICITY: Gossyplure is a natural insect pheromone that is specific for the pink bollworm. There is no evidence that it has caused any adverse effect on any non-target organism or had any adverse environmental impact.

NOMENCLATURE: Approved name: grandlure ((+)-*cis*-2-isopropenyl-1-methylcyclobutaneethanol + *cis*-3,3-dimethyl-Δ^β-cyclohexaneethanol + *cis*-3,3-dimethyl-$\Delta^{1\alpha}$-cyclohexaneacetaldehyde + *trans*-3,3-dimethyl-$\Delta^{1\alpha}$-cyclohexaneacetaldehyde). **Other names:** boll weevil sex pheromone. **CAS RN:** *[26532–22–9]*.

SOURCE: The compounds were identified from both male and female boll weevils (*Anthonomus grandis* Boheman) and their frass.

PRODUCTION: Manufactured for use in cotton.

TARGET PESTS: Boll weevils (*Anthonomus grandis*).

TARGET CROPS: Cotton.

BIOLOGICAL ACTIVITY: **Mode of action:** The pheromones are used in survey and trapping programmes in cotton. Both male and females are attracted to the volatiles and can be mass trapped, thereby reducing the population of boll weevils in the crop, or the numbers caught can be monitored, thereby identifying the best timing for the application of insecticide sprays. The grandlure baits are also used in a lure and kill strategy whereby the boll weevil adults are attracted to the lures where they come into contact with a fast-acting contact insecticide. **Efficacy:** Grandlure has been widely used in the Southern United States with over 12.5 million lures having been deployed. The use of the three pest control strategies has reduced the damage caused by boll weevils in cotton. **Key references:** 1) G H McKibben, D D Hardee, T B Davich, R C Gueldner and P A Hedin. 1971. Slow-release formulations of Grandlure, the synthetic pheromone of the boll weevil, *J. Econ. Entomol.*, **64**, 317. 2) D D Hardee, G H McKibben, D R Rummel, P M Huddleston and J R Coppedge. 1972. Boll weevils in Nature respond to Grandlure, a synthetic pheromone, *J. Econ. Entomol.*, **65**, 97.

COMMERCIALISATION: **Formulation:** Sold in slow-release dispensers for use in surveys and mass-trapping programmes. Sold in combination with insecticides in lure and kill strategies. **Tradenames:** Grandlure – International Speciality Products and IPM Technologies, Sirene-BW (plus profenfos) – IPM Technologies.

APPLICATION: The slow-release dispensers are distributed throughout the crop to attract the adults to the traps.

PRODUCT SPECIFICATIONS: The usual ratio of components is 70:30; alcohols:aldehydes. **Purity:** The chemicals are >95% pure.

COMPATIBILITY: Compatible with crop protection agents that do not repel the boll weevil.

MAMMALIAN TOXICITY: There is no evidence of allergic or other adverse toxicological effects from grandlure by researchers, manufacturers, formulators or field workers. Considered to be non-toxic.

ENVIRONMENTAL IMPACT AND NON-TARGET TOXICITY: Grandlure is a synthetic pheromone that is specific for the boll weevil (Anthonomus grandis). As such it is not expected to have any adverse effects on non-target organisms or on the environment.

2:51   (Z)-11-hexadecenal
Artichoke plume moth sex pheromone

(Z)-11-hexadecenal

NOMENCLATURE: **Approved name:** (Z)-11-hexadecenal. **Other names:** artichoke plume moth sex pheromone. **CAS RN:** [53939-28-9].

SOURCE: Isolated from the ovipositors of virgin females of the artichoke plume moth (Platyptilia carduidactyla (Riley)).

PRODUCTION: Manufactured for use in crop protection.

TARGET PESTS: Artichoke plume moth (Platyptilia carduidactyla).

TARGET CROPS: Vegetables.

BIOLOGICAL ACTIVITY: **Mode of action:** The product is the sex pheromone of the artichoke plume moth. Male moths locate and subsequently mate with female moths by following the trail or pheromone plume emitted by the virgin females. The application of the product indiscriminately interferes with this process as a constant exposure to inundative levels of pheromone makes trail following impossible (habituation/adaptation). Alternatively, the use of discrete sources of pheromone released over time presents the male with a false trail to follow (confusion). Control is subsequently achieved through the prevention of mating and the laying of fertile eggs. **Efficacy:** Very low rates are required to cause mating disruption. (Z)-11-Hexadecenal is volatile and distributes throughout the crop easily. Acts as an attractant and by disruption of mating in the disorientation mode. **Key reference:** J A Klun, K F Haynes, B A Bierl-Leonhardt, M C Birch and J R Plimmer. 1981. Sex pheromone of the female artichoke plume moth, Platyptilia carduidactyla, Environ. Entomol., **10**, 763.

COMMERCIALISATION: **Formulation:** Sold as the pheromone contained in slow-release sprayable plastic tubes. **Tradenames:** Disrupt APM – Hercon, Isomate APM – Shin-Etsu.

APPLICATION: The slow-release carriers are sprayed onto the crop to be protected at the time of adult flight.

PRODUCT SPECIFICATIONS: **Purity:** (Z)-11-Hexadecenal is >95% chemically pure.

COMPATIBILITY: It is not usual to apply the pheromone with other crop protection chemicals.

MAMMALIAN TOXICITY: There have been no reports of allergic or other adverse toxicological effects from the use of (Z)-11-hexadecenal by researchers, manufacturers, formulators or field workers. It is considered to be non-toxic.
Acute oral LD$_{50}$: rats >5,000 mg/kg. **Inhalation:** LC$_{50}$: rats >5 mg/litre.

ENVIRONMENTAL IMPACT AND NON-TARGET TOXICITY: (Z)-11-Hexadecenal is the sex pheromone of the artichoke plume moth and is specific for that species. It is considered unlikely to have any adverse effects on non-target organisms or on the environment.

2:52 (Z)-11-hexadecenal plus (Z)-9-hexadecenal plus (Z)-13-octadecenal

Rice stem borer sex pheromone

(Z)-11-hexadecenal	(Z)-9-hexadecenal	(Z)-13-octadecenal

NOMENCLATURE: **Approved name:** (Z)-11-hexadecenal; with (Z)-9-hexadecenal; with (Z)-13-octadecenal. **Other names:** rice stem borer sex pheromone. **CAS RN:** *[53939-28-9]* (Z)-11-hexadecenal.

SOURCE: The sex pheromone of the rice stem borer (*Chilo suppressalis* (Walker)) is a combination of three components. Originally isolated from the terminal segments of virgin females.

PRODUCTION: Manufactured for use in crop protection.

TARGET PESTS: Rice stem borer (*Chilo suppressalis*).

TARGET CROPS: Rice.

BIOLOGICAL ACTIVITY: **Mode of action:** (Z)-11-Hexadecenal plus (Z)-9-hexadecenal plus (Z)-13-octadecenal is the sex pheromone of the rice stem borer. Male moths locate and subsequently mate with female moths by following the trail or pheromone plume emitted by the virgin females. The application of (Z)-11-hexadecenal plus (Z)-9-hexadecenal plus (Z)-13-octadecenal makes trail following impossible (camouflage, competition between artificial and female plume, false trail following). Control is subsequently achieved through the prevention of mating and the laying of fertile eggs. **Efficacy:** Very low rates are required to cause mating disruption. The pheromone is volatile and distributes throughout the crop easily. **Key reference:** O Mochida, G S Arida, S Tatsuki and J Fukami. 1984. A field test on a third component of the female sex pheromone of the rice striped stem borer, *Chilo suppressalis*, in the Philippines, *Entomol. Exp. Appl.*, **36**, 295.

COMMERCIALISATION: **Formulation:** Sold as a mixture of the volatiles in slow-release devices such as plastic tubes or plastic laminated film. Hercon has developed a sprayable formulation. **Tradenames:** Isomate RSB – Shin-Etsu, Rice Stem Borer Monitoring Dispensers – SEDQ, Rice Stem Borer Mating Disruption Dispensers – SEDQ, Selibate CS – Thermo Trilogy, Disrupt RSB – Hercon.

APPLICATION: The devices are distributed throughout the crop at the time of moth flight.

PRODUCT SPECIFICATIONS: The pheromones are present in the ratio 250:25:30; (Z)-11-hexadecenal:(Z)-9-hexadecenal:(Z)-13-octadecenal. **Purity:** All components present in the slow-release devices are >95% chemically pure.

COMPATIBILITY: The pheromones are compatible with all crop protection agents that do not repel rice stem borers.

MAMMALIAN TOXICITY: There are no reports of the product causing allergic or other adverse toxicological effects on researchers, manufacturers, formulators or field workers. Considered to be non-toxic. **Acute oral LD$_{50}$:** rats >5,000 mg/kg (all components). **Inhalation:** LC$_{50}$: rats >5 mg/litre ((Z)-11-hexadecenal).

ENVIRONMENTAL IMPACT AND NON-TARGET TOXICITY: The product is the sex pheromone of the rice stem borer (*Chilo suppressalis*) and is specific for that species. It is not expected that it will have any adverse effects on non-target organisms or on the environment.

2:53 (Z)-11-hexadecenal plus (Z)-9-tetradecenal

Tobacco budworm sex pheromone

$$CH_3(CH_2)_3 \quad (CH_2)_7CHO$$

(Z)-9-tetradecenal

$$CH_3(CH_2)_3 \quad (CH_2)_9CHO$$

(Z)-11-hexadecenal

NOMENCLATURE: **Approved name:** (Z)-11-hexadecenal; plus (Z)-9-tetradecenal.
Other names: tobacco budworm sex pheromone; *Heliothis virescens* sex pheromone.
CAS RN: *[53939-28-9]* (Z)-11-hexadecenal.

SOURCE: Both components were first isolated from the terminal segments of virgin female *Heliothis virescens* (Fabricius) moths.

PRODUCTION: The pheromone is manufactured for use in crop protection.

TARGET PESTS: Tobacco budworm (*Heliothis virescens*).

TARGET CROPS: Cotton, maize, tobacco and tomatoes.

BIOLOGICAL ACTIVITY: **Mode of action:** The male moth locates a virgin female by following her pheromone trail. If this plume of volatiles is masked with the release of additional and random pheromones the trail is confused and the male will be unable to locate a mate or it will follow a false trail, again failing to find and mate with a female. **Efficacy:** It has been shown that the use of the sex pheromone of the tobacco budworm has been effective in maintaining the insect population at economically tolerable levels.
Key reference: J H Tumlinson, D E Hendricks, E R Mitchell, R E Doolittle and M M Brennan. 1975. Isolation, identification and synthesis of the sex pheromone of the tobacco budworm. *J. Chem. Ecol.*, **2**, 1535.

COMMERCIALISATION: **Formulation:** Sold as a combination of the two components in slow-release devices such as plastic tubes, laminated plastic or plastic film.
Tradenames: Isomate TBW – Shin-Etsu.

APPLICATION: Applied throughout the field to be treated by placing the dispensers within the crop canopy.

PRODUCT SPECIFICATIONS: Products contain the two components in the ratio 16:1; (Z)-11-hexadecenal:(Z)-9-tetradecenal. **Purity:** The components of the product are >95% chemically pure.

COMPATIBILITY: The pheromone can be used with other crop protection agents that do not repel the moths.

MAMMALIAN TOXICITY: There are no reported cases of allergic or other adverse toxicological effects from the product by researchers, manufacturers, formulators or field workers. It is considered to be non-toxic. **Acute oral LD$_{50}$:** rats >5,000 mg/kg (both components). **Inhalation:** LC$_{50}$: rats >5 mg/litre (both components).

ENVIRONMENTAL IMPACT AND NON-TARGET TOXICITY: The pheromone occurs in Nature and is specific for *Heliothis virescens*. As such it is not expected to have any adverse effects on non-target organisms or on the environment.

2:54 (Z)-11-hexadecenal plus (Z)-11-hexadecenyl acetate

Diamondback moth pheromone

$$R = \text{-CHO, -CH}_2\text{OCOCH}_3$$

NOMENCLATURE: **Approved name:** (Z)-11-hexadecenal; with (Z)-11-hexadecenyl acetate. **Other names:** diamondback moth sex pheromone; *Plutella xylostella* sex pheromone. **CAS RN:** *[53939–28–9]* (Z)-11-hexadecenal; *[34010–21–4]* (Z)-11-hexadecenyl acetate.

SOURCE: Female *Plutella xylostella* (Linnaeus) emit several volatile components shown to be attractive to males. These components were originally extracted from the whole bodies of virgin females.

TARGET PESTS: Diamondback moth (*Plutella xylostella*).

TARGET CROPS: Vegetables such as cabbage and other cruciferous crops.

BIOLOGICAL ACTIVITY: **Mode of action:** Males locate females by following a plume of air rich in the odour of a complete pheromone blend emitted by females. Permeation of the canopy of a vegetable crop with vapours of the two-component blend above is used to disrupt location of females by males and decreases mating. **Efficacy:** Several commercial formulations of the two-component blend above have been shown to be effective in maintaining populations of diamondback moths at economically tolerable levels in vegetables until harvest. **Key references:** 1) Y S Chow, Y M Lin and C L Hsu. 1977. Sex pheromone of the diamondback moth (Lepidoptera: Plutellidae), *Bull. Inst. Zool. Acad. Sinica*, **16**, 99. 2) K Kawasaki. 1984. Effects of ratio and amount of the two sex pheromone components of the diamondback moth on male behavioral response, *Appl. Entomol. Zool.*, **19**, 436.

COMMERCIALISATION: **Formulation:** Sold as slow-release formulations within slow-release devices such as laminated plastic, plastic barrier film and plastic tubes. The pheromone is produced by Hercon, Shin-Etsu, Konaga-con, Consep and Scentry Biologicals (acquired from Ecogen). **Tradenames:** NoMate DBM – Scentry Biologicals, Isomate DBM – Shin-Etsu.

APPLICATION: Pheromone dispensers are attached to sticks about 20 cm above ground. Numbers of lures recommended to be used per hectare vary with release rates.

PRODUCT SPECIFICATIONS: The commercial pheromone formulation contains the two components in the ratio 50:50. **Purity:** The pheromones used in mating disruption devices are >95% chemically pure.

COMPATIBILITY: Pheromone disruption of mating does not require insecticide but can be used with application of insecticides.

MAMMALIAN TOXICITY: Diamondback moth pheromone blend has shown no adverse toxicological effects on manufacturers, formulators or field workers. Considered to be non-toxic. **Acute oral LD$_{50}$:** rats >5,000 mg/kg ((Z)-11-hexadecenal). **Inhalation:** LC$_{50}$: rats >5 mg/litre ((Z)-11-hexadecenal).

ENVIRONMENTAL IMPACT AND NON-TARGET TOXICITY: Diamondback moth pheromone blend is a natural insect pheromone that is specific for the diamondback moth. There is no evidence that it has caused an adverse effect on non-target organisms nor had an adverse environmental impact.

2:55 (Z)-13-hexadecen-11-yn-1-ol acetate plus dodecan-1-ol acetate

Pine processionary moth sex pheromone

CH$_3$(CH$_2$)$_{11}$OCOCH$_3$

(Z)-13-hexadecen-11-yn-1-ol acetate   dodecan-1-ol acetate

NOMENCLATURE: **Approved name:** (Z)-13-hexadecen-11-yn-1-ol acetate; with dodecan-1-ol acetate. **Other names:** pine processionary moth sex pheromone.

SOURCE: Isolated from the abdomens of virgin female pine processionary moths (*Thaumetopoea pityocampa* (Denis and Schiffermüller)).

PRODUCTION: Manufactured for use in forestry management.

TARGET PESTS: Pine processionary moths (*Thaumetopoea pityocampa*).

TARGET CROPS: Pine forests.

BIOLOGICAL ACTIVITY: **Mode of action:** The presence of high levels of the processionary moth is monitored by the use of traps baited with the sex pheromone. These traps emit a a plume of the volatile components attracting males in search of virgin females for mating. The numbers of male moths captured is an indication of the size of the moth population and indicates when control measures should be taken. In addition, the pheromone can be used as a mass trapping system within the forest thereby lowering the population of adults and the numbers of viable eggs laid. **Efficacy:** The attractants are very effective at capturing males. **Key reference:** J Einhorn, P Menassieu, D Michelot and J Riom. 1983. Piégeage sexuel de la processionaire du pin, *Thaumetopoea pityocampa* Schiff. par des attractifs de synthèse. Premiers Essais dans le Sud-Ouest de la France, *Agronomie*, **3**, 499.

COMMERCIALISATION: **Formulation:** Sold as slow-release lures in which the male moths are trapped and as monitoring dispensers. **Tradenames:** Pityolure Monitoring Dispenser – SEDQ, Pityolure Mass Trapping Dispenser – SEDQ.

APPLICATION: The traps are placed within the pine plantation at chest height. A rate of one dispenser per hectare is recommended.

PRODUCT SPECIFICATIONS: The lures contain the pheromones in the ratio 1:1. **Purity:** The components are >95% chemically pure.

MAMMALIAN TOXICITY: There is no record of allergic or other adverse toxicological effects from researchers, manufacturers, formulators or field workers from the processionary moth sex pheromone. It is considered to be non-toxic. **Acute oral LD$_{50}$:** rats >5,000 mg/kg. **Acute dermal LD$_{50}$:** rats >2,000 mg/kg.

ENVIRONMENTAL IMPACT AND NON-TARGET TOXICITY: The product is the sex pheromone of the pine processionary moth and it is specific for that species. It is not expected that it will have any adverse effects on non-target organisms or on the environment.

2:56 4-(4-hydroxyphenyl)-2-butanone acetate

Melon fly pheromone

CH₃COO — [benzene ring] — (CH₂)₂COCH₃

CH_3COO — [benzene ring] — $(CH_2)_2COCH_3$

NOMENCLATURE: **Approved name:** 4-(4-hydroxyphenyl)-2-butanone acetate. **Other names:** cuelure; melon fly attractant. **CAS RN:** *[3572–06–3]*.

SOURCE: Synthetic component similar in action to the natural secretions of the male melon fly (*Dacus cucurbitae* Coquillet) that attracts females.

PRODUCTION: Manufactured for use in US federal and state insect control strategies.

TARGET PESTS: The melon fly (*Dacus cucurbitae*).

TARGET CROPS: Melons and other cucurbits.

BIOLOGICAL ACTIVITY: **Mode of action:** Cuelure is used in US-based federal and state control strategies to attract the adult melon fly to traps in a lure and kill programme. **Efficacy:** Lure and kill programmes have been shown to keep the populations of the melon fly at acceptable levels. **Key reference:** M Jacobson, L Keiser, E J Harris and D H Miyshita. 1976. Impurities in Cue-Lure attractive to female Tephritidae, *Agric. Food Chem.*, **24**, 782.

COMMERCIALISATION: **Formulation:** Distributed in federal and state control strategies as traps. **Tradenames:** Cuelure – Cyclo International, and International Speciality Products.

APPLICATION: Lure and kill strategies require placing the traps containing the pheromone in a slow-release formulation within the flight path of the adult female moths. It is usual to use sticky traps to capture the adults or to use rapid knockdown contact insecticides within the lures.

PRODUCT SPECIFICATIONS: **Purity:** The pheromone is >95% chemically pure.

COMPATIBILITY: The pheromone is not applied to the crop but is used in a lure containing an entrapment device or an insecticide.

MAMMALIAN TOXICITY: There are no reports of allergic or other adverse toxicological effects from researchers, manufacturers, formulators or field workers from the use of cuelure. It is considered to be non-toxic.

ENVIRONMENTAL IMPACT AND NON-TARGET TOXICITY: Cuelure is a synthetic pheromone that is specific for the melon fly (*Dacus cucurbitae*). It is not expected that it will have any adverse effects on non-target organisms or on the environment.

2:57   (Z)-13-eicosen-10-one

Peach fruit moth sex pheromone

$$CH_3(CH_2)_8CO(CH_2)_2 \quad \overset{H \quad H}{C=C} \quad (CH_2)_5CH_3$$

NOMENCLATURE: **Approved name:** (Z)-13-eicosen-10-one **Other names:** peach fruit moth sex pheromone; *Carposina niponensis* sex pheromone.

SOURCE: Female *Carposina niponensis* Walsingham emit several volatile components shown to be attractive to male moths. The major sex attractant, however, is (Z)-13-eicosen-10-one.

PRODUCTION: Manufactured for use in crop protection.

TARGET PESTS: Peach fruit moth (*Carposina niponensis*).

TARGET CROPS: Orchard tree crops such as peaches, apricots and apples.

BIOLOGICAL ACTIVITY: **Mode of action:** Males locate females by following a plume of air rich in the odour of a complete pheromone blend emitted by females. Permeation of the canopy of an orchard with vapours of the single component of the pheromone (Z)-13-eicosen-10-one is used to disrupt location of females by males and decreases mating. **Efficacy:** Several commercial formulations of this pheromone have been shown to be effective at maintaining populations of peach fruit moth at economically tolerable levels until harvest. **Key reference:** K Honma, K Kawasaki and Y Tamaki. 1978. Sex pheromone of the peach fruit moth, *Carposina niponensis* Walsingham [JPN], *Jpn. J. Appl. Entomol. Zool.*, **22**, 87.

COMMERCIALISATION: **Formulation:** Sold as a variety of slow-release formulations in different dispensing devices. Manufactured by Shin-Etsu and Shinkui-con. **Tradenames:** Isomate PFM – Shin-Etsu.

APPLICATION: Pheromone dispenser is attached to trees at heights recommended by formulators. Numbers of lures recommended to be used per hectare vary with release rates.

PRODUCT SPECIFICATIONS: Contains only (Z)-13-eicosen-10-one. **Purity:** The pheromone products are >95% chemically pure.

COMPATIBILITY: Pheromone disruption of mating does not require insecticide but can be used with application of insecticides and other crop protection agents.

MAMMALIAN TOXICITY: Peach fruit moth pheromone has shown no adverse toxicological effects on manufacturers, formulators or field workers. Considered to be non-toxic.

ENVIRONMENTAL IMPACT AND NON-TARGET TOXICITY: Peach fruit moth pheromone is a natural insect pheromone that is specific for peach fruit moth. There is no evidence that

(Z)-13-eicosen-10-one has caused an adverse effect on non-target organisms or had an adverse environmental impact.

2:58 ipsdienol plus *cis*-verbenol plus α-pinene

Six-spined ips aggregation pheromone

| ipsdienol | *cis*-verbenol | α-pinene |

NOMENCLATURE: **Approved name:** ipsdienol ((+)-2-methyl-6-methylene-2,7-octadien-4-ol); with *cis*-verbenol (2,6,6-trimethylbicyclo[3.1.1]hept-2-en-4-ol); with α-pinene **Other names:** six-spined ips aggregation pheromone.

SOURCE: The components of the aggregation pheromone were isolated from six-spined ips (*Ips sexdentatus* (Borner), beetles. Isolated from dissected hindguts of tree-reared beetles.

PRODUCTION: Manufactured for use in forest control strategies.

TARGET PESTS: The six-spined Ips (*Ips sexdentatus*).

TARGET CROPS: Coniferous forests.

BIOLOGICAL ACTIVITY: **Mode of action:** *Ips sexdentatus* locates new trees by following the trail of the species-specific aggregation pheromone often with some host tree volatiles present as well. These aggregation pheromones lead the adult beetles to new food sources and to other adults so that mating can take place. If these pheromones are attached to specific trees within a forest, then beetles are attracted to these baited trees and the invasion of the majority of the forest is prevented. The baited trees and those surrounding the baited trees are felled before the brood emerges thereby reducing the beetle population and protecting most of the trees. **Efficacy:** It has been shown that the baiting of trees significantly reduces the invasion of the other forest trees. **Key reference:** C Chararas. 1980. Attraction primaire et secondaire chez trois espèces de scolytidae (*Ips*) et mécanisme de colonisation, *C. R. Acad. Sci. (Paris)*, **290**, 375.

COMMERCIALISATION: **Formulation:** Sold as slow-release dispensers containing the pheromone. **Tradenames:** Stenopax – Cyanamid.

APPLICATION: The dispensers are attached to bait trees within the forest at chest height. It is usual to bait four trees per hectare. These baited trees and surrounding trees are felled before the brood emerges.

PRODUCT SPECIFICATIONS: **Purity:** The biologically active compounds in the product are >95% chemically pure.

COMPATIBILITY: It is unusual to use the pheromone with other crop protection agents.

MAMMALIAN TOXICITY: There are no reports of allergic or other adverse toxicological effects from the products by researchers, manufacturers, formulators or field workers. Considered to be non-toxic.

ENVIRONMENTAL IMPACT AND NON-TARGET TOXICITY: *Ips sexdentatus* aggregation pheromone is a naturally occurring mixture of volatile components that have a specific effect on *Ips sexdentatus*. It is not expected that the use of the product will have any adverse effects on non-target organisms or on the environment.

ipsdienol plus ipsenol plus (Z)-verbenol plus (E)-verbenol

Spruce bark beetle aggregation pheromone

ipsdienol

ipsenol

verbenol

NOMENCLATURE: **Approved name:** ipsdienol ((+)-2-methyl-6-methylene-2,7-octadien-4-ol); with ipsenol ((−)-2-methyl-6-methylene-7-octen-4-ol); with (Z)-verbenol ((Z)-(+)-2,6,6-trimethylbicyclo [3.1.1]hept-2-en-4-ol); with (E)-verbenol ((E)-(+)-2,6,6-trimethylbicyclo [3.1.1]hept-2-en-4-ol). **Other names:** spruce bark beetle aggregation pheromone.

SOURCE: All four compounds have been isolated from the hindgut of male *Ips typographus* (Linnaeus) beetles and are important aggregation pheromones.

PRODUCTION: Manufactured for use in forestry management strategies.

TARGET PESTS: Spruce bark beetle (*Ips typographus*).

TARGET CROPS: Spruce trees.

BIOLOGICAL ACTIVITY: **Mode of action:** The spruce bark beetle aggregation pheromone is vital for the insects to locate a suitable food source. The male and female adults follow a trail of the pheromone to locate suitable host trees. The release of the volatiles from a lure attached to baited trees concentrates the beetles in the baited trees and reduces their population in non-baited areas by establishing conditions for mass attack of the baited trees. **Efficacy:** At a rate of four baited trees per hectare, tree baits have been very successful in reducing insect populations and subsequent tree damage in the non-baited areas. **Key reference:** A Bakke. 1976. Spruce bark beetle, *Ips typographus*: pheromone production and field response to synthetic pheromones, *Naturwissenschaften*, **63**, 92.

COMMERCIALISATION: **Formulation:** Sold as a mixture of the volatile components in a slow-release device such as a polymer plug or a plastic bag.

APPLICATION: The baits are strapped to trees at chest height about fifty metres apart in the area where the beetles are to be concentrated. Baited trees and surrounding trees are felled and removed before the brood emerges.

PRODUCT SPECIFICATIONS: **Purity:** All components of the lures are >95% chemically pure.

MAMMALIAN TOXICITY: There have been no reports of allergic or other adverse toxicological effects from the volatiles in researchers, manufacturers, formulators or field workers. The product is considered to be non-toxic.

ENVIRONMENTAL IMPACT AND NON-TARGET TOXICITY: All components of the spruce bark beetle aggregation pheromone occur in Nature. It is not expected that they will have any adverse effects on non-target organisms or on the environment.

2:60   lineatin

Ambrosia beetle aggregation pheromone

lineatin

NOMENCLATURE: **Approved name:** lineatin ((1R,4S,5R,7R)-(+)-3,3,7-trimethyl-2,9-dioxatricyclo[3.3.1.0^{4,7}]nonane). **Other names:** ambrosia beetle aggregation pheromone. **CAS RN:** [71899-16-6].

SOURCE: Originally extracted from the frass of the ambrosia beetle, *Trypodendron lineatum* (Olivier).

PRODUCTION: Manufactured for use in forestry management.

TARGET PESTS: The ambrosia beetle (*Trypodendron lineatum*).

TARGET CROPS: Fir and pine forests.

BIOLOGICAL ACTIVITY: **Mode of action:** Lineatin is the aggregation pheromone of this ambrosia beetle. It attracts *Trypodendron lineatum* to traps. Male and female beetles locate suitable harvested host trees by following a plume of air enriched with the odour of harvested trees and containing the pheromone. Evaporation of the aggregation pheromone and vapours from host trees from lures attached to traps, attracts beetles to traps and diverts attack from harvested timber in the vicinity. The mixture of lineatin, sulcatol, S(+)-sulcatol and α-pinene is also used to attract other species of ambrosia beetle. **Efficacy:** The use of this lure has been shown to reduce the attacks by the beetles on harvested timber in commercial forests.

Key reference: T L Shore and J A McLean. 1983. A further evaluation of the interactions between the pheromones and two host kairomones of the ambrosia beetles, *Trypodendron lineatum* and *Gnathotrichus sulcatus*, *Can. Entomol.*, **115**, 1.

COMMERCIALISATION: **Formulation:** Sold as a slow-release formulation of lineatin as polymer plugs or from individual plastic bags and vials with plastic lids.
Tradenames: Linoprax – Biosystemes, and Cyanamid.

APPLICATION: Pheromone dispensers are attached to barrier traps at chest height, 50 metres apart, along the perimeter of areas containing stacked harvested pine and fir.

PRODUCT SPECIFICATIONS: **Purity:** The lineatin in the product is >95% chemically pure.

COMPATIBILITY: It is unusual to use the product in combination with other crop protection chemicals.

MAMMALIAN TOXICITY: There are no reports of allergic or other adverse toxicological effects from lineatin by researchers, manufacturers, formulators or field workers. It is considered to be non-toxic.

ENVIRONMENTAL IMPACT AND NON-TARGET TOXICITY: Lineatin is a naturally occurring insect aggregation pheromone that is specific for ambrosia beetles. It is not expected that it will have any adverse effects on non-target organisms or the environment.

2:61   lineatin plus sulcatol plus S(+)-sulcatol plus α-pinene

Ambrosia beetle aggregation pheromone and host kairomones

lineatin

sulcatol

α-pinene

NOMENCLATURE: **Approved name:** lineatin ((1R,4S,5R,7R)-(+)-3,3,7-trimethyl-2,9-dioxatricyclo[3.3.1.0^{4.7}]nonane); with sulcatol ((±)-5-methylheptan-2-ol); with S(+)-sulcatol (S(+)-5-methylheptan-2-ol); with α-pinene. **Other names:** ambrosia beetle aggregation pheromone and host kairomones. **CAS RN:** *[71899–16–6]* lineatin; *[1569–60–4]* sulcatol; *[80–56–8]* α-pinene.

SOURCE: Male *Trypodendron lineatum* (Olivier), *Gnathotrichus sulcatus* (LeConte) and *G. retusus* (LeConte) volatile components have been shown to attract male and female adult beetles.

PRODUCTION: Manufactured for use in forestry management.

TARGET PESTS: Ambrosia beetles (*Trypodendron lineatum*, *Gnathotrichus sulcatus* and *G. retusus*).

TARGET CROPS: Fir and pine forests.

BIOLOGICAL ACTIVITY: **Mode of action:** These components are the aggregation pheromones of ambrosia beetles. Lineatin, ethanol and α-pinene are used together to attract *Trypodendron lineatum* to traps. Sulcatol, ethanol and α-pinene are used to attract *Gnathotricus sulcatus* to traps and S(+)-sulcatol, ethanol and α-pinene are used to attract *G. retusus* to traps. Male and female beetles of each species locate suitable harvested host trees by following a plume of air enriched with the odour of harvested trees and containing the pheromone. Evaporation of the aggregation pheromone and vapours from host trees from lures attached to traps, attracts beetles to traps and diverts attack from harvested timber in the vicinity. **Efficacy:** The use of these lures has been shown to reduce the attacks by the beetles on harvested timber in commercial forests. **Key reference:** J H Borden, L Chong, K N Slessor, A C Oehlschlager, H D Pierce Jr. and S Lindgren. 1981. Allelochemical activity of aggregation pheromones between three sympatric species of ambrosia beetles, *Can. Entomol.*, **113**, 557.

COMMERCIALISATION: **Formulation:** Sold as a slow-release formulation of lineatin, sulcatol, S(+)-sulcatol, ethanol and α-pinene as polymer plugs or from individual plastic bags and vials with plastic lids. **Tradenames:** Ambrosia Beetle Trap Lures – PheroTech, Ambrosia Beetle Trap Lures – ChemTica, T. lineatum Lure – Boehringer.

APPLICATION: Pheromone dispensers are attached to barrier traps at chest height, 50 metres apart, along the perimeter of areas containing stacked harvested pine and fir.

PRODUCT SPECIFICATIONS: **Purity:** The insect pheromone components are >95% chemically pure.

COMPATIBILITY: Pheromone baited trap trees do not require insecticide to kill the beetles as they arrive. The same traps cannot be used to attract both *Gnathotrichus sulcatus* and *G. retusus* because of pheromone inhibition. Different traps must be baited with either sulcatol or S(+)-sulcatol.

MAMMALIAN TOXICITY: Ambrosia beetle lures have shown no allergic or other adverse toxicological effects on manufacturers, formulators or field workers.

ENVIRONMENTAL IMPACT AND NON-TARGET TOXICITY: Ambrosia beetle lures contain natural insect pheromones and host volatile components. There is no evidence that their use has had any adverse effects on non-target organisms or on the environment.

2:62   (multistriatin (–)-4-methyl-3-hepten-1-ol plus 2,4-dimethyl-5-ethyl-6,8-dioxabicyclo[3.2.1]octane)

European elm bark beetle pheromone

NOMENCLATURE: **Approved name:** multistriatin ((–)-4-methyl-3-hepten-1-ol plus 2,4-dimethyl-5-ethyl-6,8-dioxabicyclo[3.2.1]octane). **Other names:** European elm bark beetle pheromone.

SOURCE: The two components were identified from the volatiles emanating from virgin females in elm bark.

PRODUCTION: Manufactured for use in tree protection strategies.

TARGET PESTS: Smaller European elm bark beetle (*Scolytus multistriatus* (Marsham)).

TARGET CROPS: Elm trees.

BIOLOGICAL ACTIVITY: **Mode of action:** Male beetles are attracted to the virgin females by following a plume of sex pheromones. The two pheromones are mediated by the presence of volatiles from the host elm and allow males to locate and mate with females. The combination product is used to attract and trap male beetles, reduce their numbers and thereby lower the numbers of fecund female beetles. Also used for insect monitoring. **Efficacy:** The use of the product in urban settings in the United States and Canada has been very successful in lowering the incidence of bark beetle attack to tolerable levels. **Key reference:** G T Pearce, W E Gore, R M Silverstein, J W Peacock, R A Cuthbert, G N Lanier and J B Simeone. 1975. Chemical attractants for the smaller European elm bark beetle, *Scolytus multistriatus*, *J. Chem. Ecol.*, **1**, 115.

COMMERCIALISATION: **Formulation:** Sold as the attractant in male beetle traps. The beetles are trapped on sticky surfaces or killed through contact with an insecticide.

APPLICATION: The traps are placed in urban areas in the vicinity of the host elm trees and males are attracted to them.

PRODUCT SPECIFICATIONS: The pheromones are present in the ratio 1:1. **Purity:** The pheromones used in traps are >95% chemically pure.

COMPATIBILITY: As the compounds are used in pheromone traps, they are not applied with other chemicals.

MAMMALIAN TOXICITY: There is no evidence of any allergic or other adverse toxicological effect in research workers, manufacturers, formulators or field staff from their use. Considered to be non-toxic.

ENVIRONMENTAL IMPACT AND NON-TARGET TOXICITY: The smaller European elm bark beetle pheromones are naturally occuring and are specific for their target insect. Consequently it is unlikely that they will have any adverse effect on non-target organisms or the environment. In addition, the pheromones are retained within the traps and are not applied to the crop.

2:63 (Z,Z)-3,13-octadecadienyl acetate

Apple clearwing moth sex pheromone

$$CH_3(CH_2)_3 \overset{H}{\underset{}{}} = \overset{H \quad H}{\underset{(CH_2)_8}{}} = \overset{(CH_2)_2OCOCH_3}{\underset{H}{}}$$

NOMENCLATURE: **Approved name:** (Z,Z)-3,13-octadecadienyl acetate.
Other names: apple clearwing moth sex pheromone; (3Z,13Z)-18Ac.

SOURCE: The sex pheromone of the apple clearwing moth (*Synanthedon myopaeformis* (Borkhausen)). Isolated from the abdomens of virgin female moths.

PRODUCTION: Manufactured for use in crop protection.

TARGET PESTS: Apple clearwing moth (*Synanthedon myopaeformis*).

TARGET CROPS: Apple orchards.

BIOLOGICAL ACTIVITY: **Mode of action:** (Z,Z)-3,13-Octadecadienyl acetate is the sex pheromone of the apple clearwing moth. Male moths locate and subsequently mate with female moths by following the pheromone trail or plume emitted by the virgin females. The application of (Z,Z)-3,13-octadecadienyl acetate makes trail following impossible (camouflage, competition between artificial and the natural female plume, false trail following). Control is achieved by the prevention of mating and the laying of fertile eggs. **Efficacy:** Very low rates are required to cause mating disruption. The pheromone is volatile and disperses through the orchard very easily. **Key reference:** S Voerman, A K Minks, G Vanwetswinkel and J H Tumlinson. 1978. Attractivity of the 3,13-octadecadiene-1-ol acetates to the male clearwing moth *Synanthedon myopaeformis* (Borkhausen) (Lepidoptera: Sesiidae), *Entomol. Exp. Appl.*, **23**, 301.

COMMERCIALISATION: **Formulation:** Sold as a slow-release formulation of polyethylene ampoules. **Tradenames:** RAK 7 – BASF.

APPLICATION: The slow-release dispensers are attached to individual trees within the orchard at a rate of 500 per hectare.

PRODUCT SPECIFICATIONS: RAK 7 contains only (Z,Z)-3,13-octadecadienyl acetate. **Purity:** The pheromone is >95% chemically pure.

COMPATIBILITY: (Z,Z)-3,13-Octadecadienyl acetate is used alone without the need for chemical insecticides.

MAMMALIAN TOXICITY: (Z,Z)-3,13-Octadecadienyl acetate has shown no allergic or other adverse toxicological effects on manufacturers, formulators, research workers or farmers. **Acute oral LD$_{50}$:** rats >5,000 mg/kg.

ENVIRONMENTAL IMPACT AND NON-TARGET TOXICITY: (Z,Z)-3,13-Octadecadienyl acetate is a naturally occurring insect pheromone that is specific for the apple clearwing moth. There is no evidence that it has caused any adverse effects on any non-target organism or on the environment.

2:64 (E,Z)-3,13-octadecadienyl acetate plus (Z,Z)-3,13-octadecadienyl acetate

Lesser peach tree borer sex pheromone

(E,Z)- isomer   (Z,Z)- isomer

NOMENCLATURE: **Approved name:** (E,Z)-3,13-octadecadienyl acetate; with (Z,Z)-3,13-octadecadienyl acetate. **Other names:** lesser peach tree borer sex pheromone; *Synanthedon pictipes* sex pheromone.

SOURCE: Female *Synanthedon pictipes* (Grote and Robinson) emit several volatile components shown to be attractive to males. These pheromones were extracted from the ovipositors of unmated females.

PRODUCTION: Manufactured for use in crop protection.

TARGET PESTS: Lesser peach tree borer (*Synanthedon pictipes*), peach tree borer (*Sanninoidea exitiosa* (Say.)), cherry tree borer (*Synanthedon hector* (Butler)) and currant clearwing moth (*Synanthedon tipuliformis* (Clerck)).

TARGET CROPS: Stone fruit (such as peaches and apricots) orchards.

BIOLOGICAL ACTIVITY: **Mode of action:** Males locate females by following a plume of air rich in the odour of a complete pheromone blend emitted by females. Permeation of the canopy of an orchard with vapours of the two-component blend of pheromone is used to disrupt location of females by males and decreases mating. **Efficacy:** Several commercial formulations of this two-component blend have been shown to be effective at maintaining populations of lesser peach tree borer at economically tolerable levels until harvest. This blend also disrupts mating of peach tree borer (*Sanninoidea exitiosa*), cherry tree borer

(*Synanthedon hector*) and currant clearwing moth (*Synanthedon tipuliformis*).

Key reference: J H Tumlinson, C Yonce, R E Doolittle, R R Heath, C R Gentry and E R Mitchell. 1974. Sex pheromones and reproductive isolation of the lesser peachtree borer and peachtree borer, *Science (Washington)*, **185**, 614.

COMMERCIALISATION: **Formulation:** Sold as slow-release formulation in slow-release devices. Manufactured by Scentry Biologicals, Shin-Etsu and Consep. **Tradenames:** Isomate-L – Shin-Etsu, No-Mate PTB – Scentry.

APPLICATION: Pheromone dispensers are attached to trees at heights recommended by formulators. Number of lures recommended to be used per hectare varies with release rates.

PRODUCT SPECIFICATIONS: The two pheromone components are present in products in the ratio 70:30; (*E,Z*)-3,13-octadecadienyl acetate:(*Z,Z*)-3,13-octadecadienyl acetate (30%). **Purity:** The pheromones are >95% chemically pure.

COMPATIBILITY: Pheromone disruption of mating does not require insecticide but can be used with application of insecticides.

MAMMALIAN TOXICITY: Lesser peach tree borer pheromone blend has shown no adverse toxicological effects on manufacturers, formulators or field workers. Considered to be non-toxic. **Acute oral LD$_{50}$:** rats >5,000 mg/kg.

ENVIRONMENTAL IMPACT AND NON-TARGET TOXICITY: Lesser peach tree borer pheromone blend is a natural insect pheromone that is specific for lesser peach tree borer and related moths in the genera *Synanthedon* and *Sanninoidea*. There is no evidence that it has caused an adverse effect on non-target organisms or had an adverse environmental impact.

2:65   oryctalure

Rhinoceros beetle aggregation pheromone

$$CH_3(CH_2)_3CH(CH_3)(CH_2)_2COOCH_2CH_3$$

NOMENCLATURE: **Approved name:** oryctalure (ethyl 4-methyloctanoate). **Other names:** rhinoceros beetle aggregation pheromone. **CAS RN:** *[56196–53–3]*.

SOURCE: Male *Oryctes rhinoceros* (Linnaeus) volatile component that has been shown to attract both male and female adult beetles.

PRODUCTION: Manufactured for commercial use.

TARGET PESTS: Coconut rhinoceros beetle (*Oryctes rhinoceros*).

TARGET CROPS: Young oil palm plantations.

BIOLOGICAL ACTIVITY: **Mode of action:** Oryctalure is the aggregation pheromone of the coconut rhinoceros beetle. Males and females are located by following a plume of air rich in the odour of the pheromone. Evaporation of the pheromone vapours from traps attracts both male and female rhinoceros beetles to the traps. **Efficacy:** Use of pheromone-primed traps in young oil palm plantations reduces damage caused by rhinoceros beetle attack. **Key reference:** R H Hallett, A L Perez, G Gries, R Gries, H D Pierce Jr, J Yue, A C Oehlschlager, L M Gonzalez and J H Borden. 1995. Aggregation pheromone of coconut rhinoceros beetle, *Oryctes rhinoceros* (L.) (Coleoptera: Scarabaeidae), *J. Chem. Ecol.*, **21**, 1549–70.

COMMERCIALISATION: **Formulation:** Sold as a slow-release formulation of the pheromone from plastic bags. **Tradenames:** Oryctalure – ChemTica International, Coconut Rhinoceros Beetle Attract and Kill Dispensers – SEDQ.

APPLICATION: Pheromone dispensers are attached to vanes of a vaned bucket that is elevated two metres above ground at a density of one bucket trap per two hectares.

PRODUCT SPECIFICATIONS: **Purity:** The lures contain 95% chemically pure pheromone.

COMPATIBILITY: The pheromone trap does not require insecticide applications but trapping can be used with the application of insecticides to any infested palms.

MAMMALIAN TOXICITY: Oryctalure has shown no adverse toxicological effects on manufacturers, formulators or field workers.

ENVIRONMENTAL IMPACT AND NON-TARGET TOXICITY: Oryctalure is a natural insect pheromone that is specific for the coconut rhinoceros beetle. There is no evidence that it has caused any adverse effects on any non-target organisms or had any adverse environmental impact.

2:66 rhyncolure

American palm weevil aggregation pheromone

$$(CH_3)_2CHCH_2CH(OH)CH=CHCH_3$$

NOMENCLATURE: **Approved name:** rhyncolure (6-methylhept-2-en-4-ol). **Other names:** American palm weevil aggregation pheromone.

SOURCE: Rhyncolure is the male *Rhynchophorus palmarum* (Linnaeus) volatile component that has been shown to attract both male and female adult weevils.

PRODUCTION: Manufactured for use in crop protection.

TARGET PESTS: American palm weevil (*Rhynchophorus palmarum*).

TARGET CROPS: Mature oil palm plantations in which red ring disease is a problem.

BIOLOGICAL ACTIVITY: **Mode of action:** Rhyncolure is the aggregation pheromone of the American palm weevil. Adults locate males and females by following a plume of air rich in the pheromone. Evaporation of the pheromone from traps containing palm or sugarcane stalks, attracts male and female weevils to the traps. **Efficacy:** The use of rhyncolure in traps in mature oil palm plantations reduces the weevil population and also lowers the incidence of the associated red ring disease by 80% in a single year. This low level of disease is maintained as long as trapping is continued. **Key reference:** A C Oehlschlager, R S McDonald, C M Chinchilla and S N Patschke. 1995. Influence of a pheromone-based mass trapping system on the distribution of *Rhynchophorus palmarum* (L.) and the incidence of red ring disease in oil palm, *Environ. Entomol.*, **224**, 1004–12.

COMMERCIALISATION: **Formulation:** Rhyncolure is sold as a slow-release formulation from plastic bags containing liquid pheromone. **Tradenames:** Rhyncolure – ChemTica.

APPLICATION: The pheromone dispenser is attached to the inside of bucket traps that contain pieces of palm or sugarcane. These are strapped at chest height to palms in infested areas at a density of one trap per five hectares.

PRODUCT SPECIFICATIONS: **Purity:** The pheromone used in the traps is >95% chemically pure.

COMPATIBILITY: The pheromone trap does not require the additional use of insecticides but the traps can be used in combination with application of insecticides to infested palm trees.

MAMMALIAN TOXICITY: Rhyncolure has not shown any allergic or other adverse toxicological effects on manufacturers, formulators or field workers.

ENVIRONMENTAL IMPACT AND NON-TARGET TOXICITY: Rhyncolure is a natural insect pheromone that is specific for the American palm weevil. There is no evidence that it has caused any adverse effects to any non-target organism or had any adverse effect on the environment.

2:67 (Z,E)-9,12-tetradecadienyl acetate plus (Z)-9-tetradecenyl acetate

Beet armyworm sex pheromone

(Z,E)-9,12-tetradecadienyl acetate
        (Z)-9-tetradecenyl acetate

NOMENCLATURE: **Approved name:** (Z,E)-9,12-tetradecadienyl acetate; with (Z)-9-tetradecenyl acetate. **Other names:** beet armyworm sex pheromone; *Spodoptera exigua* sex pheromone. **CAS RN:** *[31654–77–0]* (Z,E)-9,12-tetradecadienyl acetate; *[16725–53–4]* (Z)-9-tetradecenyl acetate.

SOURCE: Female beet armyworm (*Spodoptera exigua* (Hübner)) emit several volatile components shown to be attractive to males. Whole body extracts of virgin females revealed the presence of many components but (Z,E)-9,12-tetradecadienyl acetate has been shown to be essential for male moth attraction.

PRODUCTION: Manufactured for use in crop protection.

TARGET PESTS: Beet armyworm (*Spodoptera exigua*).

TARGET CROPS: Vegetables such as peppers and onions.

BIOLOGICAL ACTIVITY: **Mode of action:** Males locate females by following a plume of air rich in the odour of a complete pheromone blend emitted by females. Evaporation of the pheromone blend given above from traps attracts male moths to traps. Permeation of the canopy of a crop with vapours of this two-component blend of pheromones is used to disrupt location of females by males and thereby decreases mating. **Efficacy:** Several commercial formulations of the two-component pheromone blend have been shown to be effective at maintaining populations of beet armyworm at economically tolerable levels until harvest. **Key reference:** C J Persoons, C van der Kraan, W J Nooijen, F J Ritter, S Voerman and T C Baker. 1981. Sex pheromone of the beet armyworm, *Spodoptera exigua*: isolation, identification and preliminary field evaluation, *Entomol. Exp. Appl.*, **30**, 98.

COMMERCIALISATION: **Formulation:** Sold as slow-release formulations within slow-release devices. Manufactured by Hercon, Scentry Biologicals, Shin-Etsu, Yotoh-con-S and Consep. **Tradenames:** Isomate BAW – Shin-Etsu, Hercon Disrupt BAW – Hercon, No-Mate BAW – Scentry Biologicals.

APPLICATION: Pheromone dispensers are attached to plants or sticks within canopy of crop as recommended by formulators. The number of lures recommended to be used per hectare vary with release rates.

PRODUCT SPECIFICATIONS: The product is sold with the two pheromones in the ratio 70:30; (Z,E)-9,12-tetradecadienyl acetate:(Z)-9-tetradecenyl acetate. **Purity:** The pheromones are >95% chemically pure.

COMPATIBILITY: Pheromone disruption of mating does not require insecticide but can be used with application of insecticides.

MAMMALIAN TOXICITY: Beet armyworm pheromone blend has shown no allergic or other adverse toxicological effects on manufacturers, formulators or field workers. Considered to be non-toxic.

ENVIRONMENTAL IMPACT AND NON-TARGET TOXICITY: Beet armyworm pheromone blend is a natural insect pheromone that is specific for the beet armyworm. There is no evidence that it has caused an adverse effect on non-target organisms or had an adverse environmental impact.

2:68   (Z)-7-tetradecenal

Olive moth sex pheromone

$$CH_3(CH_2)_5 \overset{H}{\diagup} = \overset{H}{\diagdown} (CH_2)_5CHO$$

NOMENCLATURE: **Approved name:** (Z)-7-tetradecenal. **Other names:** olive moth sex pheromone.

SOURCE: Originally isolated from the female glands of the olive moth (*Prays oleae* (Bernard)).

PRODUCTION: Manufactured for use in crop protection.

TARGET PESTS: Olive moth (*Prays oleae*).

TARGET CROPS: Olives.

BIOLOGICAL ACTIVITY: **Mode of action:** Males locate females by following a plume of air rich in the odour of a complete pheromone blend emitted by females. Evaporation of the pheromone blend given above from traps attracts male moths to the traps. Permeation of the canopy of an orchard with vapours of the same pheromone is used to disrupt location of females by males and decreases mating. **Efficacy:** Very low concentrations confuse male moths and thereby disrupt mating. **Key reference:** D G Campion, L J McVeigh, J Polyrakis, S Michaelakis, G N Stravarakis, P S Beevor, D R Hall and B F Nesbitt. 1979. Laboratory and field studies of the female sex pheromone of the olive moth, *Prays oleae*, *Experientia*, **35**, 1146.

COMMERCIALISATION: **Formulation:** Sold as the sex pheromone in a slow-release device.

APPLICATION: The slow-release devices are distributed throughout the olive grove and the pheromone is allowed to permeate through the grove.

PRODUCT SPECIFICATIONS: The only biologically-active volatile component in the product is (Z)-7-tetradecenal. **Purity:** (Z)-7-Tetradecenal is >95% chemically pure.

COMPATIBILITY: It is unusual to use the pheromone with other crop protection agents.

MAMMALIAN TOXICITY: There are no reports of allergic or other adverse toxicological effects from researchers, manufacturers, formulators or field workers. It is considered to be non-toxic. **Acute oral LD$_{50}$:** rats >5,000 mg/kg.

ENVIRONMENTAL IMPACT AND NON-TARGET TOXICITY: (Z)-7-Tetradecenal is the sex pheromone of the olive moth. It is not expected that it will have any adverse effects on non-target organisms or on the environment.

2:69   (E)-11-tetradecen-1-ol plus (E)-11-tetradecen-1-ol acetate

Tufted apple bud moth sex pheromone

(E)- isomer, R = -H, -COCH$_3$

NOMENCLATURE: **Approved name:** (E)-11-tetradecen-1-ol; with (E)-11-tetradecen-1-ol acetate. **Other names:** tufted apple bud moth sex pheromone.

SOURCE: Both compounds were isolated from the abdomens of the female tufted apple bud moth (*Platynota idaeusalis* (Walker)).

PRODUCTION: Manufactured for use in crop protection.

TARGET PESTS: Tufted apple bud moth (*Platynota idaeusalis*).

TARGET CROPS: Orchards, especially apple trees.

BIOLOGICAL ACTIVITY: **Mode of action:** The male moth locates the virgin females by following a plume of the sex pheromone. The use of the pheromone in orchards either confuses the males by masking the emissions from the female or causes the male to follow a false trail. In addition, the pheromone can be used as a means of trapping the males. The acetate is unattractive on its own and the (Z)- isomer of 11-tetradecen-1-ol is inhibitory to the (E)- isomer in the field. **Efficacy:** It has been shown that the use of the product in apple orchards has kept the population of moths at a level that is acceptable from flowering until harvest. **Key reference:** A S Hill, R T Cardé, A Comeau, W Bode and W L Roelofs. 1974. Sex pheromones of the tufted apple bud moth (*Platynota idaeusalis*), *Environ. Entomol.*, **3**, 249.

COMMERCIALISATION: **Formulation:** Sold as a combination product in slow-release devices such as plastic tubes, laminated plastic and plastic barrier film. **Tradenames:** NoMate TABM – Scentry.

APPLICATION: Dispensers are attached to trees throughout the orchard at a height of about three metres. The number of dispensers used depends upon the release rate of the pheromone.

PRODUCT SPECIFICATIONS: The product contains the two components in the ratio 2:1; (E)-11-tetradecen-1-ol:(E)-11-tetradecen-1-ol acetate. **Purity:** Both pheromone constituents are >95% chemically pure.

COMPATIBILITY: The product can be used with any crop protection agent that is not inhibitory to the moths.

MAMMALIAN TOXICITY: There have been no reports of allergic or other adverse toxicological effects from the product on researchers, manufacturers, formulators and field workers. It is considered to be non-toxic.

ENVIRONMENTAL IMPACT AND NON-TARGET TOXICITY: The tufted apple bud moth sex pheromone occurs in Nature and it is specific for the tufted apple bud moth. Consequently, it is not expected that the pheromone will have any adverse effects on non-target organisms or on the environment.

2:70 (Z)-11-tetradecenol acetate plus (E)-11-tetradecenol acetate

European corn borer sex pheromone

CH₃CH₂ ... H ... (CH₂)₁₀OCOCH₃

(E)- isomer

CH₃CH₂ ... (CH₂)₁₀OCOCH₃ ... H ... H

(Z)- isomer

NOMENCLATURE: **Approved name:** (Z)-11-tetradecenol acetate with (E)-11-tetradecenol acetate. **Other names:** European corn borer sex pheromone.

SOURCE: The sex pheromone of female European corn borer (*Ostrinia nubilalis* (Hübner)) moths was originally extracted from the whole, homogenised bodies of virgin females.

PRODUCTION: Manufactured for use in crop protection and insect monitoring.

TARGET PESTS: European corn borer (*Ostrinia nubilalis*).

TARGET CROPS: Maize.

BIOLOGICAL ACTIVITY: **Mode of action:** Male moths locate virgin female moths for mating by following a plume of the sex pheromone emitted by the female. If synthetic pheromones are released into the field, the higher concentration of the volatile components may confuse the males and thereby prevent them from locating the females. The European corn borer sex pheromone is more usually used, however, as a means of monitoring the flight of adults so that insecticides can be applied at the most effective timing for the control of the larvae. **Efficacy:** The monitoring of the moths is very effective allowing growers to identify the time when the population has exceeded threshold levels and spray applications are necessary. **Key reference:** J A Klun and J F Robinson. 1972. Olfactory discrimination in the European corn borer and several pheromonally analogous moths, *Ann. Entomol. Soc. Am.*, **65**, 1337.

COMMERCIALISATION: **Formulation:** Sold as slow-release lures which trap the male moths.

APPLICATION: Traps are placed around the field and the numbers of male moths captured give an indication of the intensity of the population allowing insecticide spray application to be made when, and if, necessary.

PRODUCT SPECIFICATIONS: The products contain the two components with the (Z)- isomer present in much higher concentrations than the (E)- isomer. **Purity:** Both isomers are >95% chemically pure.

COMPATIBILITY: It is unusual to use the lures in conjunction with other crop protection chemicals.

MAMMALIAN TOXICITY: There have been no reports of allergic or other adverse toxicological effects from the use, manufacture or formulation of pheromone traps containing (Z)-11-tetradecenol acetate plus (E)-11-tetradecenol acetate. The pheromones are considered to be non-toxic. **Acute oral LD$_{50}$:** rats >5,000 mg/kg.

ENVIRONMENTAL IMPACT AND NON-TARGET TOXICITY: (Z)-11-Tetradecenol acetate plus (E)-11-tetradecenol acetate is the sex pheromone of the European corn borer and is specific for that species. It is not expected that it will have any adverse effects on non-target organisms or on the environment.

2:71   (Z)-11-tetradecenyl acetate

Tortrix moth sex pheromone

$$CH_3CH_2 \diagdown \qquad \diagup (CH_2)_{10}OCOCH_3$$

$$H \qquad H$$

NOMENCLATURE: **Approved name:** (Z)-11-tetradecenyl acetate. **Other names:** tortrix moth sex pheromone; apple leaf roller sex pheromone; (Z)-11–14Ac.
CAS RN: [20711–10–8].

SOURCE: A component of the sex pheromones of tortrix moths (leaf roller) complex (*Adoxophyes orana* (Fischer von Rösslerstamm), *Pandemis heparana* (Denis and Schiffermüller) and *Archips podanus* (Scopoli)).

PRODUCTION: Manufactured for use in crop protection.

TARGET PESTS: Tortrix moth complex; leaf roller complex (*Adoxophyes orana*, *Pandemis heparana* and *Archips podanus*).

TARGET CROPS: Pome fruit (apples and pears).

BIOLOGICAL ACTIVITY: **Mode of action:** (Z)-11-Tetradecenyl acetate is a component of the sex pheromones of several tortrix moths. Male moths locate and subsequently mate with female moths by following the pheromone trail or pheromone plume emitted by the virgin females. The application of (Z)-11-tetradecenylacetate makes trail following impossible as the elevated levels of this component confuse the male moths and camouflage the female pheromone plume. Control is achieved by preventing the mating of moths and the subsequent laying of fertile eggs. **Efficacy:** Very low rates are required to cause mating disruption. (Z)-11-Tetradecenyl acetate is volatile and is easily distributed throughout the orchard. It has been shown that the (E)- isomer reduces the attraction shown by the pheromone. The presence of (Z)-9-tetradecenyl acetate (in the ratio 95:5; (Z)-11:(Z)-9) increases the activity of the pheromone to *P. heparana*, whilst the ratio of 1:3; (Z)-11:(Z)-9 was preferred by *A. orana* males. **Key reference:** M A El-Adl and P J Charmillot. 1982. Laboratory studies with the sex pheromones of the summerfruit tortrix, *Adoxophyes orana* F. v. R. and its components, *Acta Phytopathol. Acad. Sci. Hung.*, **17**, 133.

COMMERCIALISATION: **Formulation:** Sold as a slow-release formulation of polyethylene ampoules. **Tradenames:** RAK 4 – BASF, Isomate – Shin-Etsu.

APPLICATION: Dispensers are attached to individual trees within the orchard at a rate of 500 per hectare.

PRODUCT SPECIFICATIONS: The products contain only (Z)-11-tetradecenyl acetate. **Purity:** The pheromone is >95% chemically pure.

COMPATIBILITY: (Z)-11-Tetradecenyl acetate is used without the need for added chemical insecticides.

MAMMALIAN TOXICITY: (Z)-11-Tetradecenyl acetate has not shown any allergic or other adverse toxicological effects on manufacturers, formulators, research workers or farmers. **Acute oral LD$_{50}$:** rats >5,000 mg/kg.

ENVIRONMENTAL IMPACT AND NON-TARGET TOXICITY: (Z)-11-Tetradecenyl acetate is a component of natural insect pheromone systems that are specific for some Tortricid species. There is no evidence that it has had any adverse effects on non-target organisms or on the environment.

2:72　(Z)-9-tetradecenyl acetate plus (Z)-7-dodecenyl acetate

Fall armyworm sex pheromone

(Z)-9-tetradecenyl acetate

(Z)-7-dodecenyl acetate

NOMENCLATURE: **Approved name:** (Z)-9-tetradecenyl acetate; with (Z)-7-dodecenyl acetate. **Other names:** fall armyworm sex pheromone; *Spodoptera frugiperda* sex pheromone **CAS RN:** *[16725–53–4]* (Z)-9-tetradecenyl acetate; *[16974–10–0]* (Z)-7-dodecenyl acetate.

SOURCE: Several volatile components originally isolated from the terminal segments of virgin female fall armyworms (*Spodoptera frugiperda* (J. E. Smith)) have been shown to be attractive to males.

PRODUCTION: Manufactured for use in crop protection.

TARGET PESTS: Fall armyworm (*Spodoptera frugiperda*).

TARGET CROPS: Maize and cotton.

BIOLOGICAL ACTIVITY: **Mode of action:** Males locate females by following a plume of air rich in the odour of a complete pheromone blend emitted by females. Permeation of the canopy of maize or cotton with vapours of this two-component pheromone blend is used to disrupt location of females by males and decreases mating. **Efficacy:** Several commercial formulations of the two-component blend have been shown to be very effective at maintaining populations of fall armyworms at economically tolerable levels between flowering and harvest. **Key reference:** J H Tumlinson, E R Mitchell, P E A Teal, R R Heath and L J Mengelkoch. 1986. Sex pheromone of fall armyworm, *Spodoptera frugiperda* (Smith). Identification of components critical to attraction in the field, *J. Chem. Ecol.*, **12**, 1909.

COMMERCIALISATION: **Formulation:** Sold as slow-release formulations within release devices such as plastic tubes, laminated plastic or plastic barrier film. Manufactured by several companies including Hercon, Scentry (formerly Ecogen), Shin-Etsu and Consep. **Tradenames:** Isomate FAW – Shin-Etsu, No-Mate FAW – Scentry Biologicals, Hercon Disrupt FAW – Hercon.

APPLICATION: Pheromone dispensers are attached to plants at heights recommended by formulators. The number of lures recommended to be used per hectare vary with release rates.

PRODUCT SPECIFICATIONS: The product contains the pheromones in the ratio 99.4:0.6; (Z)-9-tetradecenyl acetate:(Z)-7-dodecenyl acetate. **Purity:** The pheromones in the product are >95% chemically pure.

COMPATIBILITY: Pheromone disruption of mating does not require insecticide but can be used with application of insecticides.

MAMMALIAN TOXICITY: There are no reports of fall armyworm sex pheromone causing allergic or other adverse toxicological effects to research, manufacturing or field workers. Considered to be non-toxic. **Acute oral LD$_{50}$:** rats >12,000 mg/kg (both components). **Acute dermal LD$_{50}$:** rabbits >2,000 mg/kg (both components).

ENVIRONMENTAL IMPACT AND NON-TARGET TOXICITY: Fall army worm pheromone blend is a natural insect pheromone that is specific for the fall armyworm. There is no evidence that it has caused an adverse effect on non-target organisms or had an adverse environmental impact.

2:73   11-tetradecenyl acetate
Tea tortrix sex pheromone

The Pesticide Manual - 11th edition: Entry number 696

(*E*)- isomer   (*Z*)- isomer

NOMENCLATURE: **Approved name:** 11-tetradecenyl acetate. **Other names:** tea tortrix pheromone. **CAS RN:** *[20711–10–8]* (*Z*)- isomer; *[33189–72–9]* (*E*)- isomer.

SOURCE: The product is the sex pheromone of the tea tortrix (*Homona magnanima* Diakonoff). Originally isolated from the terminal abdominal segments of virgin females.

PRODUCTION: Manufactured for use in tea plantations.

TARGET PESTS: Tea tortrix (*Homona magnanima*), smaller tea tortrix (*Adoxophyes* sp.) and leaf rollers (*Adoxophyes orana* (F. von R.) and *Platynota stultana* (Walsingham)).

TARGET CROPS: Tea.

BIOLOGICAL ACTIVITY: **Mode of action:** 11-tetradecenyl acetate is the sex pheromone of the tea tortrix. Male moths locate and subsequently mate with female moths by following the trail or pheromone plume emitted by the virgin females. The application of the product indiscriminately interferes with this process as a constant exposure to higher levels of pheromone makes trail following impossible (habituation/adaptation). Alternatively, the use of discrete sources of pheromone released over time presents the male with a false trail to follow (confusion). Control is subsequently achieved through the prevention of mating and the laying of fertile eggs. **Efficacy:** Very low rates are required to cause mating disruption. Tetradec-11-en-1-yl acetate is volatile and distributes throughout the crop easily. It acts as an attractant and by disruption of mating in the disorientation mode. **Key reference:** H Noguchi, Y Tamaki, S Arai, M Shimoda and I Ishikawa. 1981. Field evaluation of synthetic sex pheromone of the oriental tea tortrix moth, *Homona magnanima* Diakonoff [JPN], *Jpn. J. Appl. Entomol. Zool.*, **25**, 170.

COMMERCIALISATION: **Formulation:** The pheromone is sold in slow-release tubes. **Tradenames:** Hamaki-con ((*Z*)- isomer) – Shin-Etsu, Isomate-C Special ((*Z*)- isomer, mixture with codlemone) – Shin-Etsu, NoMate OLR (mainly (*E*)- isomer) – Scentry.

APPLICATION: The pheromone is sold in slow-release tubes that are distributed throughout the tea plantation. The active ingredient diffuses out of the tubes and is dispersed around the plantation.

PRODUCT SPECIFICATIONS: Composition varies according to application and may comprise either (*Z*)- or (*E*)- isomer, or both, possibly in mixture with other pheromones.

COMPATIBILITY: Can be used with any crop protection agent that does not repel the tea tortrix.

MAMMALIAN TOXICITY: The product has shown no adverse toxicological effects on research or manufacturing workers or on users.

ENVIRONMENTAL IMPACT AND NON-TARGET TOXICITY: The product is a natural insect pheromone that is specific for the tea tortrix. There is no evidence that it has caused any adverse effects on non-target organisms or had any deleterious effect on the environment.

2:74   tridec-4-en-1-yl acetate

Tomato pinworm sex pheromone

The Pesticide Manual - 11th edition: Entry number 735

$$CH_3(CH_2)_7 \quad H$$
$$H \quad (CH_2)_3OCOCH_3$$

NOMENCLATURE: **Approved name:** tridec-4-en-1-yl acetate. **Other names:** tomato pinworm pheromone, *Keiferia lycopersicella* pheromone. **CAS RN:** *[72269–48–8]* (*E*)- isomer; *[65954–19–0]* (*Z*)- isomer.

SOURCE: The sex pheromone from the tomato pinworm (*Keiferia lycopersicella*).

PRODUCTION: Manufactured for use in crop protection.

TARGET PESTS: Tomato pinworm (*Keiferia lycopersicella*).

TARGET CROPS: Tomato.

BIOLOGICAL ACTIVITY: **Mode of action:** Tridec-4-en-1-yl acetate is the sex pheromone of the tomato pinworm moth. Male moths locate and subsequently mate with female moths by following the trail or pheromone plume emitted by the virgin females. The application of the product indiscriminately interferes with this process as a constant exposure to higher levels of pheromone makes trail following impossible (habituation/adaptation). Alternatively, the use of discrete sources of pheromone released over time presents the male with a false trail to follow (confusion). Control is subsequently achieved through the prevention of mating and the laying of fertile eggs. **Efficacy:** Very low rates are required to cause mating disruption. Tridec-4-en-1-yl acetate is volatile and distributes throughout the crop easily. Acts as an attractant and by disruption of mating in the disorientation mode.

COMMERCIALISATION: **Formulation:** Sold as a microencapsulated formulation on a polymer matrix. **Tradenames:** NoMate TPW – Scentry, CheckMate TPW – Consep, Isomate TPW – Shin-Etsu, Frustrate TPW – Thermo Trilogy.

APPLICATION: Applied to the foliage of the tomato crop as adult flight commences. The pheromone diffuses out of the microencapsulated product and is dispersed throughout the field. Applied at a rate of 250 dispensers per hectare.

PRODUCT SPECIFICATIONS: Major component of the pheromone of the tomato pinworm, *Keiferia lycopersicella,* is the (*E*)- isomer; the (*Z*)- isomer is a minor component. **Purity:** The pheromone is >95% chemically pure.

COMPATIBILITY: Tridec-4-en-1-yl acetate can be used in combination with other crop protection agents that do not repel the tomato pinworm.

MAMMALIAN TOXICITY: The product has shown no adverse toxicological effects on research or manufacturing workers or on users. **Acute oral LD$_{50}$:** rats >5,000 mg/kg. **Acute dermal LD$_{50}$:** rabbits >2,000 mg/kg. **Inhalation:** LC$_{50}$ (4 hours): rats >5,000 mg/litre.

ENVIRONMENTAL IMPACT AND NON-TARGET TOXICITY: The product is a natural insect pheromone that is specific for the tomato pinworm. There is no evidence that it has caused any adverse effects on non-target organisms or had any deleterious effect on the environment.

2:75   trimedlure

Mediterranean fruit fly attractant

$$CO_2C(CH_3)_3$$

$$CH_3$$

Cl

NOMENCLATURE: **Approved name:** trimedlure (*tert*-butyl-2-methyl-4-chlorocyclohexane carboxylate). **Other names:** Mediterranean fruit fly attractant.

SOURCE: Synthetic attractant for male *Ceratitis capitata* (Wiedemann) found to be attractive by screening tests.

PRODUCTION: Manufactured for use in protection of citrus.

TARGET PESTS: Mediterranean fruit fly (*Ceratitis capitata*).

TARGET CROPS: Citrus

BIOLOGICAL ACTIVITY: **Mode of action:** Trimedlure 4-chloro-isomer is a strong attractant of male Mediterranean fruit fly. Males are attracted to traps baited with trimedlure containing this isomer where they are retained by adhesive or killed by insecticide. **Efficacy:** Monitoring helps time management decisions on insecticide application. **Key reference:** M Jacobsen, K Ohinata, D L Chambers, W A Jones and M J Fujimoto. 1973. Insect sex attractants, XIII. Isolation, identification, and synthesis of sex pheromones of the Mediterranean fruit fly, *J. Med. Chem.*, **16**, 248.

COMMERCIALISATION: **Formulation:** Slow-release formulations of attractant from polymer plug or from plastic bags containing about two milliliters of liquid trimedlure isomers. **Tradenames:** Magnet (plugs) – AgriSense, Trimedlure (liquid) – Thermo Trilogy, Trimedlure (plugs) – Farma-Tech and Thermo Trilogy, Trimedlure (bags) – ChemTica.

APPLICATION: Pheromone dispensers are attached to Jackson traps (triangular) with sticky inserts. Traps are hung in citrus trees in area to be monitored. Alternatively, two milliliters of trimedlure are applied to a dental wick which is placed in a Jackson trap (triangular). Plugs and bags emit trimedlure for about eight weeks under field conditions.

PRODUCT SPECIFICATIONS: Thirty-eight per cent of the 4-chloro- isomer is considered the minimum concentration of this active isomer in a trimedlure blend. **Purity:** Trimedlure is >95% chemically pure.

COMPATIBILITY: Trap does not require insecticide but trapping can be used with application of insecticides.

MAMMALIAN TOXICITY: Some skin irritation has been reported in California by field workers using trimedlure. Not considered to be toxic to mammals.

ENVIRONMENTAL IMPACT AND NON-TARGET TOXICITY: There is no evidence that trimedlure has caused significant adverse effects on non-target organisms or had an adverse environmental impact.

3:76 *Adoxophyes orana* granulovirus

Insecticidal baculovirus

The Pesticide Manual - 11th edition: Entry number 11

Virus: Baculoviridae: Granulovirus

NOMENCLATURE: **Approved name:** *Adoxophyes orana* granulovirus (Swiss strain).
Other names: AoGV.

SOURCE: Originally isolated from infected summer fruit tortrix larvae (*Adoxophyes orana* Fischer von Röslarstamm). Occurs relatively frequently in Nature.

PRODUCTION: *Adoxophyes orana* granulosis virus is produced commercially on larvae of the summer fruit tortrix moth.

TARGET PESTS: Used for control of summer fruit tortrix moths (*Adoxophyes orana* Fischer von Roesl.).

TARGET CROPS: Used in summer fruits.

BIOLOGICAL ACTIVITY: **Mode of action:** As with all insect baculoviruses, *Adoxophyes orana* GV must be ingested to exert an effect. Following ingestion, the virus enters the insect's haemolymph where it multiplies in the insect body leading to death. **Biology:** AoGV is more active on small larvae than later larval instars. It is ingested by the feeding larva and the protective protein matrix is dissolved in the insect's midgut (that is alkaline), releasing the virus particle still enclosed in coats. These pass through the peritrophic membrane and invade midgut cells by fusion with the microvilli. The virus particles invade the cell nuclei where they are uncoated and replicated. Initial replication produces non-occluded virus particles to hasten the invasion of the host insect, but later the virus particles are produced with protein matrices and remain infective when released from the dead insects. **Duration of development:** The length of time from ingestion to replication varies dependent upon the temperature and the development stage of the host larvae. Infection is relatively slow by comparison with chemical insecticides and insect death will follow between 6 and 12 days after ingestion in normal circumstances. **Efficacy:** AoGV acts relatively slowly as it has to be ingested before it exerts any effect on the insect host. It is important to ensure good cover of the foliage to effect good control. Monitoring of adult insect laying patterns and targeted application at newly hatched eggs gives better control than on a mixed population. **Key references:** 1) A Schmid, O Cazellos and G Benz. 1983. Mitteilungen der Schweizerischen Entomologischen Gesellschaft, **56**, 225–35. 2) R R Granados and B A Frederici (eds.). 1986. *The Biology of Baculoviruses, Vols. 1 and 2*, CRC Press, Boca Raton, Florida, USA. 3) D J Leisy and J R Fuxa. 1996. Natural and engineered viral agents for insect control. In *Crop Protection Agents from Nature: Natural Products and Analogues*, L G Copping (ed.), Royal Society of Chemistry, Cambridge, UK.

COMMERCIALISATION: **Formulation:** Sold as a suspension concentrate (= flowable concentrate) (SC) formulation. **Tradenames:** Capex 2 – Andermatt.

APPLICATION: Capex is more effective against first instar larvae and so it is recommended that adult activity is monitored and the product applied shortly after egg-laying. Ensure that the treated foliage is well covered and that the pH of the spray solution is between 6 and 8. Apply 1×10^{13} GV per hectare.

PRODUCT SPECIFICATIONS: **Purity:** The product is produced *in vivo* in *Adoxophyes orana* larvae. The product is tested to ensure that it is free from human and mammalian pathogens. Product specification is checked by bioassay on *Adoxophyes orana* larvae. **Storage conditions:** Store at temperatures below 2 °C in sealed container. **Shelf-life:** Stable for four weeks if stored at room temperature but has long term stability if stored below 2 °C.

COMPATIBILITY: Compatible with all non-copper fungicides and all pesticides which do not have a repellent effect on *Adoxophyes orana,* but not with strong oxidisers or chlorinated water. The spray solution should be maintained at a pH between 6 and 8.

MAMMALIAN TOXICITY: There is no evidence of acute or chronic toxicity, eye or skin irritation in mammals. No allergic reactions or other health problems have been observed in research or manufacturing staff or with users of the product.

ENVIRONMENTAL IMPACT AND NON-TARGET TOXICITY: *Adoxophyes orana* granulosis virus occurs in Nature. There is no evidence that it affects any organism other than summer fruit tortrix larvae. It is unstable at extreme pH and when exposed to u.v. light. It does not persist in the environment.

3:77   *Agrobacterium radiobacter*

Beneficial bacterium

Bacterium: Eubacteriales: Rhizobiacea

NOMENCLATURE: **Approved name:** *Agrobacterium radiobacter* (Beijerink and van Delden) Conn, strain K-84 and strain K1026.

SOURCE: Naturally occurring bacterium. Found widely in Nature. Strain K1026 was discovered and developed in Australia by Bio-Care Technology.

PRODUCTION: Produced by fermentation.

TARGET PESTS: Used for the control of crown gall infections caused by *Agrobacterium tumefaciens* Conn.

TARGET CROPS: Used in a variety of crops including fruit trees, nuts, vines, soft fruit and ornamentals under glass and outside.

BIOLOGICAL ACTIVITY: **Biology:** *Agrobacterium radiobacter* competes for invasion sites on damaged woody stems of a wide range of crops with the crown gall causing organism,

Agrobacterium tumefaciens, thereby preventing the pathogenic bacterium from becoming established. There is also evidence that the antagonist produces an antibacterial compound that is inhibitory to the growth of the plant pathogen. **Efficacy:** Nogall is strain K1026 and it is ineffective against crown gall disease in grapes, pome fruit and some ornamentals.
Key reference: A Kerr. 1980. Biological control of crown gall through production of agrocin 84, *Plant Dis.*, **64**, 25.

COMMERCIALISATION: **Formulation:** Sold as a water dispersible powder formulation for slurry treatment (WS) containing bacterial spores with more than 1×10^9 viable bacteria per gram. **Tradenames:** Galltrol-A – AgBioChem, Norbac 84C – IPM Laboratories, Nogall – Bio-Care Technology.

APPLICATION: Treatment involves dipping cuttings, transplants or seeds into water-based suspensions of the bacterium and planting immediately after treatment. Control is sometimes extended by soil drench treatments. A 250 gram pack suspended in twelve litres of water is sufficient to treat between 200 and 5,000 rooted cuttings or up to 10,000 seeds.

PRODUCT SPECIFICATIONS: **Purity:** Contains only living spores of the antagonist. Purity and efficacy can be determined by plating out the formulation on agar plates, incubating in the laboratory for 24 to 48 hours and counting the colonies formed.
Storage conditions: Store in a cool, dry situation out of direct sunlight. Do not freeze.
Shelf-life: If stored according to the manufacturer's recommendations the product will remain viable for a year.

COMPATIBILITY: It is unusual to mix *Agrobacterium radiobacter* with chemicals. Use non-chlorinated water to prepare suspensions. It should not be used with broad-spectrum fungicides, such as copper-based products, or bactericides or fertilisers.

MAMMALIAN TOXICITY: There has been no record of allergic or other adverse reactions from research and manufacturing staff or from users of the product.

ENVIRONMENTAL IMPACT AND NON-TARGET TOXICITY: *Agrobacterium radiobacter* occurs widely in Nature and is not expected to show any adverse effects on non-target organisms or the environment.

3:78 *Ampelomyces quisqualis*

Biological fungicide

The Pesticide Manual - 11th edition: Entry number 25

Mitosporitic fungus: formerly Deuteromycetes: Sphaeropsidales

NOMENCLATURE: **Approved name:** *Ampelomyces quisqualis* isolate number 10.
Other names: Previously known as *Cicinnobiolum cesatii* but renamed in 1959; also known as
A.q. and AQ10.

SOURCE: *Ampelomyces quisqualis* occurs widely in Nature. Isolate 10 was discovered in a
vineyard in Israel and was selected for commercialisation following the discovery of its ability
to grow and sporulate in submerged fermentation.

PRODUCTION: *Ampelomyces quisqualis* is grown commercially in semi-solid or submerged
fermentation, during which process it produces spores. The spores serve as the active
ingredient of the dispersible granule formulation.

TARGET PESTS: Selective fungal hyperparasite used to control powdery mildews. Although
different crops are attacked by a different genus or species of the powdery mildew pathogen,
Ampelomyces quisqualis may hyperparasitise all of them to a similar extent.

TARGET CROPS: Used in apples, cucurbits, grapes, ornamentals, strawberries and tomatoes.

BIOLOGICAL ACTIVITY: **Biology:** *Ampelomyces quisqualis* is a well known hyperparasite of
powdery mildews (Erysiphaceae). Following the discovery of isolate 10 in Israel in 1984, it
was licensed to and developed by Ecogen Israel Partnership, Jerusalem (a subsidiary of Ecogen
Inc.). Germinating spores of *Ampelomyces quisqualis* suppress the development of powdery
mildews through hyperparasitism. Once within the hyphae of the phytopathogen, A. *quisqualis*
propagates independently of the external environment and this leads to a cessation of the
development of the powdery mildew. Spore germination requires a humidity of at least 60%
and penetration of the powdery mildew hyphae takes 2 to 4 hours depending upon
temperature. **Efficacy:** The product works very effectively in a spray programme to control a
wide range of powdery mildews. High humidity is essential for spore germination and invasion
of powdery mildew hyphae and this can be enhanced with the addition of mineral oil
adjuvants. It is, however, recommended that the product is applied in the early morning or
late afternoon when dew is present or is expected on the crop.
Key references: 1) R A Daoust and R Hofstein. 1996. *Ampelomyces quisqualis*, a new
biofungicide to control powdery mildew in grapes, *Brighton Crop Protection Conference – Pests
& Diseases*, **1**, 33–40. 2) R Hofstein and B Fridlender. 1994. Development of production,
formulation and delivery systems, *Brighton Crop Protection Conference – Pests & Diseases*, **3**,
1273–80.

COMMERCIALISATION: **Formulation:** Sold as a water dispersible granule (WG).
Tradenames: AQ10 – Ecogen. **Patents:** US 5190754.

APPLICATION: Apply at a rate of 35 to 70 g product per hectare. Good control is achieved when disease levels are below 10%. Levels above 10% may lead to poor control. *Ampelomyces quisqualis* may give prophylactic control if applied before the powdery mildew is present in the crop, as the hyperparasite remains viable on the leaf surface for short periods. Good cover of the foliage is essential and the product should be applied when the humidity is above 60%. Addition of mineral oil and emulsifier at a rate of 0.3% v/v can be used to enhance the germination of the spores. Monitoring of the weather conditions that are conducive to the onset of powdery mildew infestations is recommended for the best results. The product has been employed as part of integrated pest management programmes and in alternation with standard chemical mildewicides. It is commonly applied by standard spray application techniques in the presence of surfactants that are compatible with the viability of the organism. Not phytotoxic or phytopathogenic.

PRODUCT SPECIFICATIONS: **Purity:** AQ10 formulation consists of 1×10^9 spores per gram. The efficacy of the formulation can be assessed using the spore germination test and/or the hyperparasitism test. The spore germination test determines the viability of the spores and involves plating out the spores on an agar plate and incubating for 48 hours during which the spores begin to germinate. The percentage germination gives an indication of spore viability of that population. The hyperparasitism test assesses performance and involves spraying cucumber plants infested with low levels of powdery mildew (*Sphaerotheca fuliginea*) and incubating the plants for ten days in the glasshouse. The hyperparasitism of the powdery mildew becomes evident and can be assessed semiquantitatively by eye. **Storage conditions:** Store in a cool dry place, preferably under refrigeration. **Shelf-life:** AQ10 has a shelf-life of ≥6 months when stored in a cool dry place and of ≥3 years if refrigerated.

COMPATIBILITY: Can be used concurrently with commercial biological insecticides such as *Bacillus thuringiensis*. However, it cannot be co-mixed with currently used fungicides such as systemic sterol biosynthesis inhibitors.

MAMMALIAN TOXICITY: AQ10 has not demonstrated evidence of toxicity, infectivity, irritation or hypersensitivity to mammals. No allergic responses or health problems have been observed by research workers, manufacturing staff or users.

ENVIRONMENTAL IMPACT AND NON-TARGET TOXICITY: *Ampelomyces quisqualis* occurs in Nature and, as such, is not expected to show any adverse effects on non-target organisms or the environment.

3:79 *Anagrapha falcifera* nucleopoly-hedrovirus
Insecticidal baculovirus

Virus: Baculoviridae: Nucleopolyhedrovirus

NOMENCLATURE: **Approved name:** *Anagrapha falcifera* nucleopolyhedrovirus.
Other names: AfNPV; AfMNPV.

SOURCE: Naturally occurring nucleopolyhedrovirus originally isolated from the alfalfa looper (*Anagrapha falcifera* (Kirby)).

PRODUCTION: Produced for commercial sale in living caterpillars cultured under controlled conditions.

TARGET PESTS: Lepidopteran larvae.

TARGET CROPS: Maize, vegetables, fruit crops and ornamentals.

BIOLOGICAL ACTIVITY: **Biology:** As with all insect baculoviruses, *Anagrapha falcifera* MNPV must be ingested to exert an effect. Following ingestion, the protective protein matrices of the polyhedral occlusion bodies (OBs) of the virus are dissolved within the midgut and the virus particles enter the insect's haemolymph. These virus particles invade nearly all cell types in the larval body where they multiply, leading to its death. Shortly after the death of the larva, the integument ruptures, releasing very large numbers of OBs. **Efficacy:** *Anagrapha falcifera* nucleopolyhedrovirus is unusual in that it is able to infect over thirty different species of Lepidoptera, thereby overcoming, to a degree, the problem of the selectivity of baculoviruses in crop protection situations. **Key references:** 1) R R Granados and B A Frederici (eds.). 1986. *The Biology of Baculoviruses, Vols. 1 and 2*, CRC Press, Boca Raton, Florida, USA. 2) D J Leisy and J R Fuxa. 1996. Natural and engineered viral agents for insect control. In *Crop Protection Agents from Nature: Natural Products and Analogues*, L G Copping (ed.), Royal Society of Chemistry, Cambridge, UK.

COMMERCIALISATION: **Formulation:** Formulated as a liquid concentrate. **Tradenames:** *Anagrapha falcifera* NPV – Thermo Trilogy.

APPLICATION: Apply in a relatively high volume to ensure good coverage of treated foliage without run off.

PRODUCT SPECIFICATIONS: **Purity:** The product contains polyhedra with no human or mammalian bacterial pathogens. Efficacy can be checked by bioassay against a susceptible caterpillar.
Storage conditions: Store in a tightly closed container in cool (<21 °C), dry and dark area. Shelf life is extended if kept frozen. Unstable at temperatures above 32 °C. **Shelf-life:** Stable for several weeks at 2 °C and several years if kept frozen.

COMPATIBILITY: Can be used with other insecticides that do not repel target species. Incompatible with strong oxidisers, acids, bases or chlorinated water.

MAMMALIAN TOXICITY: There are no reports of allergic or other adverse effects from research workers or manufacturing or field staff. Considered to be of low mammalian toxicity.

ENVIRONMENTAL IMPACT AND NON-TARGET TOXICITY: *Anagrapha falcifera* NPV occurs widely in Nature and is not expected to have any adverse effects on non-target organisms or on the environment.

3:80 *Anticarsia gemmatalis* nucleopoly-hedrovirus
Insecticidal baculovirus

Virus: Baculoviridae: Nucleopolyhedrovirus

NOMENCLATURE: **Approved name:** *Anticarsia gemmatalis* nucleopolyhedrovirus. **Other names:** AgMNPV; AgNPV.

SOURCE: Originally isolated from the velvet bean caterpillar (*Anticarsia gemmatalis* Hübner) found in a soybean crop in the USA and introduced into Brazil where *A. gemmatalis* is a significant problem. More recently, a strain of AgNPV has been identified that has good activity against the sugar cane borer (*Diatreae saccharalis* (Speyer)) and retains activity against the velvet bean caterpillar.

PRODUCTION: Produced by *in vivo* culture in *Anticarsia gemmatalis*. The newer strain is produced in *Diatreae saccaralis* an insect that is easier to culture than *A. gemmatalis*.

TARGET PESTS: *Anticarsia gemmatalis* (velvet bean caterpillar) and *Diatreae saccharalis* (sugar cane borer).

TARGET CROPS: Soybeans and sugar cane.

BIOLOGICAL ACTIVITY: **Biology:** As with all insect baculoviruses, *Anticarsia gemmatalis* MNPV must be ingested to exert an effect. Following ingestion, the protective protein matrices of the polyhedral occlusion bodies (OBs) of the virus are dissolved within the midgut and the virus particles enter the insect's haemolymph. These virus particles invade nearly all cell types in the larval body where they multiply, leading to its death. Shortly after the death of the larva, the integument ruptures, releasing very large numbers of OBs. **Key references:** 1) R R Granados and B A Frederici (eds.). 1986. *The Biology of Baculoviruses, Vols. 1 and 2*, CRC Press, Boca Raton, Florida, USA. 2) D J Leisy and J R Fuxa. 1996. Natural and engineered viral agents for insect control. In *Crop Protection Agents from Nature: Natural Products and Analogues*, L G Copping (ed.), Royal Society of Chemistry, Cambridge, UK.

COMMERCIALISATION: **Formulation:** Sold as a powder made from dried, ground infected caterpillars. **Tradenames:** Polygen – Agroggen S/A Biol Ag, Multigen – EMBRAPA.

APPLICATION: A single treatment applied to soybeans at a rate of 1×10^{10} polyhedral inclusion bodies per hectare gives control of velvet bean caterpillars for the entire season.

PRODUCT SPECIFICATIONS: **Storage conditions:** Store in a cool, dry place in a sealed container. Do not expose to direct sunlight. **Shelf-life:** Stable for over a year if stored under recommended conditions.

COMPATIBILITY: Compatible with many chemical insecticides but should not be applied with strong acids or bases or chlorinated water.

MAMMALIAN TOXICITY: There is no evidence that *Anticarsia gemmatalis* NPV has any allergic or other adverse effects on research workers, manufacturing or field staff. Considered to have low mammalian toxicity.

ENVIRONMENTAL IMPACT AND NON-TARGET TOXICITY: *Anticarsia gemmatalis* NPV occurs in Nature and is not expected to have any adverse effects on non-target organisms or on the environment.

3:81 *Autographa californica* nucleopoly-hedrovirus
Insecticidal baculovirus

Virus: Baculoviridae: Nucleopolyhedrovirus

NOMENCLATURE: **Approved name:** *Autographa californica* nucleopolyhedrovirus. **Other names:** AcNPV; AcMNPV.

SOURCE: Occurs widely in Nature; originally isolated from *Autographa californica* (Speyer).

PRODUCTION: Produced commercially by *in vivo* culture in lepidopterous larvae.

TARGET PESTS: Lepidopteran larvae.

TARGET CROPS: Maize, vegetables, fruit crops and ornamentals

BIOLOGICAL ACTIVITY: **Biology:** As with all insect baculoviruses, *Autographa californica* MNPV must be ingested to exert an effect. Following ingestion, the protective protein matrices of the polyhedral occlusion bodies (OBs) of the virus are dissolved within the midgut and the virus particles enter the insect's haemolymph. These virus particles invade nearly all cell types in the larval body where they multiply, leading to its death. Shortly after the death of the larva, the integument ruptures, releasing very large numbers of OBs. **Efficacy:** Unlike some baculoviruses, AcMNPV will infect over thirty different species of Lepidoptera. This makes it a broader spectrum product than most baculovirus-based products.
Key references: 1) R R Granados and B A Frederici (eds.). 1986. *The Biology of Baculoviruses, Vols. 1 and 2*, CRC Press, Boca Raton, Florida, USA. 2) D J Leisy and J R Fuxa. 1996. Natural and engineered viral agents for insect control, In *Crop Protection Agents from Nature: Natural Products and Analogues*, L G Copping (ed.), Royal Society of Chemistry, Cambridge, UK.

COMMERCIALISATION: **Formulation:** Formulated as a liquid concentrate.
Tradenames: VPN 80 – Agricola El Sol, Gusano – Thermo Trilogy.

APPLICATION: Good coverage of the foliage is essential to ensure the targeted caterpillars consume the virus particles.

PRODUCT SPECIFICATIONS: **Purity:** Formulated product contains the nucleopolyhedrovirus particles at 3×10^{10} PIB's per litre and no human or mammalian bacterial pathogens. **Storage conditions:** Store in a tightly closed container in cool (<21 °C), dry and dark area. Shelf-life is extended if kept frozen. Unstable at temperatures above 32 °C. **Shelf-life:** Stable for several weeks if stored at 2 °C. Great stability if stored frozen.

COMPATIBILITY: Compatible with all insecticides except those that repel the target caterpillars. Do not use with strong oxidising or reducing agents or with chlorinated water.

MAMMALIAN TOXICITY: There have been no reports of allergic or other adverse effects from research workers, manufacturing or field staff. Considered to be of low mammalian toxicity.

ENVIRONMENTAL IMPACT AND NON-TARGET TOXICITY: AcMNPV occurs widely in Nature and is not expected to have any adverse effects on non-target organisms or on the environment.

3:82 *Bacillus thuringiensis* subsp. *kurstaki*

Biological insecticide

The Pesticide Manual - 11th edition: Entry number 46

Bacterium: Schizomycetes: Eubacteriales

NOMENCLATURE: **Approved name:** *Bacillus thuringiensis* Berliner subsp. *kurstaki.*
Other names: *Btk.* **Development code:** SAN 239 I; SAN 415 I; SAN 420 I (all originally Sandoz, subsequently Novartis and now Thermo Trilogy); CGA 237218 (conjugated strain of *Btk* and *Bta,* originally Ciba, then Novartis and now Thermo Trilogy).

SOURCE: *Bacillus thuringiensis* is common in soil, mills, warehouses and other insect-rich environments. Strains that are used in crop protection are selected from those isolated in Nature on the basis of their potency in test insect species, spectrum of host insects and the ease with which they can be grown in fermenters. The insecticidal activity of *Bt* was first observed in insects associated with man, such as Japanese silkworm rearings in 1901 and flour mill moths in a German mill in 1911.

PRODUCTION: Produced by accurately controlled fermentation in deep tanks of sterilised nutrient liquid medium. The endotoxins and living spores are harvested as water dispersible liquid concentrates for subsequent formulation.

TARGET PESTS: Lepidopteran larvae, particularly the diamond back moth (*Plutella xylostella* (Linnaeus)) and other vegetable pests and forest insects. Ecogen strain EG2424 (Raven and Jackpot) is used to control Colorado potato beetle (*Leptinotarsa decemlineata* (Say)) in addition to Lepidoptera.

TARGET CROPS: Recommended for use in vegetables, fruit, maize, small grain cereals and in forests, orchards or for general tree care.

BIOLOGICAL ACTIVITY: **Mode of action:** *Bacillus thuringiensis* produces parasporal, proteinaceous, crystal inclusion bodies during sporulation. Upon ingestion, these are insecticidal to larvae of the order Lepidoptera and to both larvae and adults of a few Coleoptera. Once in the insect, the crystal proteins are solubilised and the insect gut proteases convert the original pro-toxin into a combination of up to four smaller toxins. These hydrolysed toxins bind to the insect's midgut cells at high-affinity, specific receptor binding sites where they interfere with the potassium-ion dependent, active amino acid symport mechanism. This disruption causes the formation of large cation-selective pores that increase the water permeability of the cell membrane. A large uptake of water causes cell swelling and eventual rupture, disintegrating the midgut lining. Different toxins bind to different receptors in different insect species and with varying intensities: this explains species specificities. **Biology:** The crystal inclusions derived from *Btk* are generally lepidopteran specific. Because they have to be ingested and then processed within the insect's gut, they are often slow acting (two to forty-eight hours in comparison to conventional chemicals). The toxin stops feeding and young larvae may starve to death; insects not killed by direct action of the toxin may die from bacterial infection over a longer period. Different toxins have different spectra of activity. Different strains and serotypes have been developed by different companies. For example, Novartis (products now owned by Thermo Trilogy) developed serotypes 3a, 3b and strains Int. 15–313, SA-11, SA-12 and the conjugate of *Bacillus thuringiensis* subsp. *kurstaki* and *Bt* subsp. *aizawai* GC-91; Ecogen has developed strains EG2348, EG2349, EG2371 and EG2424. In addition to producing the endotoxins, many strains of *Bt* are potent insect pathogens. (Many *Bt* genes have been isolated and used to transform crops, thereby rendering them insecticidal. These transgenic crops are included in Section 5 – Genes). **Efficacy:** Very effective when used against lepidopteran species where some damage to the crop is acceptable, such as in forestry. Light instability can cause problems if exposed to high light intensities. Rapidly hydrolysed under even mild alkaline conditions. **Key references:** 1) P Fast. 1981. The crystal toxin of *Bacillus thuringiensis*. In *Microbial Control of Pests and Plant Diseases 1970–1980*, D Burges (ed.), Academic Press, New York. 2) L F Adams, C-L Liu, S C MacIntosh and R L Starnes. 1996. Diversity and biological activity of *Bacillus thuringiensis*. In *Crop Protection Agents from Nature: Natural Products and Analogues,* L G Copping (ed.), 360–88, Royal Society of Chemistry, Cambridge, UK. 3) P F Entwistle, J S Cory, M J Bailey and S Higgs (eds.). 1993. Bacillus thuringiensis, *an Environmental Biopesticide: Theory and Practice*, Wiley, Chichester, UK, 311 pages. 4) H D Burges and K A Jones. 1989. Formulation of bacteria, viruses and protozoa to control insects, in *Formulation of Microbial Biopesticides: Beneficial Microorganisms, Nematodes and Seed Treatments*, H D Burges (ed.), 33–127, Kluwer Academic, Dordecht, the Netherlands.

COMMERCIALISATION: **Formulation:** Sold as a combination of endotoxin crystals and living bacterial spores. Formulated as a suspension concentrate (SC), a granular bait (GB), a ready to use bait (RB), a suspo-emulsion (SE), a granule (GR), an oil miscible flowable concentrate (oil miscible suspension) (OF), a dispersible powder (DP) and a wettable powder (WP). **Tradenames:** Bactospeine – Abbott, Biobit – Abbott, Foray – Abbott , DiPel – Abbott, Cordalene – Agrichem, Bactucide – Caffaro, Baturad – Cequisa, Condor [EG2348] – Ecogen, Crymax [EG7841] – Ecogen, Cutlass [EG2371] – Ecogen, Lepinox [EG7826] – Ecogen, Raven [EG2424] – Ecogen, Ecotech Bio [EG2371] – Ecogen/AgrEvo, Ecotech Pro [EG2348] – Ecogen/AgrEvo, Jackpot [EG2424] – Ecogen/Intrachem, Rapax [EG2348] – Ecogen/Intrachem, Forwarbit – Forward International, Bactosid K – Sanex, Agrobac – Tecomag, Able – Thermo Trilogy, CoStar – Thermo Trilogy, Delfin – Thermo Trilogy, Javelin – Thermo Trilogy, Thuricide – Thermo Trilogy, Vault – Thermo Trilogy, Larvo-BT – Troy Biosciences, Troy-BT – Troy Biosciences, Biobest BT – Biobest Biological Systems, Collapse – Calliope, Bactospeine Koppert – Koppert, Insectobiol – Samabiol. **Patents:** Many world-wide including US 5080897; US 5024837 (both to Ecogen).

APPLICATION: Use at rates of 100–300 g active ingredient per hectare ensuring that the crop is well covered with the spray suspension. Apply while insect larvae are small and repeat every five to seven days if infestations are high. *Bt*-based sprays can be applied up to the day of harvest.

PRODUCT SPECIFICATIONS: **Purity:** All formulations are standardised at a toxin content expressed in terms of international units active against a target pest per mg of product. Guaranteed to be free of human and mammalian pathogenic contaminants.
Storage conditions: Do not expose to direct sunlight. Keep cool but do not freeze.
Shelf-life: If stored under cool dark conditions, the products remain viable for two years or more.

COMPATIBILITY: Do not use in combination with broad spectrum biocides such as chlorothalonil. Compatible with a wide range of acaricides, insecticides, fungicides, stickers, spreaders and wetters. Do not use water with a pH above 8.0.

MAMMALIAN TOXICITY: **Oral:** No infectivity or toxicity was observed in rats at 4.7×10^{11} spores/kg. No adverse effects at doses of 1×10^8 up to 7×10^{12} colony forming units per rat. **Acute percutaneous LD$_{50}$:** rats >5,000 mg/kg; rabbits >10^9 units. Some products can cause substantial but temporary eye injury. **Skin and eye:** No infectivity or toxicity was observed in rats at 3.4×10^{11} spores/kg. **Inhalation:** No infectivity or toxicity at 5.4 mg/litre (2.6×10^7 spores/litre). **NOEL:** (2 years) rats 8.4 g/kg body weight daily; (13 weeks) rats 1.3×10^9 spores/kg body weight daily. **Other toxicological effects:** *Btk* has not shown evidence of hypersensitivity to mammals. No allergic reactions or other health problems have been shown by research workers, manufacturing staff or users. **Toxicity class:** EPA (formulation) III. Considered to be non-toxic. Tolerance exempt in the US on all raw agricultural commodities when applied to growing crops pre- or post-harvest.

ENVIRONMENTAL IMPACT AND NON-TARGET TOXICITY: **Birds:** In 63 day feeding trials, chickens receiving 5.1×10^7 spores/g diet showed no ill-effects. **Fish:** LC$_{50}$ (96 hour) water gobies (*Pomatoschistus minutus*) >400 mg/litre (as Thuricide HP). **Beneficial insects:** Non-toxic to honeybees; LD_{50} >0.1 mg/bee (Delfin WG). **Other effects:** Btk has a short persistence owing to its sensitivity to u.v. light. No adverse effects have been recorded in approved field use and none are anticipated. Btk should not be used near water-courses.

3:83   *Bacillus thuringiensis* subsp. *aizawai*
Biological insecticide

The Pesticide Manual - 11th edition: Entry number 46

Bacterium: Schizomycetes: Eubacteriales

NOMENCLATURE: **Approved name:** *Bacillus thuringiensis* Berliner subsp. *aizawai*.
Other names: *Bta*. **Development code:** SAN 401 (originally Sandoz, then Novartis and now Thermo Trilogy); CGA 237218 – conjugated strain with *Btk* (originally Ciba, then Novartis and now Thermo Trilogy).

SOURCE: *Bacillus thuringiensis* subsp. *aizawai* occurs naturally in soil and Serotype H-7, strain SA-2 has been selected for development as an insecticide.

PRODUCTION: By fermentation as for *Btk*. The endotoxins and living spores are harvested as water dispersible liquid concentrates.

TARGET PESTS: Used to control lepidopterous insects. Developed because it controls *Spodoptera* spp. and some other noctuids with only moderate susceptibility to *Btk*, because it is more active against some species recommended with *Btk* and because it controls species that have developed resistance to *Btk*.

TARGET CROPS: Recommended for use in various row crops, fruit and other trees, vegetables and cotton.

BIOLOGICAL ACTIVITY: **Mode of action:** Stomach poison; mode of action described in detail under *Btk*. **Key reference:** L F Adams, C-L Liu, S C MacIntosh and R L Starnes. 1996. Diversity and biological activity of *Bacillus thuringiensis*. In *Crop Protection Agents from Nature: Natural Products and Analogues*, L G Copping (ed.), 360–88, Royal Society of Chemistry, Cambridge, UK.

COMMERCIALISATION: **Formulation:** Sold as water dispersible liquid concentrate and wettable powder. **Tradenames:** XenTari – Abbott, Florbac – Abbott, Agree – Thermo Trilogy, Design – Thermo Trilogy.

APPLICATION: As for *Btk* and repeating every five to seven days if infestations are high.

PRODUCT SPECIFICATIONS: **Purity:** The fermentation is stopped at sporulation when, in addition to spores, crystals of protein (the delta-endotoxin) are also formed. Both are included in the product. **Storage conditions:** Store under cool, dry conditions. Do not expose to direct sunlight. **Shelf-life:** If stored as recommended by the manufacturer, the formulations will have a shelf-life of between one and three years.

COMPATIBILITY: Can be applied with a wide range of acaricides, insecticides, fungicides and spray adjuvants. Incompatible with strong oxidising agents, acids and bases.

MAMMALIAN TOXICITY: **Acute oral toxicity:** rats dosed with $>1 \times 10^8$ colony forming units per animal showed no adverse effects. **Toxicity class:** EPA (formulation) III. There has been no record of allergic or other adverse effects from researchers, manufacturers or users.

ENVIRONMENTAL IMPACT AND NON-TARGET TOXICITY: *Bacillus thuringiensis* subsp. *aizawai* is non-hazardous to birds and fish but XenTari is highly toxic to honeybees exposed directly to spray treatment. It should not be applied when honeybees are foraging in the area to be treated.

3:84 *Bacillus thuringiensis* subsp. *israelensis* *Biological insecticide*

The Pesticide Manual - 11th edition: Entry number 46

Bacterium: Schizomycetes: Eubacteriales

NOMENCLATURE: **Approved name:** *Bacillus thuringiensis* Berliner subsp. *israelensis*. **Other names:** *Bti*. **Development code:** SAN 402 I (originally Sandoz, subsequently Novartis and now Thermo Trilogy).

SOURCE: *Bacillus thuringiensis* subsp. *israelensis* occurs naturally in soil and Serotype H-14, strain SA-3 has been selected for development as an insecticide.

PRODUCTION: Produced by fermentation, as for *Btk*.

TARGET PESTS: Only Diptera: e.g. mosquito and blackfly (simuliid) larvae and fungus gnats (Gnatrol).

TARGET CROPS: Used in water bodies, sewage filters and in glasshouses.

BIOLOGICAL ACTIVITY: **Mode of action:** Insecticide with stomach action as for *Btk*. **Biology:** As for *Btk* except that the crystal inclusions derived from *Bti* are the most insoluble of any *Bt* crystals, requiring a very high pH (>11) for full solubilisation. *Bti* produces five different insecticidal proteins and all have dipteran activity although one toxin, the 27kDa cytolytic toxin, appears to synergise the others. The effects of *Bti* on larvae are as for *Btk*. Sometimes its effects are more rapid: heavily infested mosquito pools may be dramatically covered by floating, dying larvae within twenty minutes of application of *Bti* granules. Mosquito larvae cannibalise dead and dying larvae, then they, themselves, die, sometimes giving an extended period of partial control. The spores cause no significant increase in mortality and so spore-free products are marketed to minimise the weight carried during aerial application, in contrast to *Btk* in which the action of spores is significant in some host species.

Key references: 1) H de Barjac and D J Sutherland (eds.). 1990. *Bacterial Control of Mosquitoes and Blackflies: Biochemistry, Genetics Applications of* Bacillus thuringiensis israelensis *and* Bacillus sphaericus, Unwin Hyman, London. 2) P Fast. 1981. The crystal toxin of *Bacillus thuringiensis*, in *Microbial Control of Pests and Plant Diseases 1970–1980*, H D Burges (ed.), Academic Press, London. 3) L F Adams, C-L Liu, S C MacIntosh and R L Starnes. 1996. Diversity and biological activity of *Bacillus thuringiensis*. In *Crop Protection Agents from Nature: Natural Products and Analogues*, L G Copping (ed.), 360–88, Royal Society of Chemistry, Cambridge, UK. 4) P F Entwistle, J S Cory, M J Bailey and S Higgs (eds.). 1993. Bacillus thuringiensis, *an Environmental Biopesticide: Theory and Practice*, Wiley, Chichester, UK, 311 pages. 5) H D Burges and K A Jones. 1989. Formulation of bacteria, viruses and protozoa to control insects, in *Formulation of Microbial Biopesticides: Beneficial Microorganisms, Nematodes and Seed Treatments*, H D Burges (ed.), 33–127, Kluwer Academic Press, Dordecht, the Netherlands.

COMMERCIALISATION: **Formulation:** Sold as aqueous suspensions, briquettes (BR), flowable concentrates, granules (GR), wettable powders (WP) and slow release rings. **Tradenames:** Bactimos – Abbott, Gnatrol – Abbott, Skeetal – Abbott, VectoBac – Abbott, Aquabac – Becker Microbial Products, Vectocide – Sanex, Teknar – Thermo Trilogy, Acrobe – American Cyanamid, Bactis – Caffaro.

APPLICATION: Applied by air or by hand-held application equipment to expanses of water to be treated. Rates of application increase with the age of larvae to be treated and the organic content of the water. Rates between 2 and 4 kg of product per hectare are usual. Spray on to soil around germinating seedlings to control fungus gnats.

PRODUCT SPECIFICATIONS: **Purity:** *Bacillus thuringiensis* subsp. *israelensis* formulations contain delta-endotoxins with or without spores. **Storage conditions:** Store under cool, dry conditions. Do not expose to direct sunlight. **Shelf-life:** Stable for up to two years if stored under recommended conditions.

COMPATIBILITY: It is not usual to apply *Bti* with other pesticides. Incompatible with strong oxidising agents, acids and bases.

MAMMALIAN TOXICITY: **Acute oral LD$_{50}$:** rats >2.67 g/kg (1×10^{11} spores/kg); rabbits > 2×10^9 spores. **Acute percutaneous LD$_{50}$:** rats >2,000 mg/kg (4.6×10^{10} spores/kg); rabbits >6.28 g/kg. **Other toxicological effects:** Inhalation LC$_{50}$: 8×10^7 spores per rat. **NOEL:** rats (3 months) 4 g/kg body weight daily. **Toxicity class:** EPA (formulation) III (Gnatrol IV). Considered to be non-toxic. Tolerance exempt in the US on all raw agricultural commodities when applied to growing crops pre- or post-harvest.

ENVIRONMENTAL IMPACT AND NON-TARGET TOXICITY: LC$_{50}$ for water feeder guppies (*Toecilia reticulata*) >156 mg/litre (as Teknar). LC$_{50}$ (96 hours) *Daphnia pulex* >25 mg/litre (technical).

3:85 *Bacillus thuringiensis* subsp. *tenebrionis* *Biological insecticide*

The Pesticide Manual - 11th edition: Entry number 46

Bacterium: Schizomycetes: Eubacteriales

NOMENCLATURE: **Approved name:** *Bacillus thuringiensis* Berliner subsp. *tenebrionis*; Serotype 8a, 8b (Thermo Trilogy); Strains Sa-10 (Thermo Trilogy) and NovoBtt (Abbott). **Other names:** *Btt; Bacillus thuringiensis* subsp. *san diego.* **Development code:** SAN 418 I (originally Sandoz, subsequently Novartis and now Thermo Trilogy).

SOURCE: *Bacillus thuringiensis* subsp. *tenebrionis* is common in soils, particularly those rich in insects.

PRODUCTION: By fermentation, as for *Btk.*

TARGET PESTS: Used to control some Coleoptera, particularly the Colorado potato beetle (*Leptinotarsa decemlineata*).

TARGET CROPS: Solanaceous crops, mainly potatoes.

BIOLOGICAL ACTIVITY: **Mode of action:** As for *Btk.* **Biology:** As for *Btk* except that *Btt* produces a single insecticidal protein of 73 kDa that does not require activation to show its activity. The midgut environment of the target insect, *Leptinotarsa decemlineata*, is nearer to neutral pH than in Lepidoptera, being around pH 6. Ultrastructural effects on the insect midgut are similar to those of other endotoxins with a few important exceptions. No membrane lesions or microvillar damage are observed and the first cellular response (swelling and elongation) is relatively slow. Studies on the binding affinity of a susceptible coleopteran (*Leptinotarsa decemlineata*) and a tolerant one (*Diabrotica undecimpunctata howardi* – southern corn root worm) showed that susceptibility was correlated, at least in part, with increased receptor binding affinity and pore formation. Both adults and larvae are susceptible to the product. **Key reference:** L F Adams, C-L Liu, S C MacIntosh and R L Starnes. 1996. Diversity and biological activity of *Bacillus thuringiensis*. In *Crop Protection Agents from Nature: Natural Products and Analogues*, L G Copping (ed.), 360–88, Royal Society of Chemistry, Cambridge, UK.

COMMERCIALISATION: **Formulation:** Sold as a water dispersible liquid formulation. **Tradenames:** Novodor – Abbott.

APPLICATION: As for *Btk*, repeating every seven to ten days as necessary.

PRODUCT SPECIFICATIONS: **Purity:** All formulations are produced to contain a dose of the toxin that is expressed in terms of units active against a target pest per mg of product. **Storage conditions:** Store under cool, dry conditions in a sealed container. Do not expose to direct sunlight. **Shelf-life:** Stable for up to two years if stored under manufacturer's recommended conditions.

COMPATIBILITY: Can be applied with conventional agrochemicals and with spray additives. Not compatible with strong oxidising agents, acids or bases.

3. Living Systems

MAMMALIAN TOXICITY: Oral dosing of rats showed no adverse acute effects at doses of $>2 \times 10^8$ colony forming units per animal (technical) or >5 g/kg (formulation). **Toxicity class:** EPA (formulation) III. **Other toxicological effects:** Considered to be non-toxic. Tolerance exempt in the US on all raw agricultural commodities when applied to growing crops pre- or post-harvest.

ENVIRONMENTAL IMPACT AND NON-TARGET TOXICITY: Non-toxic to the environment and neither infective nor toxic to non-target organisms.

3:86 *Bacillus thuringiensis* subsp. *japonensis* strain *buibui*

Biological insecticide

Bacterium: Schizomycetes: Eubacteriales

NOMENCLATURE: **Approved name:** *Bacillus thuringiensis* Berliner subsp. *japonensis* strain *buibui*. **Other names:** Btj.

SOURCE: *Bacillus thuringiensis* subsp. *japonensis* strain *buibui* occurs naturally in soil and was originally isolated from soil in Japan.

PRODUCTION: As for *Btk*.

TARGET PESTS: Soil inhabiting beetles.

TARGET CROPS: Turf, grass, landscapes and ornamentals.

BIOLOGICAL ACTIVITY: **Mode of action:** As for *Btk*. **Biology:** As for *Btk* except that *Bacillus thuringiensis* subsp. *japonensis* strain *buibui* is specific to beetles and is very effective at controlling phytophagous soil inhabiting species. **Key reference:** P F Entwistle, J S Cory, M J Bailey and S Higgs (eds.). 1993. Bacillus thuringiensis, *an Environmental Biopesticide: Theory and Practice*, Wiley, Chichester, UK, 311 pages.

COMMERCIALISATION: **Formulation:** Sold as a powder formulation. **Tradenames:** M-Press – Mycogen.

APPLICATION: Apply to established grass when beetle damage is noticed. Repeat every seven to ten days depending upon the intensity of the attack.

PRODUCT SPECIFICATIONS: **Purity:** Guaranteed to be free of bacterial contaminants. **Storage conditions:** Store in a cool dry situation out of direct sunlight. **Shelf-life:** May be stored for twelve months.

COMPATIBILITY: Compatible with other soil active insecticides but do not apply with broad-spectrum fungicides such as copper-based compounds.

MAMMALIAN TOXICITY: *Bacillus thuringiensis* subsp. *japonensis* strain *buibui* occurs widely in Nature and there have been no reports of allergic or other adverse toxicological effects from research workers, manufacturers, formulators or field staff.

ENVIRONMENTAL IMPACT AND NON-TARGET TOXICITY: *Bacillus thuringiensis* subsp. *japonensis* strain *buibui* is not expected to have any adverse effects on non-target organisms or on the environment.

3:87   *Bacillus thuringiensis* subsp. *aizawai* encapsulated delta-endotoxins
Biological insecticide

The Pesticide Manual - 11th edition: Entry number 47

Bacterium: Schizomycetes: Eubacteriales

NOMENCLATURE: **Approved name:** *Bacillus thuringiensis* Berliner subsp. *aizawai* encapsulated delta-endotoxins.

SOURCE: *Bacillus thuringiensis* subsp. *aizawai* occurs widely in Nature, as does the bacterium *Pseudomonas fluorescens* Migula.

PRODUCTION: The gene coding for the endotoxin proteins from *Bacillus thuringiensis* subsp. *aizawai* has been used to transform the bacterium *Pseudomonas fluorescens*. The transformed bacterium expresses the gene and produces the delta-endotoxins. The cells are produced by fermentation, killed and treated with cross-linking agents to fortify the bacterial cell wall and thus give an encapsulated toxin as the product.

TARGET PESTS: Lepidopteran larvae such as *Spodoptera*, *Heliothis*, *Helicoverpa* and *Pieris* species, *Ostrinia nubialis* (Hübner) and *Plutella xylostella* (Linnaeus). This product was developed because it controls *Spodoptera* spp. and some other noctuids with only moderate susceptibility to *Btk*, because it is more active against some species recommended with *Btk* and because it controls species that have developed resistance to *Btk*.

TARGET CROPS: Soft fruit, canola, maize, soybeans, peanuts, cotton, tree fruits and nuts, tobacco, vegetables and vines.

BIOLOGICAL ACTIVITY: **Mode of action:** The mode of action is described in detail under the *Bacillus thuringiensis* subsp. *kurstaki* encapsulated delta-endotoxins entry.

COMMERCIALISATION: **Formulation:** Sold as a liquid concentrate. **Tradenames:** Maatch (*kurstaki* + *aizawai*) – Mycogen.

APPLICATION: As for *Btk*, repeating every seven to ten days depending upon the intensity of insect pressure.

3. Living Systems

PRODUCT SPECIFICATIONS: **Purity:** Contains bacterial cells cross-linked for additional strength and containing *Bta* endotoxins. Maatch (MYX 300) is a mixture of *kurstaki* Cry1A(c) and *aizawai* Cry1C toxins. **Storage conditions:** Store in a cool, dry place. Do not expose to direct sunlight. **Shelf-life:** Stable for over twelve months.

COMPATIBILITY: Compatible with most acaricides, insecticides and spray tank additives. Incompatible with strong oxidising agents, acids and bases.

MAMMALIAN TOXICITY: **Oral LD$_{50}$:** rats >5,000 mg/kg (formulation).
Acute percutaneous LD$_{50}$: rabbits >2,000 mg/kg (formulation). All animals exposed to 1×10^{11} cells by inhalation survived. **Toxicity class:** EPA (formulation) III.
Other toxicological effects: Considered to be non-toxic. Tolerance exempt in the US on all raw agricultural commodities when applied to growing crops pre- or post-harvest.

ENVIRONMENTAL IMPACT AND NON-TARGET TOXICITY: There is no evidence that the formulated product has any adverse effect on non-target organisms or on the environment.

3:88 *Bacillus thuringiensis* subsp. *kurstaki* encapsulated delta-endotoxins

Biological insecticide

The Pesticide Manual - 11th edition: Entry number 47

Bacterium: Schizomycetes: Eubacteriales

NOMENCLATURE: **Approved name:** *Bacillus thuringiensis* Berliner subsp. *kurstaki* encapsulated delta-endotoxins.

SOURCE: Produced in cells of *Pseudomonas fluorescens* Migula which has been genetically modified to produce the *Bacillus thuringiensis* serotype H-3a,3b endotoxin. For all CellCap-based products, cells are then killed in such a way that they constitute a rigid microcapsule for the enclosed insecticidal protein.

PRODUCTION: Manufactured by fermentation as for *Btk* and subsp. *aizawai* encapsulated delta-endotoxins.

TARGET PESTS: Effective against Lepidoptera and some beetles. MVP is recommended for diamond-back moth and other Lepidoptera, M/C for armyworm species (*Spodoptera* spp.), M-Trak for Colorado potato beetle and M-Peril for corn borers.

TARGET CROPS: Effective in vegetables, maize, tree fruit, vines and cotton. MVP is recommended for use in cruciferous crops, M-Trak for potatoes and M-Peril for maize. Guardjet was developed for the Japanese crucifer market.

BIOLOGICAL ACTIVITY: **Mode of action:** The mode of action is described in detail under the *Bacillus thuringiensis* subsp. *kurstaki* entry. The products contain no live cells: the infectious role of the spores in live products is partially fulfilled by gut flora derived from bacteria that live on leaves. The absence of *Bt* spores reduces potency in some species of Lepidoptera, but this is balanced by the protection given by the capsules, the net result being increased potency compared with non-encapsulated products. Encapsulation within the cell wall of *Pseudomonas fluorescens* makes formulations more robust than the standard endotoxins plus spores products produced by fermentation of the *Bacillus thuringiensis*. **Key reference:** W Gelernter. 1990. Targeting insecticide-resistant markets. In *Managing Resistance to Agrochemicals: From Fundamental Research to Practical Strategies*, M B Green, W K Moberg and H LeBaron (eds.), American Chemical Society, New York.

COMMERCIALISATION: **Formulation:** Sold as a capsule suspension (CS) (encapsulated in killed *Pseudomonas fluorescens*); and as a granule (GR). **Tradenames:** MVP (*kurstaki* – Cry 1A(c)) – Mycogen, MVP II (*kurstaki* – Cry 1A(c)) – Mycogen, M-Peril (*kurstaki* – Cry 1A(c)) – Mycogen, M-Trak (*san diego* – Cry 3A) – Mycogen, M/C (*aizawai* – Cry 1C) – Mycogen, Guardjet (*kurstaki* – Cry 1A(c)) – Mycogen/Kubota.

APPLICATION: As for Btk.

PRODUCT SPECIFICATIONS: **Purity:** MVP (MYX7275), MVP II (MYX104) and M-Peril are based on *Bacillus thuringiensis* subsp. *kurstaki* toxin Cry1A(c), as microcapsule (MVP, MVP II) and granular formulations. M-Trak is based on *Bt* subsp. *san diego* toxin Cry3A. M/C (MYX833) is based on *aizawai* toxin CryIC. **Storage conditions:** Store under cool, dark conditions. Do not expose to direct sunlight. **Shelf-life:** If stored under manufacturer's recommendation, will remain active for over twelve months.

COMPATIBILITY: Incompatible with strong oxidising agents, acids and bases. Can be used with most insecticides, acaricides, fungicides and spray tank additives.

MAMMALIAN TOXICITY: **Acute oral LD$_{50}$:** rats >5,050 mg/kg (formulation). **Acute percutaneous LD$_{50}$:** rabbits >2,020 mg/kg (formulation). **Other toxicological effects:** Inhalation: All animals survived a dose of 9.98×10^{10} cells. No formulation has shown any evidence of toxicity, infectivity or hypersensitivity to mammals. No allergic reactions or other health problems have been shown by research workers, manufacturing staff or users. **Toxicity class:** EPA (formulation) III. Considered to be non-toxic. Tolerance exempt in the US on all raw agricultural commodities when applied to growing crops pre- or post-harvest.

ENVIRONMENTAL IMPACT AND NON-TARGET TOXICITY: The formulated product has a short persistence due to its sensitivity to u.v.-light. No adverse effects have been recorded in approved field use and none are anticipated. Formulations should not be used near water courses.

3:89   *Bacillus sphaericus*   *Biological insecticide*

The Pesticide Manual - 11th edition: Entry number 44

Bacterium: Schizomycetes: Eubacteriales

NOMENCLATURE: **Approved name:** *Bacillus sphaericus* Neide, strain 2362, serotype H-5a5b.

SOURCE: *Bacillus sphaericus* is found widely in Nature and this strain (2362) was selected because of its effective control of mosquito larvae.

PRODUCTION: *Bacillus sphaericus* is produced commercially by fermentation as for *Bacillus thuringiensis* subsp. *kurstaki*.

TARGET PESTS: Mosquito larvae. Particularly active against *Culex* spp.

TARGET CROPS: Used as a public health insecticide.

BIOLOGICAL ACTIVITY: **Mode of action:** *Bacillus sphaericus* produces parasporal, proteinaceous, crystal inclusion bodies during sporulation. Upon ingestion, these are insecticidal to mosquito larvae in the same way as *Btk* is to Lepidoptera and Coleoptera. **Biology:** The crystal inclusions derived from *Bacillus sphaericus* are mosquito larva specific. Because they have to be ingested and then processed within the insect's gut, they are often slow-acting (in comparison to conventional chemicals). Strain 2362 was isolated from black fly (*Simulium* sp.) in Africa. It is active against mosquito larvae under a wide range of conditions including extended residual activity in highly organic aquatic environments. *Bacillus sphaericus* has a mode of action similar to that of *Bacillus thuringiensis* Berliner. It should be applied from first instar up to early fourth instar, with toxic symptoms often appearing within an hour of ingestion by susceptible species. The bacterium is said to recycle in the aquatic environment and this is thought to be a consequence of proliferation in susceptible insects, cannibalism and release into the water. **Efficacy:** Very effective when used against mosquito larvae in still water, even in the presence of high levels of organic matter. Light instability can cause problems if exposed to high light intensities. Rapidly hydrolysed under even mild alkaline conditions. *Bacillus sphaericus* is more effective than *Bti* for use in slow-release formulations designed to control mosquitoes.

COMMERCIALISATION: **Formulation:** Formulated as water soluble granules (SG). **Tradenames:** VectoLex CG – Abbott.

APPLICATION: Applied by air or by hand-held application equipment to expanses of water to be treated. Rates of application depend upon the stage of larvae to be treated and the organic content of the water. Rates between 2 and 4 kg of product per hectare are recommended, with the highest rates used against large larvae and in highly polluted water.

PRODUCT SPECIFICATIONS: **Purity:** Prepared as for *Btk*. The commercial product contains living spores of *Bacillus sphaericus* plus the protein endotoxin. Efficacy can be determined by bioassay on *Culex* larvae in the laboratory. **Storage conditions:** Store in cool, dry, stable conditions. **Shelf-life:** If stored under cool, dry, stable conditions, the formulated product will remain viable for ≥ 2 years.

COMPATIBILITY: Compatible with other insecticides. Do not use in conjunction with copper-based fungicides or algal control agents.

MAMMALIAN TOXICITY: No allergic reactions or other adverse health problems have been shown by research workers, manufacturing staff or users. **Oral LD$_{50}$:** rats >5,000 mg/kg (tech.). **Acute percutaneous LD$_{50}$:** rabbits >2,000 mg/kg (tech.). Mild skin irritant, eye irritant rabbits. **Inhalation LC$_{50}$:** (4 hours) *ca.* 0.09 mg/litre (technical).

ENVIRONMENTAL IMPACT AND NON-TARGET TOXICITY: *Bacillus sphaericus* has shown no adverse effects in approved field use on non-target organisms or on the environment.

3:90   *Bacillus subtilis* *Biological fungicide*

The Pesticide Manual - 11th edition: Entry number 45

Bacterium: Schizomycetes: Eubacteriales

NOMENCLATURE: **Approved name:** *Bacillus subtilis* (Ehrenberg) Cohn, strain GB03. **CAS RN:** *[68038–70–0]*. **Development code:** GUS 2000, MBI 600.

SOURCE: *Bacillus subtilis* is a common component of soil, being particularly abundant in the rhizosphere of germinating plants. The strain selected for commercialisation was chosen because of its persistence in the root zone of treated plants and because of its effectiveness at controlling fungal infections. Introduced as a seed treatment in 1994 by Christian Hansen Biosystems.

PRODUCTION: *Bacillus subtilis* is produced commercially by fermentation. The spores are used to prepare the product.

TARGET PESTS: Used as a seed treatment for the control of a range of seedling fungal pathogens including *Fusarium* spp., *Pythium* spp. and *Rhizoctonia* spp.

TARGET CROPS: Effective in a wide range of crops including soybeans, peanuts, wheat, barley, leguminous food crops and particularly cotton.

BIOLOGICAL ACTIVITY: **Mode of action:** The bacterium establishes itself in the rhizosphere of the treated crop and colonises the plant root system, competing with disease organisms that attack the developing root system. **Biology:** The rhizosphere is an environment in which a vast number of organisms thrive. It is well aerated and contains relatively high levels of nutrients supplied by the exudate from the growing plant and from the action of bacteria and fungi that colonise the region. Many plant pathogens are attracted to this region and will invade the roots of the germinating crop. *Bacillus subtilis* strain GB03, if introduced into the root zone of germinating crops as a seed treatment, persists in the rhizosphere and outcompetes fungi, allowing the crop to grow away from the pathogen.

COMMERCIALISATION: **Formulation:** Sold as seed treatments. **Tradenames:** Kodiak – Gustafson, Quantum 4000 – Gustafson, System 3 – Uniroyal, Rotor – Applied Chemicals Thailand. **Patents:** US 5215747.

APPLICATION: Applied as a seed treatment, at rates between 10 and 35 g per 100 kg of seed.

PRODUCT SPECIFICATIONS: **Purity:** Produced by fermentation and guaranteed to be free of bacterial contaminants. Viability of the bacterium within the formulation can be determined by plating out on agar and incubating at temperatures of about 25 °C for 48 hours, then counting the colonies formed. **Storage conditions:** Store under cool, dry, ambient conditions. **Shelf-life:** Stable for at least two years when stored in cool, dry conditions.

COMPATIBILITY: Incompatible with broad-spectrum seed treatments such as captan and copper-based products. Recommended for use with a range of fungicides to extend the disease control achieved with seed treatments.

MAMMALIAN TOXICITY: **Acute oral LD$_{50}$:** Not toxic or pathogenic to rats exposed to 1×10^8 colony forming units (cfu). **Acute percutaneous LD$_{50}$:** rabbits >2g/kg. **Other toxicological effects:** Not toxic to rats by inhalation at a rate of 1×10^8 cfu. **Toxicity class:** EPA (formulation) IV.

ENVIRONMENTAL IMPACT AND NON-TARGET TOXICITY: There was no pathogenicity or toxicity to young bobwhite quail by oral gavage over five days at 4×10^{11} spores per kg. *Bacillus subtilis* is a naturally occurring soil bacterium and, as such, would not be expected to cause any adverse effect on non-target organisms.

3:91   *Beauveria bassiana*   Biological insecticide

The Pesticide Manual - 11th edition: Entry number 52

Mitosporitic fungus: Previously classified as: Deuteromycetes: Moniliales

NOMENCLATURE: **Approved name:** *Beauveria bassiana* (Balsamo) Vuillemin, strains TBI, Bb 147 and GHA. **Other names:** Previously known as *Botrytis bassiana* Balsamo. **Common name:** white muscardine. **Development code:** ESC 170 GH (Ecoscience); F-7744 (Troy).

SOURCE: An isolate of *Beauveria bassiana* was obtained from a mycosed larva of the European corn borer (*Ostrinia nubilalis* (Hübner)) found in Beauce, France by INRA. A production process was developed by INRA and is now owned by Natural Plant Protection (NPP). The Troy isolate was obtained from a boll weevil (*Anthonomus grandis* (Boheman)) at the USDA-ARS Crop Insect Research Center, Lower Rio Grande Valley, Texas. The three isolates that have been commercialised are Bb 147 – NPP; ATCC 74040 (= ARSEF 3097 = FCI 7744) – Troy; and GHA – Mycotech.

PRODUCTION: *Beauveria bassiana* is cultured by solid state fermentation on clay granules.

TARGET PESTS: Strain Bb 147 is recommended for use against European corn borer (*Ostrinia nubilalis*) and Asiatic corn borer (*O. furnacalis* Guenée); strain GHA is used against whitefly, thrips, aphids and mealybugs; and ATCC 74040 is effective against a range of soft-bodied coleopteran, homopteran and heteropteran pests.

TARGET CROPS: Strain Bb 147 is recommended for use in maize in Europe; GHA is used in vegetables and ornamentals; and ATCC 74040 is used in turf and ornamentals as Naturalis-O and -T and on all raw agricultural commodities as Naturalis-L. A new formulation, Back-Off, is being developed for use in cotton, vegetables and ornamentals.

BIOLOGICAL ACTIVITY: **Biology:** The entomopathogen invades the insect body. Fungal conidia become attached to the insect cuticle and, after germination, the hyphae penetrate the cuticle and proliferate in the insect's body. High humidity or free water is essential for conidial germination and infection can take between 24 and 48 hours, depending on the temperature. The infected insect may live for three to five days after hyphal penetration and, after death, the conidiophores are produced on the outside of the insect's body and new conidia are released on the outside of the insect cadaver. The fungus is insect specific.
Key references: 1) G Riba. 1985. Thése de Doctorat d'Etat, Mention Sciences, Université Pierre et Marie Curie, France. 2) J E Wright and T A Knauf. 1994. Evaluation of Naturalis-L for control of cotton insects, *Proc. Brighton Crop Prot. Conf. – Pests & Diseases*, **1**, 45.

COMMERCIALISATION: **Formulation:** Ostrinil is an MG (a clay microgranular formulation colonised by sporulating mycelia of a pyralid active strain); Mycotrol is a WP; and Naturalis-L is an SC. **Tradenames:** Ostrinil – NPP, Calliop, Naturalis-L – Troy, Naturalis-O – Troy, Naturalis-T – Troy, BotaniGard – Mycotech, Mycotrol – Mycotech, CornGuard – Mycotech, Ago Biocontrol Bassiana – Ago Biocontrol. **Patents:** EP 9040118330.

APPLICATION: Used as foliar sprays through all types of applicators with water as the carrier. Application rates depend upon the crop and the pests to be controlled. The normal application rate on commodity crops is 750 to 1000 ml of product per hectare, for ornamentals under cover or outdoors 24 to 80 ml per 10 litres and on turf and lawns 32 to 96 ml per 100 square metres.

PRODUCT SPECIFICATIONS: **Purity:** Formulations of Naturalis contain conidia of *Beauveria bassiana* at a concentration of 2.3×10^7 spores per ml and Ostrinil formulations contain at least 5×10^8 spores per gram. Viability of the spores is determined by culture on nutrient agar and counting the colonies formed. Efficacy is checked by bioassay with an appropriate insect. Detailed identification of the specific strain in any formulation requires DNA and isoenzyme matching with the registered strain held in a type culture collection.
Storage conditions: Store in a cool, dry place. Do not freeze and do not allow the product to undergo thermal shock. **Shelf-life:** May be kept for up to one year if stored below 20 °C.

COMPATIBILITY: The products may be used alone or tank mixed with other products such as sticking agents, insecticidal soaps, emulsifiable oils, insecticides or used with beneficial insects. Do not use with fungicides and wait 48 hours after application before applying fungicides.

MAMMALIAN TOXICITY: **Acute oral LD$_{50}$:** rats >18 × 10^8 colony forming units (cfu) per kg. No infectivity of pathogenicity was observed after 21 days.
Acute percutaneous LD$_{50}$: rats >2,000 mg/kg. **Inhalation LD$_{50}$:** rats >1.2 × 10^8 cfu/animal.
Other toxicological effects: Dermal, oral and inhalation studies with Naturalis-L on rats indicated that the fungus is non-toxic and non-pathogenic. Possible irritant to eyes, skin and respiratory system.

ENVIRONMENTAL IMPACT AND NON-TARGET TOXICITY: **Birds:** Oral LD$_{50}$: (5 days) quail >2,000 mg/kg daily (by gavage). **Fish:** Naturalis-L does not affect fish embryos, larvae or adults. LC$_{50}$: (31 days) rainbow trout 7,300 mg/litre. EC$_{50}$: (14 days) *Daphnia pulex* 4,100 mg/litre. **Bees:** 30-day dietary and contact studies indicate that Naturalis-L has no significant effect; LC$_{50}$: (23 days, ingestion) 9,285 mg/kg. **Other beneficial species:** No effect observed on beneficial species after field application.

3:92 *Beauveria brongniartii*

Biological insecticide

The Pesticide Manual - 11th edition: Entry number 53

Mitosporitic fungus: Previously classified as Deuteromycetes: Moniliales

NOMENCLATURE: **Approved name:** *Beauveria brongniartii* (Saccardo) Petch strain Bb 96 (Betel), Swiss isolates. **Other names:** *Beauveria tenella* (Saccardo) McLeod *sensu* McLeod.

SOURCE: *Beauveria brongniartii* was isolated from a mycosed white grub (*Hoplochelis marginalis*) larva found in Madagascar, by CIRAD/IRAT, France. The isolated strain was particularly virulent. A fermented-rice preparation was tested successfully by INRA and a production process was developed by them. This process is now owned by Natural Plant Protection (NPP).

PRODUCTION: *Beauveria brongniartii* is cultured by solid state fermentation on clay granules.

TARGET PESTS: White grubs (*Hoplochelis marginalis* (Fairmaire)) and cockchafers (*Melolontha melolontha* (Linnaeus)).

TARGET CROPS: Sugar cane and barley.

BIOLOGICAL ACTIVITY: **Biology:** The entomopathogen invades the insect body. Fungal conidia become attached to the insect cuticle and, after germination, the hyphae penetrate the cuticle and proliferate in the insect's body. High humidity or free water is essential for conidial germination. Infection can take 24 and 48 hours depending on the temperature. The infected insect may live for three to five days after hyphal penetration and, after death, the conidiophores are produced on the outside of the insect's body and new conidia are released on the outside of the insect cadaver. The fungus is particularly effective against coleopteran pests. **Key references:** 1) O Goebel. 1989. Diplôme d'ingénieur en agronomie tropicale, CNEARC/ESAT, France. 2) B Vercambre. 1991. In *Rencontres Caraibes en Lutte Biologique*, Les Colloques de l'INRA, No 58, 371–8, Published by INRA, France.

COMMERCIALISATION: **Formulation:** *Beauveria brongniartii* is produced as a microgranule (MG) (NPP) and as inoculated barley seed (Andermatt). **Tradenames:** Engerlingspilz – Andermatt, Betel – NPP.

APPLICATION: In sugar cane, Betel may be applied at planting on the edge of the furrow or at the foot of the ratoon canes. A dose rate of 50 kg of product per hectare reduces larval populations below the damage threshold of three larvae per sugar cane. For cockchafer control, inoculated barley seed is sown in the soil.

PRODUCT SPECIFICATIONS: **Purity:** The purity of Betel is measured in terms of spore count (minimum of 0.2×10^8 spores per gram) and efficacy against *Hoplochelus marginalis* larvae. The activity of Engerlingspilz is measured by bioassay with *Melolontha melolontha*. **Storage conditions:** Store in a dry refrigerated container. **Shelf-life:** The spores remain viable for a year if stored at 2 °C.

COMPATIBILITY: Can be applied with other chemicals with the exception of fungicides.

MAMMALIAN TOXICITY: **Acute oral LD$_{50}$:** rats >5,000 mg/kg. No toxicity, infectivity or pathogenicity from a single dose of 1.1×10^9 colony forming units (cfu)/kg (rats). **Acute percutaneous LD$_{50}$:** rats >2,000 mg/kg. Mildly irritant to skin (rabbits). Considered to be non-toxic.

ENVIRONMENTAL IMPACT AND NON-TARGET TOXICITY: **Birds:** Dietary LD$_{50}$ (5 days) quail and mallard ducks >4,000 mg/kg. **Fish:** LC$_{50}$ (30 days) rainbow trout 7,200 mg/litre, **NOEL:** (30 days) rainbow trout 3,000 mg/litre. **NOEL:** (21 days) *Daphnia pulex* 500 mg/litre.

3:93 *Burkholderia cepacia*
Biological fungicide/nematicide

Bacterium: Pseudomonadales: Pseudomonadaceae

NOMENCLATURE: **Approved name:** *Burkholderia cepacia* (ex Burkholder) Yabuuchi, Kosako, Oyaizu, Yaro, Hotta, Hashimoto, Ezaki and Arakawa, Wisconsin strain. **Other names:** *Pseudomonas cepacia* (ex Burkholder) Palleroni and Holmes, Wisconsin strain.

SOURCE: A common component of the rhizosphere. An aggressive coloniser of the roots of many plants. The Wisconsin strain, isolate J82, was selected because of its ease of manufacture and effective suppression of soil-borne diseases and nematodes.

PRODUCTION: Produced by fermentation.

TARGET PESTS: Soil colonising fungal pathogens and nematodes.

TARGET CROPS: Used as a seed treatment for many different outdoor crops and also used to treat transplanted crops.

BIOLOGICAL ACTIVITY: **Biology:** *Burkholderia cepacia* is an aggressive coloniser of the root zones of growing plants. In addition, it is antagonistic to pathogenic fungi and plant parasitic nematodes preventing them from becoming established in the region of the crop and, thereafter, colonising the crop.

COMMERCIALISATION: **Formulation:** Formulated as an inert powder coated with living bacteria and used as a seed treatment and as a liquid suspension of live bacteria in nutrient broth. **Tradenames:** Deny – CCT Corp, Intercept – Soil Technologies Corp, Blue Circle Liquid Biological Fungicide – Stine Microbial Products.

APPLICATION: Used as a seed treatment or as a powder treatment for transplants. May be applied as a drench shortly after transplanting.

PRODUCT SPECIFICATIONS: **Purity:** Viability of the formulated bacterium can be determined by plating the product on to nutrient agar, culturing in the laboratory for 48 hours and counting the number of colonies that develop. **Storage conditions:** Store under cool, dry conditions in a sealed container. Powder formulations should be kept between -6 and 24 °C and liquid formulations between 1 and 24 °C. Avoid direct sunlight and do not allow liquid formulations to dry. **Shelf-life:** The powder seed treatment is stable for one year and the liquid formulation for six months.

COMPATIBILITY: Compatible with most chemical treatments. Do not apply with broad-spectrum fungicides such as copper-based products.

MAMMALIAN TOXICITY: The product has not produced any adverse allergic reactions in research workers, manufacturing or field staff. It may cause eye irritation.

ENVIRONMENTAL IMPACT AND NON-TARGET TOXICITY: *Burkholderia cepacia* occurs widely in Nature and would not be expected to cause any adverse effects on non-target organisms or on the environment.

3:94   *Candida oleophila*   *Biological fungicide*

Mitosporitic fungus: Previously classified as: Deuteromycetes: Moniliales

NOMENCLATURE: **Approved name:** *Candida oleophila* Montrocher, isolate I-82.

SOURCE: A fungus that occurs widely in Nature.

PRODUCTION: Manufactured by fermentation.

TARGET PESTS: Used to control post-harvest diseases.

TARGET CROPS: Used on citrus and pome fruit.

BIOLOGICAL ACTIVITY: **Biology:** Prevents the invasion of fruit in storage by storage disease organisms by competing for entry sites and by the production of fungicidal secondary products.

COMMERCIALISATION: **Formulation:** Sold as extruded granules. **Tradenames:** Aspire – Ecogen.

APPLICATION: Applied to harvested fruit and citrus as a spray or dip treatment.

PRODUCT SPECIFICATIONS: **Purity:** Contains only *Candida oleophila* cells. Efficacy can be determined by growing on nutrient agar in the laboratory and counting the number of colonies that develop. **Storage conditions:** Store under cool, dry conditions (4 °C) in a sealed container. Do not allow to freeze and keep out of direct sunlight. **Shelf-life:** If stored under manufacturer's recommended conditions, will remain effective for up to a year.

COMPATIBILITY: Not compatible with many chemical post-harvest antifungal fruit treatments.

MAMMALIAN TOXICITY: There have been no records of allergic or other adverse effects from the use of *Candida oleophila* by researchers, manufacturers and field workers. **Toxicity class:** EPA (formulation) III.

ENVIRONMENTAL IMPACT AND NON-TARGET TOXICITY: *Candida oleophila* is not hazardous to fish and wild-life.

3:95   *Chondostereum purpureum*
Biological herbicide

Fungus: Basidiomycetes: Agaricales

NOMENCLATURE: **Approved name:** *Chondostereum purpureum* Pouzar. **Other names:** *Stereum purpureum* Fr.; silver leaf fungus.

SOURCE: The fungus is an important source of wood-rot and is found widely in temperate forests. It is often the first fungus to show on the stumps of newly felled trees.

PRODUCTION: Produced by fermentation.

TARGET PESTS: Prevents the regrowth of undesirable forest pest trees such as the American black cherry (*Prunus serotina* Ehrh.), yellow birch (*Betula lutea* Michx.) and poplar (*Populus* spp.).

TARGET CROPS: Used in forests.

BIOLOGICAL ACTIVITY: **Biology:** *Chondostereum purpureum* invades freshly cut stumps or fresh wounds on a range of deciduous trees. The pathogen develops within the tree and spreads to the vascular system where it blocks the vessels and leads to plant death. **Duration of development:** The silver leaf pathogen will invade fresh wounds in a variety of deciduous trees, leading to plant death. After one or two years, the pathogen is replaced in the dead tree by other wood-rotting fungi. **Efficacy:** Trials have shown that about 95% of treated stumps are killed within two years of treatment.

COMMERCIALISATION: **Formulation:** Sold as a suspension of fungal mycelium in water. **Tradenames:** Biochon – Koppert.

APPLICATION: The product should be sprayed or spread on the fresh wound surface in late Spring/early Summer or in the Autumn.

PRODUCT SPECIFICATIONS: **Storage conditions:** Store in a sealed container in a cool place out of direct sunlight. **Shelf-life:** Use as soon as possible after delivery.

COMPATIBILITY: It is not necessary to apply the product with other crop protection agents.

MAMMALIAN TOXICITY: *Chondostereum purpureum* occurs widely in Nature and has not caused allergic or other adverse effects on research workers or on production or field staff.

ENVIRONMENTAL IMPACT AND NON-TARGET TOXICITY: *Chondostereum purpureum* is not expected to have any adverse effects on non-target organisms or on the environment.

3:96 *Colletotrichum gloeosporioides f. sp. aeschynomene* *Biological herbicide*

Mitosporitic fungus: Previously classified as: Deuteromycetes: Melanconiales

NOMENCLATURE: **Approved name:** *Colletotrichum gloeosporioides* (Penz.) Sacc. f. sp. *aeschynomene.*

SOURCE: Isolated from Northern joint vetch in the USA.

PRODUCTION: Produced by fermentation.

TARGET PESTS: Northern joint vetch (*Aeschynomene virginica* L.).

TARGET CROPS: Rice and soybean.

BIOLOGICAL ACTIVITY: **Mode of action:** Pathogenesis. **Biology:** *Colletotrichum gloeosporioides* f. sp. *aeschynomene* is a pathogen of Northern joint vetch. When applied to the weed, it penetrates the plant's cuticle and invades the weed, leading to plant death. The pathogen is specific to Northern joint vetch. **Key reference:** M P Greaves. 1996. Microbial herbicides: factors in development. In *Crop Protection Agents from Nature: Natural Products and Analogues*, L G Copping (ed.), 444–67, Royal Society of Chemistry, Cambridge, UK.

COMMERCIALISATION: **Formulation:** Sold as an aqueous suspension of spores. **Tradenames:** Collego – Abbott. **Patents:** US 3849104.

APPLICATION: Applied over the top of the developing weed under conditions of high humidity.

PRODUCT SPECIFICATIONS: **Storage conditions:** Store in a sealed container under cool conditions out of direct sunlight. **Shelf-life:** Use as soon as possible after receipt.

COMPATIBILITY: *Colletotrichum gloeosporioides* f. sp. *aeschynomene* is compatible with chemical herbicides but should not be used in conjunction with a fungicide.

MAMMALIAN TOXICITY: There is no report of any allergic or other adverse effects following the use of the product.

ENVIRONMENTAL IMPACT AND NON-TARGET TOXICITY: *Colletotrichum gloeosporioides* f. sp. *aeschynomene* occurs widely in Nature and is not expected to have any adverse effects on non-target organisms or the environment.

3:97 *Coniothyrium minitans*

Biological fungicide

Mitosporitic fungus: Previously classified as: Deuteromycetes: Sphaeropsidales

NOMENCLATURE: **Approved name:** *Coniothyrium minitans*.

SOURCE: Commonly occurring phylloplane fungus, isolated from the leaves of Brassicae.

PRODUCTION: Manufactured by fermentation.

TARGET PESTS: Species of the genus *Sclerotinia*.

TARGET CROPS: Oilseed rape and lettuce.

BIOLOGICAL ACTIVITY: **Biology:** The fungus is a good invader of leaf surfaces and rapidly covers the foliage of treated plants. It prevents the invasion of the pathogenic strains of *Sclerotinia* from penetrating and thereby infecting treated plants.

COMMERCIALISATION: **Formulation:** Sold as a water dispersible formulation. **Tradenames:** Contans – Prophytia.

APPLICATION: Apply as a foliar spray to plants before they are infected.

PRODUCT SPECIFICATIONS: **Purity:** Contains no contaminants. **Storage conditions:** Store in a sealed container in a cool, dry situation. Do not expose to extremes of temperature or direct sunlight. **Shelf-life:** Can be stored for twelve months under recommended conditions.

COMPATIBILITY: Incompatible with chemical fungicides.

MAMMALIAN TOXICITY: There are no reports of *Coniothyrium minitans* causing allergic or other adverse toxicological effects in research and manufacturing staff, formulators or field workers.

ENVIRONMENTAL IMPACT AND NON-TARGET TOXICITY: *Coniothyrium minitans* occurs widely in Nature and would not be expected to have any adverse effects on non-target organisms or on the environment.

3:98 *Cydia pomonella* granulovirus
Insecticidal baculovirus

The Pesticide Manual - 11th edition: Entry number 175

Virus: Baculoviridae: Granulovirus

NOMENCLATURE: **Approved name:** *Cydia pomonella* granulovirus (CpGV), Mexican strain and French isolate. **Other names:** common name is codling moth granulosis virus; also known as CmGV.

SOURCE: CpGV has been isolated from codling moth larvae in Nature.

PRODUCTION: The virus is produced by infecting codling moth larvae, harvesting the infected organisms and extracting the granular occlusion bodies by centrifugation. This technique requires very large quantities of larvae for virus production and is, thus, an expensive procedure. Trials are underway on the production of the virus in a more cost-effective way *in vivo* or through *in vitro* techniques such as insect cell culture.

TARGET PESTS: The codling moth (*Cydia pomonella* (Linnaeus)).

TARGET CROPS: Apple, pear and walnut orchards.

BIOLOGICAL ACTIVITY: **Mode of action:** Codling moth larvae are infected by the granulosis virus which was first reported in 1964 following its identification in *Cydia pomonella* larvae collected in Mexico (*J. Insect Pathol.* 1964. **6**, 373–86). **Biology:** CpGV is more active on small larvae than later larval instars that are usually inaccessible to the virus, as they burrow into the fruit. It is recommended that applications be targeted at neonate larvae by following egg-laying patterns with the use of pheromone monitoring systems (see Section 2: Pheromones). The virus is ingested by the feeding larva and the protective virus protein matrix is dissolved in the insect's midgut (that is alkaline), releasing the virus particles still enclosed in their protein coats. These pass through the peritrophic membrane and invade midgut cells by fusion with the microvilli. The virus particles invade the cell nuclei where they are uncoated and replicated. Initial replication produces non-occluded virus particles to hasten the invasion of the host insect. Later the virus particles are produced with protein matrices and remain infective when released from the dead insects. **Efficacy:** The high level of activity shown by CpGV to first instar larvae means that, if the product is applied at the correct time, good control is achieved with very low rates of application. The virus has to be consumed to be effective and death will often take many hours, even with small larvae. **Key reference:** 1) R R Granados and B A Frederici (eds.). 1986. *The Biology of Baculoviruses, Vols. 1 and 2.* CRC Press, Boca Raton, Florida, USA. 2) D J Leisy and J R Fuxa. 1996. Natural and engineered viral agents for insect control. In *Crop Protection Agents from Nature: Natural Products and Analogues,* L G Copping (ed.), Royal Society of Chemistry, Cambridge, UK.

COMMERCIALISATION: **Formulation:** Sold as a liquid and a suspension concentrate (SC) formulation. **Tradenames:** Madex 3 – Andermatt Biocontrol, Granupom – AgrEvo, Carposin – Agrichem, Carpovirusine – Calliope, Virin-Gyap – NPO Vector, CYD-X – Thermo Trilogy.

APPLICATION: The incidence of codling moth adults should be monitored using pheromone traps in order that the product can be applied at the optimum time for pest control. High volume sprays of up to 1×10^{13} GV/hectare should be applied when adults are detected. It has been suggested that rates of one-tenth of this dose can be applied at weekly intervals with good results. It may be used in ICM programmes and used on organically grown produce. Some formulations contain the virus plus specific additives to enhance the effectiveness of the product.

PRODUCT SPECIFICATIONS: **Purity:** The product is monitored to ensure that it is free of human and mammalian bacterial pathogens. It is assayed for effectiveness against codling moth larvae. **Storage conditions:** Store in sealed containers at 2 °C. **Shelf-life:** Formulations stored at 2 °C are stable for over two years. If stored at room temperature, they remain effective for one month. Infectivity is reduced by exposure to u.v. light.

COMPATIBILITY: Compatible with all crop protection agents that do not repel codling moth but not with copper-based fungicides, strong oxidisers or chlorinated water. Use water with a pH between 6 and 8.

MAMMALIAN TOXICITY: **Oral LD$_{50}$:** rats >2,000 mg/kg. **Skin and eye:** Does not penetrate the skin; mild skin irritant to rabbits. **Other toxicological effects:** Inhalation LD$_{50}$ (rats) $>2 \times 10^{12}$ GV/ml. There is no evidence of acute or chronic toxicity, eye or skin irritation in mammals. No allergic reactions or other health problems have been observed in research or manufacturing staff or users of the product.

ENVIRONMENTAL IMPACT AND NON-TARGET TOXICITY: **Birds:** *Cydia pomonella* granulovirus showed no toxicity or pathogenicity to birds at 10,000 mg/kg for five days. **Fish:** The LD$_{50}$ (96 hours) for fish was > 250 mg/litre. **Beneficial species:** LC$_{50}$ (contact) for honeybees was $>1 \times 10^{10}$ GV per ml per bee and the LC$_{50}$ for earthworms was >1,000 mg/kg soil. It was harmless to the mite predators *Typhlodromus pyri* Scheunten and *Amblyseius californicus* (McGregor). The EC$_{50}$ (48 hours) for *Daphnia pulex* was >250 mg/kg. The virus occurs widely in Nature and there is no evidence that it affects any organism other than codling moth larvae. It is unstable when exposed to u.v. light and does not persist in the environment, with no viral activity being found in soil 4 months after application. The virus particles sediment in water.

3:99   Endothia parasitica   _Biological fungicide_

Fungus: Ascomycetes: Sphaeriales

NOMENCLATURE: **Approved name:** _Endothia parasitica_ Anders. and Anders.
Other names: _Diaporthe parasitica_ Murr.; _Valsonectria parasitica_ Rehm.

SOURCE: A non-pathogenic strain of the fungus that is the causal organism of chestnut blight. Isolated from a chestnut tree in France.

PRODUCTION: Produced by fermentation.

TARGET PESTS: Chestnut blight (_Endothia parasitica_ Anders. and Anders.).

TARGET CROPS: Chestnut trees.

BIOLOGICAL ACTIVITY: **Biology:** This non-pathogenic strain of the fungus invades possible infection sites on trees and outcompetes for these sites with the pathogen, preventing the establishment of the disease.

COMMERCIALISATION: **Formulation:** Sold as spores suspended in a paste. **Tradenames:** Endothia parasitica – CNICM.

APPLICATION: Damaged or pruned areas of the tree should be treated with the product as soon as possible to allow for the establishment of the non-pathogenic strain.

PRODUCT SPECIFICATIONS: **Storage conditions:** Store in a cool, dry situation. Do not expose to bright sunlight. **Shelf-life:** One year.

COMPATIBILITY: It is unusual to apply _Endothia parasitica_ with any other treatments.

MAMMALIAN TOXICITY: There is no record of allergic or other adverse effects following the use of the product. It is considered to be of low mammalian toxicity.

ENVIRONMENTAL IMPACT AND NON-TARGET TOXICITY: _Endothia parasitica_ occurs in Nature and is not expected to have any adverse effects on non-target organisms or the environment.

3:100   Erwinia carotovora   _Microbial bactericide_

Bacterium: Eubacteriales: Bacillaceae

NOMENCLATURE: **Approved name:** _Erwinia carotovora_ Holl. **Other names:** previously known as _Bacillus carotovorus_ Jones and _Pectobacterium carotovorum_ Jones.

SOURCE: Non-pathogenic strain of _Erwinia carotovora_ isolated from Chinese cabbage.

PRODUCTION: Produced by fermentation.

TARGET PESTS: Soft rot (*Erwinia carotovora*).

TARGET CROPS: Chinese cabbage.

BIOLOGICAL ACTIVITY: **Biology:** This non-pathogenic strain of the bacterium invades possible infection sites on Chinese cabbage and outcompetes for these sites with the pathogen, preventing the establishment of the disease.

COMMERCIALISATION: **Formulation:** Sold as a suspension of spores.
Tradenames: BioKeeper – Nissan.

APPLICATION: Apply as a foliar spray ensuring good coverage of the foliage.

PRODUCT SPECIFICATIONS: **Purity:** Does not contain any contaminants.
Storage conditions: Store in a cool, dry place out of direct sunlight. **Shelf-life:** If stored correctly, the product remains viable for twelve months.

COMPATIBILITY: It is unusual to apply the product with conventional chemicals.

MAMMALIAN TOXICITY: *Erwinia carotovora* has not been reported to cause allergic or other adverse toxicological effects on research workers, manufacturers, formulators or field staff.

ENVIRONMENTAL IMPACT AND NON-TARGET TOXICITY: *Erwinia carotovora* is not expected to have any adverse effects on non-target organisms or on the environment.

3:101 *Fusarium oxysporum* Biological fungicide

The Pesticide Manual - 11th edition: Entry number 378

Mitosporitic fungus: Previously classified as: Deuteromycetes: Moniliales

NOMENCLATURE: **Approved name:** *Fusarium oxysporum* Schlechtendal, strain Fo 47.

SOURCE: *Fusarium oxysporum* strain Fo 47 is a naturally occurring mutant strain of the fungus that was found in suppressive soil of Chateaurenard, South East France by INRA researchers and was selected for commercialisation as it is not phytopathogenic and competes with other pathogenic strains of the fungus.

PRODUCTION: By solid fermentation to produce clay microgranules and by liquid fermentation to produce liquid formulation.

TARGET PESTS: For the control of vascular wilts caused by the fungal pathogens *Fusarium oxysporum* Schlechtendal and *Fusarium moniliforme* Sheldon (*Gibberella fujikuroi* Wr.).

TARGET CROPS: Fusaclean L is under development for treating rock-wool blocks and Fusaclean G for use on field and glasshouse-grown crops.

BIOLOGICAL ACTIVITY: **Mode of action:** Protects crops against pathogenic *Fusarium* spp. by three distinct mechanisms – i) soil competition at root level; *Fusarium oxysporum* strain Fo 47 is a strong root-zone coloniser and is highly competitive for nutrients with other micro-organisms, ii) competition at the surface of the root system; *Fusarium oxysporum* strain Fo 47 competes with other soil micro-organisms for access at root infection sites, iii) elicitation; *Fusarium oxysporum* strain Fo 47 activates the plant's auto-immune system, leading to the production of phytoalexins that inhibit the production of *Fusarium* digestive enzymes and detoxify the fusaric acid produced by phytopathogenic strains. **Biology:** *Fusarium oxysporum* strain Fo 47 is a non-pathogenic form of the fungus. It grows competitively within the root zones of crops, preventing the establishment of the pathogenic strains of the genus. *Fusarium oxysporum* strain Fo 47 exerts its effects by showing aggresive colonisation of the root zones and out-competing pathogenic strains for nutrients, by competing for infection sites on the crop root preventing pathogen penetration or by eliciting auto-immune responses within the crop plants, rendering them resistant to invasion by pathogenic strains.

COMMERCIALISATION: **Formulation:** Sold as a soluble concentrate (SL) and as a microgranule (MG). **Tradenames:** Fusaclean L (SL, spores, 1×10^{11} colony forming units/litre) – NPP, Fusaclean G (MG, mycelium and spores, 2.5×10^8 colony forming units/g) – NPP.

APPLICATION: Fusaclean L is added to the rock-wool blocks in which glasshouse grown crops are propagated. Fusaclean G is a granule added to the soil around both field and glasshouse-grown crops.

PRODUCT SPECIFICATIONS: **Purity:** The fermentation process is undertaken under carefully controlled conditions and no phytopathogenic strains of the fungus are included in the product. Viability of the fungus can be determined by plating onto agar, incubating in the laboratory at temperatures around 25 °C and counting the colonies formed after 48 hours. **Storage conditions:** Store under cool conditions, preferably refrigerated. Do not expose to sunlight and do not freeze. **Shelf-life:** Use as soon as possible after delivery. Dry formulations can be stored for about six months without loss of viability.

COMPATIBILITY: Incompatible with soil-applied fungicides.

MAMMALIAN TOXICITY: **Acute oral LD$_{50}$:** rats >5,000 mg/kg. **Acute percutaneous LD$_{50}$:** rats >2,000 mg/kg. **Other toxicological effects:** Not toxic by inhalation and not infective or pathogenic to rats after intra-tracheal instillation. *Fusarium oxysporum* strain Fo 47 is not pathogenic or infective to mammals.

ENVIRONMENTAL IMPACT AND NON-TARGET TOXICITY: **Birds:** oral LD$_{50}$ (5 days) quail >9,400 mg/kg (by gavage), equivalent to 1.2×10^3 colony forming units/g. **Fish:** LC$_{50}$ (96 hours) >100 mg/litre. **Other beneficial organisms:** *Fusarium oxysporum* strain Fo 47 occurs in Nature and is not expected to cause any adverse reaction to any non-target organism or to have any deleterious effect on the environment.

3:102 *Gliocladium catenulatum*

Biological fungicide

Mitosporitic fungus: Previously classified as: Deuteromycetes: Moniliales

NOMENCLATURE: **Approved name:** *Gliocladium catenulatum*.

SOURCE: Developed as a collaboration between the Agricultural Research Centre in Finland and Kemira Agro, the fungus was isolated from soil in Finland.

PRODUCTION: Produced by fermentation.

TARGET PESTS: *Pythium* spp. and *Rhizoctonia* spp. in soil and *Botrytis* spp., *Didymella* spp. and *Helminthosporium* spp. as post-harvest or foliar pathogens.

TARGET CROPS: The product has its primary use in seedling production but is also effective as a post-harvest treatment.

BIOLOGICAL ACTIVITY: **Mode of action:** Microbial fungicide with a preventative rather than curative action. Exerts its effect in three different ways. *Gliocladium catenulatum* produces an antibiotic that kills the plant pathogens. It also parasitises them in addition to competing for nutrients.

COMMERCIALISATION: **Formulation:** Sold as a granular (GR) formulation.
Tradenames: Primastop – Kemira.

APPLICATION: Apply as an overall application to seedlings as they emerge and before there is any sign of disease. Use as a foliar spray or as a dip treatment to harvested produce.

PRODUCT SPECIFICATIONS: **Purity:** Contains no contaminants. **Storage conditions:** Store under cool, dry conditions in a sealed container. Do not expose to direct sunlight.
Shelf-life: Remains viable for twelve months if stored under correct conditions.

COMPATIBILITY: It is not recommended that *Gliocladium catenulatum* be used in combination with conventional chemicals. Incompatible with broad-spectrum fungicides.

MAMMALIAN TOXICITY: There have been no reports of allergic or other adverse toxicological effects from research and manufacturing staff, formulators or field workers.

ENVIRONMENTAL IMPACT AND NON-TARGET TOXICITY: *Gliocladium catenulatum* occurs widely in Nature and is not expected to have any adverse effects on non-target organisms or on the environment.

3. Living Systems

3:103 *Gliocladium virens* *Biological fungicide*

The Pesticide Manual - 11th edition: Entry number 381

Mitosporitic fungus: Previously classified as: Deuteromycetes: Moniliales

NOMENCLATURE: **Approved name:** *Gliocladium virens* Millers, Giddens and Foster, strain GL-21. **Other names:** previously known as *Trichoderma virens*.

SOURCE: Naturally occurring soil fungus, discovered and isolated by USDA. Marketed by Thermo Trilogy.

PRODUCTION: Produced by fermentation.

TARGET PESTS: Soil-borne damping off and root rot pathogens such as *Rhizoctonia*, *Pythium*, *Fusarium*, *Thielaviopsis*, *Sclerotinia* and *Sclerotium* spp.

TARGET CROPS: Ornamentals and food crops grown in nurseries, glasshouses and interiorscapes. Outdoor use on turf and agricultural and ornamental crops.

BIOLOGICAL ACTIVITY: **Mode of action:** Microbial fungicide with a preventative rather than curative action. Exerts its effect in three different ways. *Gliocladium virens* produces an antibiotic that kills the plant pathogens. It also parasitises them in addition to competing for nutrients.

COMMERCIALISATION: **Formulation:** Sold as a granular (GR) formulation. **Tradenames:** SoilGard – Thermo Trilogy.

APPLICATION: Applied at a rate of 0.5 to 0.75 kg per square metre or 1 to 4 kg per 10 hectalitres. The product should be incorporated into soil. Apply before planting. Do not over-water and do not apply to plants that are already infested.

PRODUCT SPECIFICATIONS: **Storage conditions:** Store in a cool, dry place away from direct sunlight. **Shelf-life:** Retains biological effectiveness for a year under correct storage conditions.

COMPATIBILITY: Fungicides should not be used at the time of incorporation of the product.

MAMMALIAN TOXICITY: May cause mild, reversible irritation to the eyes and skin. No acute toxicity, infectivity or pathogenicity following inhalation.

ENVIRONMENTAL IMPACT AND NON-TARGET TOXICITY: *Gliocladium virens* occurs naturally in soil and is not expected to have any adverse effects on non-target organisms or on the environment.

3:104 *Helicoverpa zea nucleopoly-hedrovirus*   *Insecticidal baculovirus*

The Pesticide Manual - 11th edition: Entry number 393

Virus: Baculoviridae: Nucleopolyhedrovirus

NOMENCLATURE: **Approved name:** *Helicoverpa zea* nucleopolyhedrovirus.
Other names: HzSNPV; HzNPV.

SOURCE: The virus occurs naturally in *Heliothis* and *Helicoverpa* species.

PRODUCTION: The product is produced from the culture of infected *Helicoverpa zea* (Boddie) larvae under controlled conditions. Polyhedral inclusion bodies are extracted from the dead insects and formulated as a liquid concentrate.

TARGET PESTS: For control of *Heliothis* and *Helicoverpa* species including cotton boll worm (*Helicoverpa zea*) and tobacco budworm (*Heliothis virescens* Fabricius).

TARGET CROPS: Vegetables, tomatoes and cotton.

BIOLOGICAL ACTIVITY: **Mode of action:** As with all insect baculoviruses, *Helicoverpa zea* SNPV must be ingested to exert an effect. Following ingestion, the protective protein matrices of the polyhedral occlusion bodies (OBs) of the virus are dissolved within the midgut and the virus particles enter the insect's haemolymph. These virus particles invade nearly all cell types in the larval body, where they multiply leading to insect death. Shortly after the death of the larva, the integument ruptures releasing very large numbers of OBs. **Efficacy:** HzSNPV acts relatively slowly as it has to be ingested and infect before it exerts any effect on the insect host. It is important to ensure good cover of the foliage to effect good control. Monitoring of adult insect laying patterns and targeted application at newly hatched eggs gives better control than on a mixed population. **Key references:** 1) R R Granados and B A Frederici (eds.). 1986. *The Biology of Baculoviruses, Vols. 1 and 2.* CRC Press, Boca Raton, Florida, USA. 2) D J Leisy and J R Fuxa. 1996. Natural and engineered viral agents for insect control. In *Crop Protection Agents from Nature: Natural Products and Analogues*, L G Copping (ed.), Royal Society of Chemistry, Cambridge, UK.

COMMERCIALISATION: **Formulation:** Sold as a liquid concentrate (LC).
Tradenames: GemStar – Thermo Trilogy.

APPLICATION: Apply at a rate of 1,500 billion occlusion bodies per hectare (750 mls of product per hectare) ensuring good coverage of the foliage.

PRODUCT SPECIFICATIONS: **Purity:** The liquid concentrate formulation is checked to ensure that it is free from human and mammalian bacterial pathogens.
Storage conditions: Store in a tightly closed container in a cool (<21 °C), dry and dark area. Shelf-life is extended if kept frozen. Unstable at temperatures above 32 °C. **Shelf-life:** Stable for several weeks if kept cool, but has great stability if kept in a freezer.

3. Living Systems

COMPATIBILITY: Can be used with other insecticides that do not repel *Helicoverpa* and *Heliothis* species. Incompatible with strong oxidisers, acids, bases or chlorinated water.

MAMMALIAN TOXICITY: Baculoviruses are specific to invertebrates with there being no record of any vertebrate becoming infected. The virus does not infect or replicate in the cells of mammals and is inactivated at temperatures above 32 °C. There is no evidence of acute or chronic toxicity, eye or skin irritation in mammals. No allergic reactions or other health problems have been observed in research or manufacturing staff or with users of the product.

ENVIRONMENTAL IMPACT AND NON-TARGET TOXICITY: HzSNPV occurs widely in Nature and there is no evidence of the virus infecting vertebrates or plants. It has no adverse effects on fish, birds or beneficial organisms.

3:105   *Heterorhabditis bacteriophora*

Insect parasitic nematode

The Pesticide Manual - 11th edition: Entry number 396

Nematode: Rhabditida: Heterorhabditidae

NOMENCLATURE: **Approved name:** *Heterorhabditis bacteriophora* Poinar.

SOURCE: Commonly occurring soil-inhabiting nematode.

PRODUCTION: Produced by fermentation and sold as third instar larvae.

TARGET PESTS: Effective against a wide range of insect pests but targeted at Japanese beetles.

TARGET CROPS: Used in a wide range of crops, ornamentals and turf.

BIOLOGICAL ACTIVITY: **Biology:** The third stage larvae are the infectious stage and only these can survive outside the host insect as they do not require food. They enter a host through one of its natural openings or through the skin. The nematode larva then releases bacteria into the insect's body and toxins produced by these bacteria kill the insect within 48 hours. The bacteria then digest the insect's body into material that the nematode can feed upon, and the nematode's fourth stage develops within the dead insect. These fourth stage larvae develop into hermaphrodite nematodes which lay as many as 1,500 eggs each. These eggs develop into males and females that are able to reproduce sexually. After mating, the males die and the females will lay eggs in the dead insect if there is enough food available or, if not, the first and second stage larvae develop inside the female nematode's body. As soon as the larvae reach the third stage, they leave the dead insect and seek out a new host. **Predation:** The nematode is a very aggressive parasite and the third instar larvae are able to travel several tens of centimetres in search of a new host. **Duration of development:** The development of the nematode is very dependent on temperature and availability of food.

Efficacy: Very effective for the control of beetles and other insects. Particularly effective against phytophagous insects that are gregarious in habit. **Key reference:** R Gaugler and H K Kaya. 1990. Entomopathogenic nematodes. In *Biological Control*, CRC Press, Boca Raton, Florida, 365 pages.

COMMERCIALISATION: **Formulation:** Sold as water dispersible clay formulation. **Tradenames:** Heteromask – BioLogic, Cruiser – Ecogen, Lawn Patrol – Hydro-Gardens, Nema-top – e-nema, Nema-green – e-nema.

APPLICATION: Apply at a rate of 5×10^5 juveniles per square metre as an overall drench when target insects are present. Ensure that soil temperatures remain above 12 °C and air temperatures should be between 12 and 30 °C for two weeks after application.

PRODUCT SPECIFICATIONS: **Purity:** Sold as infective third instar larvae with no bacterial contaminants. The effectiveness of the formulation can be determined by bioassay on Japanese beetles or other susceptible insects. **Storage conditions:** Store in a refrigerator at 3 to 5 °C. Do not freeze or expose to direct sunlight. **Shelf-life:** Use as soon as possible after delivery.

COMPATIBILITY: Incompatible with broad-spectrum insecticides or benzimidazole-based fungicides.

MAMMALIAN TOXICITY: There are no records of allergic or other adverse reactions in researchers, producers or users of the product.

ENVIRONMENTAL IMPACT AND NON-TARGET TOXICITY: *Heterorhabditis bacteriophora* occurs in Nature and is not expected to show any adverse effects on non-target organisms or the environment.

3:106   *Heterorhabditis megidis*

Insect parasitic nematode

The Pesticide Manual - 11th edition: Entry number 396

Nematode: Rhabditida: Heterorhabditidae

NOMENCLATURE: **Approved name:** *Heterorhabditis megidis* Poinar, Jackson and Klein, MicroBio Strain UK 211 and HW79 (Dutch strain). **Other names:** *Heterorhabditis bacteriophora* Poinar; parasitic nematode.

SOURCE: Widespread throughout the world.

PRODUCTION: Produced by fermentation in a liquid diet or sometimes reared in soil on weevils. Sold as third stage infectious juveniles.

TARGET PESTS: Soil insects such as the larvae and pupae of black vine weevils (*Otiorhynchus sulcatus* (Fabricius)).

TARGET CROPS: Ornamentals and vegetables in glasshouses and outdoors.

BIOLOGICAL ACTIVITY: **Biology:** The third stage larvae are the infectious stage and only these can survive outside the host insect as they do not require food. They enter a host through one of its natural openings or through the skin. The nematode larva then releases bacteria (*Photorhabdus luminescens* Boenare Akhurst and Mourani) into the insect's body and toxins produced by these bacteria kill the insect within 48 hours. The bacteria then digest the insect's body into material that the nematode can feed upon, and the nematode's fourth stage develops within the dead insect. These fourth stage larvae develop into hermaphrodite nematodes which lay as many as 1,500 eggs each. These eggs develop into males and females that are able to reproduce sexually. After mating, the males die and the females will lay eggs in the dead insect if there is enough food available or, if not, the first and second stage larvae develop inside the female nematode's body. As soon as the larvae reach the third stage, they leave the dead insect and seek out a new host. **Predation:** Infectious nematodes can travel distances of several tens of centimetres in the soil in search of new food sources.
Duration of development: Growth rate is very dependent upon temperature and it is likely that the nematode will complete its lifecycle in 14 to 20 days in the presence of sufficient soil insects. **Efficacy:** Very effective predators that can be used to eradicate vine weevil populations. **Key reference:** R Gaugler and H K Kaya. 1990. Entomopathogenic nematodes. In *Biological Control*, CRC Press, Boca Raton, Florida, 365 pages.

COMMERCIALISATION: **Formulation:** Sold as infective third stage larvae. **Tradenames:** Dickmaulrüsslernematoden – Andermatt, Larvanem – Koppert, Nemasys H – MicroBio and Biobest, Heterorhabditis megidis – Neudorff.

APPLICATION: Apply as a drench overall when target insects are present. The area to be treated must be moist at application and must not be allowed to dry out after treatment. The temperature of the soil or compost should be between 12 and 30 °C at application and for 14 days after application. Apply at a rate of 5×10^5 juveniles per square metre, repeated every two weeks as necessary.

PRODUCT SPECIFICATIONS: **Purity:** Product contains only third stage infective larvae. Efficacy of the product may be checked by a bioassay on vine weevils (*Otiorhyncus sulcatus*) or on larvae of *Galleria mellonella* (Linnaeus) or *Tenebrio molitor* Linnaeus. Actual nematode numbers may be determined by direct counting under a microscope.
Storage conditions: Store in a refrigerator at 3 to 5 °C. Do not freeze or expose to direct sunlight. **Shelf-life:** Use as soon as possible after delivery.

COMPATIBILITY: Incompatible with soil insecticides. Soil moisture is necessary for the nematodes to move and infect their hosts.

MAMMALIAN TOXICITY: No allergic or other adverse reaction has been reported by researchers, production staff or users following the use of *Heterorhabditis megidis* or its associated bacterium.

ENVIRONMENTAL IMPACT AND NON-TARGET TOXICITY: It is not expected that *Heterorhabditis megidis* or its associated bacterium will have any adverse effect on non-target organisms or on the environment.

3:107 *Lymantria dispar* nucleopoly-hedrovirus
Insecticidal baculovirus

Virus: Baculoviridae: Nucleopolyhedrovirus

NOMENCLATURE: **Approved name:** *Lymantria dispar* nucleopolyhedrovirus.
Other names: gypsy moth virus; LdMNPV; LdNPV.

SOURCE: Isolated from infected gypsy moth (*Lymantria dispar* (Linnaeus)) larvae by the USDA. The "expanded gypsy moth research, development and application program" was part of the USDA "combined forest pest research and development program" co-ordinated by the Forest Insect and Disease Research Laboratory, Hampden, Connecticut and culminated in the registration of the product in 1978 by the EPA.

PRODUCTION: Produced *in vivo* in gypsy moth larvae reared under controlled conditions.

TARGET PESTS: Gypsy moth (*Lymantria dispar* (Linnaeus)).

TARGET CROPS: Forestry and landscape trees.

BIOLOGICAL ACTIVITY: **Mode of action:** As with all insect baculoviruses, *Lymantria dispar* MNPV must be ingested to exert an effect. Following ingestion, the protective protein matrices of the polyhedral occlusion bodies (OBs) of the virus are dissolved within the midgut and the virus particles enter the insect's haemolymph. These virus particles invade nearly all cell types in the larval body where they multiply, leading to its death. Shortly after the death of the larva, the integument ruptures releasing very large numbers of OBs. **Efficacy:** The virus infects only gypsy moth. **Key references:** 1) R R Granados and B A Frederici (eds.). 1986. *The Biology of Baculoviruses, Vols. 1 and 2.* CRC Press, Boca Raton, Florida, USA. 2) D J Leisy and J R Fuxa. 1996. Natural and engineered viral agents for insect control. In *Crop Protection Agents from Nature: Natural Products and Analogues*, L G Copping (ed.), Royal Society of Chemistry, Cambridge, UK.

COMMERCIALISATION: **Formulation:** Sold through the US Forestry Service as a liquid suspension. **Tradenames:** Gypcheck – US Forestry Service.

APPLICATION: Two aerial applications of 2.5×10^{11} polyhedral inclusion bodies (PIBs) per hectare will typically restrict defoliation to below 55 to 60% and sometimes below 30%.

PRODUCT SPECIFICATIONS: **Purity:** Products contain polyhedral inclusion bodies and no contaminating human and mammalian bacterial pathogens. **Storage conditions:** Store in a refrigerator in a sealed container. Do not freeze and do not expose to direct sunlight.
Shelf-life: Formulations can be stored for up to six months.

COMPATIBILITY: It is unusual to apply *Lymantria dispar* MNPV with other insecticides. Incompatible with strong oxidisers, acids, bases or chlorinated water.

MAMMALIAN TOXICITY: There are no reports of allergic or other adverse reactions to *Lymantria dispar* MNPV from research workers or manufacturing or field staff. Considered to be non-toxic to mammals.

ENVIRONMENTAL IMPACT AND NON-TARGET TOXICITY: *Lymantria dispar* MNPV occurs in Nature and is not expected to have any adverse effects on non-target organisms or the environment.

3:108 *Mamestra brassicae* nucleopoly-hedrovirus *Insecticidal baculovirus*

The Pesticide Manual - 11th edition: Entry number 450

Virus: Baculoviridae: Nucleopolyhedrovirus

NOMENCLATURE: **Approved name:** *Mamestra brassicae* nucleopolyhedrovirus. **Other names:** MbMNPV.

SOURCE: Occurs in Nature as a natural parasite of the cabbage moth. It was first isolated from virosed larvae of the cabbage moth (*Mamestra brassicae* (Linnaeus)) collected in France by INRA researchers. The virus isolate was developed by NPP (Natural Plant Protection), France. It is also able to infect other lepidopteran species.

PRODUCTION: MbNPV is multiplied *in vivo* on *Mamestra brassicae* infested at the larval stage and isolated by centrifugation techniques. The product is then formulated as a suspension comprising the entomopathogenic virus particles and specific additives.

TARGET PESTS: Mamestrin is registered in France for the control of *Mamestra brassicae* and may be used against *Helicoverpa armigera* (Hübner), *Phthorimaea operculella* Zeller and *Plutella xylostella* (Linnaeus).

TARGET CROPS: Mamestrin can be used on a variety of crops including vegetables, potatoes, brassicae and ornamentals.

BIOLOGICAL ACTIVITY: **Mode of action:** As with all insect baculoviruses, *Mamestra brassicae* NPV must be ingested to exert an effect. Following ingestion, the virus enters the insect's haemolymph where it multiplies in the insect body, leading to its death. **Biology:** MbMNPV is more active on small larvae than later larval instars. The virus is ingested by the feeding larva and the virus protein matrix is dissolved in the insect's midgut (that is alkaline), releasing the virus particles still enclosed in their protein coats. These pass through the peritrophic membrane and invade midgut cells by fusion with the microvilli. The virus particles invade the cell nuclei where they are uncoated and replicated. Initial replication produces non-occluded virus particles to hasten the invasion of the host insect but later the virus particles are produced with protein matrices and remain infective when released from the dead insects. **Duration of development:** First to third instar larvae die within seven days of treatment. **Efficacy:** MbMNPV acts relatively slowly as it has to be ingested and infect its host before it exerts any effect on the insect. **Key references:** 1) R R Granados and B A Frederici (eds.). 1986. *The Biology of Baculoviruses, Vols. 1 and 2*, CRC Press, Boca Raton, Florida, USA. 2) D J Leisy and J R Fuxa. 1996. Natural and engineered viral agents for insect control. In *Crop*

Protection Agents from Nature: Natural Products and Analogues, L G Copping (ed.), Royal Society of Chemistry, Cambridge, UK.

COMMERCIALISATION: **Formulation:** Sold as a liquid formulation. **Tradenames:** Mamestrin – NPP and Calliope, Virin-EKS – NPO Vector. **Patents:** FR 8717748; EP 90401016.

APPLICATION: Mamestrin should be applied to foliage at a dose of 4 litres product/ha/application. It has potential for integrated crop management (ICM). Monitoring of adult insect laying patterns and targeted application at newly hatched eggs gives better control than on a mixed age population. It is important to ensure coverage of the foliage to effect good control.

PRODUCT SPECIFICATIONS: **Purity:** Mamestrin contains 2.5×10^{12} polyhedral inclusion bodies (PIBs)/litre. The infectivity of the formulated product is assessed by bioassay against *Mamestra brassicae* larvae. **Storage conditions:** Store under dry conditions at 4 °C. **Shelf-life:** The product has a shelf-life of 2 years when stored under the appropriate conditions.

COMPATIBILITY: Compatible with most crop protection agents that do not repel the target insects. Do not apply with copper-based fungicides. Use non-chlorinated water with a neutral pH as a carrier.

MAMMALIAN TOXICITY: **Acute oral LD$_{50}$:** male rats $>10.2 \times 10^9$ polyhedral inclusion bodies (PIBs)/kg body weight, female rats $>10.95 \times 10^9$ PIBs/kg body weight. **Skin and eye:** Mamestrin shows no skin penetration. **Other toxicological effects:** Inhalation LD$_{50}$ rats $>7.5 \times 10^{10}$ PIBs/kg body weight. No toxicity, infectivity or pathogenicity was detected after an intranasal installation in rats of 7.5×10^{10} PIBs/kg body weight. The NOEL (99 days) for mice was $>1.5 \times 10^9$ PIBs/kg body weight daily. There is no evidence of acute or chronic toxicity, eye or skin irritation to mammals although Mamestrin may induce a slight hypersensitive reaction. No allergic symptoms or health problems have been observed with research workers, manufacturing staff or users.

ENVIRONMENTAL IMPACT AND NON-TARGET TOXICITY: *Mamestra brassicae* NPV is not toxic or infective to birds and is not toxic to fish. The LD$_{50}$ (oral and contact) to honeybees is $>5 \times 10^4$ PIBs/bee.

3:109   *Metarhizium anisopliae*

Fungal insecticide

Mitosporitic fungus: Previously classified as: Deuteromycetes: Moniliales

NOMENCLATURE: **Approved name:** *Metarhizium anisopliae* Sorok.
Other names: previously known as *Penicillium anisopliae* Vuill. and *Entomophthora anisopliae* Metsch. **Common name:** green muscardine fungus.

SOURCE: Commonly occurring fungus often associated with dead insects.

PRODUCTION: Produced by controlled, deep fermentation.

TARGET PESTS: Effective against a range of Coleoptera and Lepidoptera. BioBlast is used to control termites.

TARGET CROPS: Used in a variety of different crops including glasshouse-grown vegetables and ornamentals.

BIOLOGICAL ACTIVITY: **Mode of action:** *Metarhizium anisopliae* is a very effective entomopathogen. It attacks the target insect by penetrating its cuticle and invading the haemolymph. **Efficacy:** Applied as a foliar spray to infested crops, the entomopathogen invades and immobilises the insect within two days. Death occurs after seven to ten days. The mycosed insects remain adhered to the crop and additional spores are released to maintain a high level of infective material on the crop. Following treatment of a termite infestation, infection of as few as 5 to 10% of the population will lead to the destruction of the entire colony over a two-week period.

COMMERCIALISATION: **Formulation:** Sold as an injectable formulation for termite control and as a suspension of spores for control of foliar pests. **Tradenames:** BioBlast – EcoScience and Terminex, Ago Biocontrol Metarhizium 50 – Ago Biocontrol.

APPLICATION: *Metarhizium anisopliae* is applied as a foliar spray when insects are present on the crop. It is also injected into termite galleries and areas with termite mud tubes.

PRODUCT SPECIFICATIONS: **Purity:** Free from contaminants. **Storage conditions:** Store in a cool, dry place out of direct sunlight. **Shelf-life:** If stored under recommended conditions, the formulation will remain viable for 12 months.

COMPATIBILITY: Used alone.

MAMMALIAN TOXICITY: There are no reports of allergic or other adverse toxicological effects from research, manufacturing, formulation or field staff.

ENVIRONMENTAL IMPACT AND NON-TARGET TOXICITY: *Metarhizium anisopliae* occurs widely in Nature and is not expected to have any adverse effects on non-target organisms or on the environment.

3:110　*Metarhizium flavoviride*

Mitosporitic fungus: Previously classified as: Deuteromycetes: Moniliales

NOMENCLATURE: **Approved name:** *Metarhizium flavoviride*.

SOURCE: Widely occurring entomopathogen isolated from mycosed insects.

PRODUCTION: Produced by fermentation.

TARGET PESTS: Grasshoppers and locusts.

BIOLOGICAL ACTIVITY: **Mode of action:** *Metarhizium flavoviride* is a very effective entomopathogen. It attacks the target insect by penetrating its cuticle and invading the haemolymph. Conditions of high humidity are essential for cuticular penetration and this is effected by the appropriate formulation technique. The strain that is being commercialised for use against grasshoppers and locusts has been shown to be highly virulent under tropical conditions. **Efficacy:** The entomopathogen invades the cuticle of the target insect relatively quickly and the insect will become lethargic and cease feeding within two to three days of invasion. Death follows after seven to ten days with the sporulation of the fungus outside the cadaver providing a source of spores for continued infestation.

COMMERCIALISATION: **Formulation:** Sold as an ultra-low volume (ULV) formulation of the dried fungal spores in mineral oils. **Tradenames:** Green Muscle – International Institute of Biological Control.

APPLICATION: Applied using controlled droplet application techniques to optimise droplet size to facilitate insect invasion.

PRODUCT SPECIFICATIONS: **Purity:** Contains no contaminants. **Storage conditions:** Store in a cool, dry situation out of direct sunlight. **Shelf-life:** If stored correctly, the formulation will remain effective for twelve months.

COMPATIBILITY: *Metarhizium flavoviride* can be applied with low rates of conventional insecticides as this has been shown to reduce the time taken to kill the target insects from more than a week to three to four days. However, it is usual to recommend the use of the product alone.

MAMMALIAN TOXICITY: *Metarhizium flavoviride* occurs widely in Nature. There have been no reports of allergic or other adverse toxicological effects by research or manufacturing staff, formulators or field workers.

ENVIRONMENTAL IMPACT AND NON-TARGET TOXICITY: *Metarhizium flavoviride* is not expected to have any adverse effects on non-target organisms or the environment.

3:111   *Myrothecium verrucaria*

Biological nematicide

Mitosporitic fungus: Previously classified as: Deuteromycetes: Moniliales

NOMENCLATURE: **Approved name:** *Myrothecium verrucaria* (von Albertini and von Schweinitz) Ditmar ex von Stendel.

SOURCE: The fungus occurs in soil and the commercial strain was isolated from a nematode in the USA.

PRODUCTION: Produced by fermentation.

TARGET PESTS: Plant parasitic nematodes including root-knot (*Meloidogyne* spp.), cyst (*Heterodera* spp.), sting (*Belonolaimus longicaudatus* Rau) and burrowing (*Radopholus similis* (Cobb)) nematodes.

TARGET CROPS: Developed for use in turf, tobacco, grapes, citrus, brassicae and bananas.

BIOLOGICAL ACTIVITY: **Biology:** *Myrothecium verrucaria* has direct contact activity against nematodes. The fungal spores germinate in the rhizosphere and the mycelium invades any nematodes that are present. In addition, the fungus modifies the microflora of the root zone, leading to a beneficial plant response. **Key reference:** P Warrior, R M Beach, P A Grau, J M Conley and G W Kirfman. 1998. Commercial development and introduction of DiTera, a new nematicide. In *9th International Congress of Pesticide Chemistry*, Royal Society of Chemistry, Cambridge, UK.

COMMERCIALISATION: **Formulation:** Sold as a powder formulation. **Tradenames:** DiTera – Abbott.

APPLICATION: Applied as a seed treatment or as a soil drench.

PRODUCT SPECIFICATIONS: **Purity:** Contains only spores of *Myrothecium verrucaria*. Viability can be checked by plating out on nutrient agar, incubating in the laboratory and counting the number of colonies that develop. **Storage conditions:** Store in a cool, dry, sealed container. Do not freeze and keep out of direct sunlight. **Shelf-life:** Retains viability for up to one year.

COMPATIBILITY: Can be applied with other compounds but not fungicides. It is usual not to mix with chemicals as it has a role in integrated crop management systems.

MAMMALIAN TOXICITY: Toxicological studies indicate a very favourable acute and non-acute toxicological profile. There is no evidence of allergic reactions.

ENVIRONMENTAL IMPACT AND NON-TARGET TOXICITY: *Myrothecium verrucaria* occurs widely in Nature and is not expected to have any adverse effects on non-target organisms or on the environment.

3:112 Neodiprion sertifer/N. lecontei nucleopolyhedrovirus

Insecticidal baculovirus

Virus: Baculoviridae: Nucleopolyhedrovirus

NOMENCLATURE: **Approved name:** *Neodiprion sertifer* nucleopolyhedrovirus and *Neodiprion lecontei* nucleopolyhedrovirus. **Other names:** sawfly virus; NsMNPV; NlMNPV; NsNPV; NlNPV, NeseNPV, NeleNPV.

SOURCE: Naturally occurring virus isolated from sawflies in forests in the USA and Canada. Nucleopolyhedroviruses have been isolated from 25 species of sawfly.

PRODUCTION: The virus is produced from the propagation of sawflies in the field. Selected high-density populations are treated with the virus and, several days later, the diseased insects are collected and frozen. Before application, the larvae are freeze-dried and ground into a fine powder.

TARGET PESTS: Sawflies (*Neodiprion* spp.).

TARGET CROPS: Forests.

BIOLOGICAL ACTIVITY: **Mode of action:** The virus is ingested by the feeding larva and the protective protein matrix is dissolved in the insect's midgut (that is alkaline), releasing the virus particles. These pass through the peritrophic membrane and invade midgut cells by fusion with the microvilli. The virus particles invade the cell nuclei of the epithelial cells where they are uncoated and replicated. Initial replication produces non-occluded virus particles but later the virus particles are produced with protein matrices and remain infective when released from the dead insects. **Biology:** As with all insect baculoviruses, *Neodiprion sertifer* and *Neodiprion lecontei* NPV must be ingested to exert an effect. Following ingestion, the virus is unusual in that it infects only the epithelial cells of the larval midgut. However, the infection is sufficient to lead to larval mortality. **Efficacy:** Sawflies are gregarious forest pests and this makes them particularly vulnerable to viral epizootics. The infection of a single larva will always lead to the death of an entire colony, which gives the advantage that low rates of use are sufficient for population control. **Key references:** 1) R R Granados and B A Frederici (eds.). 1986. *The Biology of Baculoviruses, Vols. 1 and 2.* CRC Press, Boca Raton, Florida, USA. 2) D J Leisy and J R Fuxa. 1996. Natural and engineered viral agents for insect control. In *Crop Protection Agents from Nature: Natural Products and Analogues*, L G Copping (ed.), Royal Society of Chemistry, Cambridge, UK.

COMMERCIALISATION: **Formulation:** Sold as a powder derived from ground, freeze dried infected larvae. Neochek-S (derived from *N. sertifer* (Geoffrey)) is sold and used only under the supervision of the US-EPA and Leconteivirus (derived from *N. lecontei* (Fitch)) is sold and used under supervision from the Canadian Forestry Service. **Tradenames:** Neochek-S – US Forest Service, Leconteivirus – Canadian Forestry Service, Monisarmiovirus – Kemira, Virox – Oxford Virology.

3. Living Systems

APPLICATION: The recommended rate of application is 5×10^9 polyhedral inclusion bodies (PIBs) or 50 virus-killed larvae per hectare. A single application will keep a forest free of sawflies for several years.

PRODUCT SPECIFICATIONS: **Purity:** The products contain ground, freeze-dried, infected larvae. **Storage conditions:** Store in a cool, dry situation. May be frozen. Do not expose to direct sunlight or high temperatures. **Shelf-life:** The product retains its viability for up to two years.

COMPATIBILITY: It is unusual to use the product in combination with other crop protection agents. Not compatible with strong acids or alkalis.

MAMMALIAN TOXICITY: There are no reports of allergic or other adverse effects of the products on research workers or manufacturing or field staff. Considered to be a product of low mammalian toxicity.

ENVIRONMENTAL IMPACT AND NON-TARGET TOXICITY: It is not expected that any of the products will have any adverse effects on non-target organisms or on the environment.

3:113   *Nosema locustae*   Biological insecticide

Microspora: Microsporida: Nosematicae

NOMENCLATURE: **Approved name:** *Nosema locustae* Canning.
Development code: SHA 117001.

SOURCE: Isolated from grasshoppers in the USA.

PRODUCTION: *Nosema locustae* is produced by *in vivo* rearing in grasshoppers.

TARGET PESTS: Grasshoppers.

TARGET CROPS: Pastures, rangeland and many other crops.

BIOLOGICAL ACTIVITY: **Mode of action:** *Nosema locustae* has to be ingested to be effective. Second and third instar, wingless nymphs are the most susceptible. The microsporidial spores germinate in the grasshopper's midgut and invade the insect's body, leading to lethal infections. The response of the grasshoppers to infection varies with some dying shortly after infection whilst others become weakened and sluggish. In this condition, the insects do not feed but are often cannibalised by healthy grasshoppers that subsequently become infected. Egg production is reduced by 60 to 80% in the surviving adults and, in many cases, the *Nosema locustae* parasite is passed on to new generations through the eggs. Once established in the population, the microsporidium will usually survive for at least a year.
Biology: *Nosema locustae* is a microsporidial pathogen that infects approximately 60 different species of grasshopper as well as Mormon crickets. Death follows shortly after infection.
Efficacy: *Nosema locustae* is effective against many species of grasshopper and Mormon

crickets. It will not control the Southern lubber grasshopper or other cricket species.

Key reference: W M Brooks. 1988. Entomogenous protozoa. In C M Ignoffo (ed.), *Handbook of Natural Pesticides Volume V, Microbial Insecticides, Part A, Entomogenous Protozoa and Fungi,* CRC Press Inc, Boca Raton, Florida, USA, pp. 1–149.

COMMERCIALISATION: **Formulation:** Sold as baits with *Nosema locustae* spores sprayed onto the surface of bran and thickened with 0.25% hydroxymethyl cellulose as a sticker. **Tradenames:** Nolo Bait – M&R Durango, Grasshopper Control Semaspore Bait – Beneficial Insect Company.

APPLICATION: The bait is distributed throughout the crop to be protected either by hand or with a spreader. Better control is achieved if the bait is applied in the early morning. When grasshopper populations reach more than eight per square metre, apply 1 kg product per hectare. Repeat after four to six weeks if the population remains high.

PRODUCT SPECIFICATIONS: **Purity:** Product contains *Nosema locustae* spores attached to bran bait. Efficacy can be determined by bioassay on grasshopper nymphs. **Storage conditions:** Store in a sealed container at 0 to 6 °C. Do not expose to direct sunlight. **Shelf-life:** Spores remain infective for up to 18 months if stored according to the manufacturer's recommendations.

COMPATIBILITY: It is unusual to apply *Nosema locustae* with other pest control agents.

MAMMALIAN TOXICITY: *Nosema locustae* does not irritate, replicate or accumulate in rats, guinea pigs or rabbits. **Oral LD$_{50}$:** rats >5 g/kg (4.49×10^9 spores/kg). Considered to be non-toxic to mammals. **Toxicity class:** EPA (formulation) IV.

ENVIRONMENTAL IMPACT AND NON-TARGET TOXICITY: *Nosema locustae* does not replicate or accumulate in rainbow trout or bluegill sunfish. Honeybees and other beneficial organisms are not infected.

3:114   *Paecilomyces fumosoroseus*
Biological insecticide

The Pesticide Manual - 11th edition: Entry number 549

Mitosporitic fungus: Previously classified as: Deuteromycetes: Moniliales

NOMENCLATURE: **Approved name:** *Paecilomyces fumosoroseus* (Wise) Bronn and Smith strain Apopka 97 (PFR 97).

SOURCE: *Paecilomyces fumosoroseus* has been isolated from a range of infected insects around the world. The Apopka 97 strain was isolated in 1986 from the mealybug, *Phenacoccus solani* Ferris, on *Gynura* (a velvet plant) growing in a conservatory in Apopka, Florida. This strain was licensed to Thermo Trilogy Corporation (formerly W R Grace and Co) who developed the production and formulation. European development has been undertaken by Biobest.

PRODUCTION: *Paecilomyces fumosoroseus* is produced by fermentation and is sold as a suspension of spores in a WG formulation.

TARGET PESTS: For control of whitefly (*Trialeurodes vaporariorum* (Westwood) and *Bemisia tabaci* (Gennadius)). Also shows some activity against aphids, thrips and spider mites.

TARGET CROPS: Recommended for use on ornamentals and food crops in glasshouses and outdoors.

BIOLOGICAL ACTIVITY: **Mode of action:** *Paecilomyces fumosoroseus* spores germinate on the body of the target insect and it exerts its insecticidal action through penetration of the cuticle and subsequent fungal growth within the haemolymph and other tissues of the infested insects. Sporulation from dead insects leads to infection of epidemic proportions. **Biology:** *Paecilomyces fumosoroseus* cannot grow at temperatures above 32 °C. It exerts its effects on whitefly larvae by enzymic and mechanical entry through the insect cuticle and subsequently invades the haemolymph. After insect death, the fungus releases spores following penetration of the insect exoskeleton by the conidiophores. *Paecilomyces fumosoroseus* does not produce mycotoxins. **Key references:** 1) K Bolkmans and G Sterk. 1995. PreFeRal WG (*Paecilomyces fumosoroseus* strain Apopka 97), a new microbial insecticide for the biological control of whiteflies in greenhouses. *Medische Faculteit Landbouwwetenschappen Rijksuniversiteit Gent*, **60**, 707–11. 2) G Sterk, K Bolkmans and J Eyals. 1996. A new microbial insecticide, *Paecilomyces fumosoroseus* strain Apopka 97, for the control of greenhouse whitefly. *Brighton Crop Protection Conference – Pests & Diseases*. **2**, 461–6.

COMMERCIALISATION: **Formulation:** Sold as a water dispersible granule (WG) containing 1×10^9 colony forming units per gram. **Tradenames:** PreFeRal – Thermo Trilogy.

APPLICATION: High volume sprays ensuring good coverage of the foliage should be applied at a dose rate of 10 g product per litre (14 oz. per 100 gallons).

PRODUCT SPECIFICATIONS: **Purity:** The fermentation procedure is carried out under controlled conditions and only spores of *Paecilomyces fumosoreus* are found within the product. The viability of the spores can be determined by plating out on agar, incubating in the laboratory for 48 hours and counting the colonies formed. **Storage conditions:** The formulated product should be stored in dry, refrigerated conditions at 4 °C. Do not freeze. **Shelf-life:** If stored under the correct conditions, the formulated product will remain biologically active for over 6 months.

COMPATIBILITY: Cannot be tank-mixed or applied with fungicides. *Paecilomyces fumosoroseus* does not infect beneficial insects or insect parasites and predators and so it can be used in combination with other whitefly control measures such as *Encarsia formosa* Gahan and *Macrolophus caliginosus*.

MAMMALIAN TOXICITY: *Paecilomyces fumosoroseus* shows no oral toxicity, pathogenicity or infectivity to any tested animals at 1×10^6 colony forming units (cfu)/animal. **Skin and eye:** No dermal toxicity, pathogenicity or infectivity at 1×10^9 cfu/animal. Slight dermal irritancy reversible within 72 hours at 1×10^8 cfu/animal. Practically non-irritating to the eye at $>1 \times 10^7$ cfu/animal. **Other toxicological effects:** Not a dermal sensitiser at 1×10^9 cfu/animal.

ENVIRONMENTAL IMPACT AND NON-TARGET TOXICITY: *Paecilomyces fumosoroseus* strain Apopka 97 is harmless to non-target organisms, including predatory and beneficial insects, mammals and birds. It is a soil fungus that is widespread in Nature and is not expected to show any adverse environmental effects.

3:115 *Phasmarhabditis hermaphrodita*
Mollusc parasitic nematode

Nematode: Rhabdita: Phasmarhabditidae

NOMENCLATURE: **Approved name:** *Phasmarhabditis hermaphrodita* (Schneider) Andrassy. **Other names:** mollusc parasitic nematode.

SOURCE: Found widely in soil, a natural pathogenic nematode.

PRODUCTION: Produced by fermentation and sold as third stage juveniles.

TARGET PESTS: Very effective against slugs.

TARGET CROPS: Vegetables and ornamentals in glasshouses and outdoors.

BIOLOGICAL ACTIVITY: **Biology:** *Phasmarhabditis hermaphrodita* third stage juveniles invade slugs through the dorsal pore (the raised area on the slug's back). Once inside the host, the nematodes release bacteria that produce toxins which prevent the slugs from feeding within 72 hours. The nematodes feed on the immobilised and dying slugs and the juvenile nematodes develop into adults that breed producing eggs which hatch into juvenile nematodes. The mantle of the infected slugs swells during this process with the slugs dying underground after seven to ten days. The nematodes may continue to reproduce in the body of the slug or infective third stage juveniles may pass into the soil to seek more hosts depending, upon the availability of food. **Predation:** Infective nematodes can travel several centimetres in search of new hosts. **Duration of development:** The development of the nematodes is very dependent upon soil temperatures. In the presence of sufficient slugs and at temperatures between 5 and 25 °C, it would be expected that the life-cycle would be completed within 14 to 20 days. **Efficacy:** Very effective predators of slugs with rates of 3×10^5 nematodes per square metre reducing slug damage to less than 1% within 15 days. **Key reference:** R Gaughler and H K Kaya. 1990. Entomopathogenic nematodes. In *Biological Control*, CRC Press, Boca Raton, Florida, 365 pages.

COMMERCIALISATION: **Formulation:** Sold as infective third stage juveniles in a moist, inert carrier. **Tradenames:** Nemaslug – MicroBio.

APPLICATION: For crops that are attacked during germination or immediately after emergence or planting out, apply four days prior to emergence or transplanting. Applications to crops that are susceptible later in the season, such as potatoes, should be made six to seven weeks before harvest or when the crop is most sensitive to slug attack. Apply to moist soil or compost at a rate of 3×10^5 juveniles per square metre, as a drench, when the soil temperature is between 5 and 25 °C. A single application is effective for up to six weeks. For plants that require prolonged protection, a second treatment may be necessary. Apply within four hours of diluting the formulation and stir to prevent sedimentation. For best activity, apply in the evening. Do not use close to ponds, as this may reduce the beneficial water snail population.

PRODUCT SPECIFICATIONS: **Purity:** Formulations contain third stage infective nematode juveniles in an inert carrier. Efficacy can be measured by bioassay on host slugs and numbers confirmed by counting under a microscope. **Storage conditions:** Store for no more than two days in a cool dark place. If kept for longer than two days, the product must be stored in a refrigerator at temperatures around 5 °C. Do not freeze and avoid direct sunlight and temperatures above 35 °C. **Shelf-life:** The juvenile nematodes remain infective for relatively short periods after delivery.

COMPATIBILITY: Compatible with a wide range of conventional agrochemicals but should not be used with benzimidazole-based fungicides or soil-applied insecticides. Compatible with all IPM or biological crop protection strategies.

MAMMALIAN TOXICITY: *Phasmarhabditis hermaphrodita* and its associated bacterium have not caused any allergic or other adverse reactions in researchers, production staff or users.

ENVIRONMENTAL IMPACT AND NON-TARGET TOXICITY: *Phasmarhabditis hermaphrodita* and its associated bacterium would not be expected to have any effects on non-target organisms nor any adverse environmental effects.

3:116   *Phlebiopsis gigantea* Biological fungicide

The Pesticide Manual - 11th edition: Entry number 569

Fungus: Basidiomycetes: Agaricales

NOMENCLATURE: **Approved name:** *Phlebiopsis gigantea* (Fr.) Jul. **Other names:** previously known as *Phlebia gigantea* and *Peniophora gigantea*.

SOURCE: The strain used in the product Rotstop was originally isolated in 1987 by the Finnish Forest Research Institute from Norway spruce log left in the forest. It was used as a stump treatment on pine and spruce in 1988 and was re-isolated in 1989 from a Norway spruce stump. In 1991, it was formulated into the product by Kemira Oy.

PRODUCTION: Produced by fermentation and formulated as fungal spores.

TARGET PESTS: Developed for the control of *Heterobasidion annosum* Bref. also known as *Fomes annosus* Cke.

TARGET CROPS: Pine and spruce tree stumps.

BIOLOGICAL ACTIVITY: **Mode of action:** *Phlebiopsis gigantea* exerts its effect by competing for the entry sites of the pathogen on the cut stumps of pine and spruce trees. **Biology:** The fungus invades the cut surface of spruce and pine trees and prevents the subsequent invasion of the damaged surface by the pathogenic fungus *Heterobasidium annosum*, the causal organism of root and butt rot. **Efficacy:** Very effective if applied at harvest when the temperature is above 8 °C. **Key reference:** K Korhonen *et al.* 1993. Control of *Heterobasidium annosum* by stump treatment with Rotstop, a new commercial formulation of *Phlebiopsis gigantea*. In *Proc. of 8th International Conference on Root and Butt Rots*, Wik, Sweden and Haikko, Finland, August 9th – 16th, 1993, M Johanson and J Stenlid (eds.), IUFRO, Uppsala, Sweden, pp. 675–85.

COMMERCIALISATION: **Formulation:** Formulated as a wettable powder (WP) containing 1×10^6 to 1×10^7 colony forming units (cfu) per gram. **Tradenames:** Rotstop – Kemira.

APPLICATION: Recommended application time is when *Heterobasidium annosum* is capable of spreading or growing on stumps (during the vegetative period when the temperature is above 8 °C). The product is mixed with water and the suspension is sprayed on the stump surface with a spraying device on the harvester head at tree felling or manually after felling.

PRODUCT SPECIFICATIONS: **Purity:** The viability and purity of the product is tested by determining the number of colony forming units following plating out on agar and incubation. The agar used should contain milled wood as the sole energy source to confirm the viability of the fungus. If the test is run in the presence of *Heterobasidium annosum*, an indication of the competitive efficacy of the fungus can be made. The efficacy of the product can also be determined by treating the upper surface of freshly cut tree stem pieces and exposing these to spores of *Heterobasidium annosum*. **Storage conditions:** Store for short periods (one to two weeks) at room temperature. Store unopened packages at temperatures below 8 °C. **Shelf-life:** One to two weeks at room temperature. Up to twelve months in unopened container at <8 °C.

COMPATIBILITY: Rotstop is not compatible with chemical fungicides. There has been no application for authorisation to use Rotstop with any other pesticide.

MAMMALIAN TOXICITY: Application of the product does not cause exposure of man and mammals to the fungus above that which occurs naturally. There have been no reports of allergic or other adverse toxicological effects from research workers, manufacturing staff or users. Inhalation of the product and skin contact should be avoided by use of standard protective equipment.

ENVIRONMENTAL IMPACT AND NON-TARGET TOXICITY: *Phlebiopsis gigantea* is a natural component of the microflora of coniferous forests and, as such, is not expected to have any effect on non-target organisms nor show any adverse environmental properties. It is possible that the long-term use of Rotstop will reduce the occurrence of the fungus in treated areas and lead to an enhanced suppression of *Heterobasidion annosum*.

3:117 *Phytophthora palmivora*

Biological herbicide

Fungus: Oomycetes: Peronosporales

NOMENCLATURE: **Approved name:** *Phytophthora palmivora* (Butl.) Butl.

SOURCE: Naturally occurring soil pathogenic fungus. Isolated from strangler vine (*Morrenia odorata* (H&A) Lindl.) in a Florida citrus grove.

PRODUCTION: Manufactured by fermentation.

TARGET PESTS: *Morrenia odorata*, the strangler vine or milkweed vine.

TARGET CROPS: Citrus and other perennial crops.

BIOLOGICAL ACTIVITY: **Biology:** *Phytophthora palmivora* invades the strangler vine via the roots. It is specific to the weed and may take six to ten weeks to kill it. After application, populations of *Morrenia odorata* will continue to fall but complete control in an orchard may not be achieved for up to a year after treatment. **Key references:** 1) M P Greaves. 1996. Microbial herbicides – factors in development. In *Crop Protection Agents from Nature: Natural Products and Analogues*, L G Copping (ed.), Royal Society of Chemistry, Cambridge, UK, pp. 444–67. 2) W H Ridings, D J Mitchell, C L Schoulties and N E El-Gholl. 1976. Biological control of milkweed vine in Florida citrus groves with a pathotype of *Phytophthora citrophthora*. In *Proceedings IV International Symposium of Biological Control of Weeds*.

COMMERCIALISATION: **Formulation:** Sold as a liquid suspension containing 6.7×10^5 living chlamydospores per ml. **Tradenames:** DeVine – Abbott.

APPLICATION: Apply to soil between May and September after the strangler vine has germinated. Ensure that the soil is wet at the time of application and it may be necessary to irrigate after three days to maintain soil moisture content. Apply at a rate of 750 mls/ha (about 1×10^9 chlamydospores per hectare). DeVine can be applied by a boom sprayer using at least 80 litres per hectare of water, by chemigation ensuring that the product is applied towards the end of the irrigation or through sprinkler irrigation. Apply only once a season.

PRODUCT SPECIFICATIONS: **Purity:** The product contains 6.7×10^5 living chlamydospores of *Phytophthora palmivora* per ml. **Storage conditions:** Store under refrigeration, prevent from freezing and do not expose to direct sunlight. **Shelf-life:** Use as soon as possible after delivery.

COMPATIBILITY: Do not mix with chlorinated water or apply with any other pesticide, fertiliser or spray adjuvant. Do not use within 30 metres of susceptible plants such as cucurbit vegetables.

MAMMALIAN TOXICITY: There is no evidence that *Phytophthora palmivora* has any allergic or other adverse effects on mammals. Considered to be of low mammalian toxicity.

ENVIRONMENTAL IMPACT AND NON-TARGET TOXICITY: *Phytophthora palmivora* occurs naturally in the soil and there is no evidence that its use as a mycoherbicide has any effect on non-target organisms or on the environment.

3:118 *Pseudomonas cepacia*
Biological fungicide

Bacterium: Pseudomonadales: Pseudomonadaceae

NOMENCLATURE: **Approved name:** previously known as *Pseudomonas cepacia* Palleroni and Holmes; reclassified as *Burkholderia cepacia*; Wisconsin strain.

See *Burkholderia cepacia*.

3:119 *Pseudomonas chloraphis*
Biological fungicide

Bacterium: Pseudomonadales: Pseudomonadaceae

NOMENCLATURE: **Approved name:** *Pseudomonas chloraphis*.

SOURCE: Frequently occurring soil bacterium isolated from rhizosphere.

PRODUCTION: Manufactured by fermentation.

TARGET PESTS: Soil- and seed-borne fungal pathogens.

TARGET CROPS: Cereals.

BIOLOGICAL ACTIVITY: **Biology:** *Pseudomonas chloraphis* is a vigorous rhizosphere-inhabiting bacterium that rapidly colonises the root zone of treated plants. It outcompetes phytopathogenic species by depriving them of the nutrients necessary for their growth and by producing antifungal secondary metabolites.

COMMERCIALISATION: **Formulation:** Sold as a seed treatment. **Tradenames:** Cedoman – BioAgr.

APPLICATION: Treated seed are sown. The bacterium rapidly colonises the rhizosphere and prevents the establishment of phytophagous species.

PRODUCT SPECIFICATIONS: **Purity:** Contains no contaminants. **Storage conditions:** Store in a cool, dry, sealed container out of direct sunlight. **Shelf-life:** Remains viable for twelve months if stored under recommended conditions.

COMPATIBILITY: Incompatible with broad-spectrum fungicide treatments.

MAMMALIAN TOXICITY: *Pseudomonas chloraphis* has not had any reports of allergic or other adverse toxicological effects from research and manufacturing staff, formulators or field workers.

ENVIRONMENTAL IMPACT AND NON-TARGET TOXICITY: *Pseudomonas chloraphis* is a commonly occurring soil bacterium. It is not expected that its use as a seed treatment will have any adverse effects on non-target organisms or on the environment.

3:120   *Pseudomonas fluorescens*

Biological fungicide/bactericide

Bacterium: Pseudomonadales: Pseudomonadaceae

NOMENCLATURE: **Approved name:** *Pseudomonas fluorescens* (Trevisan) Migula.

SOURCE: A naturally and widely occurring bacterium. A strain that was naturally non-ice nucleating was isolated and registered in the USA for suppression of frost damage (FrostBan). Other strains with anti-fungal or anti-bacterial activity have been isolated and commercialised in the USA.

PRODUCTION: Produced by fermentation.

TARGET PESTS: Fire-blight (*Erwinia amylovora* Winsl.), soil-borne *Fusarium* and *Rhizoctonia* spp. and frost damage.

TARGET CROPS: Fruit tree crops, particularly pears and apples, cotton and vegetables.

BIOLOGICAL ACTIVITY: **Mode of action:** Bacteria on the leaves of crops often serve as nucleation sites for ice formation and ice crystals often form when they are present and the temperature falls below freezing, with resulting damage to the leaf. If these bacteria are replaced on plant leaves with competitive antagonists that lack the ice-nucleating protein, frost is prevented, even at temperatures as low as -5 °C. Other strains of *Pseudomonas fluorescens* are antagonistic to foliar or rhizosphere bacteria and fungi through the production of siderophores and antibiotics.

COMMERCIALISATION: **Formulation:** Sold as seed treatments or WPs of bacterial spores. **Tradenames:** Dagger – Ecogen (withdrawn), BlightBan – Plant Health Technologies, Biocure – Stanes.

APPLICATION: Apply non-nucleating bacteria to foliage of tree crops and vegetables before the temperature falls below freezing. A single application will protect from frost damage to temperatures as low as -5 °C for up to two months. The bacterium must be established on the foliage before freezing temperatures occur. Soil-borne pathogens are controlled with the use of seed treatments or hopper-box applications and foliar pathogens by spray applications. Fire blight sprays should be applied before flowering.

PRODUCT SPECIFICATIONS: **Storage conditions:** Store in a cool, dry place in a sealed container. Do not expose to extremes of temperature or direct sunlight. **Shelf-life:** If stored under recommended conditions, the product remains viable for a year.

COMPATIBILITY: It is unusual to apply *Pseudomones fluorescens* with other chemical treatments.

MAMMALIAN TOXICITY: There are no records of allergic or other adverse effects following use of *Pseudomones fluorescens*. It is regarded as being of low mammalian toxicity.

ENVIRONMENTAL IMPACT AND NON-TARGET TOXICITY: *Pseudomonas fluorescens* occurs widely in Nature and is not expected to have any adverse effects on non-target organisms or on the environment.

3:121 *Pseudomonas gladioli*

Bacterial herbicide

Bacterium: Pseudomonadales: Pseudomonadaceae

NOMENCLATURE: **Approved name:** *Pseudomonas gladioli.*

SOURCE: Isolated from *Poa annua* L. in Japanese turf.

PRODUCTION: Manufactured by controlled fermentation.

TARGET PESTS: *Poa annua* (annual meadow grass).

TARGET CROPS: Golf courses and similar areas of fine grasses.

BIOLOGICAL ACTIVITY: **Mode of action:** *Pseudomonas gladioli* invades the weed's xylem water transporting system where it multiplies, eventually blocking the tissues, leading to plant death. It does not invade the xylem of other turf grass species. **Biology:** *Pseudomonas gladioli* is a pathogen of annual meadow grass (*Poa annua*).

COMMERCIALISATION: **Tradenames:** AM 301 – Japan Tobacco, Camperico – Microgen.

APPLICATION: Apply to turf as a drench through an irrigation system.

PRODUCT SPECIFICATIONS: **Purity:** The product contains spores of *Pseudomonas gladioli* and no other bacterial contaminants. **Storage conditions:** Store in a cool, dark, dry place. Do not expose to direct sunlight or extremes of temperature. **Shelf-life:** If stored under manufacturer's recommended conditions, may be kept for up to one year.

COMPATIBILITY: Incompatible with broad-spectrum fungicides.

MAMMALIAN TOXICITY: There are no reports of allergic or other adverse toxicological effects from research workers, manufacturers or field staff.

ENVIRONMENTAL IMPACT AND NON-TARGET TOXICITY: *Pseudomonas gladioli* occurs widely in Nature and is not expected to have any adverse effects on non-target organisms or on the environment.

3:122 *Pseudomonas syringae*

Bacterial fungicide

Bacterium: Pseudomonadales: Pseudomonadaceae

NOMENCLATURE: **Approved name:** *Pseudomonas syringae* Van Hall.
Other names: *Pseudomonas cerasi* Griff.

SOURCE: Occurs widely in Nature.

PRODUCTION: Produced by fermentation.

TARGET PESTS: Used to control fungal pathogens of stored produce.

TARGET CROPS: Post-harvest crops such as citrus and other fruit and vegetables.

BIOLOGICAL ACTIVITY: **Biology:** The bacterium competes with pathogenic fungi for occupation of the surface of the treated crop. This coverage of the treated plant surface also prevents access to entry sites. **Efficacy:** *Pseudomonas syringae* covers the surface of treated harvested produce and presents a barrier to invasion by pathogenic fungi.

COMMERCIALISATION: **Formulation:** Sold as a suspension concentrate of spores.
Tradenames: BioBlast – EcoScience.

APPLICATION: Sprayed onto fruit and vegetables after harvest or used as a dip treatment.

PRODUCT SPECIFICATIONS: **Purity:** Contains no contaminants. **Storage conditions:** Store under cool, dry conditions out of direct sunlight. **Shelf-life:** May be stored for twelve months.

COMPATIBILITY: It is recommended that the product be used alone.

MAMMALIAN TOXICITY: There are no reports of allergic or other adverse toxicological effects from research or manufacturing staff, formulators or field workers.

ENVIRONMENTAL IMPACT AND NON-TARGET TOXICITY: *Pseudomonas syringae* occurs widely in Nature and is not expected to have any adverse effects on non-target organisms or on the environment.

3:123 *Pythium oligandrum* *Biological fungicide*

Fungus: Oomycetes: Peronosporales

NOMENCLATURE: **Approved name:** *Pythium oligandrum.*

SOURCE: Occurs widely in Nature.

PRODUCTION: Manufactured by fermentation.

TARGET PESTS: A wide range of soil-borne fungal pathogens.

TARGET CROPS: Glasshouse and outdoor vegetables, cereals and non-food tree crops.

BIOLOGICAL ACTIVITY: **Mode of action:** *Pythium oligandrum* outcompetes pathogenic soil fungi and also stimulates the growth of crops, rendering them less susceptible to disease attack. **Biology:** The product is applied to the soil and rapidly becomes established in the crop rhizosphere, preventing the growth and pathogenicity of soil fungi.

COMMERCIALISATION: **Formulation:** Sold as a wettable powder (WP).
Tradenames: Polyversum – Remeslo ssro.

APPLICATION: Apply five grams product per kg of seeds. For individual established plants, suspend five g of product in ten litres of water and apply five ml per plant. A single application is usually sufficient for a season.

PRODUCT SPECIFICATIONS: **Storage conditions:** Store in a sealed container in a cool, dry place. Do not expose to extremes of temperature or direct sunlight. **Shelf-life:** Retains viability for a year under correct storage conditions.

COMPATIBILITY: Do not apply with chemical fungicides. Use non-chlorinated water to prepare suspensions.

MAMMALIAN TOXICITY: *Pythium oligandrum* has not caused allergic or other adverse effects in research workers, manufacturing or field staff. It is considered to be of low mammalian toxicity.

ENVIRONMENTAL IMPACT AND NON-TARGET TOXICITY: *Pythium oligandrum* occurs in Nature and is not thought to have any adverse effects on non-target organisms or on the environment.

3. Living Systems

3:124 *Serratia entomophila*

Biological insecticide

Bacterium: Eubacteriales: Enterobacteriaceae

NOMENCLATURE: **Approved name:** *Serratia entomophila* Grimont, Jackson, Ageron and Noonan. **Other names:** commonly known as the causal organism of amber disease.

SOURCE: *Serratia entomophila* is a soil-inhabiting, non-spore forming, aerobic bacterium that has specific activity against – and was isolated from – the New Zealand grass grub, *Costelytra zealandica* White (Coleoptera: Scarabaeidae).

PRODUCTION: *Serratia entomophila* is manufactured and formulated by Industrial Research Ltd and produced by fermentation.

TARGET PESTS: The New Zealand grass grub, *Costelytra zealandica*.

TARGET CROPS: Established pasture.

BIOLOGICAL ACTIVITY: **Biology:** The bacterium enters the insect *per os* and adheres to the surface of the foregut, where it inhibits feeding, the biosynthesis of digestive enzymes and, finally, invades the insect haemocoel. **Efficacy:** After death, the infected larvae disintegrate, passing additional bacteria into the soil to infect new grub larvae. The genes associated with the disease process are encoded on a single plasmid.

COMMERCIALISATION: **Formulation:** Formulated as a liquid suspension containing 4×10^{13} live cells per litre. **Tradenames:** Invade – Coated Seed.

APPLICATION: The formulated product is applied at a rate of 1 litre per hectare.

PRODUCT SPECIFICATIONS: **Purity:** The bacterium is produced by fermentation, with checks made on the quality of the product prior to formulation. The product is evaluated for efficacy by bioassay against the grass grub. **Storage conditions:** Store in a refrigerator. Do not freeze. **Shelf-life:** Sealed containers can be stored for up to six months if kept under cool conditions.

COMPATIBILITY: The product should not be used in conjunction with broad-spectrum biocides.

MAMMALIAN TOXICITY: There have been no adverse toxic reactions to the bacterium from research workers, manufacturers or users.

ENVIRONMENTAL IMPACT AND NON-TARGET TOXICITY: *Serratia entomophila* occurs in Nature and is not expected to have any adverse effects on non-target organisms or to have any deleterious effects on the environment.

3:125 *Spodoptera exigua* nucleopoly-
hedrovirus *Insecticidal baculovirus*

The Pesticide Manual - 11th edition: Entry number 657

Virus: Baculoviridae: Nucleopolyhedrovirus

NOMENCLATURE: **Approved name:** *Spodoptera exigua* multicapsid nucleopolyhedrovirus.
Other names: *Spodoptera exigua* nucleopolyhedrovirus; SeNPV; SeMNPV.

SOURCE: Baculovirus that occurs widely in Nature, originally isolated from the beet
armyworm, *Spodoptera exigua* (Hübner).

PRODUCTION: Produced in larvae of *Spodoptera exigua* under controlled conditions. The
baculovirus is separated from the larval cadavers by centrifugation.

TARGET PESTS: For control of beet armyworm (*Spodoptera exigua*).

TARGET CROPS: Recommended for use in various outdoor crops, including cotton,
vegetables, grapes, ornamentals and glasshouse vegetables and ornamentals.

BIOLOGICAL ACTIVITY: **Mode of action:** As with all insect baculoviruses, *Spodoptera exigua*
NPV must be ingested to exert an effect. Following ingestion, the virus enters the insect's
haemolymph where it multiplies in the insect body, leading to insect death. **Biology:** SeMNPV
is more active on small larvae than later larval instars. The virus is ingested by the feeding larva
and the protective protein matrix is dissolved in the alkaline insect midgut, releasing the virus
particles. These pass through the peritrophic membrane and invade midgut cells by fusion
with the microvilli. The virus particles invade the cell nuclei, where they are uncoated and
replicated. Initial replication produces non-occluded virus particles to hasten the invasion of
the host insect but later the virus particles are produced with protein matrices and remain
infective when released from the dead insects. **Duration of development:** Caterpillars cease
feeding approximately four days after infection and die after five to ten days. **Efficacy:**
SeMNPV acts relatively slowly as it has to be ingested and infect before it exerts any effect on
the insect host. It is important to ensure good cover of the foliage to effect good control.
Monitoring of adult insect laying patterns and targeted application at newly hatched eggs gives
better control than on a mixed population. **Key references:** 1) R R Granados and
B A Frederici (eds.). 1986. *The Biology of Baculoviruses, Vols. 1 and 2*, CRC Press, Boca Raton,
Florida, USA. 2) D J Leisy and J R Fuxa. 1996. Natural and engineered viral agents for insect
control. In *Crop Protection Agents from Nature: Natural Products and Analogues*, L G Copping
(ed.), Royal Society of Chemistry, Cambridge, UK.

COMMERCIALISATION: **Formulation:** Formulated as wettable powder formulations (WP)
and liquid concentrates. **Tradenames:** Spod-X – Thermo Trilogy and Brinkman, Ness-A –
Applied Chemicals Thailand, Ness-E – Applied Chemicals Thailand.

APPLICATION: Monitor the occurrence of adults and apply during egg laying. It is important
to ensure that the foliage is well covered.

3. Living Systems

PRODUCT SPECIFICATIONS: **Purity:** Rod-shaped, elongated particles enclosed in a protein crystalline matrix (occlusion body) with no human or mammalian pathogenic bacteria. Efficacy of the formulation can be detemined by bioassay on *Spodoptera exigua* larvae.
Storage conditions: Store in a cool, dry place. Keep liquid formulations refrigerated but do not freeze. Dry formulations can be stored frozen. Do not expose to sunlight.
Shelf-life: Wettable powder formulations are stable for up to one year. Liquid formulations should be used within three months.

COMPATIBILITY: Compatible with most crop protection agents that do not exert a repellent effect on *Spodoptera exigua* but do not use with copper-based fungicides or chlorinated water. Should be applied in water at a neutral pH.

MAMMALIAN TOXICITY: *Spodoptera exigua* MNPV has not demonstrated evidence of toxicity, infectivity, irritation or hypersensitivity to mammals. No allergic responses or other adverse health problems have been observed by research workers, manufacturing staff or users.

ENVIRONMENTAL IMPACT AND NON-TARGET TOXICITY: *Spodoptera exigua* MNPV occurs in Nature and, as such, is not expected to show any adverse effects on non-target organisms or the environment.

3:126 *Steinernema carpocapsae*

Insect parasitic nematode

The Pesticide Manual - 11th edition: Entry number 659

Nematode: Nematoda: Steinernematidae

NOMENCLATURE: **Approved name:** *Steinernema carpocapsae* (Weiser).
Other names: *Neoaplectana carpocapsae* Weiser; beneficial nematodes.

SOURCE: *Steinernema carpocapsae* is widespread throughout the world.

PRODUCTION: Produced commercially by fermentation. Sold as third instar larvae.

TARGET PESTS: Black vine weevil (*Otiorhynchus sulcatus* (Fabricius)) and other soil insects such as cutworms (*Agrotis* spp.). Also used to control *Gryllotalpa gryllotalpa* (Linnaeus), *Tipula* spp., mint borer, armyworms, billbugs, root weevils, fleas, stem borers and fungus gnats.

TARGET CROPS: Glasshouse vegetables and ornamentals and outdoor strawberries, vegetables and blackcurrants. Also recommended for use in turf.

BIOLOGICAL ACTIVITY: **Biology:** The third stage larvae are the infectious stage and only these can survive outside the host insect as they do not require food. They enter a host through one of its natural openings. The nematode larva then releases bacteria (*Xenorhabdus* spp.) into the insect's body and toxins produced by these bacteria kill the insect within 48 hours.

The bacteria then digest the insect's body into material that the nematode can feed upon, and the nematode's fourth stage develops within the dead insect. These fourth stage larvae develop into males and females that reproduce sexually. After mating, the males die and the females will lay eggs in the dead insect if there is enough food available or, if not, the first and second stage larvae develop inside the female nematode's body. When larvae reach the third stage, they are able to leave the dead insect and seek out a new host. However, there may be two or more generations within the host dependent upon the availability of food. The third stage is always the infective stage. **Predation:** Infectious nematodes can travel distances of several centimetres and lie in wait for new food sources. **Duration of development:** Growth rate is very dependent upon temperature and it is likely that the nematode will complete its life-cycle in 14 to 20 days in the presence of sufficient soil insects. **Efficacy:** Very effective predators that can be used to eradicate vine weevil populations. Also parasitise other soil-inhabiting insects. **Key reference:** R Gaugler and H K Kaya. 1990. Entomopathogenic nematodes. In *Biological Control*, CRC Press, Boca Raton, Florida, 365 pages.

COMMERCIALISATION: **Formulation:** Supplied as third instar larvae encapsulated within a granule. **Tradenames:** Exhibit SC-WDG – Novartis BCM, Bio Safe WG (for turf – Japan) – Thermo Trilogy, BioVector WG 20% (for cranberries and mint) – Thermo Trilogy, Vector TL, WG (for turfgrass and ornamentals) – Thermo Trilogy, Savior WG (for turfgrass and ornamentals) – Thermo Trilogy, Horticultural Scanmask (for commercial horticulture) – BioLogic, Lawn & Garden Scan mask (for amateur use) – BioLogic, Ecomask (for use at temperatures of 15–30 °C) – BioLogic, Guardian – Hydro-Gardens, Steinernema carpocapsae – Neudorff.

APPLICATION: Disperse the granules in water and apply by watering evenly over soil to be treated at a rate of about 1×10^7 infective juvenile nematodes for each 20 square metres.

PRODUCT SPECIFICATIONS: **Purity:** Products contain only third instar infectious nematode larvae. Product efficacy can be determined by bioassay on black vine weevil or other coleopteran larvae. **Storage conditions:** Store under cool conditions but do not freeze. Keep out of direct sunlight and do not allow temperatures to exceed 35 °C. **Shelf-life:** *Steinernema carpocapsae* can be stored for two weeks at 6 to 8 °C. Granular formulations extend the shelf life to 60 days at room temperature and 125 to 180 days at 5 °C.

COMPATIBILITY: Will not survive in manure. High humidity and temperatures above 15 °C are necessary for effective control.

MAMMALIAN TOXICITY: No allergic or other adverse reactions have been reported by researchers, production staff or users from use in glasshouse or outdoor crops from *Steinernema carpocapsae* or its associated bacterium.

ENVIRONMENTAL IMPACT AND NON-TARGET TOXICITY: It is not expected that the use of products containing *Steinernema carpocapsae* will have any effects on non-target organisms nor have any adverse effects on the environment.

3:127 *Steinernema feltiae*

Sciarid fly parasitic nematode

The Pesticide Manual - 11th edition: Entry number 659

Nematode: Nematoda: Steinernematidae

NOMENCLATURE: **Approved name:** *Steinernema feltiae* Filipjev. MicroBio Strain UK 76.
Other names: *Neoaplectana bibionis*; *Neoaplectana feltiae*.

SOURCE: *Steinernema feltiae* is widespread throughout the world.

PRODUCTION: Produced commercially by fermentation. Sold as third instar larvae.

TARGET PESTS: Sciarid flies (*Bradysia* spp., *Lycoriella* spp. and *Sciara* spp.) and other soil insects. Also sold as a preventative control for vine weevils (*Otiorhynchus sulcatus* (Fabricius)).

TARGET CROPS: Glasshouse vegetables and ornamentals, mushrooms and outdoor strawberries, vegetables and turf.

BIOLOGICAL ACTIVITY: **Biology:** The third stage larvae are the infectious stage and only these can survive outside the host insect as they do not require food. They enter a host through one of its natural openings. The nematode larva then releases bacteria (*Xenorhabdus* spp.) into the insect's body and toxins produced by these bacteria kill the insect within 48 hours. The bacteria then digest the insect's body into material that the nematode can feed upon, and the nematode's fourth stage develops within the dead insect. These fourth stage larvae develop into males and females that reproduce sexually. After mating, the males die and the females will lay eggs in the dead insect if there is enough food available or, if not, the first and second stage larvae develop inside the female nematode's body. The larvae may leave the host when they reach the third stage but two or three generations may develop within the host, depending upon the availability of food. **Predation:** Infectious nematodes can travel distances of centimetres in search of new food sources.
Duration of development: Growth rate is very dependent upon temperature and it is likely that the nematode will complete its life-cycle in 14 to 20 days in the presence of sufficient soil insects. **Efficacy:** Very effective predators that can be used to eradicate sciarid fly populations. Also parasitise other soil-inhabiting insects. **Key reference:** R Gaugler and H K Kaya. 1990. Entomopathogenic nematodes. In *Biological Control*, CRC Press, Boca Raton, Florida, 365 pages.

COMMERCIALISATION: **Formulation:** Supplied as third instar larvae or as a granular formulation with partially dehydrated nematodes in the centre of a clay granule.
Tradenames: Nemasys (for horticultural crops) – MicroBio and Biobest, Nemasys M (for mushrooms) – MicroBio and Biobest, Sciarid (for mushrooms) – Koppert, Entonem – Koppert, Traunem – Andermatt, Exhibit SF-WDG – Novartis BCM, Magnet (for mushrooms) – Thermo Trilogy, X-Gnat (for ornamentals) – Thermo Trilogy, Scanmask – BioLogic and IPM Laboratories, BotaniGard – Mycotech, Steinernema feltiae – Neudorff, Nema-plus – e-nema.

APPLICATION: Apply by watering evenly over soil to be treated at a rate of about 1×10^7 juvenile nematodes for each 25 square metres. Disperse granules in water before treatment. For best control, ensure that the soil or compost is moist and that the temperature remains between 10 and 30 °C.

PRODUCT SPECIFICATIONS: **Purity:** Products contain only third instar infectious nematode larvae. Product efficacy can be determined by bioassay against sciarid larvae. **Storage conditions:** Store under cool conditions for a few days but do not freeze. Keep out of direct sunlight and temperatures above 35 °C. **Shelf-life:** *Steinernema feltiae* can be stored for two weeks at 6 to 8 °C. Larvae remain infectious for only a short period after delivery. Granules remain active for 60 days at room temperature and up to six months at 5 °C.

COMPATIBILITY: Will not survive in manure. High humidity and temperatures above 15 °C are necessary for effective control.

MAMMALIAN TOXICITY: No allergic or other adverse reactions have been reported by research staff, producers or users of *Steinernema feltiae* or its associated bacterium in glasshouse or outdoor crops.

ENVIRONMENTAL IMPACT AND NON-TARGET TOXICITY: It is not expected that *Steinernema feltiae* or its associated bacterium will have any adverse effects on non-target organisms nor damage the environment.

3:128   *Steinernema glaseri*
White grub parasitic nematode

The Pesticide Manual - 11th edition: Entry number 659

Nematode: Nematoda: Steinernematidae

NOMENCLATURE: **Approved name:** *Steinernema glaseri* (Steiner) Wouts, Mracek, Gardin and Bedding strain B-326. **Other names:** white grub parasitic nematode. **Development code:** B-326.

SOURCE: Isolated from soil in New Jersey, USA.

PRODUCTION: Produced commercially by fermentation in 30,000 to 60,000 litre fermenters on an undefined growing medium.

TARGET PESTS: Used for the control of white grubs (Scarabaeidae).

TARGET CROPS: Recommended for use in turf.

BIOLOGICAL ACTIVITY: **Biology:** The third stage larvae are the infectious stage and only these can survive outside the host insect as they do not require food. They measure 1.1 mm in length and 0.42 mm in width and enter their host through one of its natural openings (the mouth, anus or spiracles). The nematode larva then releases bacteria (*Xenorhabdus* spp.) into the insect's body. The bacteria are medium to long motile rods with peritrichous flagellae. They are gram negative facultative anaerobes that form sphaeroplasts in older cultures. They are non-spore formers, have no resistant stage and are found only in the nematodes or the insect host. The bacteria proliferate within the insect causing septicaemia and death within 24 to 72 hours. The nematode's fourth stage develops within the dead insect. These fourth stage larvae develop into males and females that reproduce sexually. After mating, the males die and the females will lay eggs in the dead insect if there is enough food available or, if not, the first and second stage larvae develop inside the female nematode's body. The larvae may leave the host when they reach the third stage but usually two or three generations develop within the host depending upon the availability of food. **Duration of development:** At 22 to 28 °C, the life-cycle takes approximately six days in most insects.

Key references: 1) R Gaugler and H K Kaya. 1990. Entomopathogenic nematodes. In *Biological Control*, CRC Press, Boca Raton, Florida, 365 pages. 2) R Georgis, C T Redmond and W T Martin. 1992. *Steinernema* B-326 and B-319 (Nematoda): new biological soil insecticides. *Brighton Crop Protection Conference – Pests & Diseases*, **1**, 73–9.

COMMERCIALISATION: **Formulation:** Prepared as a gel polymer encasing the immobilised third stage infective juvenile nematodes. **Tradenames:** Steinernema glaseri – Praxis, Steinernema glaseri – Thermo Trilogy, Steinernema glaseri – Greenfire, Steinernema glaseri – Integrated Pest Management.

APPLICATION: Apply at a rate of 2.5×10^9 infective juveniles per hectare to moist soil when the temperature is between 15 and 35 °C. The best control is achieved at temperatures of 25 to 35 °C. Applications may be made using standard irrigation systems or with common spraying systems at pressures up to 2068 kPa with nozzle sizes of 50 μm or greater.

PRODUCT SPECIFICATIONS: **Purity:** The product contains only third stage infective nematode juveniles encased in a water soluble gel. **Storage conditions:** Store for short periods at room temperature or for longer periods under refrigeration. Do not freeze or store at temperatures above 37 °C. The nematodes are very susceptible to desiccation. **Shelf-life:** The product may be kept for three months at room temperature and for twelve months if refrigerated.

COMPATIBILITY: Compatible with a wide range of biological and chemical pesticides.

MAMMALIAN TOXICITY: Tests conducted on rats, mice, rabbits and pigs showed no symptoms or mortality caused by the nematodes or their associated bacteria by oral, intradermal, subcutaneous or intraperitoneal inoculation. The nematode/bacterium complex cannot withstand body temperatures of 37 °C and is eliminated by the immune system upon injection. The gut of mammals will not allow nematode penetration.

ENVIRONMENTAL IMPACT AND NON-TARGET TOXICITY: *Steinernema glaseri* strain B-326 was isolated from soil and occurs in Nature. It will not survive in birds and caused no mortality or symptoms following oral, dermal, subcutaneous or intraperitoneal inoculation. It is highly sensitive to desiccation and u.v. light and shows significant mortality in exposed environments. In aquatic environments, nematode survival is poor due to low oxygen levels.

3:129   *Steinernema riobrave*

Soil insect parasitic nematode

The Pesticide Manual - 11th edition: Entry number 659

Nematode: Nematoda: Steinernematidae

NOMENCLATURE: **Approved name:** *Steinernema riobrave* Cabarillas, Poinar and Raulston.
Other names: soil insect parasitic nematode.

SOURCE: Originally isolated from soil.

PRODUCTION: Produced by fermentation in 30,000 to 60,000 litre fermenters in undefined medium.

TARGET PESTS: Control of large nymph and adult mole crickets (*Scapteriscus* spp.) in turf; and citrus weevils (*Pachnaeus litus* Germar), sugar cane rootstalk borer (*Diaprepes abbreviatus* (Linnaeus)) and other pests in citrus.

TARGET CROPS: Recommended for use in turf, citrus and sugar cane.

BIOLOGICAL ACTIVITY: **Biology:** The third stage larvae are the infectious stage and only these can survive outside the host insect as they do not require food. They enter their host through one of its natural openings (the mouth, anus or spiracles). The nematode larva then releases bacteria (*Xenorhabdus* spp.) into the insect's body. The bacteria are medium to long motile rods with peritrichous flagellae. They are non-spore forming, gram negative facultative anaerobes and are found only in the nematodes or the insect host. The bacteria proliferate within the insect, causing death within 24 to 72 hours. The nematode's fourth stage develops within the dead insect. These fourth stage larvae develop into males and females that reproduce sexually. After mating the males die and the females lay eggs in the dead insect if there is enough food available or, if not, the first and second stage larvae develop inside the female nematode's body. The larvae may leave the host when they reach the third stage but usually two or three generations develop within the host, depending upon the availability of food. **Duration of development:** The timing of the life-cycle is very dependent upon soil conditions and temperature. *Steinernema riobrave* is very susceptible to desiccation. At temperatures between 22 and 28 °C, the life-cycle will take about six to ten days.
Key reference: R Gaugler and H K Kaya. 1990. Entomopathogenic nematodes. In *Biological Control*, CRC Press, Boca Raton, Florida, 365 pages.

COMMERCIALISATION: **Formulation:** Sold as a water dispersible granule (WG).
Tradenames: Biovector 355 WG – Thermo Trilogy, Devour WG – Thermo Trilogy, Vector MC, WG – Thermo Trilogy.

APPLICATION: Apply at a rate of 2.5×10^9 infective juveniles per hectare to moist soil when the temperature is between 15 and 35 °C. The best control is achieved at temperatures of 22 to 28 °C. Applications may be made using standard spraying systems at pressures up to 2068 kPa with nozzle sizes of 50 μm or greater.

PRODUCT SPECIFICATIONS: **Purity:** The product contains third stage infective juveniles on an inert carrier. The purity of the formulation can be determined by examination under a microscope and its efficacy through bioassay on susceptible insect larvae.
Storage conditions: Store under dry conditions at room temperature or, if stored for longer than a few days, refrigerate. Do not freeze and do not allow the temperature to exceed 37 °C. **Shelf-life:** If stored at room temperature, the product will remain viable for up to two to three months. If refrigerated, the product will remain active for up to a year.

COMPATIBILITY: Compatible with all biological control systems and many chemical pesticides. Do not apply in a tank mix with copper- or benzimidazole-based fungicides, or with soil insecticides.

MAMMALIAN TOXICITY: Tests conducted on rats, mice, rabbits and pigs showed no symptoms or mortality caused by the nematodes or their associated bacteria by oral, intradermal, subcutaneous or intraperitoneal inoculation. The nematode/bacterium complex cannot withstand body temperatures of 37 °C and is eliminated by the immune system upon injection. The gut of mammals will not allow nematode penetration.

ENVIRONMENTAL IMPACT AND NON-TARGET TOXICITY: *Steinernema riobrave* was isolated from soil and occurs in Nature. It will not survive in birds and showed no mortality or symptoms following oral, dermal, subcutaneous or intraperitoneal inoculation. It is highly sensitive to desiccation and u.v. light and shows significant mortality in exposed environments. In aquatic environments, nematode survival is poor owing to low oxygen levels.

3:130   *Steinernema scapterisci*

Mole cricket parasitic nematode

The Pesticide Manual - 11th edition: Entry number 659

Nematode: Nematoda: Steinernematidae

NOMENCLATURE: **Approved name:** *Steinernema scapterisci* strain B-319.
Other names: mole cricket parasitic nematode.

SOURCE: Naturally occurring nematode isolated in South America by University of Florida researchers from mole crickets during a natural epizootic. Originally reported by R Georgis (*Proc. Brit. Crop Prot. Conf. – Pests & Diseases*, 1992, **1**, 73). Introduced by Biosys (now Thermo Trilogy, who no longer manufacture it) and licensed to Ecogen.

PRODUCTION: Manufactured by fermentation in sterile undefined medium. Infective juveniles are harvested by concentration of the fermentation broth.

TARGET PESTS: Mole crickets (*Scapteriscus vicinus* Scudder and *Gryllotalpa* spp.).

TARGET CROPS: Turf grass, particularly golf courses.

BIOLOGICAL ACTIVITY: **Biology:** The third stage larvae are the infectious stage and only these can survive outside the host insect as they do not require food. They enter a host through one of its natural openings (mouth, anus, spiracles) and penetrate the body cavity. The nematode larva then releases its symbiotic bacteria (*Xenorhabdus* spp.) into the insect's body and toxins produced by these bacteria kill the insect within 36 to 48 hours. The bacteria then digest the insect's body into material that the nematode can feed upon, and the nematode's fourth stage develops within the dead insect. These fourth stage larvae develop into males and females that reproduce sexually. After mating, the males die and the females will lay eggs in the dead insect if there is enough food available or, if not, the first and second stage larvae develop inside the female nematode's body. When larvae reach the third stage, they are able to leave the dead insect and seek out a new host. However, there may be two or more generations within the host dependent upon the availability of food. The third stage is always the infective stage. **Predation:** Infective juveniles can travel distances of several tens of centimetres in search of new insect hosts. **Duration of development:** Growth rate is dependent upon soil temperature and moisture levels. In the presence of sufficient host insects and soil temperatures of between 15 and 35 °C, it is usual for the nematode to complete its life-cycle within 15 to 20 days. Optimal temperatures for *Steinernema scapterisci* are between 25 and 35 °C. **Efficacy:** *Steinernema scapterisci* is a very efficient pathogen of mole crickets. **Key references:** 1) R Georgis, C T Redmond and W R Martin. 1992. Steinernema B-326 and B-319 (Nematoda): New Biological Soil Insecticides. In *Brighton Crop Protection Conference – Pests & Diseases*, **1**, 73–9. 2) R Gaugler and H K Kaya. 1990. Entomopathogenic nematodes. In *Biological Control*, CRC Press, Boca Raton, Florida, 365 pages.

COMMERCIALISATION: **Formulation:** Sold as a clay-based formulation containing 60 million infective stage nematodes per pack. **Tradenames:** Otinem S – Ecogen.

APPLICATION: Apply to moist soil at a rate of 2.2×10^9 infective juveniles per hectare. Ensure that the soil is irrigated every three to four days after treatment unless rain occurs. Apply using standard spray application equipment at spray pressures not exceeding 2068 kPa.

PRODUCT SPECIFICATIONS: **Purity:** Efficacy of the formulation can be measured by bioassay against a target pest. Nematode numbers can be determined by counting juveniles under a microscope. **Storage conditions:** Store the formulation at 10 °C. Keep out of direct sunlight and avoid desiccation. **Shelf-life:** Stable for 2 months under recommended storage conditions.

COMPATIBILITY: Should not be tank mixed with benzimidazole-based fungicides or soil insecticides/nematicides. Compatible with other IPM/biological control strategies.

MAMMALIAN TOXICITY: Neither *Steinernema scapterisci* nor its bacterial symbiote have shown evidence of toxicity, infectivity, irritation, or hypersensitivity to mammals. No allergic responses or health problems have been observed by research workers, manufacturing staff or users.

ENVIRONMENTAL IMPACT AND NON-TARGET TOXICITY: *Steinernema scapterisci* and its associated bacterium have shown no adverse effects on any non-target organism nor any deleterious effects on the environment.

3:131 *Streptomyces griseoviridis*

Biological fungicide

The Pesticide Manual - 11th edition: Entry number 660

Bacterium: Actinomycetales: Streptomycetaceae

NOMENCLATURE: **Approved name:** *Streptomyces griseoviridis* Anderson *et al.* strain K 61.

SOURCE: Isolated from Finnish light-coloured *Sphagnum* peat that had been reported to have disease suppressing properties. Several strains of *Streptomyces* shown to possess antagonistic properties against seed- and soil-borne fungal pathogens were isolated by the Department of Plant Pathology of the University of Helsinki and the strain K 61 was selected for development.

PRODUCTION: Produced by fermentation followed by freeze drying of the organism.

TARGET PESTS: Various seed- and soil-borne fungal pathogens and particularly *Fusarium* spp. that cause wilt, root and basal rots. It also shows activity against other seed- and soil-borne pathogens such as *Alternaria* spp, *Pythium* spp. and *Phomopsis* spp.

TARGET CROPS: Vegetables, ornamentals and herbs.

BIOLOGICAL ACTIVITY: **Mode of action:** The effect is due to a combination of factors including competition for "living space and nutrients", lysis of the cell walls of pathogenic fungi by extracellular fungi and the production of antifungal metabolites. **Biology:** *Streptomyces griseoviridis* strain K 61 exerts its effect through a number of different modes of action. It competes for essential nutrients with plant pathogenic fungi, produces extracellular enzymes that cause the cell walls of these pathogens to lyse and it produces antifungal secondary metabolites. It is also suggested that *Streptomyces griseoviridis* strain K 61 increases the vigour and the rate of growth of healthy crops, rendering them less susceptible to attack by soil pathogens. **Duration of development:** *Streptomyces griseoviridis* strain K 61 establishes itself in the rhizosphere and develops with the growing crop root. **Efficacy:** Effective inhibition of the growth and pathogenesis of several plant pathogens is enhanced by growth stimulation of healthy crops. **Key reference:** O Mohammadi. 1994. *Proc. 3rd International Workshop on Plant Growth-Promoting Rhizobacteria*, 282–4.

COMMERCIALISATION: **Formulation:** Sold as a wettable powder (WP). **Tradenames:** Mycostop – Kemira.

APPLICATION: *Streptomyces griseoviridis* can be applied as a dry seed treatment at five to ten g per kg of seed or as an aqueous suspension for the spraying or drenching of growth substrates or via drip irrigation to give a dose of one to two g per ten square metres.

PRODUCT SPECIFICATIONS: **Purity:** The product contains a minimum of 1×10^8 colony forming units (cfu) per gram. Viability of the product is determined by plating out on agar and counting the number of colonies produced following incubation in the laboratory for 48 hours. Biological efficacy is tested using a bioassay with artificially infested cauliflower seeds.

Storage conditions: Store the unopened packages below 8 °C. **Shelf-life:** The formulated material is stable for 12 months when stored under the recommended conditions.

COMPATIBILITY: It is not recommended that Mycostop be applied as a tank mix with other pesticides or concentrated fertiliser solutions.

MAMMALIAN TOXICITY: Not hazardous to animals. No allergic or health problems have been observed in research workers, manufacturing staff or users. Inhalation of the fine powder and skin contact should be avoided by using recommended protective equipment.

ENVIRONMENTAL IMPACT AND NON-TARGET TOXICITY: **NOEL:** for bobwhite quail or mallard ducks was 2.45×10^9 colony forming units (cfu)/kg. Not toxic to fish with NOEL to rainbow trout being 5,000 cfu/ml. NOEL for Daphnia 1×10^4 cfu/ml. NOEL to honeybees was 9.8×10^8 cfu/kg. As the fungus is a natural component of the soil microflora, it is not expected that use of the product will lead to any adverse effects on the environment.

3:132 *Syngrapha falcifera* nucleopoly-hedrovirus *Insecticidal baculovirus*

Virus: Baculoviridae: Nucleopolyhedrovirus

NOMENCLATURE: **Approved name:** *Syngrapha falcifera* nucleopolyhedrovirus. **Other names:** SfNPV.

SOURCE: Originally isolated from the celery looper (*Syngrapha falcifera*) in the USA. Selected for use as a biological insecticide because of its relatively wide host range and its persistence on leaf surfaces.

PRODUCTION: Manufactured by *in vivo* methods using celery loopers. The virus is separated from the insect cadavers by centrifugation.

TARGET PESTS: For control of *Heliothis* and *Helicoverpa* species including cotton boll worm (*Helicoverpa zea* Boddie) and tobacco budworm (*Heliothis virescens* Fabricius).

TARGET CROPS: Cotton, tomatoes and other vegetables.

BIOLOGICAL ACTIVITY: **Mode of action:** As with all insect baculoviruses, *Syngrapha falcifera* NPV must be ingested to exert an effect. Following ingestion, the protective protein matrix of the polyhedral occlusion bodies (OBs) of the virus is dissolved within the midgut and the virus particles enter the insect's haemolymph. These virus particles invade nearly all cell types in the larval body where they multiply leading to death. Shortly after the death of the larva, the integument ruptures releasing very large numbers of OBs. **Efficacy:** SfNPV acts relatively slowly as it has to be ingested and then has to infect before it exerts any effect on the insect host. It is important to ensure good cover of the foliage to effect good control. Monitoring of adult insect laying patterns and targeted application at newly hatched eggs gives better control than on a mixed population. **Key references:** 1) R R Granados and B A Frederici (eds.). 1986. *The Biology of Baculoviruses, Vols. 1 and 2*, CRC Press, Boca Raton, Florida, USA. 2) D J Leisy and J R Fuxa. 1996. Natural and engineered viral agents for insect control. In *Crop Protection Agents from Nature: Natural Products and Analogues*, L G Copping (ed.), Royal Society of Chemistry, Cambridge, UK.

COMMERCIALISATION: **Formulation:** Under development by Novartis in collaboration with Thermo Trilogy (originally Biosys).

APPLICATION: Apply as a spray ensuring good cover of the foliage. The virus will remain infective on the surface of leaves for seven to fourteen days if not exposed to full sunlight.

PRODUCT SPECIFICATIONS: **Purity:** Free from human and mammalian bacterial pathogens. **Storage conditions:** Store in sealed containers under cool, dark conditions. May be stored frozen. **Shelf-life:** Stable for several weeks if kept cool, but has long-term stability if kept in a freezer.

COMPATIBILITY: Can be used with other insecticides that do not repel target insect species. Incompatible with strong oxidisers, acids, bases or chlorinated water.

MAMMALIAN TOXICITY: Baculoviruses are specific to invertebrates with there being no record of any vertebrate becoming infected. The virus does not infect or replicate in the cells of mammals and is inactivated at temperatures above 32 °C. There is no evidence of acute or chronic toxicity, eye or skin irritation in mammals. No allergic reactions or other health problems have been observed in research or manufacturing staff or with users of the product.

ENVIRONMENTAL IMPACT AND NON-TARGET TOXICITY: SfNPV occurs widely in Nature and there is no evidence of the virus infecting vertebrates or plants. It has no adverse effects on fish, birds or beneficial organisms.

3:133 *Trichoderma harzianum*

Biological fungicide

The Pesticide Manual - 11th edition: Entry number 731

Mitosporitic fungus: Previously classified as: Deuteromycetes: Moniliales

NOMENCLATURE: **Approved name:** *Trichoderma harzianum* Tul, variety TH11 (Harzan), strain T-39. **Other names:** previously known as *Trichoderma lignorum* (Tode) Harz. **Development code:** ABG-8007 (Makhteshim).

SOURCE: *Trichoderma harzianum* occurs widely in Nature and this isolate was selected for commercialisation because of its ability to compete with phytopathogenic fungi.

PRODUCTION: *Trichoderma harzianum* is produced by fermentation.

TARGET PESTS: Recommended for the control of soil-inhabiting *Botrytis* and *Sclerotinia* species.

TARGET CROPS: Recommended for use on vines and vegetables.

BIOLOGICAL ACTIVITY: **Mode of action:** Competes in the soil for nutrients and rhizosphere dominance with phyto-pathogenic fungi. **Biology:** *Trichoderma harzianum* is a widely distributed member of the soil microflora and it exerts its effect by competing for nutrients with phytopathogenic species.

COMMERCIALISATION: **Formulation:** Formulated as an MG. **Tradenames:** Harzan – NPP, Trichodex – Makhteshim, Ago Biocontrol Trichoderma 50 – Ago Biocontrol.

APPLICATION: Apply to soil using conventional application equipment. Ensure that the soil is moist and that the temperature is at least 12 °C.

PRODUCT SPECIFICATIONS: **Purity:** The product contains only spores of *Trichoderma harzianum*. Viability of the formulation is determined by plating the product out on agar and counting the number of colonies formed after incubation in the laboratory for 48 hours. **Storage conditions:** Store under dry, stable conditions as unopened packs. **Shelf-life:** Vacuum packs maintain product viability for one year if stored at 20 °C and if unopened.

COMPATIBILITY: Not to be used with any fungicidal treatment.

MAMMALIAN TOXICITY: **Acute oral LD$_{50}$:** rats >500 mg/kg. **Skin and eye:** Eye irritant, not a skin irritant. Possible skin sensitiser. **Other toxicological effects:** Inhalation LC$_{50}$ >0.89 mg/litre. *Trichoderma harzianum* is non-infectious and non-pathogenic.

ENVIRONMENTAL IMPACT AND NON-TARGET TOXICITY: Acute oral LD$_{50}$ mallard ducks and bobwhite quail >2,000 mg/kg. LC$_{50}$ (96 hours) zebra fish 1.23×10^5 colony forming units (cfu)/ml. LC$_{50}$ (10 days) *Daphnia pulex* 1.6×10^4 cfu/ml. *Trichoderma harzianum* was not toxic to honeybees at 1,000 ppm.

3:134 *Trichoderma harzianum* and *Trichoderma viride* *Biological fungicide*

The Pesticide Manual - 11th edition: Entry number 731

Mitosporitic fungi: Previously classified as: Deuteromycetes: Moniliales

NOMENCLATURE: **Approved name:** *Trichoderma harzianum* Rifai (strain ATCC 20475) and *Trichoderma viride* Tul (strain ATCC 20476). **Other names:** *Trichoderma harzianum/polysporum* (Link) Rifai and *Trichoderma lignorum* (Tode) Harz.

SOURCE: Both are naturally occurring soil fungi that were isolated from soil.

PRODUCTION: Manufactured by fermentation.

TARGET PESTS: A wide range of soil and foliar pathogens including *Armillaria mellea* Kumm. (honey fungus), *Phytophthora* spp., *Chondrostereum purpureum* Pouzar (silver leaf), *Pythium* spp., *Fusarium* spp., *Rhizoctonia* spp. and *Sclerotium rolfsii* Sacc.

TARGET CROPS: Orchards, vineyards, ornamental, vegetable, glasshouse and horticultural use. Post-harvest fruit and vegetables.

BIOLOGICAL ACTIVITY: **Mode of action:** The beneficial effects of the combination of *Trichoderma harzianum* and *Trichoderma viride* is through competition in the soil or on newly pruned stems with pathogenic fungi. The beneficial fungi outcompete the pathogens for nutrients and rhizosphere/wound dominance thereby preventing or significantly reducing the impact of the pathogens. *Trichoderma* species also enhance tissue development in treated crops through the enhancement of natural auxin release. **Efficacy:** It is claimed that treatment of soil with *Trichoderma* species shows greater than 90% cure of silver leaf in pome fruit and greater than 50% in stone fruit. Injections reduced the incidence of *Armillaria* in a variety of crops. Wound treatments must be allowed to become established for at least 48 hours. **Key references:** 1) A Siven and I Chet. 1986. *Trichoderma harzianum*: an effective biocontrol agent of *Fusarium* spp., In V Jensen et al. (eds.), *Microbial Communities in Soil*, Elsevier, London. 2) A Tronsmo and C Dennis. 1977. The use of *Trichoderma* species to control strawberry fruit rots, *Netherlands Journal of Plant Pathol.*, **83** (Suppl. 1), 449–55.

COMMERCIALISATION: **Formulation:** Formulated as a dry powder (Trisan, Trichoseal), in pellet form (Trichopel), as an injectable (Trichoject) and impregnated dowels (Trichodowels). **Tradenames:** Trichodowels – Agrimms Biologicals, Trichoseal – Agrimms Biologicals, Trichoject – Agrimms Biologicals, Trichopel – Agrimms Biologicals, Trisan – Applied Chemicals (Thailand), BINAB T – Bio-Innovation AB, Bio-Trek HB – Wilbur-Ellis.

APPLICATION: It is important to apply the products early in the growing season or immediately after pruning. *Trichoderma* species are very effective at protecting crops from the onset of disease and application before the plant pathogens are visible always gives the best control. For control of soil borne diseases the product is applied at rates of 6 to 12 kg product per hectare or the pellets or dowells are placed in the soil around the germinating seeds or close to the established trees. The wound sealant is applied as soon as possible after pruning and ideally within five minutes. Woody crops should be injected in mid to late Spring with 20 ml of the product at ground level into plants up to three rows away from the infection treated. Injection should be supplemented with soil treatment. Soil should be moist at the time of treatment.

PRODUCT SPECIFICATIONS: **Storage conditions:** Store under cool, dry conditions in a sealed container. Do not freeze or expose to direct sunlight. **Shelf-life:** If stored under recommended conditions the product should remain viable for up to 12 months.

COMPATIBILITY: It is unusual to apply *Trichoderma* species with other crop protection chemicals. Do not apply fungicides within four weeks of use.

MAMMALIAN TOXICITY: **Acute oral LD$_{50}$:** rats >500 mg/kg. **Skin and eye:** *T. harzianum* is an eye irritant but not a skin irritant. It is a possible skin sensitiser. **Other toxicological effects:** Inhalation LC$_{50}$ >0.89 mg/litre. *T. harzianum* is non-infectious and non-pathogenic. **Toxicity class:** EPA (formulation) III-IV.

ENVIRONMENTAL IMPACT AND NON-TARGET TOXICITY: *T. harzianum* acute oral LD$_{50}$ for mallard ducks and bobwhite quail >2,000 mg/kg. LC$_{50}$ (96 hours) zebra fish 1.23×10^5 colony forming units (cfu)/ml. It was non-toxic to bees by oral administration at 1,000 ppm. LC$_{50}$ (10 days) *Daphnia pulex* 1.6×10^4 cfu/ml.

3:135 *Verticillium lecanii* *Biological insecticide*

The Pesticide Manual - 11th edition: Entry number 750

Mitosporitic fungus: Previously classified as: Deuteromycetes: Moniliales

NOMENCLATURE: **Approved name:** *Verticillium lecanii* (Zimmerman) Viegas, whitefly strain or aphid strain. **Other names:** previously known as *Cephalosporium lecanii*.

SOURCE: *Verticillium lecanii* occurs widely in Nature. Two commercial strains were isolated by R A Hall, the first from the aphid, *Macrosiphoniella sanborni*, during a natural epidemic and the second from the glasshouse whitefly, *Trialeurodes vaporariorum* (Westwood). The two isolates had different host ranges and were initially developed by Tate and Lyle Ltd, who no longer produce or market them.

PRODUCTION: *Verticillium lecanii* isolates are cultured on a sterile undefined medium and the spores harvested by concentration and drying.

TARGET PESTS: Mycotal is used for control of whitefly, with a side-effect on thrips. Vertalec is used to control aphids. A mutant form is under development by the USDA for control of cyst nematode in soybean.

TARGET CROPS: Mycotal and Vertalec are used on glasshouse crops. The USDA mutant form is under development for use in soybean.

BIOLOGICAL ACTIVITY: **Mode of action:** Insecticide, acting through penetration of cuticle and subsequent fungal growth in haemolymph and tissues of insects. If conditions are sufficiently humid, nutrients incorporated in the formulation support growth and sporulation of microcolonies on foliage: these, together with sporulation from dead insects, lead to infection of epidemic proportions. **Biology:** *Verticillium lecanii* is an entomopathogenic fungus that exerts its effect by invasion of the living insect. Spores adhere to the cuticle of the insect and, under ideal conditions, germinate producing a germ tube that penetrates the host insect's cuticle by either physical of enzymic processes and subsequently invades the haemolymph and other tissues. The fungal hyphae develop in the insect and sporulation takes place through the dead insect's cuticle providing infectious spores to continue the epidemic.

Key references: 1) R A Hall. 1976. *J. Invertebr. Pathol.*, **27**, 41. 2) R A Hall. 1979. *J. Invertebr. Pathol.*, **101**, 1.

COMMERCIALISATION: **Formulation:** Sold as a wettable powder (WP) formulation. **Tradenames:** Mycotal (whitefly strain) – Koppert, Vertalec (aphid strain) – Koppert, Ago Biocontrol Vorticillium 50 – Ago Biocontrol.

APPLICATION: The products are applied at high volume in the presence of the target insect pests. Invasion of the pests is better under conditions of high humidity. Non-phytotoxic and non-phytopathogenic.

PRODUCT SPECIFICATIONS: **Purity:** Products contain spores of *Verticillium lecanii* whose activity is measured in terms of spore count and efficacy against insects. Spore count is determined by plating on agar and counting the colonies formed after 48 hours incubation in the laboratory using standard techniques. Efficacy assays are conducted against *Aphis fabae* for Vertalec and against pupae of *Trialeurodes vaporariorum* for Mycotal. **Storage conditions:** Refrigerate for long periods of storage. Do not allow temperature to reach 35 °C. Do not freeze. **Shelf-life:** The product is stable at 4 °C for up to six months.

COMPATIBILITY: Susceptible to some fungicides, especially dithiocarbamates.

MAMMALIAN TOXICITY: No skin or eye irritation has been observed. There is no evidence of acute or chronic toxicity, infectivity or hypersensitivity to mammals. No allergic responses or health problems have been observed by research workers, manufacturing staff or users.

ENVIRONMENTAL IMPACT AND NON-TARGET TOXICITY: *Verticillium lecanii* is widespread in Nature and is not pathogenic to non-target species. It has not shown adverse effects within the environment.

4:136   *Amblyseius barkeri*   *Thrips predator*

Predatory mite: Mesostigmata: Phytoseiidae

NOMENCLATURE: **Approved name:** *Amblyseius barkeri* (Hughes). **Other names:** Previously known as *Neoseiulus barkeri*. **Common names:** thrips predator; thrips predatory mite.

SOURCE: *Amblyseius barkeri* is cosmopolitan and occurs widely in Nature, being found in Europe, northern and equatorial Africa, California and Israel. It thrives under conditions of high humidity, but enters diapause when days shorten and temperatures fall below 15 °C.

PRODUCTION: Reared on living non-phytophagous prey mites such as *Tyrophagus* spp. or *Acarus siro* Linnaeus in a ratio of 1:1 to 1:5 predator:prey, excluding eggs. Small quantities of bran are provided as food for the prey mites.

TARGET PESTS: Main prey are thrips including *Frankliniella occidentalis* (Pergande), *F. intosa* (Trybom), *Thrips tabaci* Lindeman, *T. palmi* Karny and *Parthenothrips dracaenae* (Hegeer), although the predator can survive on pollen.

TARGET CROPS: Glasshouse-grown crops such as tomatoes, cucumbers, peppers and ornamentals. Also used for thrips control in interiorscapes.

BIOLOGICAL ACTIVITY: **Biology:** Eggs (oval and about 0.14 mm in diameter) are laid in the axils of the midvein and the lateral veins on the underside of leaves. The first active stage (larva) has six legs and does not feed but remains near the place of emergence. Proto- and deutonymphs and adults have eight legs, are very mobile and consume food actively.
Predation: Predatory mites pierce their prey and suck the contents. They consume between 1 and 5 thrips per day, depending on prey-instar, temperature and humidity, giving a total of about 85 in their lifetime. They do not feed on adults. **Egg laying:** Female predatory mites lay between 22 (at 15 to 16 °C) and 47 (at 25 to 26 °C) eggs throughout their lives.
Duration of development: Eggs hatch after 2 or 3 days, followed by 4 days for immature development at 25 °C. Adults live up to 30 days, depending on the temperature.
Efficacy: Because *Amblyseius barkeri* can survive on pollen, it can be introduced before the thrips populations build up. However, in crops that produce large quantities of pollen, its effectiveness is reduced because of this alternative food source, so higher populations must be introduced. *Amblyseius barkeri* consumes first instar thrips larvae more readily than later instars. **Key references:** 1) R J Jacobson. 1997. Integrated pest management (IPM) in greenhouses. In T Lewis (ed.), *Thrips as Crop Pests*, 639–66, CABI, Wallingford, UK.
2) J Riudavets. 1995. Predators of *Frankliniella occidentalis* (Perg.) and *Thrips tabaci* Lind: a Review. In A J M Loomans et al. *Biological Control of Thrips Pests*, **95–1**, 44–87, Wageningen Agricultural University Press, the Netherlands.

COMMERCIALISATION: **Formulation:** Sold as a vermiculite formulation with 10,000 to 50,000 predators per litre and as a specially formulated slow-release breeding colony of the predatory mite. Sometimes sold in bran in combination with *Amblyseius cucumeris* (Oudemans). **Tradenames:** Thripex-C – Koppert, Broad Mite Biocontrol (Neoseiulus

4. Insect Predators

barkeri) – IPM Laboratories, Thrips Predator – Arbico, Amblyseius barkeri (plus Amblyseius cucumeris) – Neudorff, Spical – Koppert.

APPLICATION: In glasshouses, sprinkle culture/carrier carefully on the leaves of the crop in early Spring at a rate of 50 to 120 predatory mites per plant and repeat every two to three weeks. Release on peppers immediately after the appearance of the first flowers. Often a high level early release gives the best results. In interiorscapes, a release rate of 1,000 to 10,000 predators per 50 square metres every two weeks is recommended.

PRODUCT SPECIFICATIONS: **Purity:** No phytophagous mites, no mould or other contaminants. **Storage conditions:** Store at 15 to 20 °C. Do not refrigerate. Do not place containers in direct sunlight. **Shelf-life:** Will remain viable for five days if received within one day of shipping and if stored under recommended conditions.

COMPATIBILITY: Very sensitive to insecticides and benzimidazole-based fungicides. Do not release if methomyl or a synthetic pyrethroid has been used. Most effective on smooth-leaved plants.

MAMMALIAN TOXICITY: Allergic reactions have been noted in production workers but this may be due to the prey rather than the predator. There have been no reports of allergic or other adverse reactions following field use.

ENVIRONMENTAL IMPACT AND NON-TARGET TOXICITY: *Amblyseius barkeri* is now wide-spread in Nature and there have been no reports of any adverse impact on the environment or on non-target organisms.

4:137 *Amblyseius californicus* Mite predator

The Pesticide Manual - 11th edition: Entry number 19

Predatory mite: Mesostigmata: Phytoseiidae

NOMENCLATURE: **Approved name:** *Amblyseius californicus* (McGregor).

SOURCE: *Amblyseius californicus* is a native of Mediterranean climates.

PRODUCTION: Reared on phytophagous mites such as *Tetranychus urticae* Koch on bean plants or on non-phytophagous acarid mites on bran.

TARGET PESTS: Preferred growth stages of spider mites, *Tetranychus urticae*, are the eggs and immature stages. *Amblyseius californicus* will survive on other small arthropods and on pollen, but it will not reproduce in the absence of spider mites.

TARGET CROPS: Glasshouse-grown crops, particularly those grown at relatively high temperatures and low relative humidities such as cucumbers, peppers and ornamentals. Also effective in field crops grown under high temperature conditions, such as strawberries.

BIOLOGICAL ACTIVITY: **Biology:** Eggs are laid on the hairs in the axils of the midvein and the lateral veins on the underside of leaves. The eggs hatch into six-legged larvae that do not feed and remain in groups near their place of emergence. Proto- and deutonymphal stages and adults have eight legs, are mobile and feed. **Predation:** At 26 °C, immature predatory mites consume, on average, 11.4 spider mite eggs and nymphs before reaching adulthood. An adult female can consume in excess of 150 prey over a 16 day period. *Amblyseius californicus* feeds on phytophagous mites by piercing the prey and sucking the contents. **Egg laying:** Egg laying varies with temperature from less than one per day (to yield a total of 48 throughout the female life-cycle) at 13 °C to over 3.5 per day (to yield a total of 65 throughout the female life-cycle) at 33 °C. Duration of development, egg laying and longevity will depend upon temperature, the type and availability of food and the ambient humidity.
Duration of development: *Amblyseius californicus* development is more rapid at high temperature, taking about 15 days at 15 °C, 8 days at 20 °C and 5.5 days at 25 °C.
Efficacy: *Amblyseius californicus* is particularly useful where food is scarce, temperatures are high, humidity is low and when the phytophagous mites are concealed in the terminal shoots of the crop.

COMMERCIALISATION: **Formulation:** Minimum of 2,000 live adults and juvenile predators per unit in vermiculite or corn husks. Contains an unspecified number of predator eggs. DoE licence required for release in the UK. **Tradenames:** Ambly-line cal 2000 – Novartis BCM, Californicus-System – Biobest, Spider Mite Predator – Arbico, Ambsure (cal) – Biological Crop Protection.

APPLICATION: Predatory mites are fragile and should be carefully mixed with the carrier material and sprinkled over the crop such that the carrier settles on the foliage, allowing the predators to move onto the crop. If there are hot-spots in the crop, the material can be poured into a box hanging within the crop where the phytophagous mites are most abundant. If reared on phytophagous mites on bean leaves, lay the leaves carefully on the leaves of the crop.

PRODUCT SPECIFICATIONS: **Purity:** No significant phytophagous mites, no mould and no other contaminants. **Storage conditions:** Store at 5 to 8 °C, 65 to 80% relative humidity, out of direct sunlight. **Shelf-life:** Use within 18 hours of receipt.

COMPATIBILITY: Incompatible with foliar-applied insecticides and acaricides and insecticidal smokes. Can be used with systemic soil applied insecticides such as imidacloprid.

MAMMALIAN TOXICITY: Allergic reactions have been noted in production workers, but this may be due to the prey rather than the predator. There have been no reports of allergic or other adverse reactions following glasshouse or field use.

ENVIRONMENTAL IMPACT AND NON-TARGET TOXICITY: *Amblyseius californicus* is wide-spread in Nature and there have been no reports of adverse environmental impact nor effects on non-target organisms.

4. Insect Predators

4:138   *Amblyseius cucumeris*   *Thrips predator*

The Pesticide Manual - 11th edition: Entry number 19

Predatory mite: Mesostigmata: Phytoseiidae

NOMENCLATURE: **Approved name:** *Amblyseius cucumeris* (Oudemans).
Other names: also known as *Neoseiulus cucumeris* (Oudemans). **Common names:** thrips predator; thrips predatory mite.

SOURCE: *Amblyseius cucumeris* is cosmopolitan, occurs widely in Nature and is found in Europe, North Africa, California and Australia. It thrives under conditions of high humidity but some strains enter diapause when days shorten to 12.5 hours, day temperatures fall below 22 °C and night temperatures drop to 17 °C. A strain that does not enter diapause has been selected for commercial application.

PRODUCTION: Reared on living non-phytophagous prey mites such as *Tyrophagus* spp. or *Acarus farris* (Oudemans) in a ratio of 1:1 to 1:5 predator:prey, excluding eggs. Small quantities of bran are provided as food for the prey mites. Up to 100,000 Phytoseiids per litre can be produced in this way.

TARGET PESTS: Main prey are thrips including *Frankliniella occidentalis* (Pergande), *F. tritici* (Fitch), *Thrips tabaci* Lindeman and *T. obscuratus* Crawford but the predator will eat spider mites, *Tetranychus urticae* Koch, and can survive on pollen.

TARGET CROPS: Glasshouse crops such as tomatoes, cucumbers, peppers and ornamentals. Also used for thrips control in interiorscapes.

BIOLOGICAL ACTIVITY: **Biology:** Eggs are laid in the axils of the midvein and the lateral veins on the underside of leaves. The eggs hatch into six-legged larvae that do not feed but remain aggregated near their place of emergence. Proto- and deutonymphs and adults have eight legs, are very mobile and consume food actively. *Amblyseius cucumeris* cannot survive below 0 °C but it can be stored at 9 °C with low mortality. **Predation:** Predatory mites pierce their prey and suck the contents. This species feeds only on first instar thrips,consuming between one and five thrips per day, depending on temperature and humidity.
Egg laying: Female predatory mites lay between 22 (at 15 to 16 °C) and 47 (at 25 to 26 °C) eggs throughout their lives. Eggs are laid close to recently-hatched thrips larvae.
Duration of development: Eggs hatch after two or three days, larvae mature after 0.5 to 1.5 days, protonymphs and deutonymphs each take two to 3.5 days to develop and adults live for six to eleven days, depending on the temperature. The lowest threshold temperature for larval development is 7.7 °C. **Efficacy:** Because *Amblyseius cucumeris* can survive on pollen, it can be introduced before the thrips allowing the predator population to build up. However, in crops that produce large quantities of pollen, its effectiveness is reduced because of this alternative food source and higher populations must be introduced. *Amblyseius cucumeris* feeds on only first instar thrips and, as a consequence, it may take a few months to control *Thrips tabaci*. **Key references:** 1) R J Jacobson. 1997. Integrated pest management (IPM) in greenhouses. In T Lewis (ed.), *Thrips as Crop Pests*, 639–66, CABI, Wallingford, UK.

2) M W Sabelis and P J C van Rijn. 1997. Predation by insects and mites. In T Lewis (ed.), *Thrips as Crop Pests*, 259–354, CABI, Wallingford, UK.

COMMERCIALISATION: **Formulation:** Sold as a vermiculite formulation with 10,000 to 50,000 predators per litre and as a specially formulated slow-release breeding colony of the predatory mite. The controlled release sachets are commercially more important for crops such as cucumbers and peppers. The loose product is more important in ornamentals. Sometimes sold in bran in combination with *Amblyseius barkeri*. **Tradenames:** Ambly-line cu 25000 – Novartis BCM, Thripex-C – Koppert, Thripex Plus – Koppert, Amblyseius-C – Applied Bio-Nomics, Thrips Destroyer – Nature's Alternative Insectary, Ambsure (abs) – Biological Crop Protection, Ambsure (c) – Biological Crop Protection, Amblyseius Thrips Predators – English Woodlands Biocontrol, Amblyseius System – Biobest, Amblyseius Breeding System (ABS 5) – Biobest, Neoseiulus cucumeris (thrips predator) – M&R Durango, Thrips Biocontrol (Neoseiulus cucumeris) – IPM Laboratories, Amblyseius cucumeris mite (in bags), Amblyseius cucumeris (in tubes) and Amblyseius cucumeris (in controlled-release satchets) – Rincon-Vitova Insectaries, Amblyseius cucumeris (non-diapause strain) – Sautter & Stepper, Thrips Predator – Arbico, Amblyseius barkeri (plus Amblyseius cucumeris) – Neudorff.

APPLICATION: In glasshouses, place bran carefully on the leaves of the crop in early Spring at a rate of 500 mites per plant and repeat every 2 to 3 weeks. Release on peppers immediately after the appearance of the first flowers. Often a high-level early release gives the best results. In glasshouses and interiorscapes, a release rate of 1,000 predators per 50 square metres weekly is recommended. For cucumbers, an initial application of 250 predators per plant followed by subsequent applications of 50 per plant every 15 days. Field applications of 150,000,000 predators per hectare per season are recommended. The use of controlled-release sachets gives longer periods of control in crops such as peppers and cucumbers.

PRODUCT SPECIFICATIONS: **Purity:** No phytophagous mites, no mould or other contaminants. **Storage conditions:** Store at 10 to 15 °C; do not refrigerate. Do not place containers in direct sunlight. **Shelf-life:** Use within five days if received within one day of shipping and if stored under recommended conditions. *Amblyseius cucumeris* cannot survive temperatures below 0 °C but can be stored at 9 °C with only low mortality.

COMPATIBILITY: Very sensitive to insecticides and benzimidazole-based fungicides. Do not release if methomyl or a synthetic pyrethroid has been used. Most effective on smooth-leaved plants.

MAMMALIAN TOXICITY: Allergic reactions have been noted in production workers but this may be due to the prey rather than the predator. There have been no reports of allergic or other adverse reactions following field use.

ENVIRONMENTAL IMPACT AND NON-TARGET TOXICITY: *Amblyseius cucumeris* is now wide-spread and there is no evidence of adverse environmental effects nor adverse effects on non-target organisms.

4:139 *Amblyseius degenerans* Thrips predator

The Pesticide Manual - 11th edition: Entry number 19

Predatory mite: Mesostigmata: Phytoseiidae

NOMENCLATURE: **Approved name:** *Amblyseius degenerans* (Berlese). **Other names:** also known as *Iphiseius degenerans* Berlese. **Common names:** thrips predator; thrips predatory mite.

SOURCE: *Amblyseius degenerans* occurs naturally in Africa and the Mediterranean. It thrives under conditions of high humidity but tolerates lower humidities than *Amblyseius cucumeris* (Oudemans). It will not enter diapause under glasshouse vegetable growing conditions (16 to 25 °C).

PRODUCTION: Usually reared on pollen.

TARGET PESTS: Main prey are thrips, in particular *Frankliniella occidentalis* (Pergande). *Thrips tabaci* Lindeman are less favoured as prey. The predator will eat spider mites, *Tetranychus urticae* Koch, and can survive on pollen.

TARGET CROPS: Glasshouse crops such as peppers and ornamentals. Also used for thrips control in interiorscapes.

BIOLOGICAL ACTIVITY: **Biology:** Eggs (oval and about 0.14 mm in diameter) are laid in the axils of the midvein and the lateral veins on the underside of leaves. The eggs hatch into six-legged larvae that do not feed but remain aggregated near their place of emergence. Pro- and deuto-nymphs and adults have eight legs. These stages are very mobile and consume food actively. **Predation:** Predatory mites pierce their prey and suck their contents. They consume between one and five thrips per day depending on temperature and humidity. Larger and more aggressive than *Amblyseius cucumeris*. **Egg laying:** Female predatory mites lay between 22 (at 15 to 16 °C) and 47 (at 25 to 26 °C) eggs throughout their lives. Females require multiple matings for egg laying. **Duration of development:** Eggs hatch after two or three days, larvae mature after 0.5 to 1.5 days, protonymphs and deutonymphs take two to 3.5 days to develop and adults live for over 20 days, depending on the temperature. **Efficacy:** Because *Amblyseius degenerans* can survive on pollen, it can be introduced before the thrips appear allowing the predator population to build up. *Amblyseius degenerans* consumes first stage thrips larvae more often than later stages. **Key references:** 1) R J Jacobson. 1997. Integrated pest management (IPM) in greenhouses. In T Lewis (ed.), *Thrips as Crop Pests*, 639–66, CABI, Wallingford, UK. 2) M W Sabelis and P J C van Rijn. 1997. Predation by insects and mites. In T Lewis (ed.), *Thrips as Crop Pests*, 259–354, CABI, Wallingford, UK.

COMMERCIALISATION: **Formulation:** Sold as a vermiculite formulation with 10,000 to 50,000 predators per litre. Also sold in small 30 to 60 ml vials. **Tradenames:** Ambly-line d – Novartis BCM, Degenerans L – Applied Bio-Nomics, Iphiseius degenerans – Rincon-Vitova Insectaries, Degerans System – Biobest, Thripans – Koppert.

APPLICATION: Place predators carefully on the leaves of the crop in early Spring, ensuring that they are well distributed, at a rate of one mite per plant and repeat every 2 to 3 weeks. Release on peppers immediately after the appearance of the first flowers. Often a high level early release gives the best results. As the females require multiple matings, it is recommended that introductions are concentrated on a few plants per row rather than evenly distributed through the crop. In glasshouses and interiorscapes, a release rate of 1,000 predators per 100 square metres weekly is recommended. Normally only one or two introductions are made on peppers.

PRODUCT SPECIFICATIONS: **Purity:** No phytophagous mites, no mould or other contaminants. **Storage conditions:** Store at 15 to 20 °C. Do not refrigerate. Do not place containers in direct sunlight. **Shelf-life:** Viable for five days if received within one day of shipping and if stored under recommended conditions.

COMPATIBILITY: Very sensitive to insecticides and benzimidazole-based fungicides. Do not release if methomyl or a synthetic pyrethroid has been used. Most effective on smooth-leaved plants.

MAMMALIAN TOXICITY: There have been no reports of allergic or other adverse reactions following field use. If bred on non-phytophagous mites there have been cases of rhinitis or skin irritation or both in production workers. This is believed to be due to the prey mite rather than *Amblyseius degenerans*.

ENVIRONMENTAL IMPACT AND NON-TARGET TOXICITY: *Amblyseius degenerans* is wide-spread in Nature and has not shown any adverse effects on non-target organisms or on the environment.

4:140   *Amblyseius fallacis*   *Mite predator*

Predatory mite: Mesostigmata: Phytoseiidae

NOMENCLATURE: **Approved name:** *Amblyseius fallacis* (Garman).

SOURCE: Predatory mite that occurs widely in Nature, particularly in orchards.

PRODUCTION: Bred on spider mites (*Tetranychus urticae* Koch) under controlled conditions.

TARGET PESTS: Spider mites and, in particular, *Tetranychus urticae* and *Panonychus ulmi* (Koch).

TARGET CROPS: Orchard crops, especially apples and pears, strawberries, ornamentals and protected vegetable crops.

BIOLOGICAL ACTIVITY: **Biology:** Eggs are laid on the hairs in the axils of the midvein and the lateral veins on the underside of leaves. The eggs hatch into six-legged larvae that do not feed and remain in groups near their place of emergence. Proto- and deutonymphal stages and adults have eight legs, are mobile and feed. **Predation:** At 26 °C, immature predatory mites consume an average of 11.4 spider mite eggs and nymphs before reaching adulthood. An adult female can consume in excess of 150 prey over a 16-day period. *Amblyseius fallacis* feeds on phytophagous mites by piercing the prey and sucking the contents.

Duration of development: *Amblyseius fallacis* development is most rapid under high temperature conditions taking about 15 days at 15 °C, 8 days at 20 °C and 5.5 days at 25 °C. It prefers conditions of high humidity. **Efficacy:** *Amblyseius fallacis* is particular useful where food is scarce, temperature and humidity are high and when the phytophagous mites are concealed in the terminal shoots of the crop.

COMMERCIALISATION: **Formulation:** Minimum of 2,000 live adults and juvenile predators per unit in vermiculite or corn husks. Contains an unspecified number of predator eggs. **Tradenames:** Amblyseius fallacis – IPM Laboratories, Amblyseius fallacis – Rincon-Vitova, Amblyseius fallacis – Praxis.

APPLICATION: Distribute leaves on which *A. fallacis* has been bred carefully within the crop.

PRODUCT SPECIFICATIONS: **Purity:** Commercial product contains only adult *Amblyseius fallacis* with no mould or other contaminants and no significant phytophagous mites. **Storage conditions:** Keep between 8 and 10 °C out of direct sunlight. Do not freeze. **Shelf-life:** Use within two days of delivery.

COMPATIBILITY: Compatible with most agrochemicals. Do not apply with acaricides or persistent insecticides.

MAMMALIAN TOXICITY: *Amblyseius fallacis* has shown no allergic or other adverse effects on research workers, manufacturing or field staff. It is considered to be of low mammalian toxicity.

ENVIRONMENTAL IMPACT AND NON-TARGET TOXICITY: *Amblyseius fallacis* occurs in Nature and is not expected to have any adverse effects on non-target organisms or the environment.

4:141   *Anagrus atomus*   Leafhopper parasite

The Pesticide Manual - 11th edition: Entry number 26

Parasitic wasp: Hymenoptera: Mymaridae

NOMENCLATURE: **Approved name:** *Anagrus atomus* (Linnaeus). **Other names:** leafhopper egg parasitoid.

SOURCE: *Anagrus atomus* occurs widely in Nature and is a very effective parasite of leafhoppers.

PRODUCTION: *Anagrus atomus* is reared under controlled conditions on leafhopper eggs.

TARGET PESTS: For control of leafhoppers *Hauptidia maraccana* Melichar and *Empoasca decipiens* Paoli.

TARGET CROPS: Recommended for use on glasshouse-grown tomatoes, peppers and ornamentals.

BIOLOGICAL ACTIVITY: **Biology:** The adults are small (2 mm) and the females search for leafhopper eggs and lay their eggs inside the leafhopper eggs. Parasitised eggs are bright red in colour. The wasp develops in the leafhopper egg. Following pupation, the adults emerge from the parasitised eggs, mate and the females seek out new host eggs. **Duration of development:** The adult females are short-lived (2 to 3 days). **Efficacy:** The females are mobile and are very effective at seeking out host eggs.

COMMERCIALISATION: **Formulation:** Sold as pupae close to emergence on leaf pieces, in units of 50 to 100. **Tradenames:** Anagrus atomus native Species – English Woodland Biocontrol, Anagsure (a) – Biological Crop Protection.

APPLICATION: The leaf pieces containing the Anagrus atomus pupae are laid out within the crop and the adults are allowed to emerge and seek host eggs. The parasite may be applied to protected edible and ornamental crops at any time of the year.

PRODUCT SPECIFICATIONS: **Purity:** Formulations contain only parasitised leafhopper eggs with Anagrus atomus pupae close to emergence. **Storage conditions:** Keep cool and out of direct sunlight. Do not allow to freeze. **Shelf-life:** Use immediately upon receipt.

COMPATIBILITY: Incompatible with residual insecticides.

MAMMALIAN TOXICITY: Anagrus atomus has not demonstrated evidence of toxicity, infectivity, irritation or hypersensitivity to mammals. No allergic responses or other adverse health problems have been observed by research workers, manufacturing staff or users.

ENVIRONMENTAL IMPACT AND NON-TARGET TOXICITY: Anagrus atomus occurs in Nature and, as such, is not expected to show any adverse effects on non-target organisms.

4:142 *Aphelinus abdominalis* Aphid parasite

The Pesticide Manual - 11th edition: Entry number 30

Parasitic wasp: Hymenoptera: Aphelinidae

NOMENCLATURE: **Approved name:** Aphelinus abdominalis (Dalman). **Other names:** aphid parasitic wasp.

SOURCE: Widespread in Europe.

PRODUCTION: Reared in insectaries on aphids such as Macrosiphum euphorbiae (Thomas).

TARGET PESTS: Aphids, with particular activity against 'large' aphids such as Macrosiphum euphorbiae and Aulacorthum solani (Kaltenbach).

TARGET CROPS: Protected vegetable and ornamental crops.

BIOLOGICAL ACTIVITY: **Biology:** Eggs are laid within the aphid and the wasp passes through four larval stages after egg hatch, during which time the aphid continues to feed. The adult emerges from its pupal stage within the mummified aphid, which is always black.
Predation: Female wasps are more effective parasites of large than small aphids. Eggs are laid within aphid colonies and the female can parasitise between 10 and 15 aphids a day. The adult wasps also predate aphids. **Egg laying:** Adults mate within a day of emergence. Unfertilised females lay only male eggs, whilst fertilised females lay eggs that can develop into either males or females dependent upon the size of the aphid to be parasitised. As a rule, eggs laid in large aphids are fertilised and develop into females whilst those laid in smaller aphids are not fertilised and develop into males. **Duration of development:** An adult wasp will emerge between 13 and 15 days after oviposition, depending upon the temperature. The pupal stage takes about five days to hatch. **Efficacy:** A very efficient flyer and seeker of aphids. The relatively large ovipositor restricts the size of aphid that can be parasitised.
Key references: 1) E B Hågvar and T Hofsvang. 1991. Aphid parasitoids (Hymenoptera, Aphidiidae): Biology, host selection and use in biological control, *Biocontrol News and Information*. **12** (1), 13–41. 2) P Stary. 1988. Aphelinidae. In *Aphids: their Biology, Natural Enemies and Control*. A K Minks and P Harrewijn (eds.), Vol. B, 185–8, Elsevier, Amsterdam, the Netherlands.

COMMERCIALISATION: **Formulation:** Supplied as mummies that hatch during and after shipment. **Tradenames:** Aphel-line ab – Novartis BCM, Aphelinus-System – Biobest, Aphelinus – Sautter & Stepper, Aphelinus – IPM Laboratories, Aphelinus – Praxis, Aphelsure (a) – Biological Crop Protection, Aphilin – Koppert.

APPLICATION: Allow adult wasps to fly from the container close to the aphid colonies. Rest bottles or vials in the crop so the remaining adults can enter the crop as they emerge from the mummies.

PRODUCT SPECIFICATIONS: **Purity:** Adult wasps with no contaminants or pure mummies with no carrier. **Storage conditions:** Store in the dark at 8 to 10 °C. **Shelf-life:** Use as soon as possible. *Aphelinus abdominalis* will remain active for two to three days if stored as recommended.

COMPATIBILITY: Incompatible with residual insecticides. Ants will protect aphids from parasitism.

MAMMALIAN TOXICITY: No allergic or other adverse reactions have been noted with research and production staff or users.

ENVIRONMENTAL IMPACT AND NON-TARGET TOXICITY: *Aphelinus abdominalis* is not expected to have any adverse effects on non-target organisms or on the environment.

4:143 *Aphidius colemani* *Aphid parasitoid*

The Pesticide Manual - 11th edition: Entry number 31

Parasitic wasp: Hymenoptera: Aphidiidae

NOMENCLATURE: **Approved name:** *Aphidius colemani* Viereck. **Other names:** *Aphidius platensis* (Bréthes); *Aphidius transcaspicus* (Telenga). **Common name:** aphid parasitoid.

SOURCE: This parasitic wasp was thought to have originated in India but the species *Aphidius platensis* and *A. transcaspicus* were re-classified as junior synonyms of *A. colemani* and this extended its geographical range from Central Asia to the Mediterranean. The wasp has been introduced into Australia, Africa, Central America, California, England, Norway and the Netherlands. Traditionally, *Aphidius matricariae* Haliday was the principal commercial agent but recently strains selected from commercial colonies for their superior performance against *Aphis gossypii* Glover were shown to be *Aphidius colemani* contaminants and this species has generally superseded *A. matricariae.*

PRODUCTION: *Aphidius colemani* is reared on *Aphis gossypii* Glover or *Myzus persicae* (Sulzer) under controlled glasshouse conditions. Mummies of known age are collected, packaged in bottles or vials and despatched to the customer.

TARGET PESTS: Aphids. The primary hosts are *Myzus persicae*, *Myzus nicotianae* Blackman and *Aphis gossypii*. *Aulacorthum solani* (Kaltenbach) and *Rhopalosiphum padi* (Linnaeus) are also parasitised.

TARGET CROPS: Glasshouse-grown crops such as tomatoes, cucumbers, peppers, aubergines and ornamentals. Also effective in interiorscapes.

BIOLOGICAL ACTIVITY: **Biology:** Female adults lay single eggs within an aphid. Parasitised aphids continue to feed and can transmit viruses. After egg hatch, the wasp larva progresses through four stages within the aphid before pupating within the aphid's body, the mummy stage. At parasite pupation, the parasite larva spins a silk cocoon within the aphid cuticle. The cuticle of the aphid host then hardens and the body swells, providing a protective case from which the adult wasp emerges. The adult leaves the mummy through a small round hole cut in the dorsum of the mummified host. **Predation:** Female wasps can parasitise 100 to 200 aphids within seven days, although this will vary with host. The presence of *Aphidius colemani* will often disturb the aphid colony leading to the production of an aphid alarm pheromone that causes aphids to migrate from or fall off the leaf. **Egg laying:** Females mate within one day of emergence and begin to lay eggs within a few hours of mating. Fertilised females can lay both unfertilised eggs, that develop into males, and fertilised eggs, that develop into females. Females can lay viable eggs without mating, but these always develop into males. **Duration of development:** It takes between 13 and 15 days from parasitism or egg laying to adult emergence. It is usual for the mummy to exist for five to six days at 20 °C. **Efficacy:** Particularly effective against *Aphis gossypii*, *Myzus persicae* and *Myzus nicotianae* although it will parasitise over 40 different aphid species. Very effective searchers that work well against small, well-dispersed populations. Can be attacked by hyperparasitic wasps.

4. Insect Predators

Key references: 1) E B Hågvar and T Hofsvang. 1991. Aphid parasitoids (Hymenoptera, Aphidiidae): Biology, host selection and use in biological control, *Biocontrol News and Information.* **12** (1), 13–41. 2) P Stary. 1988. Aphidiidae. In *Aphids: their Biology, Natural Enemies and Control*, A K Minks and P Harrewijn (eds.), Vol. B, 171–184. Elsevier, Amsterdam, the Netherlands. 3) P M J Ramakers. 1989. Biological control in greenhouse. In *Aphids: their Biology, Natural Enemies and Control*, A K Minks and P Harrewijn (eds.), Vol. C, 199–208, Elsevier, Amsterdam, the Netherlands.

COMMERCIALISATION: **Formulation:** Most frequently sold as freshly-collected aphid mummies of known age with no carrier in bottle with a feeder ring in the cap. Sometimes supplied as newly-emerged adult wasps. **Tradenames:** Aphi-line c – Novartis BCM, Aphipar – Koppert, Aphibank – Koppert, Aphidius colemani – English Woodland Biocontrol, Aphisure (c) – Biological Crop Protection, Aphid Destroyer – Nature's Alternative Insectary, Adult Aphidius – Applied Bio-Nomics, Aphidius System – Biobest, Aphidius aphid parasite – M&R Durango, Aphidius colemani – IPM Laboratories, Aphidius colemani – Praxis, Aphidius colemani wasps – Rincon-Vitova Insectaries, Aphidius – Sautter & Stepper, Aphidius colemani – Neudorff, AAP 2539 – BioSafer.

APPLICATION: Release near infested areas early in the season. Less effective at high than low aphid populations. Release throughout treated area by allowing parasites to escape from the shipping vial. Treat every other week at a rate of between 2 and 3 wasps per square metre. Can be used at lower rates as a preventative treatment.

PRODUCT SPECIFICATIONS: **Purity:** Aphid mummies with no non-parasitised aphids. Absence of hyperparasites is essential. Percentage hatch should be greater than 70%. Adults of known age with no hyperparasites. **Storage conditions:** Maintain at 5 to 10 °C and do not expose to direct sunlight. **Shelf-life:** Use as soon as possible and within five days if received within 1 day of despatch and stored under recommended conditions. Adults must be applied immediately. Release in the early morning or in the late evening when glasshouse vents are closed.

COMPATIBILITY: Do not use sticky yellow traps as these attract *Aphidius colemani*. Blue sticky traps can be used. Ants will reduce the effectiveness of *A. colemani*.

MAMMALIAN TOXICITY: There have been no reports of acute or chronic toxicity, eye or skin irritation or allergic or other adverse reactions to *Aphidius colemani* in research, production or horticultural staff.

ENVIRONMENTAL IMPACT AND NON-TARGET TOXICITY: *Aphidius colemani* has no effects on non-target organisms and no adverse environmental effects are expected from its use.

4:144 *Aphidius ervi* *Aphid parasite*

Parasitic wasp: Hymenoptera: Aphidiidae

NOMENCLATURE: **Approved name:** *Aphidius ervi* Haliday. **Other names:** aphid parasite.

SOURCE: The parasitic wasp is native to Europe and Asia. Introduced and established in Chile, Canada, USA and Australia.

PRODUCTION: Supplied as freshly-emerged adults.

TARGET PESTS: Aphids, including *Acyrthosiphon pisum* (Harris), *A. kondoi* Shinji, *Aulacorthum solani* (Kaltenbach), *Sitobion avenae* (Fabricius) and *Macrosiphum euphorbiae* (Thomas).

TARGET CROPS: Glasshouse grown crops such as peppers. May be used in ornamentals under glass in the Spring. *Aphidius ervi* was widely released in the past in classical biological control programmes and is used in cereal and legume crops in South America.

BIOLOGICAL ACTIVITY: **Biology:** Female adults lay single eggs within an aphid. Parasitised aphids continue to feed and can transmit viruses. After egg hatch, the wasp larva progresses through four stages within the aphid before pupating within the aphid's body, the mummy stage. The adult leaves the mummy through a small round hole. **Predation:** Female wasps can parasitise 100 to 200 aphids within seven days, although this varies with the host aphid. The presence of *Aphidius ervi* will often disturb the aphid colony, leading to the production of an aphid alarm pheromone that causes aphids to migrate from or fall off the leaf.
Egg laying: Females mate within one day of emergence and begin to lay eggs within a few hours of mating. Fertilised females can lay both unfertilised eggs, that develop into males, and fertilised eggs, that develop into females. Females can lay viable eggs without mating but these all develop into males. **Duration of development:** It takes between 13 and 15 days from egg hatch to adult emergence. It is usual for the mummy to exist for five to six days at 20 °C.
Efficacy: Particularly effective against *Acyrthosiphon pisum*, *Aulacorthum solani* and *Macrosiphum euphorbiae* although it will parasitise many different aphid species. Very effective searchers that work well against small, well-dispersed populations. Can be attacked by hyperparasitic wasps.
Key references: 1) E B Hågvar and T Hofsvang. 1991. Aphid parasitoids (Hymenoptera, Aphidiidae): Biology, host selection and use in biological control. *Biocontrol News and Information.* **12(1)**, 13–41. 2) P Stary. 1988. Aphidiidae. In *Aphids: their Biology, Natural Enemies and Control*, A K Minks and P Harrewijn (eds.), Vol. B, 171–184. Elsevier, Amsterdam, the Netherlands. 3) P M J Ramakers. 1989. Biological control in greenhouses. In *Aphids: their Biology, Natural Enemies and Control*, A K Minks and P Harrewijn (eds.), Vol C, 199–208, Elsevier, Amsterdam, the Netherlands.

COMMERCIALISATION: **Formulation:** Freshly collected adult wasps or mixed mummies and adults. **Tradenames:** Aphi-line e – Novartis BCM, Ervi-System – Biobest, Aphidius ervi – Rincon-Vitova, Aphidius ervi – IPM Laboratories, Aphidius ervi – Praxis, Aphipar – Koppert, Ervipar – Koppert, Aphisure (e) – Biological Crop Protection.

APPLICATION: Release near infested areas early in the season. Less effective at high than low aphid populations. Release throughout treated area by allowing parasites to escape from the

4. Insect Predators

shipping vial. Treat every other week at a rate of between two and three wasps per square metre.

PRODUCT SPECIFICATIONS: **Purity:** Adult wasps with no non-parasitised aphids. Absence of hyperparasites is essential. **Storage conditions:** Maintain at 5 to 10 °C and do not expose to direct sunlight. **Shelf-life:** Five days if received within one day of despatch and stored under recommended conditions.

COMPATIBILITY: Do not use sticky yellow traps as these attract *Aphidius ervi*. Blue sticky traps can be used.

MAMMALIAN TOXICITY: There have been no reports of allergic or other adverse reactions following field use.

ENVIRONMENTAL IMPACT AND NON-TARGET TOXICITY: *Aphidius ervi* occurs in Nature and is not expected to show any parasitism of non-target species or any adverse environmental effects.

4:145   *Aphidius matricariae*   Aphid parasite

Parasitic wasp: Hymenoptera: Aphidiidae

NOMENCLATURE: **Approved name:** *Aphidius matricariae* Haliday. **Other names:** aphid parasite.

SOURCE: Occurs widely in Europe. Generally replaced as an aphid parasite by *Aphidius colemani* Viereck that was isolated from a commercial strain of *Aphidius matricariae* that had been selected for its more effective control of aphids.

PRODUCTION: Reared under controlled conditions on aphids such as *Myzus persicae* (Sulzer).

TARGET PESTS: Aphids, particularly *Myzus persicae* and *Myzus nicotianae* Blackman.

TARGET CROPS: Glasshouse-grown crops such as tomatoes, aubergines, cucumbers, peppers and ornamentals. Also effective in interiorscapes.

BIOLOGICAL ACTIVITY: **Biology:** Female adults lay single eggs within an aphid. Parasitised aphids continue to feed and can transmit viruses. After egg hatch, the wasp larva progresses through four stages within the aphid before pupating within the aphid's body, the mummy stage. The adult leaves the mummy through a small round hole. **Predation:** Female wasps can parasitise 100 to 200 aphids within seven days. The presence of *Aphidius matricariae* will often disturb the aphid colony leading to the production of aphid alarm pheromone that causes aphids to migrate from or fall off the leaf. **Egg laying:** Females mate within one day of emergence and begin to lay eggs within a few hours of mating. Fertilised females can lay both unfertilised eggs, that develop into males, and fertilised eggs, that develop into females. Females can lay viable eggs without mating but these develop only into males.

Duration of development: It takes between 13 and 15 days from egg hatch to adult emergence depending upon the host species and the temperature. It is usual for the mummy to exist for five to six days at 20 °C. **Efficacy:** Particularly effective against *Myzus persicae*, although it will parasitise several different species of aphid. Ineffective against *Aphis gossypii* Glover. Very effective searcher that works well against low-density, well-dispersed populations. Can be attacked by hyperparasitic wasps. Less effective and narrower host range than *Aphidius colemani*. **Key references:** 1) E B Hågvar and T Hofsvang. 1991. Aphid parasitoids (Hymenoptera, Aphidiidae): Biology, host selection and use in biological control. *Biocontrol News and Information*. **12(1)**, 13–41. 2) P Stary. 1988. Aphidiidae. In *Aphids: their Biology, Natural Enemies and Control*, A K Minks and P Harrewijn (eds.), Vol. B, 171–184, Elsevier, Amsterdam, the Netherlands. 3) P M J Ramakers. 1989. Biological control in greenhouses. In *Aphids: their Biology, Natural Enemies and Control*, A K Minks and P Harrewijn (eds.), Vol C, 199–208, Elsevier, Amsterdam, the Netherlands.

COMMERCIALISATION: **Formulation:** Sold as adults. **Tradenames:** Aphidius matricariae – Applied Bio-nomics.

APPLICATION: Release near infected areas early in the season. Less effective at high than low aphid populations. Release throughout treated area by allowing parasites to escape from the shipping vial. Treat every other week at a rate of between two and three wasps per square metre. Can be used at lower rates as a preventative treatment.

PRODUCT SPECIFICATIONS: **Purity:** Adults only with no hyperparasites.
Storage conditions: Maintain at 5 to 10 °C and do not expose to direct sunlight.
Shelf-life: Can be stored for up to five days under recommended conditions, although the parasite is more effective if used immediately.

COMPATIBILITY: Do not use sticky yellow traps as these attract *Aphidius matricariae*. Blue sticky traps can be used. Control ants, as these will protect aphids from parasitism.

MAMMALIAN TOXICITY: No allergic or other adverse reactions have been reported following release of *Aphidius matricariae* by research, maufacturing or field staff.

ENVIRONMENTAL IMPACT AND NON-TARGET TOXICITY: *Aphidius matricariae* occurs widely in Nature and is not expected to have any adverse effects on non-target organisms or the environment.

4:146 *Aphidoletes aphidimyza*

Aphid predator

The Pesticide Manual - 11th edition: Entry number 32

Predatory gall-midge: Diptera: Cecidomyiidae

NOMENCLATURE: **Approved name:** *Aphidoletes aphidimyza* Rondani. **Other names:** gall midge; aphid midge; aphid gall-midge.

SOURCE: Native to northern parts of North America and Europe. *Aphidoletes aphidimyza* was originally developed as an aphid control measure in Finland and Russia in the 1970s, culminating in its commercial sale in Finland in 1978. Subsequently, commercial trials were conducted in Northern Europe and Canada alongside new breeding strategies. This led to the release of commercial products from the mid 1980s.

PRODUCTION: Raised on *Aphis gossypii* Glover or other suitable aphid and sold as pupae within a vermiculite carrier or moist cotton. Often raised on *Myzus persicae* (Sulzer) or *Aphis fabae* Scopoli on sweet peppers, aubergines or beans.

TARGET PESTS: Aphids, all genera and species.

TARGET CROPS: Glasshouse vegetables such as tomatoes, peppers and cucumbers. Recommended for use on ornamentals and within interiorscapes. In Canada, it has been used successfully in parks on flowers, trees and shrubs. It is also used in home gardens and apple orchards.

BIOLOGICAL ACTIVITY: **Biology:** *Aphidoletes aphidimyza* adults are active at night and so mating and egg-laying occur at night and at dusk. In the day, the adults seek refuge within the crop, usually hanging under leaves or in spider webs low over the ground. Oval eggs (0.3 × 0.1 mm) are laid near or under the aphids. Newly emerged larvae are 0.3 mm long and reach 2.5 mm in length when fully grown. They attack aphids by injecting them with a paralysing toxin through the knee joints. Within ten minutes of the injection, the body contents of the aphid are dissolved and the gall-midge sucks them out. *Aphidoletes aphidimyza* will consume more aphids as it grows and, if prey are plentiful will inject and kill more aphids than it can eat. *Aphidoletes aphidimyza* enters diapause in the Autumn with falling temperatures and shortening days. In the Autumn, fully-grown larvae tunnel into the soil where they hibernate about two cm underground in a cocoon. In glasshouse or interiorscapes, Winter diapause can be avoided with low level supplemental lighting (60 watts for 20 square metres). **Predation:** *Aphidoletes aphidimyza* larvae will eat between ten and 100 aphids from egg-hatch to pupation. The preferred temperature for predation is between 19 and 28 °C. The adults feed on honey-dew. **Egg laying:** The number of eggs laid by a female depends on the weather, the amount of food consumed as a larva and the amount of honey-dew absorbed as an adult. Most eggs are laid in the first two to four days of adulthood. Females live for about ten days and lay up to 250 eggs. **Duration of development:** Development time is very dependent on temperature. At 21 °C, the egg stage takes two to three days, the larval stage takes seven to 14 days and the pupal stage takes 14 days. Females live for about ten days and males for about seven days. **Efficacy:** The searching behaviour of the adult female gall-midge is very effective with infested plants being found easily within uninfested plants. Large aphid populations are preferred for egg-laying. This allows for the rapid spread of the midges throughout the glasshouse. Larvae can move about six cm without feeding and can detect aphids from a distance of 2.5 cm. **Key reference:** P M J Ramakers. 1989. Biological control in greenhouses. In *Aphids: their Biology, Natural Enemies and Control*, A K Minks and P Harrewijn (eds.), Vol C, 199–208, Elsevier, Amsterdam, the Netherlands.

COMMERCIALISATION: **Formulation:** Pupae stored in vermiculite in bottles, in damp cotton or in moist peat. Sometimes sold as adults. **Tradenames:** Aphido-line a 250 – Novartis

BCM (in vermiculite in bottles), Aphidoletes-V – Applied Bio-Nomics (in vermiculite in bottles), Aphidoletes Aphid Parasites – English Woodland Biocontrol, Aphidoletes Gallmücken – Neudorff, Aphidoletes Gallmücken – Sautter & Stepper, Aphidoletes aphidomyza Midge AA250 – Rincon-Vitova Insectaries, Aphidoletes aphidomyza Midge AA1 – Rincon-Vitova Insectaries, Aphidoletes aphidomyza – IPM Laboratories, Aphidoletes aphidomyza Predatory Gall Midge – M&R Durango, Aphidoletes-System – Biobest, Aphid Predator – Arbico, Aphidoletes aphidomyza (adults) – Applied Bio-Nomics, Aphidosure (a) – Biological Crop Protection, Aphidend – Koppert, Aphidoletes aphidomyza – Praxis.

APPLICATION: Apply one to six midges per plant weekly for two to four weeks. A guide for release is about one midge for ten aphids. Keep packing material moist for two weeks following opening. For overall application, release one to four midges per square metre but use higher rates to control established colonies. Distribute the carrier onto the growing medium or into release boxes. Early application is recommended in aphid hot-spots. Pupae survive best when organic matter is present for a pupation site. Keep conditions moist but not wet.

PRODUCT SPECIFICATIONS: **Purity:** No live aphids, only viable pupae.
Storage conditions: Can be stored for up to five days in a refrigerator. Will emerge from pupa within a week at room temperature. **Shelf-life:** Up to five days in a refrigerator (10 °C). Cold storage reduces female egg laying and delays emergence. Should be used as soon after delivery as possible.

COMPATIBILITY: Avoid residual pesticides. Do not hose down the crop as this will dislodge the larvae. Use in conjunction with other aphid parasites.

MAMMALIAN TOXICITY: No allergic or other adverse effect has been recorded with research or manufacturing staff nor through its use in the field. There is no evidence of acute or chronic toxicity, eye or skin irritation or hypersensitivity in mammals.

ENVIRONMENTAL IMPACT AND NON-TARGET TOXICITY: No adverse environmental or non-target effects have been recorded from the use of *Aphidoletes aphidomyza*.

4:147   *Aphytis lignanensis*   Red scale parasite

Parasitic wasp: Hymenoptera: Aphelinidae

NOMENCLATURE: **Approved name:** *Aphytis lignanensis* Compere.
Other names: armoured scale parasite; red scale parasite; scale parasite; golden chalid.

SOURCE: Native to India and Pakistan.

PRODUCTION: Reared on scale insects and sold as adult wasps fed on honey for 24 hours prior to shipment.

TARGET PESTS: Scale insects, particularly of citrus, olives, nut crops and passion fruit, including *Aonidiella aurantii* (Maskell), *Aonidiella orientalis* (Newstead) and *Aspidiotus nerii* (Bouché).

TARGET CROPS: Citrus, ornamentals, orchard crops and passion fruit.

BIOLOGICAL ACTIVITY: **Biology:** The female wasp lays eggs under the scale cover and onto the body of second instar and unmated female scales. The unmated female scale releases a pheromone to attract the males and this also attracts the parasitic female wasp. The eggs develop into legless larvae that feed on the scale by sucking its body fluids. All stages of scale are parasitised by the larvae, except the crawlers. The larvae pupate within the scale and later emerge to mate and continue the cycle. Adults also feed on scales. **Predation:** One parasite will destroy an average of 30 scales in its lifetime. **Egg laying:** The female wasp lays its eggs under the female scale when it loosens to allow the male to mate. Between one and five eggs are laid dependent upon the size of the scale. Approximately six scales will be attacked per day. **Duration of development:** Egg to adult takes about 12 to 13 days and the adult has a life span of 26 days in the presence of an adequate food source. **Efficacy:** *Aphytis lignanesis* can move as far as six trees from the point of introduction. It is attracted to female scales by the scale sex pheromone. Less effective under conditions of high or low temperature or low humidity. Adults also feed on nectar and the presence of nectar-producing plants aids their parasitism. More effective parasite in hot, humid conditions than *Aphytis melinus* DeBach.

COMMERCIALISATION: **Formulation:** Supplied in boxes lined with wet newspaper and packed in ice or in plastic, sealed capsules. **Tradenames:** Aphytis lignanesis – Bugs for Bugs.

APPLICATION: Apply by hanging container on a twig of the plant to be treated on the shaded side of the tree. Apply one capsule to every nine or twelve trees. Begin release before flowering and continue until the Autumn. Most effective if released before male scale flight. Recommended release rate 12,000 to 25,000 wasps per hectare. Young trees represent poor candidates for biological control because they offer little natural shelter for the beneficial wasp.

PRODUCT SPECIFICATIONS: **Purity:** Adult wasps with no contaminants.
Storage conditions: Can be stored in a cooled, insulated container at 15 to 19 °C away from direct sunlight. **Shelf-life:** Adults will survive for 26 days after emergence.

COMPATIBILITY: Extreme cold or low humidity will limit activity. Ants interfere with the parasites and reduce their performance. Generally, copper and foliar feeds will not harm *Aphytis lignanesis* but organophosphates are toxic. If an OP has been applied a minimum of four weeks should elapse before release of the parasites.

MAMMALIAN TOXICITY: No allergic or other adverse reactions have been noted with workers in the field. There is no evidence of acute or chronic toxicity, eye or skin irritation or hypersensitivity in mammals.

ENVIRONMENTAL IMPACT AND NON-TARGET TOXICITY: *Aphytis lignanesis* occurs widely in Nature and is not expected to parasitise non-target organisms or have any adverse effects on the environment.

4:148 *Aphytis melinus* *Red scale parasite*

Parasitic wasp: Hymenoptera: Aphelinidae

NOMENCLATURE: **Approved name:** *Aphytis melinus* DeBach. **Other names:** armoured scale parasite; red scale parasite; scale parasite; golden chalcid.

SOURCE: Native to India and Pakistan.

PRODUCTION: Reared on scale insects and sold as adult wasps fed on honey for 24 hours prior to shipment.

TARGET PESTS: Red scale and oriental scale insects, particularly of citrus, olives, nut crops and passion fruit including *Aonidiella aurantii* (Maskell), *Aonidiella orientalis* (Newstead) and *Aspidiotus nerii* (Bouché).

TARGET CROPS: Citrus, ornamentals, orchard and nut crops and passion fruit.

BIOLOGICAL ACTIVITY: **Biology:** The female wasp lays eggs under the scale cover and onto the body of second instar and unmated female scales. The unmated female scale releases a pheromone to attract the males and this also attracts the parasitic female wasp. The eggs develop into legless larvae that feed on the scale by sucking its body fluids. All stages of scale are parasitised by the larvae, except the crawlers. The larvae pupate within the scale and later emerge to mate and continue the cycle. Adults also feed on scales. **Predation:** One parasite will destroy an average of 30 scales in its lifetime. **Egg laying:** The female wasp lays its eggs under the female scale when it loosens to allow the male to mate. Between one and five eggs are laid dependent upon the size of the scale. Approximately six scales will be attacked per day. **Duration of development:** Egg to adult takes about 12 to 13 days and the adult has a life span of 26 days in the presence of an adequate food source. **Efficacy:** *Aphytis melinus* can move as far as six trees from the point of introduction. It is attracted to female scales by the scale sex pheromone. Less effective under conditions of high or low temperature or low humidity. Adults also feed on nectar and the presence of nectar-producing plants aids their parasitism. *Aphytis melinus* is more suited to cooler, less humid regions than *Aphytis lignanensis* Compere.

COMMERCIALISATION: **Formulation:** Supplied in boxes lined with wet newspaper and packed in ice or in plastic, sealed capsules. **Tradenames:** Aphytis melinus – Biological Services, Aphytis melinus – Arbico, Aphytis melinus – IPM Laboratories, Aphytis melinus – Praxis.

APPLICATION: Apply by hanging container on a twig of the plant to be treated on the shaded side of the tree. Apply one capsule to every nine or twelve trees. Begin release before flowering and continue until the Autumn. Most effective if released before male scale flight. Recommended release rate 12,000 to 25,000 wasps per hectare. Young trees represent poor candidates for biological control because they offer little natural shelter for the beneficial wasp.

PRODUCT SPECIFICATIONS: **Purity:** Adult wasps with no contaminants.
Storage conditions: Can be stored in a cooled, insulated container at 15 to 19 °C away from direct sunlight. **Shelf-life:** Adults will survive for 26 days after emergence.

Aphytis melinus 201

COMPATIBILITY: Extreme cold or low humidity will limit activity. Ants interfere with the parasites and reduce their performance. Very effective in dry conditions. Do not release within four weeks of organophosphate spray. Can be released following application of copper or foliar fertilisers.

MAMMALIAN TOXICITY: No allergic or other adverse reactions have been noted with workers in the field. There is no evidence of acute or chronic toxicity, eye or skin irritation or hypersensitivity in mammals.

ENVIRONMENTAL IMPACT AND NON-TARGET TOXICITY: *Aphytis melinus* occurs widely in Nature and is not expected to parasitise non-target organisms or have any adverse effects on the environment.

4:149 *Chrysoperla carnea* Aphid predator

The Pesticide Manual - 11th edition: Entry number 143

Predatory lacewing: Neuroptera: Chrysopidae

NOMENCLATURE: **Approved name:** *Chrysoperla carnea* (Stephens). **Other names:** also known as *Chrysopa carnea* Stephens. **Common name:** green lacewing; aphid lions; golden eyes.

SOURCE: Widespread general insect predator.

PRODUCTION: Reared on aphids or on artificial diet and sold as eggs or, more usually, as larvae.

TARGET PESTS: All species of aphid. *Chrysoperla carnea* is a voracious predator and will also consume a variety of other slow-moving, soft-bodied arthropods including whitefly, scales, thrips, mites, beetles and caterpillar eggs.

TARGET CROPS: Particularly useful in interiorscapes. Can be used in protected and outdoor crops especially strawberries, hops and top fruit.

BIOLOGICAL ACTIVITY: **Biology:** Eggs are laid on slender stalks on the undersides of leaves. The larvae grow to about one cm in length and feed on aphids. The larvae camouflage themselves by covering their bodies in prey debris. After pupation they emerge as adults that feed only on nectar and pollen. **Predation:** Larvae will consume over 400 aphids during development. Older larvae can consume between 30 and 50 aphids per day. **Egg laying:** The adult lays more than 100 eggs. **Duration of development:** Larvae feed for three to four weeks undergoing three moults before pupation. Adults emerge after about seven days, begin to lay eggs after a further six days and live for about 14 days depending upon temperature. **Efficacy:** Very active and aggressive predator of aphids and other insects. Will consume beneficial as well as phytophagous insects and may even be cannibalistic although most beneficials move too quickly for *C. carnea* to catch them. The common name, aphid lion, relates to its voracious appetite. **Key reference:** R A Sundby. 1966. A comparative study of the efficiency of three predatory insects *Coccinella septempunctata* (Coleoptera: Coccinellidae), *Chrysopa carnea* St. (Neuroptera: Chrysopidae) and *Syrphus ribesii* L. (Diptera: Syrphidae) at two different temperatures. *Entomophaga*, **11**, 395–404.

COMMERCIALISATION: **Formulation:** Sold as eggs in bran, rice hulls or other material and with moth eggs present as a source of food. More usually sold as larvae in the same carrier or as individuals in cells of cardboard trays. **Tradenames:** Green Lacewing – Arbico, Chryosure (c) – Biological Crop Protection, Chrysopa MC-500 – System – Biobest, Lacewing – Kunafin, Chrysoperla carnea (Card) – Novartis BCM, Chrysoperla – Sautter & Stepper, Lacewing – Rincon-Vitova Insectaries, Chrysoperla carnea – Neudorff, Chrysoperla carnea – IPM Laboratories, Chrysoperla carnea – Praxis, Chrysoperla carnea – Koppert.

APPLICATION: Release 1 lacewing for 10 aphids or 10 eggs per plant or five larvae per square metre every other week. Repeat applications after 14 days if the population has not been checked. More frequent application may lead to the older larvae consuming the younger ones. Eggs and larvae can be applied in the field by aircraft using equipment designed for pollen application. Adults tend to migrate away from release sites. Often used to control "hot-spots".

PRODUCT SPECIFICATIONS: **Purity:** No contaminants. **Storage conditions:** Adults can be stored in the refrigerator for up to two days. **Shelf-life:** Pupae hatch within five days. Adults should be released within two days.

COMPATIBILITY: Lacewing eggs are eaten by ants. Incompatible with many other beneficial insects as the larvae will eat these as well as pest species. Incompatible with persistent insecticides.

MAMMALIAN TOXICITY: No allergic or other adverse reactions have been noticed following their use in the field. Occasionally, the larvae will sting people.

ENVIRONMENTAL IMPACT AND NON-TARGET TOXICITY: Lacewings are common in Nature and are not expected to have any adverse effects on non-target organisms or on the environment.

4:150   *Cotesia* species   *Lepidopteran parasite*

Parasitic wasp: Hymenoptera: Aphidiidae

NOMENCLATURE: **Approved name:** *Cotesia* species. **Other names:** lepidopteran parasitic wasp.

SOURCE: Natural parasite of the larvae of Lepidoptera. A number of species have been commercialised including *C. plutella* Kurdjmov, a parasite of diamondback moth larvae (*Plutella xylostella* Linnaeus) and *C. marginiventris* Cresson, a parasite of several caterpillars including *Trichoplusia ni* (Hübner), *Spodoptera* spp. and *Helicoverpa* spp.

PRODUCTION: Reared under controlled conditions on host caterpillars.

TARGET PESTS: Various caterpillar pests.

TARGET CROPS: Brassicae and other vegetables in glasshouses and outdoors.

BIOLOGICAL ACTIVITY: **Predation:** It is usual for the adult female to be attracted to the host by chemical stimuli produced when the phytophagous insect host damages the crop by feeding. There is also evidence that the frass of host insects attracts the female wasps. **Duration of development:** The level of parasites within a crop is enhanced by leaving old plants in or near new plantings so the pupae can hatch and enter the establishing crop. **Efficacy:** An effective parasite of Lepidoptera with good mobility and ability to find larvae. Can be parasitised by hyperparasites. **Key reference:** R G van Driesche and T S Bellows (eds.). 1996. *Biological Control*, Chapman & Hall, London. ISBN 0–412–02861–1.

COMMERCIALISATION: **Formulation:** Sold as adult wasps. **Tradenames:** Cotesia plutella – Arbico, Cotesia plutella – Biofac, Cotesia plutella – Caltec, Cotesia plutella – Praxis, Cotesia marginiventris – Arbico, Cotesia marginiventris – Biofac, Cotesia marginiventris – Caltec, Cotesia marginiventris – Praxis.

APPLICATION: Release 400 adults per hectare per week during periods of infestation. Release on the upwind side of the area to be treated.

PRODUCT SPECIFICATIONS: **Storage conditions:** Store at temperatures between 10 and 20 °C. **Shelf-life:** Use as soon as possible after delivery.

COMPATIBILITY: Compatible with *Bacillus thuringiensis* sprays but do not use with persistent chemical insecticides.

MAMMALIAN TOXICITY: There is no record of allergic or other adverse toxicological effects in research workers or production or field staff. Considered to be of low mammalian toxicity.

ENVIRONMENTAL IMPACT AND NON-TARGET TOXICITY: *Cotesia* species occur naturally and are not expected to have any adverse effects on non-target organisms or the environment.

4:151   *Cryptolaemus montrouzieri*

Mealybug predator

The Pesticide Manual - 11th edition: Entry number 165

Predatory beetle: Coleoptera: Coccinellidae

NOMENCLATURE: **Approved name:** *Cryptolaemus montrouzieri* Mulsant.
Other names: Australian ladybird beetle; mealybug predator; mealybug destroyer.

SOURCE: *Cryptolaemus montrouzieri* is a native of Australia.

PRODUCTION: Reared on mealybugs and shipped as live beetles or larvae with a food source.

TARGET PESTS: Will consume all species of mealybug. *Cryptolaemus montrouzieri* has been known to consume other phytophagous insects such as aphids and the young stages of soft scales.

TARGET CROPS: Widely used to control mealybug in Californian citrus plantations and in US grape orchards. Effective against mealybug infestations in a wide range of situations including orchards and plantations, glasshouse-grown crops and interiorscapes. Not effective on tomatoes.

BIOLOGICAL ACTIVITY: **Biology:** Eggs are laid within the egg pouches of the mealybug. There are four larval stages and larvae can reach a length of 13 mm and their bodies are covered with wax-like projections. They pupate on sheltered regions on stems or on the undersides of leaves. The adult insect is dark brown with an orange head, thorax and abdomen. It is about 4 mm long. **Predation:** All stages of *Cryptolaemus montrouzieri* consume mealybugs. Young larvae and adult beetles prefer host eggs and young larvae, but older *Cryptolaemus montrouzieri* larvae will consume all stages. They will also consume insects in families related to mealybugs such as aphids and it has been reported that they will eat their own kind. **Egg laying:** Females copulate shortly after emergence and begin egg-laying within five days. The number of eggs laid is very dependent upon the female's diet and food shortages cause a reduction in eggs laid. The egg-laying capacity of a female varies between 200 and 700 eggs in its lifetime, with between seven and eleven eggs being laid each day. **Duration of development:** The duration of development is dependent upon the temperature. Eggs hatch in eight to nine days at 21 °C and in five to six days at 27 °C. At the same temperatures, full larval development takes 19 to 26 and 12 to 17 days. The pupae take 14 to 20 and seven to ten days respectively and the full cycle from egg to adult takes between 28 and 47 days. The adults live for between 27 and 70 days. **Efficacy:** Because the adults can fly, large areas can be covered in the search for food. At 21 °C, a larva will consume more than 250 mealybug larvae through its development to an adult. All stages are most active in sunlight and between temperatures of 21 and 29 °C with relative humidities between 70 and 80%. *Cryptolaemus montrouzieri* is not effective at temperatures below 21 °C. Mealybugs are completely devoured.

COMMERCIALISATION: **Formulation:** Sold as adults or larvae with a food and water source in bottles, vials or punnets containing at least 40 beetles. **Tradenames:** Cryptobug – Koppert,

Crypto-line m – Novartis BCM, Cryptolaemus montrouzieri Mealy Bug Predator – M&R Durango, Cryptosure (m) – Biological Crop Protection, Cryptolaemus-System – Biobest, Cryptolaemus montrouzieri – Arbico, Cryptolaemus montrouzieri – IPM Laboratories, Cryptolaemus montrouzieri – Praxis, Cryptolaemus montrouzieri – Rincon-Vitova, Cryptolaemus montrouzieri – Neudorff.

APPLICATION: Make first application in the Spring when mealybug populations are low at a rate of five beetles per infested plant or two to five beetles per square metre or at 1,200 to 12,000 beetles per hectare. Repeat as necessary, usually twice a week, if populations are high and twice a year as a prophylatic treatment.

PRODUCT SPECIFICATIONS: **Purity:** Should contain adult beetles only although larvae are sometimes introduced to aid identification. **Storage conditions:** Store under cool conditions but do not refrigerate. Keep temperature above 15 °C. **Shelf-life:** Release as soon as possible.

COMPATIBILITY: Control ants as these protect mealybugs for their honeydew. Do not release following application of residual insecticides. *Cryptolaemus montrouzieri* is particularly sensitive to diazinon. Attracted to light colours. Often used in combination with *Leptomastix dactylopii* Howard.

MAMMALIAN TOXICITY: There have been no reports of allergic or other adverse reactions following use of *Cryptolaemus montrouzieri* in enclosed or field situations.

ENVIRONMENTAL IMPACT AND NON-TARGET TOXICITY: *Cryptolaemus montrouzieri* occurs widely in Nature and is not expected to have any adverse effects on non-target organisms or the environment.

4:152   *Dacnusa sibirica*   Leafminer parasite

Parasitic wasp: Hymenoptera: Braconidae

NOMENCLATURE: **Approved name:** *Dacnusa sibirica* Telenga. **Other names:** leafminer parasite; leafminer wasp parasite.

SOURCE: Common in temperate climates.

PRODUCTION: Produced on leafminers and supplied as adult wasps.

TARGET PESTS: Leafminers such as *Liriomyza bryoniae* (Kaltenbach), *Liriomyza huidobrensis*, *Liriomyza trifolii* (Burgess) and *Phytomyza syngenesiae* (Hardy).

TARGET CROPS: Glasshouse-grown vegetables and ornamentals. Also effective in interiorscapes.

BIOLOGICAL ACTIVITY: **Biology:** Eggs are laid in leafminer larvae by adult female wasps. Females are able to distinguish between parasitised and non-parasitised larvae. The wasp larva develops within the leafminer larva which is not killed until it pupates. The wasp pupa is formed within the pupated leafminer and can hibernate therein. **Predation:** Females lay between 50 and 225 eggs within leafminer larvae in their lifetime depending on temperature. The eggs hatch and the larvae feed on the leafminer larvae. The parasite prefers leafminer larvae at the first or second larval stage. **Egg laying:** Eggs are laid throughout the year in heated glasshouses. Optimal temperatures are between 15 and 20 °C.

Duration of development: Development time from egg hatch to adult emergence is dependent upon temperature taking about 16 days at 22 °C. Adults live for between 8 and 20 days. **Efficacy:** The wasps are very mobile and, once an infested plant is located, the leafminer larvae are rapidly parasitised. *Dacnusa sibirica* will parasitise leafminers at low temperatures.

COMMERCIALISATION: **Formulation:** Live adults supplied with a food source in bottles. **Tradenames:** Minusa – Koppert, Dac-line s – Novartis BCM, Minex – Koppert (in combination with *Diglyphus isaea*), Dac-line s and Dig-line i – Novartis BCM (in combination with *Diglyphus isaea*), Dacnusa-System – Biobest, Dacsure (si) – Biological Crop Protection, Dacnusa sibirica – Schlupfwespen – Neudorff, Dacnusa/Diglyphus (225:25) – Neudorff, Dacnusa – Sautter & Stepper, Diglyphus/Dacnusa – Sautter & Stepper, Dacnusa sibirica – Praxis.

APPLICATION: Release in Winter and Spring at a rate of 1,200 to 5,000 parasites per hectare weekly, or at a rate of one wasp per 10 leafminer mines.

PRODUCT SPECIFICATIONS: **Purity:** No contaminating insects. **Storage conditions:** Keep cool but do not refrigerate. Keep out of direct sunlight. **Shelf-life:** Release immediately.

COMPATIBILITY: Avoid the use of residual insecticides for four weeks prior to release. Often used in combination with *Diglyphus isaea* (Walker).

MAMMALIAN TOXICITY: There have been no reports of allergic or other adverse reactions following use in glasshouses or interiorscapes.

ENVIRONMENTAL IMPACT AND NON-TARGET TOXICITY: *Dacnusa sibirica* occurs widely in Nature and is not expected to have any adverse effects on non-target organisms or the environment.

4:153 *Delphastus pusillus* Whitefly predator

Predatory beetle: Coleoptera: Coccinellidae

NOMENCLATURE: **Approved name:** *Delphastus pusillus* Leconte. **Other names:** whitefly predatory beetle; black lady beetle.

SOURCE: Widely distributed across Central and Southern United States of America and Central and South America.

PRODUCTION: Reared on glasshouse-grown whitefly (*Trialeurodes vaporariorum* (Westwood) or *Bemisia tabaci* (Gennadius)) under controlled conditions.

TARGET PESTS: Glasshouse whitefly (*Trialeurodes vaporariorum* and *Bemisia tabaci*).

TARGET CROPS: Cucumbers, peppers and other glasshouse vegetable crops, ornamentals and interiorscapes.

BIOLOGICAL ACTIVITY: **Biology:** Adult and larval stages feed on whitefly eggs and pupae, with the adults preferring eggs. Older larvae migrate down the plant and pupate on the undersides of older leaves. Adults avoid feeding on whitefly parasitised by *Encarsia formosa* Gahan. **Predation:** Whitefly eggs and larvae are eaten by adult and larval stages. Adults also feed on honeydew produced by their prey but females must feed on whitefly eggs for maximum egg production. **Egg laying:** Females lay an average of three eggs per day to give a total of about 180 eggs in their life-span. Eggs are laid amongst whitefly eggs and larvae. **Duration of development:** The develoment time from egg to adult is 21 days at 23 °C. Adult beetles can live for up to 60 days. **Efficacy:** Adults and larvae search actively for prey. Consumption of 100 to 150 whitefly eggs per day is required to maintain adult oviposition. Individual beetles can consume as many as 10,000 whitefly eggs or 700 whitefly scales during their lifetime.

COMMERCIALISATION: **Formulation:** Sold as adult beetles in bottles. A DoE licence is required for release in the UK. **Tradenames:** Delphastus-A – Applied Bio-Nomics, Delphastus pusillus – IPM Laboratories, Whitefly Destroyer – Nature's Alternative Insectary, Delphastus-System – Biobest, Delsure (si) – Biological Crop Protection, Delphastus pusillus Beetles – Rincon-Vitova Insectaries, Delphastus pusillus Predator Beetle – M&R Durango, Delphastus pusillus – Arbico, Delphastus pusillus – Praxis, Delphastus pusillus – Koppert.

APPLICATION: Adult beetles are released within infested crops at a rate of one beetle per 10 square metres as a preventative treatment and five beetles per 10 square metres as a curative treatment.

PRODUCT SPECIFICATIONS: **Purity:** Adults only, no host material present. **Storage conditions:** Use as soon as possible after receipt. **Shelf-life:** May be stored for a few days at 10 °C. Longer periods reduce egg-laying and predator viability.

COMPATIBILITY: Incompatible with residual insecticides. May be used with other whitefly parasites. Most effective at high populations of whitefly.

MAMMALIAN TOXICITY: There have been no reports of any adverse or allergic reaction from laboratory, manufacturing or field trial staff.

ENVIRONMENTAL IMPACT AND NON-TARGET TOXICITY: *Delphastus pusillus* occurs widely in Nature and there is no evidence of adverse environmental effects nor of effects on non-target organisms.

4:154 *Diglyphus isaea* — Leafminer parasite

The Pesticide Manual - 11th edition: Entry number 234

Ectoparasitic wasp: Hymenoptera: Eulophidae

NOMENCLATURE: **Approved name:** *Diglyphus isaea* (Walker). **Other names:** eulophid wasp, leafminer predator and leafminer parasite.

SOURCE: Widely distributed in Europe, North Africa and Japan. Introduced throughout the world.

PRODUCTION: Reared on leafminers and sold as adult wasps.

TARGET PESTS: Leafminer larvae such as *Liriomyza bryoniae* (Kalkenbach), *Liriomyza trifolii* (Burgess) *Liriomyza huidobrensis* (Blan.) and *Phytomyza syngenesiae* Hardy.

TARGET CROPS: Vegetables and ornamentals in glasshouses, in interiorscapes and may control leafminers on outdoor crops.

BIOLOGICAL ACTIVITY: **Biology:** Female wasps are about 2 mm long. They paralyse the leafminer larva and then lay one or more eggs next to the host, usually late second and third larval stages. After egg-hatch, the wasp larva lies next to the leafminer and feeds on it. The leafminer larva stops feeding after it is paralysed. The wasp larva moves away from the parasitised leafminer to pupate using the mine of the host. The adult wasp leaves the leaf through a round hole in the upper surface of the leaf. **Predation:** Wasps sting leafminer larvae to lay eggs and as a food source. Larvae of the second larval stages are preferred. When conditions are optimal for the wasp, a female will kill about 360 leafminer larvae of which 290 are used for egg-laying and 70 as food. The higher the population of leafminers the greater the predation and it is possible that *Diglyphus isaea* can select areas with high leafminer populations. **Egg laying:** *Diglyphus isaea* will lay between 200 and 300 eggs in its lifetime. **Duration of development:** The duration of the life cycle is dependent upon temperature with *Diglyphus isaea* being particularly active at temperatures above 22 °C. At 15 °C the time taken from egg hatch to adult emergence is about 26 days whilst at 25 °C it is about 10.5 days. Eggs hatch after about two days and moult three times as larvae. The pupal stage is about six days. **Efficacy:** *Diglyphus isaea* is a very effective ectoparasite of leafminers particularly at temperatures above 22 °C. The leafminers cease feeding upon paralysis by the females and the female is a very efficient locator of its host.

COMMERCIALISATION: **Formulation:** Sold as adults in shaker bottles. **Tradenames:** Miglyphus – Koppert, Dig-line i – Novartis BCM, Minex – Koppert (in combination with *Dacnusa sibirica*), Dac-line s and Dig-line i – Novartis BCM (in combination with *Dacnusa sibirica*), Digsure (I) – Biological Crop Protection, B.C.P. Dacnusa (& 10% Diglyphus) – Biological Crop Protection, Diglyphus isaea – Neudorff, Dacnusa/Diglyphus (225:25) – Neudorff, Diglyphus/Dacnusa – Sautter & Stepper, Leafminer Parasite – Arbico, Diglyphus-System – Biobest, Diglyphus isaea – Praxis.

4. Insect Predators

APPLICATION: Release when tunnels are first seen in the crop at a rate of 1,200 to 2,400 wasps per hectare evenly distributed throughout the crop. Repeat applications on a weekly basis for three weeks. Control should be seen within 15 days of application.

PRODUCT SPECIFICATIONS: **Purity:** Product contains only *Diglyphus isaea* adults. **Storage conditions:** Keep cool but do not refrigerate. Do not expose to direct sunlight. **Shelf-life:** Release immediately.

COMPATIBILITY: Do not use residual insecticides four weeks before or after release. Often used in conjunction with *Dacnusa sibirica* Telenga. Most effective at high temperatures.

MAMMALIAN TOXICITY: No allergic or other adverse reaction has been reported following use in glasshouses, interiorscapes or outdoors.

ENVIRONMENTAL IMPACT AND NON-TARGET TOXICITY: *Diglyphus isaea* occurs widely in Nature and is not expected to show any adverse effects on non-target organisms or the environment.

4:155   *Encarsia formosa*   *Whitefly parasite*

The Pesticide Manual - 11th edition: Entry number 269

Parasitic wasp: Hymenoptera: Aphelinidae

NOMENCLATURE: **Approved name:** *Encarsia formosa* Gahan. **Other names:** glasshouse whitefly parasite.

SOURCE: Thought to have evolved in the same location as its host in tropical or subtropical regions. Now can be found in Europe, Australia, New Zealand and North America.

PRODUCTION: Reared on whitefly larvae under controlled glasshouse conditions.

TARGET PESTS: Glasshouse whitefly, *Trialeurodes vaporariorum* (Westwood). *Bemisia tabaci* (Gennadius) is also parasitised but is a poor host and higher numbers of *Encarsia formosa* are required.

TARGET CROPS: Tomatoes, cucumbers, peppers and other vegetable crops and ornamentals in glasshouses and also used in interiorscapes.

BIOLOGICAL ACTIVITY: **Biology:** Adult female wasps can lay eggs in all larval stages of the whitefly, but it is usual to select third and fourth larval stages. The parasite develops within the whitefly larva, passing through six developmental stages (egg, four larval stages and the pupal stage). When the wasp pupates within the whitefly, the host "pupa" turns black. The adult wasp emerges from the parasitised "pupa" and feeds on honeydew and the body fluids of whitefly larvae; some hosts are killed by this feeding. **Predation:** *Encarsia formosa* adult females attack young whitefly larvae by stinging and laying eggs within them. Adult wasps also feed directly on the scales. **Egg laying:** The adult wasp will not fly at temperatures below

15 °C. Activity is low below 18 °C but adults continue to search by walking on the leaves. It is normal for the adult female wasp to lay between 60 and 100 eggs.

Duration of development: The life-cycle takes between two and four weeks depending upon the temperature. At temperatures above 30 °C, the female lives only for a few days.

Efficacy: The parasitic wasp searches actively for a host. It can cover distances of 10 to 30 metres and is very effective in locating whitefly. The presence of honeydew restricts the movement of the adult and consequently large infestations are more difficult to control.

Key references: 1) R G van Driesche and T S Bellows (eds.). 1996. *Biological Control*, Chapman & Hall, London. ISBN 0–412–02861–1. 2) M Malais and W J Ravensberg (eds.). 1992. *Knowing and Recognising: the Biology of Glasshouse Pests and their Natural Enemies*, Koppert Biological Systems, Berkel en Rodenrijs, the Netherlands. 3) P Stary. 1988. Aphelinidae. In *Aphids: their Biology, Natural Enemies and Control*, A K Minks and P Harrewijn (eds.), Vol. B, 185–8, Elsevier, Amsterdam, the Netherlands.

COMMERCIALISATION: **Formulation:** Sold as pupae or on small cards either attached to the surface or protected within a well in the card. **Tradenames:** Encar-line f 10000 – Novartis BCM, Encar-line f 6000 – Novartis BCM, En-Strip – Koppert, Para-strip – Applied Bio-Nomics, Para-bulk – Applied Bio-Nomics, Encarsia formosa Glasshouse Whitefly Parasite – M&R Durango, Sweet Potato Whitefly Predator – Arbico, Encarsia formosa Whitefly Parasite – Biofac, Encarsia Whitefly Parasites – English Woodland Biocontrol, Encarsia formosa Wasps – Rincon-Vitova Insectaries, Encarsia-System – Biobest, Encarsia Cards – Biobest Encsure (f) – Biological Crop Protection, Encsure (cf) – Biological Crop Protection, Encarsia formosa – Praxis.

APPLICATION: Cards are hung within the crop and the adults emerge into the infested crops. Preventative applications at 0.5 to 1 per square metre from planting tomatoes. Increase to one to five per square metre when whitefly are seen and repeat every other week. Continue until 90% parasitism is achieved. Removal of lower leaves may affect control. Double these rates for cucumbers. For Poinsettia, use 0.3 *E. formosa* per plant each week.

PRODUCT SPECIFICATIONS: **Purity:** Pupae of *Encarsia formosa* with no live whitefly and no debris. **Storage conditions:** May be stored for a few days at 6 to 8 °C within a sealed container. Longer periods of storage reduce viability. Emergence occurs at room temperature. **Shelf-life:** Use as soon as possible after receipt. Three to four days maximum at 6 to 8 °C.

COMPATIBILITY: Incompatible with residual insecticides. Less effective at high populations of whitefly because of high levels of honeydew. Do not release if methomyl or a synthetic pyrethroid has been used.

MAMMALIAN TOXICITY: No allergic or other adverse reactions have been reported by producers or formulators nor from the use of *Encarsia formosa* in glasshouses or interiorscapes.

ENVIRONMENTAL IMPACT AND NON-TARGET TOXICITY: *Encarsia formosa* occurs widely in Nature and it is unlikely that any adverse environmental effects will result from its use.

4:156 *Eretmocerus* sp. nr *californicus*

Whitefly parasite

The Pesticide Manual - 11th edition: Entry number 275

Parasitic wasp: Hymenoptera: Aphelinidae

NOMENCLATURE: **Approved name:** *Eretmocerus* sp. nr *californicus* Howard.
Other names: *Eretmocerus eremicus*; whitefly parasite.

SOURCE: Species identification is difficult and the species definition *Eretmocerus* near *californicus* has been recognised since at least 1980 and is the dominant species in the South Western United States where it occurs in the desert regions of California and Arizona.

PRODUCTION: *Eretmocerus* sp. nr *californicus* is an obligate parasite of whitefly and the species is reared on *Bemisia tabaci* (Gennadius) or *Trialeurodes vaporariorum* (Westwood) under controlled conditions.

TARGET PESTS: For control of whitefly *Bemisia tabaci*; it is also capable of parasitising *Trialeurodes vaporariorum*.

TARGET CROPS: Recommended for use in vegetables, ornamentals and interiorscapes.

BIOLOGICAL ACTIVITY: **Biology:** All *Eretmocerus* species are obligate parasites of whitefly. When the egg hatches, the first instar parasite larva burrows into the host, where it completes its development. **Egg laying:** Adult females lay single eggs beneath the immobile second or third instar larvae of the host. **Efficacy:** The female wasp is very mobile and actively seeks whitefly eggs as food. The adults also feed directly on the scales.

COMMERCIALISATION: **Formulation:** Sold as parasitised whitefly pupae. A DoE licence is required for release in the UK. **Tradenames:** Ercal – Koppert, Eret-line cal – Novartis BCM, Eretmocerus californicus Small Parasitic Wasp – M&R Durango, Eretmocerus californicus – IPM Laboratories, Eretsure (c) – Biological Crop Protection, Eretmocerus californicus – Praxis, Eretmocerus californicus – Beneficial Insectary.

APPLICATION: The parasite is sold as parasitised *Bemisia tabaci* or *Trialeurodes vaporariorum* pupae. These should be placed on the infested plants and the adult wasps allowed to move into the area to be treated.

PRODUCT SPECIFICATIONS: **Purity:** Containers contain parasitised pupae in bran and no other impurity.

COMPATIBILITY: Incompatible with residual insecticides.

MAMMALIAN TOXICITY: *Eretmocerus californicus* has not demonstrated evidence of toxicity, infectivity, irritation or hypersensitivity to mammals. No allergic responses or other adverse health problems have been observed by research workers, manufacturing staff or users.

ENVIRONMENTAL IMPACT AND NON-TARGET TOXICITY: *Eretmocerus californicus* occurs in Nature and, as such, is not expected to show any adverse effects on non-target organisms or the environment.

4:157   *Feltiella acarisuga*   *Mite predator*

Predatory gall-midge: Diptera: Cecidomyiidae

NOMENCLATURE: **Approved name:** *Feltiella acarisuga* (Vallot) **Other names:** previously known as *Therodiplosis persicae* Kieffer. **Common name:** red spider mite gall midge predator.

SOURCE: Widely occurring in Northern Europe.

PRODUCTION: Reared under controlled conditions on red spider mites, *Tetranychus urticae* Koch.

TARGET PESTS: Spider mites including *Tetranychus urticae* and *T. cinnabarinus* (Boisduval).

TARGET CROPS: Glasshouse-grown vegetable and ornamental crops.

BIOLOGICAL ACTIVITY: **Biology:** Adult *Feltiella acarisuga* lay yellowish eggs (about 0.25 mm long) in colonies of red spider mites. The creamy brown larvae have four stages and each predates spider mites. Pupae appear as white fluff near the veins of the leaves. **Predation:** All larval stages of the midge consume eggs, nymphs and adult spider mites. Overwintered mites are also controlled. The predator consumes about five times as many mites per individual as the predatory mite *Phytoseiulus persimilis* Athios-Herriot. **Egg laying:** Eggs are laid in spider mite colonies. **Duration of development:** Under normal temperature conditions eggs hatch within two days and the four larval stages together last for approximately seven days. The total life-cycle from egg to egg is between two and four weeks. **Efficacy:** *Feltiella acarisuga* is a very mobile predator that tracks its prey whilst in flight. It is effective under cold and dark conditions in the Spring and Autumn and is able to locate its prey in crops that are difficult to monitor such as ornamentals. It is easy to see within the crop and provides long-lasting protection from spider mite damage.

COMMERCIALISATION: **Formulation:** Sold as larvae in tubs. **Tradenames:** Therodiplosis-System – Biobest, Felsure (a) – Biological Crop Protection, Felti-line a – Novartis BCM.

APPLICATION: Tubs containing pupae or cocoons are opened in the shade of the crop and the emerging adults are allowed to escape. In the Spring, release 500 to 750 adults per hectare, weekly. It is best to place the tubs near spider mite colonies. As temperatures increase, release the midges less frequently.

PRODUCT SPECIFICATIONS: **Purity:** It is essential that the product contains only *Feltiella acarisuga* pupae and not the parasitoid *Aphanogmus parvulus* Roberti, a natural enemy of *F. acarisuga*.

4. Insect Predators

Storage conditions: Keep tubs under cool, dark conditions. Do not expose to direct sunlight. **Shelf-life:** Use as soon as possible after receipt.

COMPATIBILITY: It is essential that the parasite of *Feltiella acarisuga* is not present. Most fungicides have no effect on the midge but acaricides delay the population build up by removing its prey.

MAMMALIAN TOXICITY: There has been no evidence of adverse allergic or other effects following the rearing or release of *Feltiella acarisuga* under glasshouse conditions.

ENVIRONMENTAL IMPACT AND NON-TARGET TOXICITY: *Feltiella acarisuga* occurs widely in Nature and is not expected to have any advese effects on non-target organisms or on the environment.

4:158 *Galendromus occidentalis*

Mite predator

Predatory mite: Acarina: Phytoseiidae

NOMENCLATURE: **Approved name:** *Galendromus occidentalis* (Nesbitt).
Other names: synonymous with *Typhlodromus occidentalis* Nesbitt and *Metaseiulus occidentalis*.

SOURCE: A widespread mite predator found primarily in regions of high temperature and humidity.

PRODUCTION: Reared on phytophagous mites under controlled conditions.

TARGET PESTS: *Tetranychus* species, particularly *T. urticae* Koch and *T. cinnabarinus* (Boisduval).

TARGET CROPS: Glasshouse and outdoor vegetables and ornamentals, grape vines and nut crops.

BIOLOGICAL ACTIVITY: **Biology:** Eggs are laid near a food source on the surface of the leaves. These hatch into larvae with three pairs of legs. They do not eat. The protonymph emerges from the larva and begins to feed. The adults emerge from the nymphal stage, mate within a few hours and the females then begin to lay eggs. *Galendromus occidentalis* is a slower-acting predator than *Phytoseiulus persimilis* but all stages are able to withstand wider ranges of temperature and are more tolerant of starvation. **Predation:** The nymphal stages consume eggs, larvae and protonymphs of the spider mite and adults eat all stages of the prey. Adult *G. occidentalis* consume between one and three adult mites or six eggs per day. **Efficacy:** *Galendromus occidentalis* is a very versatile predator of spider mites and is well adapted to high temperature and humidity. It can exist in the absence of mites as food.

COMMERCIALISATION: **Formulation:** Sold as adults. **Tradenames:** Galendromus occidentalis – Arbico, Galendromus occidentalis – IPM Laboratories, Galendromus occidentalis – Praxis, Galendromus occidentalis – Rincon-Vitova.

APPLICATION: Release at a rate of about ten predators per square metre every two weeks in glasshouses. Between two and three applications should be sufficient. Outside, rates of between 12,000 and 50,000 adults per hectare every two weeks should be used. Again, two to three applications should be sufficient. It is common to apply in conjunction with a faster-acting predator such as *Phytoseiulus persimilis* particularly if mite infestations are high.

PRODUCT SPECIFICATIONS: **Storage conditions:** Do not expose to extremes of temperature. Do not expose to direct sunlight. **Shelf-life:** As *Galendromus occidentalis* can survive in the absence of a food source, it may be kept for several days before release.

COMPATIBILITY: Used in conjunction with other mite predators. Do not use with persistent insecticides or acaricides.

MAMMALIAN TOXICITY: There are no records of allergic or other adverse effects from *Galendromus occidentalis* in research workers, production or field staff. It is regarded as being of low mammalian toxicity.

ENVIRONMENTAL IMPACT AND NON-TARGET TOXICITY: *Galendromus occidentalis* occurs in Nature and is not expected to have any adverse effects on non-target organisms or on the environment.

4:159   *Harmonia axyridis*   Aphid predator

Predatory ladybird: Coleoptera: Coccinellidae

NOMENCLATURE: **Approved name:** *Harmonia axyridis* Pallas. **Other names:** predatory ladybird; Chinese ladybird.

SOURCE: Originated from Asia (probably China) but now introduced into North America and Europe.

PRODUCTION: Reared in insectaries under controlled conditions on eggs of moths such as *Ephestia kuehniella* or on aphids.

TARGET PESTS: Many species of aphid.

TARGET CROPS: A wide variety of protected crops and ornamentals.

BIOLOGICAL ACTIVITY: **Biology:** As soon as larvae emerge from eggs they begin to consume aphids and they continue until pupation. Released larvae are active at temperatures above 11 to 12 °C. In the absence of food, the larvae can become cannibalistic but adults can survive some days without food. **Predation:** Both adults and larvae consume aphids but they may also prey on other insects such as scales and lepidopteran eggs. **Egg laying:** Adult females will lay approximately 20 eggs a day throughout a life-time of two to three months. **Duration of development:** At 25 °C, it takes 15 to 20 days from egg hatch to adult. Adults live for several months. **Efficacy:** Larvae are very mobile and prospect widely for prey from their release point. They reduce aphid populations very quickly being comparable to chemical treatments.

COMMERCIALISATION: **Formulation:** Sold as larvae in boxes containing a food source (usually *Ephestia* eggs) to allow development during transportation. **Tradenames:** Harmonia – Biotop.

APPLICATION: Release second or third instar larvae on infested plants. Rate of release depends upon plant size and the extent of the aphid infestation.

PRODUCT SPECIFICATIONS: **Purity:** Only larvae of *Harmonia axyridis* with no contaminants. **Storage conditions:** Store in the dark under cool conditions. Do not expose to bright sunlight. **Shelf-life:** Can be kept for several days if stored under recommended conditions.

COMPATIBILITY: Incompatible with foliar insecticides.

MAMMALIAN TOXICITY: No allergic or other adverse reaction has been reported from the use of *Harmonia axyridis* in glasshouses or outdoor conditions.

ENVIRONMENTAL IMPACT AND NON-TARGET TOXICITY: *Harmonia axyridis* occurs widely in Nature and would not be expected to have any significant effect on non-target organisms or on the environment.

4:160 *Hippodamia convergens*

Insect predator

The Pesticide Manual - 11th edition: Entry number 402

Predatory ladybird: Coleoptera: Coccinellidae

NOMENCLATURE: **Approved name:** *Hippodamia convergens* Guérin. **Other names:** ladybird; ladybug beetle.

SOURCE: Native to North America.

PRODUCTION: Usually collected in the wild rather than insectary-reared.

TARGET PESTS: Polyphagous, eating a wide variety of prey including aphids, beetles, chinch bugs, whiteflies and mites.

TARGET CROPS: Many outdoor and protected crops.

BIOLOGICAL ACTIVITY: **Biology:** Adults are about 5 mm in length and are orange-brown in colour with black spots and white stripes on the head shield. They mate and lay large numbers of oval, orange eggs in clusters on the undersides of leaves. Eggs hatch into black larvae with orange spots. **Predation:** Adults and larvae eat insects. A larva will consume about 400 aphids in its larval stage and an adult will consume over 5,000. **Egg laying:** Eggs are laid under leaves shortly after mating. **Duration of development:** At optimum temperatures the life-cycle takes about 30 days. The adults can live for 3 months. **Efficacy:** Very efficient, polyphagous insect. It requires a source of nectar or pollen to mature to the adult stage and this must be provided if not available within the crop. Particularly effective under cool conditions. Mobile insects that often migrate from site of application.

COMMERCIALISATION: **Formulation:** Adults collected in the wild and sold packed in a suitable substrate such as wood-wool. **Tradenames:** Ladybugs – Kunafin, Hippodamia convergens Lady Beetle – M&R Durango, Hippodamia System – Biobest, Hippodamia convergens (Ladybugs) Aphid Destroyer – Nature's Alternative Insectary, Ladybird Beetle – Arbico, Ladybug – BioPac, Aphidamia – Koppert.

APPLICATION: Release at a rate of between 180,000 and 500,000 per hectare. An early evening release is preferred. If used in glasshouses, cover openings to prevent escape. If used in the field, the wings can be sealed together by sugar solutions as a temporary measure to encourage feeding and egg laying and to reduce migration. Ensure there is moisture in the release environment.

PRODUCT SPECIFICATIONS: **Purity:** Dependent upon harvesting site.
Storage conditions: Store in a refrigerator for up to 3 months. Do not expose to direct sunlight. **Shelf-life:** Remain active for up to 3 months if stored under suitable conditions. Release within two days if stored at room temperature.

COMPATIBILITY: Do not use residual foliar insecticides for one month before or after release.

MAMMALIAN TOXICITY: No allergic or other adverse reaction has been reported following their use in glasshouse crops or outdoors.

ENVIRONMENTAL IMPACT AND NON-TARGET TOXICITY: *Hippodamia convergens* occurs widely in Nature and is unlikely to show any adverse effects on non-target organisms or the environment.

4:161   *Hypoaspis aculeifer*

Fungus gnat predator

Predatory mite: Mesostigmata: Phytoseiidae

NOMENCLATURE: **Approved name:** *Hypoaspis aculeifer* (Canestrini). **Other names:** fungus gnat predator; thrips predator.

SOURCE: *Hypoaspis aculeifer* is cosmopolitan and occurs widely in Nature in Europe and North America. It is a soil-dwelling predatory mite and is often found in association with decaying plants.

TARGET PESTS: Main prey are fungus gnat or sciarid flies (*Bradysia* spp.) although other soil-inhabiting arthropods such as thrips pupae (*Frankliniella occidentalis* Pergande), collembola and nematodes may also be preyed upon.

TARGET CROPS: Glasshouse vegetable crops and ornamentals.

BIOLOGICAL ACTIVITY: **Biology:** A predatory mite that feeds on a wide range of insect, mite and nematode species in the soil. *Hypoaspis aculeifer* lays its eggs in the soil and these hatch into motile larval stages. There are three immature stages, reddish-brown in colour, and these will feed upon soil arthropods but eat less than the adults. The adult mite reaches a size of about 1 mm. The mite does not enter diapause. **Egg laying:** An adult female will lay up to 87 eggs in her lifetime at optimal temperatures (22 °C). **Duration of development:** The ideal temperature range for the mite is between 17 and 26 °C and development stops when the temperature falls below 7 or 8 °C. **Efficacy:** *Hypoaspis aculeifer* is very effective at controlling a range of soil insects and mites. It will reduce thrips populations by predating the pupae when they fall to the ground.

COMMERCIALISATION: **Formulation:** Sold as a vermiculite formulation with 10,000 predatory mites (all stages) in a one litre bottle. **Tradenames:** Entomite – Koppert, Hyposure (a) – Biological Crop Protection.

APPLICATION: Turn and shake bottle gently before use. Spread material carefully and evenly on to the soil or rockwood blocks. Recommended rates of use are 100 mites per square metre as a preventative treatment and 200 to 250 mites per square metre as a curative treatment. Apply once per season.

PRODUCT SPECIFICATIONS: **Purity:** No phytophagous mites, mould or other contaminants. **Storage conditions:** Store at 10 to 15 °C in the dark. **Shelf-life:** Use within three days of receipt if stored under recommended conditions.

COMPATIBILITY: *Hypoaspis aculeifer* is sensitive to most conventional pesticides.

MAMMALIAN TOXICITY: No allergic or other adverse reaction has been reported following the use of *Hypoaspis aculeifer* in glasshouse crops by producers, research workers or growers.

ENVIRONMENTAL IMPACT AND NON-TARGET TOXICITY: *Hypoaspis aculeifer* has a wide geographical distribution and there is no evidence of adverse effects on non-target organisms or on the environment.

4:162   *Hypoaspis miles*   *Sciarid fly predator*

Predatory mite: Mesostigmata: Phytoseiidae

NOMENCLATURE: **Approved name:** *Hypoaspis miles* (Berlese). **Other names:** sometimes referred to as *Geolaelaps* sp. **Common names:** fungus gnat predator; fungus fly predator; sciarid fly predator.

SOURCE: Originally found in a decaying oat spillage at Leith, Scotland. Recorded in the literature from a variety of habitats in Europe, the Former Soviet Union and the USA.

PRODUCTION: Produced in mixtures of peat and vermiculite and fed on grain mites such as *Tyrophagus putrescentriae* (Schrank). Supplied as mixed stages in moist carrier.

TARGET PESTS: Sciarid flies (*Bradysia* spp.), springtails, mites and thrips pupae.

TARGET CROPS: Glasshouse-grown vegetables and, in some interiorscapes.

BIOLOGICAL ACTIVITY: **Biology:** A predatory mite that feeds on a wide range of insect and mite species in the soil. *Hypoaspis miles* lays its eggs in the soil and these hatch into motile larval stages. These immature stages will feed upon soil arthropods but eat less than the adults. The adult mite reaches a size of about 1 mm. **Predation:** One adult *Hypoaspis miles* can kill up to seven sciarid fly larvae per day. The juvenile stages also predate but consume fewer larvae. Adults can survive for long periods without feeding but will not reproduce in the absence of food. **Egg laying:** Female mites lay eggs in soil and these hatch within one to two days at temperatures of 25 °C. The nymphs become adults within five to six days and inhabit the upper 1 to 2 cm of the soil surface. Development is slower at lower temperatures and no development occurs at all at 10 °C and lower. **Efficacy:** *Hypoaspis miles* is very effective at controlling a range of soil insects and mites. It will reduce thrips populations by predating the pupae when they fall to the ground.

COMMERCIALISATION: **Formulation:** Mixed populations of growth stages supplied in peat and/or vermiculite. **Tradenames:** Hypo-line m – Novartis BCM, Hypoaspis Sciarid Fly Predators – English Woodland Biocontrol, Hyposure (m) – Biological Crop Protection, Hypoaspis miles – Applied Bio-nomics, Hypoaspis miles – Neudorff, Geolaelaps sp. (= Hypoaspis sp.)-Fungus Gnat Destroyer – Nature's Alternative Insectary, Entomite – Svenska Predator, Hypex – Svenska Predator, Hypoaspis-System – Biobest.

APPLICATION: Apply 25 *Hypoaspis miles* for preventive treatment and 55 for curative treatment per 100 to 300 square metre of growing medium or bench area. Rates of 150 per square metre are recommended for high populations of pests. Apply evenly to the soil of glasshouse-grown crops. A single application should be suffcient to establish a population for the season.

PRODUCT SPECIFICATIONS: **Purity:** Mixed population of different growth stages plus some soil insects as a food source. **Storage conditions:** Hold at room temperature and do not cool. **Shelf-life:** Use as soon as possible after delivery.

COMPATIBILITY: Do not use soil insecticides. Killed by freezing conditions but well adapted to moist soil. *Hypoaspis miles* can survive in dry soil.

MAMMALIAN TOXICITY: Allergic reactions have been recorded following use although this is thought to be caused by the prey mites rather than *Hypoaspis miles*.

ENVIRONMENTAL IMPACT AND NON-TARGET TOXICITY: *Hypoaspis miles* occurs widely in Nature and has no adverse effects on non-target organisms or the environment.

4:163   *Leptomastix dactylopii*

Mealybug parasite

The Pesticide Manual - 11th edition: Entry number 444

Parasitic wasp: Hymenoptera: Encyrtidae

NOMENCLATURE: **Approved name:** *Leptomastix dactylopii* Howard. **Other names:** chalcid mealybug parasite.

SOURCE: Native to South America, probably Brazil and introduced into California in 1934. It has since spread around the world.

PRODUCTION: Reared on its only known host, the citrus mealybug, *Planococcus citri* (Risso).

TARGET PESTS: The citrus mealybug, *Planococcus citri*.

TARGET CROPS: Ornamentals and vegetables in glasshouses and in interiorscapes. Also released to protect citrus plantations from attack.

BIOLOGICAL ACTIVITY: **Biology:** Females lay eggs in third instar mealybug larvae as their ovipositors often pass through younger instars. The egg hatches and the larva goes through four larval stages before pupating within the mummified mealybug. The adult emerges through a round hole in the mummy. Unfertilised females lay only male eggs. **Predation:** The mealybug into which an egg is laid is consumed by the developing wasp larva.
Egg laying: Under ideal conditions, a female wasp will lay between 60 and 100 eggs in 10 to 14 days. It is unusual for more than a single egg to be laid within a single mealybug.
Duration of development: The duration of development is dependent upon temperature varying from about 45 days at 17 °C to 12 days at 30 °C. **Efficacy:** The adult parasitic wasp is a very good flyer and has excellent searching ability. Even low wasp densities can control mealybug populations.

COMMERCIALISATION: **Formulation:** The parasite is supplied as both adults or pupae within the mummified mealybug. **Tradenames:** Leptopar – Koppert, Mealybug Parasite – Arbico, Leptomastix – Sautter & Stepper, Lepsure (d) – Biological Crop Protection,

Leptomastix-System – Biobest, Leptomastix dactylopii – IPM Laboratories, Leptomastix dactylopii – Neudorff, Leptomastix dactylopii – Bugs for Bugs, Lepto-line d – Novartis BCM.

APPLICATION: Release between one and two wasps per square metre or up to five wasps per plant if pest populations are high. Release weekly for four to six weeks, twice a year.

PRODUCT SPECIFICATIONS: **Purity:** No contaminating insects should be present. **Storage conditions:** Do not expose to direct sunlight or freeze. Keep cool if not used immediately. **Shelf-life:** Use as soon as possible after delivery.

COMPATIBILITY: Do not use residual insecticides. Often used in combination with *Cryptolaemus montrouzieri* Mulsant.

MAMMALIAN TOXICITY: No allergic or other adverse reactions have been reported from the use of *Leptomastix dactylopii* in glasshouse or field conditions.

ENVIRONMENTAL IMPACT AND NON-TARGET TOXICITY: *Leptomastix dactylopii* occurs widely in Nature and is not thought to pose any threat to non-target organisms nor to have an adverse effect on the environment.

4:164 *Metaphycus bartletti*

Scale insect parasite

Wasp parasite: Hymenoptera: Encyrtidae

NOMENCLATURE: **Approved name:** *Metaphycus bartletti* Annecke and Mynhardt. **Other names:** soft scale parasite; black scale parasite; scale parasitoid.

SOURCE: Widely occurring scale parasite.

PRODUCTION: Reared in insectaries under controlled conditions on scale insects.

TARGET PESTS: *Saissetia olea* (Bernard) (black scale of olives).

TARGET CROPS: Olive plantations and on ornamentals such as laurel.

BIOLOGICAL ACTIVITY: **Biology:** The larvae consume scale insects from the egg to the adult stage and the adult wasps feed on honey. The life-cycle of the wasp is between 25 and 40 days depending on the temperature. **Predation:** The larvae eat the inside of parasitised scales. Females will parasitise only third instar larvae and very young scales. **Egg laying:** The female wasp is very long-lived and can lay over 100 eggs in her life-time. **Duration of development:** Development time is very dependent on the temperature. The egg can develop into an adult in 11 days and the adult wasp can survive for over 50 days. **Efficacy:** The adult female wasp is very mobile and very effective at seeking and parasitising its prey.

COMMERCIALISATION: **Formulation:** Sold as adult wasps or as parasitised scales. **Tradenames:** Metaphycus bartletti – Biotop.

APPLICATION: Apply to infested olive trees at a rate of five to ten wasps per tree in the Spring and Autumn. Introduce as soon as scales reach the third larval instar.

PRODUCT SPECIFICATIONS: **Purity:** Adults consist of fecund females. All scales supplied are parasitised. **Storage conditions:** Adults may be kept under normal conditions in the presence of a suitable food source. Very active in direct sunlight. **Shelf-life:** Adults may be kept for a few days if fed on honey solution.

COMPATIBILITY: Incompatible with foliar insecticides.

MAMMALIAN TOXICITY: No allergic or other adverse reaction has been reported following the release of *Metaphycus bartletti* in glasshouses or outdoors.

ENVIRONMENTAL IMPACT AND NON-TARGET TOXICITY: *Metaphycus bartletti* occurs widely in Nature and is not expected to have any adverse effect on non-target organisms or on the environment.

4:165   *Metaphycus helvolus*

Scale insect parasite

Parasitic wasp: Hymenoptera: Encyrtidae

NOMENCLATURE: **Approved name:** *Metaphycus helvolus* (Compere). **Other names:** black scale parasite; soft scale parasite; scale parasitoid.

SOURCE: Originated in South Africa but now widely introduced.

PRODUCTION: Reared in insectaries on scale insects.

TARGET PESTS: Citrus black scale and soft scales such as *Saisettia coffeae* (Walker), *S. oleae* (Bernard) and *Coccus hesperidum* Linnaeus. Not effective against hard scale insects.

TARGET CROPS: Citrus plantations, fruit orchards, ornamentals outdoors and under glass.

BIOLOGICAL ACTIVITY: **Biology:** The larvae consume scale insects from the egg to the adult stage and the adults feed on older scales. The adults can survive on nectar. The life-cycle of the wasp is very rapid, particularly at temperatures above 25 °C, varying from 11 to 33 days. **Predation:** Larvae eat eggs and larvae of soft scale species and the adults feed on older scales. Females will parasitise only second and third instar scale larvae. **Egg laying:** The female wasp is very long-lived and can lay over 400 eggs in her lifetime. Eggs are laid in young nymphal instars. **Duration of development:** Very dependent on the temperature, the egg can develop into an adult wasp in 11 days. Adults can live for over 50 days. **Efficacy:** *Metaphycus helvolus* is very mobile and very effective at seeking and parasitising its prey.

COMMERCIALISATION: **Formulation:** Sold as adult wasps. **Tradenames:** Metsure (h) – Biological Crop Protection, Metaphycus helvolus wasps – Rincon-Vitova, Metaphycus helvolus – IPM Laboratories.

APPLICATION: Apply to infested citrus trees at a rate of 1,000 to 3,000 wasps per tree in the Spring. Under glasshouse conditions, release about five wasps per square metre, repeating three times at two week intervals. Introduce as soon as scales are seen.

PRODUCT SPECIFICATIONS: **Purity:** Fecund female adults. **Storage conditions:** Adults may be kept under warm conditions in the presence of a food source. Very active in direct sunlight. **Shelf-life:** Use as soon as possible as quality declines with storage.

COMPATIBILITY: Extremely low humidity and temperature reduce the wasp's activity. Control ants, as they attack *Metaphycus helvolus*. Do not use in areas of dull light.

MAMMALIAN TOXICITY: No allergic or other adverse reaction has been reported following release of *Metaphycus helvolus* in glasshouses or outdoors.

ENVIRONMENTAL IMPACT AND NON-TARGET TOXICITY: *Metaphycus helvolus* occurs widely in Nature and there is no evidence that it affects non-target organisms or that it has any adverse effects on the environment.

4:166 *Orius albidipennis* Thrips predator

The Pesticide Manual - 11th edition: Entry number 535

Predatory bug: Hemiptera: Anthocoridae

NOMENCLATURE: **Approved name:** *Orius albidipennis* (Reuter). **Other names:** minute pirate bug.

SOURCE: Palaearctic species, found mainly in the Southern Mediterranean from North Africa to the Near East, Iran and Russian Asia Minor. It is also found in the Canary Islands, Cape Verde and Spain. *Orius* spp. were first reported as predators of thrips in 1914. Subsequent work in the USA in the late 1970s and early 1980s led to the introduction of *Orius* spp. as commercial products in Canada and Europe in the 1990s.

PRODUCTION: Bred in insectaries on soft-bodied phytophagous adult, larval, nymphal and egg-stage insects. Lepidopteran eggs are a common food source.

TARGET PESTS: Thrips are the main prey but it will also consume a wide range of arthropods including aphids, mites and the eggs of some lepidopteran species.

TARGET CROPS: Glasshouse-grown vegetables and ornamentals.

BIOLOGICAL ACTIVITY: **Biology:** There are seven development stages; egg, five nymphal stages and the adult. Eggs are laid within the plant tissue, usually in the leaf stem or in the main vein on the underside of the leaf. Eggs are usually laid separately. All the nymphal stages have characteristic red eyes. Adults vary in size from 2 to 3 mm with the females being larger than the males. Males are clearly asymmetrical. **Predation:** All growth stages catch and kill small insects, holding them motionless with their forelegs and sucking them dry. If insect numbers are high, the bugs will kill more insects than they need to eat and they also kill other *Orius* species and other beneficial insects. Prey is located by touch rather than by sight. The larvae and adults are relatively fast-moving. **Egg laying:** Eggs are laid usually singly with only their tops protruding above the plant surface two to three days after mating. Temperature and food supply have a significant effect on the number of eggs laid by a female, with the normal number being between 125 and 160 eggs in its lifetime.

Duration of development: Development is very dependent upon temperature and at 28 °C, total preimaginal development takes 14.5 days whilst at 20 °C, it takes 23 days. A poor food supply slows this development timescale significantly. Females live for 20 to 23 days.

Efficacy: The adults can fly reasonably well and can locate new infested plants very easily. *Orius albidipennis* is able to survive in the absence of prey. **Key references:** 1) R Chyzik, M Klein and Y Ben-Dov. 1995, Reproduction and survival of the predatory bug *Orius albidipennis* on various arthropod prey. *Entomologia Experimentalis et Applicata*, **75**, 27–31. 2) M Salim, S A Masud and H M Khan. 1987. *Orius albidipennis* (Reut.) (Hemiptera: Anthocoridae) – a predator of cotton pests. *Philippine Entomologist*, **7**, 37–42. 3) J Riudavets. 1995. Predators of *Frankliniella occidentalis* (Perg.) and *Thrips tabaci* Lind.: a review. *Wageningen Agric. Univ. Papers,* **95–1**, 43–87.

COMMERCIALISATION: **Formulation:** Sold as adults in packaging material with a food supply **Tradenames:** Minute Pirate Bug – Arbico (species not stated), Orius – Sautter & Stepper (species not stated), Orius-System – Biobest (species not stated), Ori-line a – Novartis BCM, Orius-Raubwanzen – Neudorff (species not stated).

APPLICATION: Spread carrier material onto plants or place in release boxes. Apply at rate of one adult per two infested plants. Release close to site of infestation in early morning or late evening under low light conditions and when the glasshouse vents are closed.

PRODUCT SPECIFICATIONS: **Purity:** Containers include adult bugs in a carrier plus a food source and no contaminants. **Storage conditions:** Store at 5 to 10 °C. Do not expose to direct sunlight. **Shelf-life:** Use as soon as possible.

COMPATIBILITY: Do not use residual insecticides. Adults are easily disturbed. Egg laying is optimal in the presence of a high-quality food source and at temperatures around 22 °C.

MAMMALIAN TOXICITY: No allergic or other adverse reaction has been reported following its use under glasshouse conditions.

ENVIRONMENTAL IMPACT AND NON-TARGET TOXICITY: *Orius albidipennis* occurs widely in Nature and has not shown any adverse effects on the environment but it will consume other insects.

4:167 *Orius insidiosus* *Thrips predator*

The Pesticide Manual - 11th edition: Entry number 535

Predatory bug: Hemiptera: Anthocoridae

NOMENCLATURE: **Approved name:** *Orius insidiosus* (Say). **Other names:** minute pirate bug.

SOURCE: Nearctic, very widespread in Nature.

PRODUCTION: Bred in insectaries on soft-bodied phytophagous adult, larval, nymphal and egg-stage insects.

TARGET PESTS: Many thrips, including *Frankliniella occidentalis* (Pergande), *Sericothrips variabilis* (Beach) and *Thrips tabaci* Lindeman, but will also consume a wide range of arthropods including aphids, mites and the eggs of some lepidopteran species.

TARGET CROPS: Glasshouse-grown vegetables and ornamentals. Widely used in glasshouses in Canada.

BIOLOGICAL ACTIVITY: **Biology:** There are seven development stages; egg, five nymphal stages and the adult. Eggs are laid within the plant tissue usually in the leaf stem or in the main vein on the underside of the leaf. Eggs are usually laid separately. All the nymphal stages have characteristic red eyes. Adults vary in size from 2 to 3 mm with the females being larger than the males. In the field, *Orius insidiosus* are slightly aggregated with the crowding of nymphs being slightly greater than the adults. **Predation:** All growth stages catch and kill small insects holding them motionless with their forelegs and sucking them dry with little difference in the numbers of prey consumed by adults and nymphs. If insect numbers are high, the bugs will kill more insects than they need to eat and they also kill other *Orius* species and other beneficial insects. Prey is located by touch rather than by sight. The larvae and adults move rapidly. **Egg laying:** Eggs are laid usually singly with only their tops protruding above the plant surface two to three days after mating. Eggs are laid in or adjacent to the growing tips with very few eggs laid in flowers and fruits. Temperature and food supply have a significant effect on the number of eggs laid by a female with the normal being about one to three eggs per day giving a total of 30 to 40 eggs in its lifetime. **Duration of development:** Development is very dependent upon temperature with development time between 28 and 32 °C being 12 days and at 24 °C being 20 days. Development ceases at temperatures below 10 °C. Adult longevity and female fecundity at 26 °C vary with diet, being respectively 42 days and 144 eggs on *Ephestia kuehniella* Zeller eggs and 17 days and 66 eggs on *Frankliniella occidentalis* adults. Female longevity is significantly longer on diets of pollen alone whilst fecundity is higher in diets of *Heliothis virescens* (Fabricius) eggs than pollen. Nymphs can complete their development on diets of pollen. **Efficacy:** The adults can fly reasonably well and can locate new infested plants easily. **Key references:** 1) R J Jacobson. 1997. Integrated pest management (IPM) in greenhouses. In T Lewis (ed.), *Thrips as Crop Pests*, 639–66, CABI, Wallingford, UK. 2) M W Sabelis and P J C van Rijn. 1997. Predation by insects and mites. In T Lewis (ed.), *Thrips as Crop Pests*, 259–354, CABI, Wallingford, UK. 3) J Riudavets. 1995. Predators of

4. Insect Predators

Frankliniella occidentalis (Perg.) and *Thrips tabaci* Lind.: a review. *Wageningen Agric. Univ. Papers,* **95–1**, 43–87.

COMMERCIALISATION: **Formulation:** Sold as adults in packaging material with a food supply of buckwheat in a vermiculite carrier. **Tradenames:** Ori-line i – Novartis BCM, Predatory Minute Pirate Bug – M&R Durango, Orius insidiosus Pirate Bug – Nature's Alternative Insectary, Orius insidiosus – IPM Laboratories, Minute Pirate Bug – Arbico (species not stated), Orius – Sautter & Stepper (species not stated), Orius-System – Biobest (species not stated), Orius-Raubwanzen – Neudorff (species not stated).

APPLICATION: Sprinkle carrier onto plants or use release boxes, allowing adults to escape on their own. Apply at rate of one adult per two infested plants. Release close to site of infestation in the early morning or late evening, under low light conditions and with the glasshouse vents closed.

PRODUCT SPECIFICATIONS: **Purity:** Containers include adult bugs in a carrier plus a food source and no contaminants. **Storage conditions:** Store at 5 to 10 °C. Do not expose to direct sunlight. **Shelf-life:** Use as soon as possible.

COMPATIBILITY: Do not use residual insecticides. Adults are easily disturbed. Egg laying is optimal in the presence of a high-quality food source and at temperatures around 22 °C.

MAMMALIAN TOXICITY: No allergic or other adverse reaction has been reported following its use under glasshouse conditions.

ENVIRONMENTAL IMPACT AND NON-TARGET TOXICITY: *Orius insidiosus* occurs in Nature and is not expected to have any adverse effects on non-target organisms or the environment.

4:168   *Orius laevigatus*   *Thrips predator*

The Pesticide Manual - 11th edition: Entry number 535

Predatory bug: Hemiptera: Anthocoridae

NOMENCLATURE: **Approved name:** *Orius laevigatus* (Fieber). **Other names:** minute pirate bug.

SOURCE: West palaearctic in areas with marine influence. Widespread throughout the Mediterranean area, especially in the Iberian Peninsula and Atlantic coasts of Western Europe. Very widely spread in Nature.

PRODUCTION: Bred in insectaries on soft-bodied phytophagous adult, larval, nymphal and egg-stage insects.

TARGET PESTS: Thrips, especially *Frankliniella occidentalis* (Pergande), *Thrips tabaci* Lindeman and *Caliothrips fasciatus* (Pergande), but will also consume a wide range of insects including aphids, mites and the eggs of some lepidopteran species.

TARGET CROPS: Glasshouse-grown vegetables and ornamentals. *Orius laevigatus* has also found success in strawberry tunnels.

BIOLOGICAL ACTIVITY: **Biology:** There are seven development stages; egg, five nymphal stages and the adult. Eggs are laid within the plant tissue usually in the leaf stem or in the main vein on the underside of the leaf. Eggs are usually laid separately. All the nymphal stages have characteristic red eyes. Adults vary in size with the females being larger than the males. *Orius laevigatus* adapts very well to a protected environment and it can survive, even without thrips prey. **Predation:** All growth stages catch and kill small insects, holding them motionless with their forelegs and sucking their contents. Nymphs and adults consume about two *Frankliniella occidentalis* larvae or adults per day at 20 °C. If insect numbers are high, the bugs will kill more insects than they need to eat and they also kill other *Orius* species and other beneficial insects. Prey is located by touch rather than by sight. The larvae and adults are relatively fast-moving. **Egg laying:** Eggs are laid usually singly with only their tops protruding above the plant surface two to three days after mating. Temperature and food supply have a significant effect on the number of eggs laid by a female. Oviposition periods range from 18 to 33 days. A female will lay about 150 eggs in its lifetime. **Duration of development:** Development is very dependent upon temperature and at 27 °C the egg will hatch in about 4 days and the five larval stages together take about 13 days. Males do not live as long as females. Lower temperatures and a poor food supply slows this development timescale significantly. *Orius laevigatus* enters reproductive diapause in daylengths of less than 16 hours and this limits its use in more Northerly countries during the early part of the season. It hibernates as adults in European climates. **Efficacy:** The adults can fly reasonably well and can locate new infested plants very easily. **Key references:** 1) R J Jacobson. 1997. Integrated pest management (IPM) in greenhouses. In T Lewis (ed.), *Thrips as Crop Pests*, 639–66, CABI, Wallingford, UK. 2) J Riudavets. 1995. Predators of *Frankliniella occidentalis* (Perg.) and *Thrips tabaci* Lind.: a review. *Wageningen Agric. Univ. Papers,* **95–1**, 43–87.

COMMERCIALISATION: **Formulation:** Sold as adults in packaging material with a food supply. **Tradenames:** Ori-line I – Novartis BCM, Orisure (I) – Biological Crop Protection, Minute Pirate Bug – Arbico (species not stated), Orius – Sautter & Stepper (species not stated), Orius-System – Biobest (species not stated), Orius-Raubwanzen – Neudorff (species not stated), Thripor – Koppert.

APPLICATION: Sprinkle carrier over crops or place in a release box and allow adults to escape from packaging on their own. Apply at rate of one adult per two infested plants. Release close to site of infestation in early morning or late evening, when light intensity is low and the glasshouse vents are closed.

PRODUCT SPECIFICATIONS: **Purity:** Containers include adult bugs in a carrier plus a food source and no contaminants. **Storage conditions:** Store at 5 to 10 °C. Do not expose to direct sunlight. **Shelf-life:** Use as soon as possible.

COMPATIBILITY: Do not use residual insecticides. Adults are easily disturbed. Egg laying is optimal in the presence of a high-quality food source and at temperatures around 22 °C.

4. Insect Predators

MAMMALIAN TOXICITY: No allergic or other adverse reaction has been reported following its use under glasshouse conditions.

ENVIRONMENTAL IMPACT AND NON-TARGET TOXICITY: *Orius laevigatus* occurs widely in Nature and has not shown any adverse effects on non-target organisms or on the environment.

4:169 *Orius majusculus* Thrips predator

The Pesticide Manual - 11th edition: Entry number 535

Predatory bug: Hemiptera: Anthocoridae

NOMENCLATURE: **Approved name:** *Orius majusculus* Reuter. **Other names:** minute pirate bug.

SOURCE: Palaearctic. Common throughout Central Europe, parts of the British Isles and Southern Scandinavia. Also found in Southern Europe but not in North Africa.

PRODUCTION: Bred in insectaries on soft-bodied phytophagous adult, larval, nymphal and egg-stage insects.

TARGET PESTS: Thrips, including *Frankliniella occidentalis* (Pergande), but will also consume a wide range of insects including aphids, mites and the eggs of some lepidopteran species.

TARGET CROPS: Glasshouse-grown vegetables and ornamentals.

BIOLOGICAL ACTIVITY: **Biology:** There are seven development stages; egg, five nymphal stages and the adult. Eggs are laid within the plant tissue usually in the leaf stem or in the main vein on the underside of the leaf. Eggs are usually laid separately. All the nymphal stages have characteristic red eyes. Adults vary in size, with the females being larger than the males. Winter populations in the wild consist mainly of females that become active in March to April. Oviposition begins in May. **Predation:** All growth stages catch and kill small insects, holding them motionless with their forelegs and sucking them dry. The immature stages of *Orius majusculus* will consume about 130 *Frankliniella occidentalis* larvae at 25 °C. If prey are abundant, the bugs will kill more insects than they need to eat and they also kill other *Orius* species and other beneficial insects. Prey is located by touch rather than by sight. The larvae and adults are relatively fast-moving. **Egg laying:** Eggs are laid, two to three days after mating, usually singly, with only their tops protruding above the plant surface. Temperature and food supply have a significant effect on the number of eggs laid by a female. At 15 °C, 20 °C and 25 °C, females fed on caterpillar eggs laid 195, 158 and 237 eggs respectively.
Duration of development: Development is temperature dependent and, at 25 °C, the eggs will hatch in about four days whilst, at 15 °C, it takes 9 to 10 days. The duration of the five nymphal stages together is between 14 and 15 days. Adult longevity is dependent on food supply and temperature. At 26 °C, with caterpillar eggs as food, *Orius majusculus* lives for

about 50 days but, with *Frankliniella occidentalis* adults as food, it only lives for about 20 days.
Efficacy: The adults can fly reasonably well and can locate new infested plants very easily.
Key references: 1) R J Jacobson. 1997. Integrated pest management (IPM) in greenhouses. In T Lewis (ed.), *Thrips as Crop Pests*, 639–66, CABI, Wallingford, UK. 2) J Riudavets. 1995. Predators of *Frankliniella occidentalis* (Perg.) and *Thrips tabaci* Lind.: a review. *Wageningen Agric. Univ. Papers,* **95–1**, 43–87.

COMMERCIALISATION: **Formulation:** Sold as adults in packaging material with a food supply. **Tradenames:** Ori-line m – Novartis BCM, Minute Pirate Bug – Arbico (species not stated), Orius – Sautter & Stepper (species not stated), Orius-System – Biobest (species not stated), Orius-Raubwanzen – Neudorff (species not stated).

APPLICATION: Sprinkle carrier onto crops or place in release boxes and allow adults to escape on their own. Apply at rate of one adult per two infested plants. Release close to site of infestation in the early morning or late evening when the light intensity is low and the glasshouse vents are closed. Best results in glasshouses were obtained with one predator per 100 thrips when starting with infestations of ten thrips per leaf. Do not release in early crops (before late March in Northern Europe) as the bugs often do not establish.

PRODUCT SPECIFICATIONS: **Purity:** Containers include adult bugs in a carrier plus a food source and no contaminants. **Storage conditions:** Store at 5 to 10 °C. Do not expose to direct sunlight. **Shelf-life:** Use as soon as possible.

COMPATIBILITY: Do not use residual insecticides. Adults are easily disturbed. Egg laying is optimal in the presence of a high-quality food source and at temperatures around 22 °C. *Orius majusculus* has occasionally been observed to be phytophagous on chrysanthemums in Holland.

MAMMALIAN TOXICITY: No allergic or other adverse reaction has been reported following its use under glasshouse conditions.

ENVIRONMENTAL IMPACT AND NON-TARGET TOXICITY: *Orius majusculus* occurs widely in Nature and has not shown any adverse effects on non-target organisms or on the environment.

4:170   *Phytoseiulus persimilis*

Spider mite predator

The Pesticide Manual - 11th edition: Entry number 577

Predatory mite: Mesostigmata: Phytoseiidae

NOMENCLATURE: **Approved name:** *Phytoseiulus persimilis* Athios-Henriot.
Other names: red spider mite predator; Chilean mite.

SOURCE: First identified on roots of orchids imported into Germany from Chile in 1958. Subsequently, exported around the world.

PRODUCTION: Reared in insectaries on *Tetranychus urticae* Koch on beans.

TARGET PESTS: Red spider mites (*Tetranychus urticae*).

TARGET CROPS: Glasshouse-grown vegetables and ornamentals, interiorscapes and outdoor crops such as strawberries, cotton, vegetables and ornamentals.

BIOLOGICAL ACTIVITY: **Biology:** Eggs are laid near a food source on the surface of the leaves. These hatch into larvae with three pairs of legs. They do not eat. The protonymph emerges from the larva and immediately starts to eat. At the second nymphal stage the predator searches for food constantly. The adults emerge from the nymphal stage, mate within a few hours and the females then begin to lay eggs. In the absence of food the predator can survive for some time on water and honey but reproduction then ceases. **Predation:** Larvae do not feed, the nymphal stages consume eggs, larvae and protonymphs of the spider mite and adults eat all stages of the prey. *Phytoseiulus persimilis* is almost completely dependent on the spider mite. **Egg laying:** A female will lay eggs for the duration of its life following mating. No eggs are laid by unfertilised females. A female can deposit up to five eggs per day under ideal conditions of temperature, humidity and food supply and will lay a maximum of 60 eggs in its life. **Duration of development:** Rate of development is very dependent upon the temperature. At 15 °C, the period of time from egg to egg is about 25 days but, at 30 °C, this is reduced to about five days. **Efficacy:** The rapid breeding rate of *Phytoseiulus persimilis* means that it is a very effective predator of spider mites. It reproduces much faster than the pest mite and the nymphal stages remain on the leaf on which they hatch. The adults move from plant to plant through physical contact of adjacent plants and along spider mite webs. An adult female predator will consume five adult spider mites or 20 young larvae and eggs in a day. Under ideal conditions of temperature (15 to 25 °C) and relative humidity (60 to 70%), the predator can destroy an infestation and will subsequently starve to death.

COMMERCIALISATION: **Formulation:** Sold as adults in bags, paper sachets, bottles and vials with suitable carrier and *Tetranychus urticae* eggs as a food source. Also supplied on bean leaves that can be distributed throughout the crop. **Tradenames:** Phyto-line p – Novartis BCM, Spidex – Koppert, Spidex Plus – Koppert, Phytoseiulus-System – Biobest, Phytosure (p) – Biological Crop Protection, Phytosure (pt) – Biological Crop Protection, Phytoseiulus persimilis – Neudorff.

APPLICATION: Under glasshouse conditions, release one predatory mite for every 15 to 25 spider mites or five predatory mites per square metre. Shake adults carefully and evenly throughout the crop. Outdoors, release between 2,500 and 50,000 mites per hectare.

PRODUCT SPECIFICATIONS: **Purity:** Fecund adults with carrier and a few red spider mite eggs. No other contaminants. **Storage conditions:** Store at 12 to 15 °C and protect from freezing and high temperatures. **Shelf-life:** Use as soon as possible, as the prey mites on leaf pieces will soon be consumed and the predators may turn to cannabalism.

COMPATIBILITY: Incompatible with benzimidazole fungicides and residual insecticides. Humidities below 60% slow life-cycle and inhibit egg hatch. Mites go dormant below 10 °C. May be used in conjunction with *Amblyseius californicus*.

MAMMALIAN TOXICITY: No allergic or other adverse reaction has been reported from its use in glasshouse or outdoor crops.

ENVIRONMENTAL IMPACT AND NON-TARGET TOXICITY: *Phytoseiulus persimilis* is widespread in Nature and is not thought to be damaging to non-target species nor to the environment.

4:171   *Podisus maculiventris*

Caterpillar predatory bug

Predatory bug: Heteroptera: Pentatomidae

NOMENCLATURE: **Approved name:** *Podisus maculiventris* (Say). **Other names:** caterpillar predator.

SOURCE: *Podisus maculiventris* occurs widely in Nature in North and South America. It is a plant-dwelling, predatory bug.

TARGET PESTS: Lepidoptera and Coleoptera.

TARGET CROPS: Vegetable, agronomic and ornamental crops in glasshouses and in open fields.

BIOLOGICAL ACTIVITY: **Biology:** At temperatures between 21 and 27 °C, eggs take about five days to hatch. There are five nymphal stages taking together between twenty and twenty eight days. Young nymphs are red with a black pattern on the abdomen. Older nymphs have a pattern of black, white, orange and yellow on their abdomens. The development threshold for *Podisus maculiventris* is 11 to 12 °C with a temperature optimum between 17 and 26 °C. A constant temperature of 33 °C is lethal. *Podisus maculiventris* does not enter diapause. **Predation:** Nymphs and adults consume prey eggs and small larvae. **Egg laying:** Yellow eggs are deposited in clusters (20 to 25 eggs per cluster) with the cluster bearing a crop of spines. **Efficacy:** A very mobile predator of Lepidoptera and Coleoptera.

COMMERCIALISATION: **Formulation:** Sold as mixed instar nymphs (third and fourth instar) and adults mixed with paper scraps. Each box contains 100 predatory bugs. **Tradenames:** Podibug – Koppert.

APPLICATION: Open box carefully at the site of application and introduce the packing material plus bugs to the infested plants. Adult bugs may fly away from the place of introduction. Use one bug per square metre for light infestations and five per square metre for heavy infestations or hot spots, both as curative treatments.

4. Insect Predators

PRODUCT SPECIFICATIONS: **Purity:** No phytophagous mites, moulds or other contaminants. **Storage conditions:** Store at 8 to 10 °C in the dark. **Shelf-life:** Use within three days if stored as recommended.

COMPATIBILITY: Sensitive to most conventional pesticides.

MAMMALIAN TOXICITY: There have been no reports of allergic or other adverse toxicological effects arising from contact with *Podisus maculiventris* from research staff, producers or users.

ENVIRONMENTAL IMPACT AND NON-TARGET TOXICITY: *Podisus maculiventris* has a wide distribution in Nature and there is no evidence that it has any adverse effects on non-target organisms or on the environment.

4:172 *Trichogramma brassicae*

Lepidopteran egg parasite

The Pesticide Manual - 11th edition: Entry number 732

Parasitic wasp: Hymenoptera: Trichogrammatidae

NOMENCLATURE: **Approved name:** *Trichogramma brassicae* Bezdenko. **Other names:** previously known as *Trichogramma maidis* Pintureau and Voegelé. **Common name:** moth egg predator; lepidopteran egg parasite; trichogramms.

SOURCE: Widely occurring parasitic wasp.

PRODUCTION: Reared in insectaries under controlled conditions on the eggs of moths such as *Ephestia kuehniella* Zeller.

TARGET PESTS: Eggs of lepidopteran pests particularly *Ostrinia nubilalis* (Hübner) (European corn borer), *Mamestra brassicae* (Linnaeus) and *Helicoverpa armigera* (Hübner).

TARGET CROPS: Maize, pepper, tomatoes, and ornamentals. The main use is in maize.

BIOLOGICAL ACTIVITY: **Biology:** Adult female wasps are about 0.5 mm long. They lay their eggs into a lepidopteran egg, preferring recently-laid eggs. When the wasp egg hatches, the wasp larva consumes the developing caterpillar inside the egg. It pupates inside the egg and emerges as an adult wasp. Adults feed on nectar. **Predation:** Most lepidopteran eggs can be parasitised by *Trichogramma brassicae*. **Egg laying:** Adult wasps mate shortly after emergence and fertilised females lay eggs that develop into either males or females. Unfertilised females also lay viable eggs that develop only into males. A female wasp will parasitise over 50 eggs in its lifespan of 5 to 14 days. **Duration of development:** The time from egg lay to wasp emergence varies with temperature from as little as seven to as long as 20 days. **Efficacy:** If the recommendations for use are followed, *Trichogramma brassicae* will destroy about 80% of pest eggs and will keep the lepidopteran population in check. The adults are very mobile and are expert at locating insect eggs.

COMMERCIALISATION: **Formulation:** Sold as parasitised eggs fixed on cardboard or in capsules. **Tradenames:** Trig – UNCAA and Biotop, Trichocap – BASF, Pyratyp – BASF, TR 16 – UNCAA.

APPLICATION: Spread cardboard carrier or capsules within the crop. The release rate should be between 12,000 and 500,000 parasitised eggs per hectare depending on the stage of growth of the crop, the area to be treated, the type of pest targeted, the development stage of the pest and the climatic conditions.

PRODUCT SPECIFICATIONS: **Purity:** Only parasitised, non-phytophagous lepidopteran eggs with no contaminants. **Storage conditions:** Diapausing *Trichogramma brassicae* must be stored at 3 °C, 75% relative humidity. Always store following the manufacturer's instructions. **Shelf-life:** Diapausing parasites can be kept under recommended storage conditions for several months. Re-activated *Trichogramma brassicae* must be used within a few days of delivery.

COMPATIBILITY: Incompatible with foliar insecticides.

MAMMALIAN TOXICITY: No allergic or other adverse reaction has been recorded from the production of *Trichogramma brassicae* or its use in glasshouse or field conditions.

ENVIRONMENTAL IMPACT AND NON-TARGET TOXICITY: *Trichogramma brassicae* occurs widely in Nature and is unlikely to cause any adverse effects on non-target organisms or on the environment.

4:173 *Trichogramma evanescens*
Lepidopteran egg parasite

The Pesticide Manual - 11th edition: Entry number 732

Parasitic wasp: Hymenoptera: Trichogrammatidae

NOMENCLATURE: **Approved name:** *Trichogramma evanescens* Westwood. **Other names:** moth egg parasite; trichogramms.

SOURCE: Widely occurring parasitic wasp.

PRODUCTION: Reared in insectaries on the eggs of moths such as *Ephestia kuehniella* Zeller.

TARGET PESTS: Eggs of lepidopteran pests such as *Helicoverpa zea* (Boddie), *Heliothis virescens* (Fabricius) and *Ostrinia nubilalis* (Hübner).

TARGET CROPS: A wide range of field and glasshouse grown crops.

BIOLOGICAL ACTIVITY: **Biology:** Adult female wasps are about 0.5 mm long. They lay their eggs into a lepidopteran egg, preferring freshly-laid eggs. Upon hatching, the wasp larva consumes the developing caterpillar within the egg. It pupates inside the egg and emerges as an adult wasp. Adults feed on nectar. **Predation:** Most lepidopteran eggs are parasitised by *Trichogramma evanescens*. **Egg laying:** Adult wasps mate shortly after emergence and fertilised females lay eggs that develop into both males and females. Unfertilised females lay eggs that develop only into males. A female wasp will parasitise over 50 eggs in its life of 5 to 14 days. **Duration of development:** The time from egg lay to wasp emergence varies with temperature from 7 to 20 days. **Efficacy:** The parasite will have 30 or more generations in a season and, if numbers are high, will keep a lepidopteran population in check. The adults are very mobile and are expert locaters of insect eggs.

COMMERCIALISATION: **Formulation:** Sold as parasitised eggs fixed to a card.
Tradenames: Tricho-strip – Koppert, Tricho-line – Novartis BCM.

APPLICATION: Hang cards within the crop evenly distributed. Release rates of about 12,000 to 500,000 parasitised eggs per hectare depending upon the incidence of caterpillars. Use pheromone traps to monitor the population of Lepidoptera within the crop.

PRODUCT SPECIFICATIONS: **Purity:** Only parasitised non-phytophagous lepidopteran eggs with no contaminants. **Storage conditions:** Store in the dark at 10 to 15 °C.
Shelf-life: Can be kept for three to four days under recommended storage conditions.

COMPATIBILITY: Incompatible with foliar insecticides.

MAMMALIAN TOXICITY: No allergic or other adverse reaction has been reported from the use of *Trichogramma evanescens* in glasshouse or field conditions. Allergies associated with host Lepidoptera are known in production.

ENVIRONMENTAL IMPACT AND NON-TARGET TOXICITY: *Trichogramma evanescens* is widespread in Nature and is not thought to be damaging to non-target species or to the environment.

4:174   *Typhlodromus occidentalis*

Mite predator

Predatory mite: Mesostigmata: Phytoseiidae

NOMENCLATURE: **Approved name:** *Typhlodromus occidentalis* Nesbitt.
Other names: synonymous with *Galendromus occidentalis* and *Metaseiulus occidentalis*; predatory mite. See also *Galendromus occidentalis* entry.

SOURCE: Occurs widely, particularly in warm climates.

PRODUCTION: Reared in insectaries on red spider mites feeding on bean plants.

TARGET PESTS: Spider mites including *Tetranychus urticae* Koch.

TARGET CROPS: Tree crops in hot, dry climates, outdoor vegetable crops where temperatures are high and humidity is low and glasshouse vegetables and ornamentals where humidity is low.

BIOLOGICAL ACTIVITY: **Biology:** Eggs are laid in the vicinity of red spider mite eggs. These hatch into larvae. The nymphs develop from larvae and consume spider mite eggs, larvae, nymphs and adults. Adults live for 17 to 20 days and predate spider mite eggs, larvae, nymphs and adults. At low temperatures adults will enter diapause. **Predation:** Predatory mites pierce their prey and suck them empty. Adults can consume between 5 and 15 spider mites or eggs each day. More effective than *Phytoseiulus persimilis* under conditions of low humidity and high temperature. **Egg laying:** Female *Typhlodromus occidentalis* will lay about 50 eggs in its lifetime at the rate of two to three per day. **Duration of development:** Eggs hatch within a few days of laying and adults develop within seven to eight days under ideal conditions. Optimum temperatures are between 27 and 32 °C.

COMMERCIALISATION: **Formulation:** Sold as adults, nymphs and eggs on bean leaves. **Tradenames:** Typhlodromus occidentalis – Biological Services.

APPLICATION: In tree crops, apply at the rate of 25,000 predators per hectare, in outdoor vegetables, 25,000 to 50,000 per hectare and, in glasshouse crops, 10 predators per 10 sq m distributed evenly throughout the crop with additional predators applied to heavily-infested plants.

PRODUCT SPECIFICATIONS: **Purity:** Supplied on bean leaves as adults, nymphs and eggs with no significant phytophagous mites or other contaminants. **Storage conditions:** May be stored for up to 3 days on leaves out of direct sunlight and under cool conditions. Ensure that the leaves are separated from each other. **Shelf-life:** It is recommended that *Typhlodromus occidentalis* is used immediately.

COMPATIBILITY: *Typhlodromus occidentalis* is tolerant of many organophosphate insecticides and some acaricides but pyrethroids, carbaryl and other carbamates should not be used. Do not release within two weeks of the application of residual insecticides. Ideal for use in hot, dry conditions.

MAMMALIAN TOXICITY: No allergic or other adverse reactions have been reported following release of *Typhlodromus occidentalis*.

ENVIRONMENTAL IMPACT AND NON-TARGET TOXICITY: *Typhlodromus occidentalis* occurs widely in Nature and is not expected to have any adverse effects on non-target organisms or on the environment.

Predatory mite: Mesostigmata: Phytoseiidae

NOMENCLATURE: **Approved name:** *Typhlodromus pyri* Scheuten (Mikulov strain).
Other names: synonymous with *Galendromus pyri* and *Metaseiulus pyri*. **Common name:** fruit tree predatory mite.

SOURCE: Occurs widely, particularly in warm climates. Frequently found in fruit trees.

PRODUCTION: Reared under controlled conditions on red spider mites.

TARGET PESTS: Spider mites: *Tetranychus urticae* Koch, *Panonychus ulmi* (Koch), *Calepitrimerus vitis* (Nalepa), *Eriophyes vitis* (Prendergast) and *Aculus schlechtendali* (Nalepa).

TARGET CROPS: Fruit trees, especially top fruit, and vineyards.

BIOLOGICAL ACTIVITY: **Biology:** Eggs are laid in the vicinity of red spider mite eggs. These hatch into larvae. The nymphs develop from larvae and consume spider mite eggs, larvae, nymphs and adults. Adults live for 17 to 20 days and predate spider mite eggs, larvae, nymphs and adults. Depending upon climatic conditions, there are between two and four generations per season. At low temperatures, adults will enter diapause with the females overwintering in the bark of trees. All stages of *Typhlodromus pyri* can survive on pollen and fungi.
Predation: Predatory mites pierce their prey and suck them empty. Adults will consume about eight spider mites or eggs each day. More effective than *Phytoseiulus persimilis* under conditions of low humidity and high temperature. **Egg laying:** Female *Typhlodromus pyri* will lay about 50 eggs in its lifetime at the rate of two to three per day.
Duration of development: Eggs hatch within a few days of laying and adults develop within 7 to 8 days under ideal conditions. Optimum temperatures are between 27 and 32 °C.
Efficacy: *Typhlodromus pyri* is a very effective predator of spider mites but control in orchards and vineyards takes time. Often good control is not achieved until the season following application.

COMMERCIALISATION: **Formulation:** Sold as packs containing textile belts with 10 to 20 predatory female mites in diapause. **Tradenames:** Typhlodromus-System – Biobest, Typex – Svenska Predator.

APPLICATION: Apply at a rate of 25,000 predators per hectare. Attach textile strips to the trunks or branches of the crop to be treated in the late Winter or early Spring.

PRODUCT SPECIFICATIONS: **Purity:** Supplied as adult female mites in diapause.
Storage conditions: *Typhlodromus pyri* is supplied only in Winter and should be stored in a cooled room, an unheated cellar or in the open air. Do not allow the temperature to rise above 10 °C. Do not expose to direct sunlight **Shelf-life:** May be stored for two months under recommended storage conditions.

COMPATIBILITY: *Typhlodromus pyri* is very sensitive to chemical pesticides although the Mikulov strain is 200 times less sensitive than the wild type. Nevertheless, it is recommended that chemical pesticides are not applied following the release of the predator.

MAMMALIAN TOXICITY: There have been no reports of adverse allergic or other reactions from research workers, manufacturing staff or from the field release of *Typhlodromus pyri*.

ENVIRONMENTAL IMPACT AND NON-TARGET TOXICITY: *Typhlodromus pyri* occurs widely in Nature and is not expected to have any adverse effect on non-target organisms or the environment.

5:176 *als 1* gene

Introduces tolerance to sulfonylurea herbicides

NOMENCLATURE: **Approved name:** *als 1* gene. Also known as sulfonylurea tolerance gene and STS. **Promoter:** not applicable.

SOURCE: Crops that showed resistance to sulfonylurea herbicides were used to identify a tolerance gene coded *als 1* gene. This trait was selected rather than introduced through molecular biology and resistant crops were used as parents in breeding programmes designed to introduce the sulfonylurea-tolerance into elite varieties of soybean and cotton. Tobacco plants expressing this herbicide-tolerance have been used as the source of the material in breeding programmes in crops such as cotton.

TARGET PESTS: All weeds and in particular broad-leaved weeds.

TARGET CROPS: Soybean and cotton.

BIOLOGICAL ACTIVITY: **Biological activity:** The *als 1* gene codes for the enzyme acetolactate synthase (ALS) that is insensitive to the sulfonylurea herbicides, inhibitors of this natural enzyme. Acetolactate synthase is key in the biosynthesis of branched chain amino acids and its inhibition leads to rapid plant death. **Biology:** Resistance to over-the-top application of sulfonylurea herbicides is through the presence of a gene coding for the acetolactate synthase (ALS) enzyme that is insensitive to the sulfonylurea herbicides. This insensitivity has been demonstrated by *in vitro* enzyme bioassays and cosegregation of enzyme and whole plant tolerance. **Mode of action:** *Als 1* plants are not inhibited by the sulfonylurea herbicides and are, therefore, not affected by over-the-top applications that prevent the growth of many weeds of soybean and cotton fields. **Efficacy:** Homozygous mutants with *als 1* genes are 10 to 100 times more tolerant to sulfonylureas tested. **Key reference:** *Crop Science*, **29**, 1403–8, 1989.

COMMERCIALISATION: **Tradenames:** STS tolerant Soybeans – AgraTech Seeds, AgriPro Seeds, AgVenture, Asgrow Seeds, Beck's Hybrids, Campbell Seeds, Chemgro Seeds, Countrymark Cooperative, Croplan Genetics, Dairyland Seed Co, DEKALB Genetics, Deltapine Seed, Garst Seed, Golden Harvest Seeds, Growmark, Hoegmeyer Hybrids, Hoffman Seeds, Latham Seeds, Merscham Seeds, Midwest Seeds, Mycogen Seeds, NC+ Hybrids, Pioneer Hi-Bred International, Rupp Seed, Sands of Iowa, Scott's Quality Seeds, Sieben Hybrids.
STS tolerant Cotton – Du Pont.
STS tolerant Canola – Cargill Hybrid Seeds.
Patents: US 5084082

PRODUCT SPECIFICATIONS: Selected sulfonylurea-tolerance trait bred into elite crop varieties.

COMPATIBILITY: Compatible with over-the-top applications of sulfonylurea herbicides such as chlorimuron-methyl (Classic) and thifensulfuron-methyl (Pinnacle).

MAMMALIAN TOXICITY: There is no evidence that STS crops have any unusual characteristics that will render them different from conventional crops. There have been no reports of allergic or other adverse effects from researchers, breeders or users of the products.

ENVIRONMENTAL IMPACT AND NON-TARGET TOXICITY: There is no evidence that the use of STS crops will have any deleterious effect on non-target organisms or the environment.

5:177   *Bacillus thuringiensis* gene

Introduces resistance to insects

NOMENCLATURE: **Approved name:** *Bacillus thuringiensis* endotoxin genes; *Bt* genes. **Promoter:** cauliflower mosaic virus (CaMV) 35S.

SOURCE: *Bacillus thuringiensis* produces parasporal, protein aceous, crystal inclusion bodies during sporulation. Upon ingestion, these are insecticidal. Different endotoxins have different biological spectra and different toxin genes are used in different crops to afford protection from attack by different insects. For example, Monsanto has used *cry1A(c)* genes from *Btk* in cotton and tomatoes and *crylIIA* genes from *Btt* in potatoes and Novartis and Mycogen used *cry1A(b)* genes from *Btk* and Monsanto *crylIA* and *crylA(b)* genes, both from *Btk*, in maize. AgrEvo (Plant Genetic Systems) is also using *cry9C* toxin genes from *Bacillus thuringiensis* var. *tolworthi* in transgenic maize.

PRODUCTION: The gene is isolated from *Bacillus thuringiensis*, is often truncated and introduced into the crop associated with the promoter, usually cauliflower mosaic virus 35S promoter. Before introduction into crops it is common to increase the number of constructs in bacterial fermentation. The transgenic bacteria may be identified by use of a selectable marker such as antibiotic-resistance linked to a bacterium-specific promoter. The plants are produced by insertion of the *Bt* nucleic acid using transformed and disabled *Agrobacterium tumefasciens*, bombardment using a particle gun or other accepted transformation technique. Transgenic crops are identified using a selectable marker such as a herbicide-tolerance or an antibiotic-resistance gene. Elite varieties are bred from these transgenic crops. Novartis launched transgenic insect-resistant maize that contained two selectable markers, glufosinate-tolerance and ampicillin-resistance, *Bt* 176. More recently, it has developed a second maize line, *Bt* 11, that contains no anti-biotic resistance genes.

TARGET PESTS: Colorado potato beetle (*Leptinotarsa decemlineata* (Say)), European corn borer (*Ostrinia nubilalis* Hübner), pink corn borer (*Sesamia cretica*) and noctuids (*Heliothis* spp. and *Helicoverpa* spp.).

TARGET CROPS: The main target crops are potatoes, cotton and maize.

BIOLOGICAL ACTIVITY: **Biological activity:** The gene is expressed constitutively throughout the plant such that susceptible insects that feed upon the crop succumb. Different genes are used for different phytophagous insects. (For a full description of the mode of action and insect specificity of *Bt*-endotoxins see the *Bacillus thuringiensis* Berliner entries in section 3. Living Systems). **Biology:** The *cry1A(b)* gene codes for the full endotoxin that is hydrolysed by the gut digestive enzymes to form the toxin. It is active against a wide variety of Lepidoptera and is used to transform maize to give resistance to European corn borer (*Ostrinia nubilalis*). The *cry1A(c)* gene codes for the endotoxin that is particularly active against tobacco budworm (*Heliothis virescens* (Fabricius)), a major pest of cotton. The *cryIIIA* gene codes for a coleopteran specific endotoxin and is used in potatoes against Colorado potato beetle (*Leptinotarsa decemlineata*). Many crops are now being introduced that contain both *Bt*-genes and herbicide tolerance genes and there is a potato variety that contains *Bt*-genes and virus coat protein genes. **Mode of action:** Once in the insect, the crystal proteins are solubilised and the insect gut proteases convert the original pro-toxin into a smaller toxin. These hydrolysed toxins bind to the insect's midgut at high affinity specific receptor binding sites where they interfer with the potassium ion dependent active amino acid symport mechanism. This disruption causes the formation of a large, cation-selective pore that increases the water permeability of the membrane. A large uptake of water causes cell swelling and eventual rupture and the subsequent disintegration of the midgut lining. Different toxins bind to different receptors and this explains the selectivity of different *Bt* strains. This differential binding is described by those working in the field as different modes of action. Different genes coding for these proteins have been isolated and used to transform various crop plants such that the crops produce insecticidal proteins throughout their lives. In some cases the truncated genes have been used so that the insect-active toxin is produced in the crop rather than the pro-toxin that requires hydrolysis in the insect gut. **Efficacy:** Field studies and initial commercial use have shown good control of the target insects in the absence of additional chemical applications. Where other insect pests have appeared in the crop additional chemical treatment is usually recommended.

COMMERCIALISATION: Conditional approval for Monsanto's transgenic cotton seed was granted in the USA in late 1995 with the first introduction of BollGard cotton in 1996 by Delta and Pineland as NUCOTN 33B and NUCOTN 35B. Ciba (now Novartis) was granted approval to sell *Bt*-transformed maize in the USA in 1995 and in Canada in 1996.
Tradenames: BollGard Cotton (*cryIA(c)*) – Deltapine, Paymaster Cottonseed and Stoneville Pedigreed Seed.
InGard Cotton (*cryIA(c)*) – Deltapine Australia.
BollGard plus Roundup Ready Cotton (*cryIA(c)*) – Deltapine and Paymaster Cottonseed.
Bt plus Buctril BXN System Cotton (*cryIA(c)*) – Stoneville Pedigreed Seed.
NewLeaf Potatoes (*cryIIIA*) – NatureMark.
NewLeaf Plus Potatoes (*cryIIIA* plus PLRV coat protein) – NatureMark.
NewLeaf Y Potatoes (*cryIIIA* plus PVY coat protein) – NatureMark.
YieldGard Corn (*cryIA(b)*) – Asgrow Seeds, Beck's Hybrids, Cargill Hybrid Seeds, Countrymark Cooperative, Croplan Genetics, DEKALB Genetics, Golden Harvest Seeds, Growmark, Hoffman Seeds, Mycogen Seeds and Pioneer Hi-Bred International.
Maximizer Corn (*cryIA(b)*) – Novartis Seeds.

MaizeGard Corn (*crylA(b)*) – Novartis Seeds.
MaisGard Corn (*crylA(b)*) – Novartis Seeds.
Bt plus Liberty Link Corn (*crylA(b)*) – Garst Seeds.
Bt Corn plus IMI Tolerance (*crylA(b)*) – Garst Seeds, Mycogen Seeds and Novartis Seeds.
Bt-Xtra Corn (*crylA(b)*) – DEKALB Genetics and Mycogen.
StarLink Corn (*cry9C* plus glufosinate-tolerance) – AgrEvo and Plant Genetic Systems.
NatureGard – Mycogen.
KnockOut Bt – Northrup King.

APPLICATION: Seeds expressing the endotoxins from *Bacillus thuringiensis* are resistant to phytophagous insects particularly from the orders Lepidoptera and Coleoptera. Their use often results in reduced applications of conventional insecticides.

COMPATIBILITY: Compatible with most crop protection agents. Cotton growers are recommended to plant 75% of their crop to *Bt*-cotton and to apply conventional insecticides to the remaining 25% and those insecticides should not include *Bacillus thuringiensis* based products. Alternatively they may sow 96% of their cotton to *Bt*-cotton and leave the remaining 4% completely untreated as refugia. These restrictions are designed to reduce the possibility of the onset of insect resistance to *Bt* toxins. In maize, there is no recommendation to leave non-*Bt* crop refugia for insects but a strategy will be implemented. *Bt*-maize cannot be grown in areas where *Bt*-cotton is grown. It is likely that the recommendation will call for growers to plant up to 75% of their maize to *Bt*-varieties and leave 25% untreated with these refugia planted adjacent to or within *Bt*-maize fields. Refugia should also be present on every 130 hectares of maize. In potatoes, Monsanto has recommended to farmers that they plant at least 20% of their land to non-*Bt*-potatoes and that these must be planted adjacent or as close as possible to the *Bt*-crop. These refugia may be treated as the farmer deems appropriate. Some seed is sold conditional on the acceptance of restrictions.

MAMMALIAN TOXICITY: *Bacillus thuringiensis* based products are considered to be safe insecticides. There are no reports of allergic or other adverse reactions from the use of these transgenic products.

ENVIRONMENTAL IMPACT AND NON-TARGET TOXICITY: The transgenic crops are not expected to cause any adverse effects on non-target organisms or the environment.

5:178   bromoxynil tolerance gene

Introduces tolerance to bromoxynil

NOMENCLATURE: **Approved name:** bromoxynil tolerance gene; *bxn* gene; nitrilase gene. **Promoter:** cauliflower mosaic virus (CaMV) 35S.

SOURCE: The gene used to transform cotton and tobacco was isolated from the soil bacterium, *Klebsiella ozaenae*.

PRODUCTION: The gene was characterised in and isolated from the originating organism, *Klebsiella ozaenae*, and then amplified in bacterial culture. Cotton callus was transformed using *Agrobacterium tumefasciens* and transformants grown on in a collaborative programme between Rhône-Poulenc Agro and Calgene. The transformed plants were then used as one parent in a breeding programme and elite varieties were selected for commercialisation.

TARGET PESTS: Hard-to-kill broad-leaved weeds such as morning-glory (*Ipomoea* spp.) and cocklebur (*Xanthium* spp.).

TARGET CROPS: Cotton and tobacco.

BIOLOGICAL ACTIVITY: **Biological activity:** The *bxn* gene codes for a nitrilase enzyme that detoxifies bromoxynil converting it to the non-herbicidal metabolite, dibromohydroxybenzoic acid. **Biology:** Preliminary work on *bxn*-tobacco conducted by Rhône-Poulenc working with the French tobacco company, SEITA, showed that transformed tobacco, known as dark "ITB", would tolerate applied bromoxynil. This tobacco was granted a licence in Europe in March 1994 and was the first transgenic crop to achieve this status. Rhône-Poulenc worked closely with Calgene on the development of *bxn*-cotton and this was deregulated by USDA in February 1994. It is expected that the gene will be introduced into other crops such as oilseed rape. **Mode of action:** Transformed crops express the gene constitutively and are, therefore, tolerant of bromoxynil applied over-the-top at recommended rates. **Efficacy:** Very effective at controlling hard-to-kill broad-leaved weeds without damage to the crop.

COMMERCIALISATION: Introduced into US cotton growing regions in 1998.
Tradenames: BXN-Cotton – Stoneville Pedigreed Seed.

COMPATIBILITY: Compatible with a wide variety of crop protection chemicals used in cotton cultivation.

MAMMALIAN TOXICITY: There is no evidence that transformed cotton or tobacco plants show any differences from conventionally-bred cultivars and, therefore, do not show any greater hazards.

ENVIRONMENTAL IMPACT AND NON-TARGET TOXICITY: *Bxn*-cotton has not been shown to have any adverse effects on non-target organisms or on the environment.

5:179   class II EPSP synthase gene
Introduces tolerance to glyphosate

NOMENCLATURE: **Approved name:** class II EPSP synthase gene; CP4-EPSPS gene; Roundup Ready gene. **Promoter:** cauliflower mosaic virus (CaMV) 35S. Because EPSP synthase is located in the chloroplasts of plants, the CP4-EPSP gene has been linked to a promoter that operates within the chloroplast thereby ensuring that the gene is functional only where the enzyme is active.

SOURCE: The class II EPSP synthase gene was extracted from *Agrobacterium tumefaciens* strain CP4 isolated from the glyphosate production facilities and cloned into *E. coli*. The promoter was isolated from the cauliflower mosaic virus and found to be very effective at enhancing transcription levels of foreign genes in plants.

TARGET PESTS: A wide variety of weeds.

TARGET CROPS: The introduction of this glyphosate insensitive gene into elite crop varieties allows the grower to apply over-the-top applications of glyphosate for weed control. Major crops commercially available include soybeans, maize, cotton and canola.

BIOLOGICAL ACTIVITY: **Biology:** The transformed crops are tolerant of glyphosate application because the EPSP synthase gene expressed in the crop is not inhibited by the herbicide at the rates at which it is applied. **Mode of action:** The mutant EPSP synthase isolated from *Agrobacterium tumefaciens* has an affinity for glyphosate that is over 2,000 times less than natural plant EPSP synthase but with no adverse effects on the growth of transformed crop plants. Hence, transformed crops treated with rates of glyphosate of up to 1.68 kg acid equivalent/hectare show no visible signs of injury and no yield reduction. There are trials in progress with crops such as maize that contain both the class II EPSP synthase gene and the glyphosate oxidoreductase gene isolated from *Achromobacter* sp. strain LBAA. This enzyme catalyses the cleavage of the C-N bond in glyphosate to give the non-herbicidal aminomethylphosphonic acid (AMPA). **Efficacy:** The recommended use rate of glyphosate is 0.34–1.12 kg acid equivalent/hectare. At these application rates all weeds infesting transformed crops are well controlled with no adverse effects on the crop. If the application is timed to coincide with small weed size and just prior to crop canopy cover, lower rates give excellent control. **Key reference:** G Kishore *et al.* 1988. EPSP synthase: from biochemistry to genetic engineering of glyphosate tolerance. In *Biotechnology for Crop Protection*, ACS Symp. Series No. 379, P A Hedin, J J Menn and R M Hollingsworth (eds.), 37–48, American Chemical Society, Washington DC, USA.

COMMERCIALISATION: Roundup Ready soybeans were first commercialised in the USA in 1996 and were followed by Roundup Ready canola in Canada, Roundup Ready cotton, Roundup Ready soybeans and Roundup Ready maize in the USA. Trials are in progress with Roundup Ready potatoes in the USA and Roundup Ready sugar beet, maize and oilseed rape for use in Europe. Cotton and maize crops containing the class II EPSP synthase and *Btk* genes have been commercialised in the USA. **Tradenames:** Roundup Ready Soybeans – AgraTech Seeds, AgriPro Seeds, AgVenture, Asgrow Seeds, Callahan Seeds, Campbell Seeds, Chemgro Seeds, Countrymark Cooperative, Croplan Genetics, Dairyland Seed Company, DEKALB Genetics, Deltapine Seed, Farmers Cooperative, Garst Seed, Golden Harvest Seeds, Gutwein Seeds, Hoegemeyer Hybrids, Hoffman Seeds, Interstate Seed, Merschman Seeds, Midwest Seeds, NC+ Hybrids, Novartis Seeds, Patriot Seeds, Sands of Iowa, Scott's Quality Seeds, Stine Seed, Terra Industries and Trisler Seed Farms.
Roundup Ready plus BollGard Cotton – Paymaster.
Roundup Ready Cotton – Paymaster.

Roundup Ready Canola – Monsanto.
Roundup Ready Corn – DEKALB Genetics.

PRODUCT SPECIFICATIONS: Elite varieties of crop containing the strain CP4 Class II EPSP synthase gene driven by CaMV 35S promoter.

COMPATIBILITY: Roundup Ready crops are guaranteed tolerant of glyphosate only as Roundup. Other herbicides that are recognised as being selective in a particular crop can still be used.

MAMMALIAN TOXICITY: There is no evidence that Roundup Ready crops have any unusual characteristics that will render them different from conventional crops. There have been no reports of allergic or other adverse effects from researchers, breeders or users of the products.

ENVIRONMENTAL IMPACT AND NON-TARGET TOXICITY: There is no evidence that the use of Roundup Ready crops will have any deleterious effect on non-target organisms or the environment.

5:180   *CpTI* gene   *Introduces resistance to insects*

NOMENCLATURE: **Approved name:** cowpea trypsin inhibitor gene; *CpTI* gene.
Promoter: cauliflower mosaic virus 35S (CaMV 35S).

SOURCE: The cowpea trypsin inhibitor gene was isolated from the cowpea (*Vigna unguiculata* I. Walp.) following observations that the bruchid beetle (*Callosobruchus maculatus* F.) feeding on stored cowpeas failed to develop normally and often died.

PRODUCTION: The full-length cDNA clone encoding the trypsin inhibitor from cowpea was placed under the control of a CaMV 35S promoter and used in a construct for transfer into plants. The construct used the *Agrobacterium tumefaciens* Ti plasmid with kanamycin-resistance as the selectable marker.

TARGET PESTS: Many insect pests especially Lepidoptera and Coleoptera.

TARGET CROPS: Potatoes, oilseed rape, rice, strawberries and other crops.

BIOLOGICAL ACTIVITY: **Biological activity:** Cowpea trypsin inhibitor is a protease that interferes with the digestion of insects. Trypsin is an important digestive enzyme and its inhibition results in the failure of treated insects to incorporate consumed material into useable materials. **Mode of action:** The gene expressed in plants leads to the production of the trypsin inhibitor throughout the transgene. Insects that feed upon these plants have their gut trypsin inhibited and this leads to a failure to grow and reproduce. Intoxicated insects cease to feed shortly after eating. **Efficacy:** Broad-spectrum insect control has been achieved with various transgenic crops. **Key reference:** V A Hilder, A M R Gatehouse, S E Sherman,

R F Barker and D Boulter. 1987. A novel mechanism for insect resistance engineered into tobacco, *Nature*, **330**, 160–3.

COMMERCIALISATION: The original work was undertaken at the University of Durham with support from the Agricultural Genetics Company (now Pestax). Agreements for the development of *CpTI* have been signed with several companies but no product has been commercialised. **Patents:** EP 272144; US 5218104 and US 4640836.

COMPATIBILITY: Transformed plants can be treated with conventional chemicals and there is evidence that the use of *CpTI* genes as one component of a dual gene insertion stategy gives more than additive insect control.

MAMMALIAN TOXICITY: There are no reports of allergic or other adverse toxicological properties associated with the use of *CpTI* genes by research workers, plant breeders or field workers.

ENVIRONMENTAL IMPACT AND NON-TARGET TOXICITY: Cowpea trypsin inhibitor occurs widely in Nature and it is not expected to have any adverse effects on non-target organisms or on the environment when expressed in transgenic crops.

5:181   *GNA* gene   *Introduces resistance to insects*

NOMENCLATURE: **Approved name:** snowdrop lectin gene; *GNA* gene.
Promoter: cauliflower mosaic virus 35S (CaMV 35S) promoter for overall expression in the plant and maize sucrose synthase 1 (Sh-1) promoter for expression in the phloem and subsequently for sucking insect control.

SOURCE: The snowdrop (*Galanthus nivalis* Linnaeus) lectin gene was originally identified and characterised at the Katholieke Universiteit, Leuven, Belgium. The lectin is found in most parts of the snowdrop but is particularly abundant in the bulb. Lectins had been recognised as possessing insecticidal activity but often this was associated with adverse mammalian toxicity. Collaboration with the Agricultural Genetics Company (now Pestax) has led to the development of transgenic crop plants that contain the gene expressed constitutively or specifically in the phloem.

PRODUCTION: The gene was isolated as cDNA and cloned into *E. coli*. It was then cloned into an *Agrobacterium tumefasciens* plasmid containing the appropriate promoter. Plants were then transformed using classical transformation technology.

TARGET PESTS: Sucking insects such as aphids and whitefly, other phytophagous insects and nematodes.

TARGET CROPS: Potatoes, tobacco, tomatoes, maize, rice, cereals and top fruit.

BIOLOGICAL ACTIVITY: **Biological activity:** Lectins exert their effects in insects and mammals by binding to glycoproteins in the guts of animals that consume them. The advantage

of *GNA* is that it binds specifically to α-1,3-mannose residues and these are not components of the mammalian gut. *GNA* is a tetrameric protein and does not bind to α-linked glucose.
Mode of action: The exact mode of action of *GNA* is not certain but it is likely that the insecticidal effects are associated with the binding of the lectin to mannose residues in the gut epithelial cells leading to a disruption of epithelial cell function and death. **Efficacy:** Bioassays have shown that *GNA* is very active against members of the order Homoptera having an oral LC_{50} against the brown planthopper (*Nilaparvata lugens*) of 6mM.
Key references: 1) A M R Gatehouse, R E Down, K S Powell, N Sauvion, Y Rahbe, C A Newell, A Merryweather, D Boulter and J A Gatehouse. 1996. Effects of GNA expressing transgenic potato plants on peach-potato aphid, *Myzus persicae*, *Entomol. Exp. Appl.*, **79**, 295–307. 2) W J Peumans and E J M Van Damme. 1995. The role of lectins in plant defence, *Histochem. J.*, **27**, 253–71. 3) Y Shi, M B Wang, K S Powell, E Van Damme, V A Hilder, A M R Gatehouse, D Boulter and J A Gatehouse. 1994. Use of the rice sucrose synthase-1 promoter to direct phloem-specific expression of β-glucuronidase and snowdrop lectin genes in transgenic tobacco plants, *J. Exp. Bot.*, **45**, 623–31.

COMMERCIALISATION: Pestax has entered into a number of collaborative agreements with several companies for the development of *GNA* but no product has been commercialised. **Patents:** US 5545820; Australia 668096.

COMPATIBILITY: Transgenic plants expressing the *GNA* gene can be treated with agrochemicals in the usual way. It is unlikely that insecticides will be needed. Transgenic plants containing *GNA* plus another gene coding for an insect-specific toxin may be developed as a method for avoiding the onset of resistance.

MAMMALIAN TOXICITY: *GNA* is a mannose-specific binding lectin and as such is not considered to represent a toxicological hazard to mammals. There are no reports of allergic or other adverse toxic effects from research workers, breeders or field workers.

ENVIRONMENTAL IMPACT AND NON-TARGET TOXICITY: *GNA* occurs in Nature and its expression in transgenic crops is not expected to have any adverse effects on non-target organisms or on the environment.

5. Genes

5:182   IMI-tolerance gene
Introduces tolerance to imidazolinone herbicides

NOMENCLATURE: **Approved name:** imidazolinone-tolerance gene or *IMI* gene. **Promoter:** not relevant as the trait was selected rather than introduced.

SOURCE: In the 1980s, Cyanamid funded Molecular Genetics to select maize cell lines that were tolerant of imidazolinone herbicides using *in vitro* selection techniques. These cell lines were grown on to produce mature maize plants that were shown to possess a modified acetolactate synthase gene coding for an enzyme that was not inhibited by the imidazolinones.

These mature plants were used as one parent in a breeding programme undertaken by Pioneer Hi-Bred International that led to the launch of IMI-corn in the USA in 1995. The same technique has been used to produce other IMI-tolerant crops.

TARGET PESTS: All types of weed.

TARGET CROPS: Maize.

BIOLOGICAL ACTIVITY: **Biology:** The plants are tolerant of the herbicides by virtue of an enzyme that is not inhibited by the herbicides. **Mode of action:** The selected plants contain an acetolactate synthase enzyme that is not inhibited by the imidazolinone herbicides and as such they can tolerate over-the-top applications of these herbicides. Cyanamid held a major share of the soybean herbicide market with these compounds but none has had selectivity in maize. The introduction of these varieties allowed these herbicides to be used in maize crops. **Efficacy:** Tolerance is so complete that there have been reports of imazethapyr-tolerant maize occurring in conventional soybean crops.

COMMERCIALISATION: Introduced by Pioneer and Garst in 1995 and now commercialised by over 60 seed companies in the USA. Work is now underway to introduce the trait into oilseed rape, wheat, rice, potatoes, cotton and sugar beet. **Tradenames:** IMI-tolerant Corn – AgriPon Seeds, AgVenture Seed, Asgrow Seeds, Beck's Hydrid Seeds, Callahan Seeds, Cargill Hybrid Seeds, Chemgro Seeds, Countrymark Cooperative, Croplan Genetics, DEKALB Genetics, Garst Seed, Golden Harvest Seeds, Growmark, Hoegmeyer Hybrids, Hoffman Seeds, Interstate Seed, Midwest Seed Genetics, Mycogen Seeds, NC+ Hybrids, Pioneer Hi-Bred International, Sands of Iowa, Scott's Quality Seeds, Trisler Seed Farms, Wilson Seeds. IMI-tolerance plus Bt – Asgrow Seeds, Beck's Hybrid Seeds, Garst Seed, Mycogen Seeds, Novartis Seeds.

PRODUCT SPECIFICATIONS: Selected imidazolinone-tolerance trait bred into elite maize varieties.

COMPATIBILITY: Compatible with all imidazolinone herbicides and herbicides generally used to control weeds in maize.

MAMMALIAN TOXICITY: IMI-tolerant varieties have been shown to be substantially identical to related varieties and are not expected to show any adverse toxicological effects. There have been no reports of allergic or other adverse toxicological effects from research workers, breeders or growers.

ENVIRONMENTAL IMPACT AND NON-TARGET TOXICITY: IMI-tolerant varieties are not expected to have any adverse effects on non-target organisms or on the environment.

5:183 papaya ringspot potyvirus coat protein gene

Introduces resistance to papaya ringspot potyvirus

NOMENCLATURE: **Approved name:** papaya ringspot potyvirus coat protein gene; papaya ringspot virus coat protein gene; PRSV coat protein gene. **Promoter:** cauliflower mosaic virus 35S (CaMV 35S).

SOURCE: The coat protein gene was isolated from mild PRSV strain 5–1 that had been shown to protect papaya plants from severe attacks if used as an inoculant for each plant each season.

PRODUCTION: The gene was isolated and used to transform parents of the Sunrise variety. These transformants were used as parents in a breeding programme.

TARGET PESTS: Papaya ringspot potyvirus.

TARGET CROPS: Papaya.

BIOLOGICAL ACTIVITY: **Biological activity:** The papaya ringspot potyvirus causes one of the most serious diseases in limiting the commercial production of papayas world-wide. It is difficult to control and is aphid-vectored. Management practices such as roguing when initial outbreaks occurred kept the disease in check but did not control it. Two mild strains of the virus, HA-5–1 and HA-6–1 were developed by treating crude infected tissue extracts with nitrous acid. Inoculation with these mild strains protected the crop from severe infections and maintained yields but this protection was not shown by the preferred variety Sunrise. The introduction of the coat protein gene from the mild strain HA-5–1 into breeding stock produced varieties that were high-yielding and protected from PRSV. These two transgenic varieties were coded 55–1 and 63–1. **Mode of action:** Transformed crops expressing the coat protein gene show good resistance to attack from this aphid-transmitted virus. **Efficacy:** The transgenic papaya varieties 55–1 and 63–1 have shown good resistance to PRSV from Hawaii but do not show resistance to strains from other regions of the world. **Key references:** 1) P Tennant, C Gonsalves, K Ling, M Fitch, R Manshardt, J L Slighthom and D Gonsalves. 1994. Differential protection against papaya ringspot virus isolates in coat protein gene transgenic papaya and classically cross-protected papaya, *Phytopath.*, **84**, 1359–66. 2) A Strating. 1996. Availability of determination of nonregulated status for papaya lines genetically engineered for virus resistance, *Federal Register*, **61**, 48663–4.

COMMERCIALISATION: The transgenic lines were deregulated for use in Hawaii in 1996 and so became the first transgenic perennial crop to be registered in the USA. The work was undertaken by a collaboration between the University of Hawaii and Cornell University and the transgenic varieties have been named SunUp. **Tradenames:** SunUp 55–1 and SunUp 63–1 – University of Hawaii, Rainbow – University of Hawaii.

COMPATIBILITY: The transgenic papayas are compatible with all compounds registered for use in the papaya crop.

5. Genes

MAMMALIAN TOXICITY: The transgenic crops are substantially similar to crops of non-genetically engineered varieties and as such are not considered to pose any greater risk to mammals. Considered to be non-toxic.

ENVIRONMENTAL IMPACT AND NON-TARGET TOXICITY: The transgenic crops do not exhibit pathogenic properties, should not lead to the emergence of new plant viruses, are not more likely to become weeds than other papaya varieties, should not harm threatened or endangered species and should not cause damage to processed agricultural commodities.

5:184 phosphinothricin acetyl transferase gene

Introduces tolerance to glufosinate-ammonium

NOMENCLATURE: **Approved name:** phosphinothricin acetyl transferase (*pat*) gene. Also known as bilanafos acetyl reductase (*bar*) gene and Liberty Link gene. **Promoter:** cauliflower mosaic virus (CaMV) 35S.

SOURCE: The bilanafos acetyl reductase (*bar*) gene was isolated by De Block *et al.* in 1987 and was shown to be identical to the phosphinothricin acetyl transferase (*pat*) isolated from the source organism of bilanafos, *Streptomyces viridochromogenes* in 1988 by Strauch *et al.* The gene is now synthesised rather than derived from the host bacterium but is identical in its action. The promoter was isolated from the cauliflower mosaic virus and has been found to be very effective at enhancing transcription levels of foreign genes in plants.

TARGET PESTS: A wide variety of weeds.

TARGET CROPS: This gene codes for an enzyme that catalyses a highly specific acetylation of the herbicide glufosinate yielding the herbicidally inactive metabolite N-acetyl-L-glufosinate. The gene has been used to transform a variety of different crops.

BIOLOGICAL ACTIVITY: **Biology:** The transformed crops are tolerant of applied glufosinate herbicide because they are able to acetylate it very rapidly into a non-phytotoxic metabolite. **Mode of action:** The bacterium that produces the related natural herbicide, bilanafos (or phosphinothricin) (see section 1), produces an enzyme that acetylates the herbicide as a defence mechanism from its effect on the enzyme, glutamine synthetase. This enzyme was isolated from *Streptomyces viridochromogenes* which produces it and was used to transform elite varieties of several crops. These transformed crops are able to acetylate the herbicide when it is sprayed on them and escape its effects. **Efficacy:** The gene expressed in transgenic crops renders the crops tolerant of over-the-top application of the herbicide glufosinate-ammonium, as it is acetylated very rapidly before any deleterious effects on the enzyme glutamine synthetase can occur. **Key references:** 1) M De Block, J Bottermann, M Vandewiele, T Dockx, C Thoen, V Gossele, N R Movva, C Thompson, M Van Montagu and J Leemans.

1987. Engineering herbicide resistance into plants by expression of a detoxifying enzyme, *EMBO Journal*, **6**, 2513–8. 2) E Strauch, W Arnold, R Alijah, W Wohlleben, A Pühler, G Donn, E Uhlmann, F Hein and F Wengenmayer. 1988. *Chemical Abstracts*, **110**, 34815z. 3) E Rasche and M Gadsby. 1997. Glufosinate-ammonium tolerant crops – international developments and experiences, *The 1997 Brighton Crop Protection Conference – Weeds*, **3**, 941–6.

COMMERCIALISATION: Liberty Link canola was the first transgenic crop to be introduced commercially when it was approved by Canadian authorities in 1995. Introductions of glufosinate-tolerant maize in the USA followed in 1997 and soybean and sugar beet crops will be commercialised in the USA shortly. European registrations for transgenic oilseed rape, maize and sugar beet are expected in the next few years.
Tradenames: Liberty Link Canola – Plant Genetic Systems.
Liberty Link Field Corn – AgVenture, Asgrow Seeds, Callahan Seeds, Campbell Seeds, Cargill Hybrid Seeds, Chemgro Seeds, Croplan Genetics, DEKALB Genetics, Garst Seeds, Golden Harvest Seeds, Gutwein Seeds, Hoegemeyer Hybrids, Hoffman Seeds, Interstate Seeds, Merschman Seeds, Midwest Seed Genetics, NC+ Hybrids, Pioneer Hi-Bred International, Rupp Seeds, Sands of Iowa, Stine Seed and Wilson Seeds. Liberty Link Field Corn plus *Bt* (Lightning) – Garst Seeds. **Patents:** EP 275957.

COMPATIBILITY: Liberty Link varieties of crops are tolerant of over-the-top applications of glufosinate-ammonium, sold by AgrEvo as Liberty.

MAMMALIAN TOXICITY: There is no evidence that Liberty Link crops have any unusual characteristics that will render them different from conventional crops. There have been no reports of allergic or other adverse effects from researchers, breeders or users of the products.

ENVIRONMENTAL IMPACT AND NON-TARGET TOXICITY: There is no evidence that the use of Liberty Link crops will have any deleterious effect on non-target organisms or the environment.

5:185 potato leafroll virus coat protein gene

Introduces resistance to potato leafroll virus luteovirus

NOMENCLATURE: **Approved name:** potato leafroll virus luteovirus coat protein gene; PLRV coat protein gene. **Promoter:** cauliflower mosaic virus 35S (CaMV 35S).

SOURCE: The coat protein gene was isolated from the potato leafroll virus luteovirus and multiplied in *E. coli*. It was then used to transform potato crops using conventional techniques. The promoter was isolated from the cauliflower mosaic virus and has been found to be very effective at enhancing transcription levels of foreign genes in plants.

PRODUCTION: The transformed potato plants were used as parents in classical breeding programmes.

TARGET PESTS: Potato leafroll virus luteovirus.

TARGET CROPS: Potatoes.

BIOLOGICAL ACTIVITY: **Biological activity:** It has been demonstrated that the presence of the coat protein from viruses reduces or eliminates the symptoms of the virus.
Mode of action: Host resistance genes against potato leafroll luteovirus are polygenic and this makes conventional breeding for resistance difficult. Transformed crops expressing the coat protein gene, however, show good resistance to attack from this aphid-transmitted virus.
Efficacy: Good resistance has been shown to potato leafroll luteovirus. Sold in crops also expressing the endotoxin gene of *Btt* for protection against Colorado potato beetle (*Leptinotarsa decemlineata* (Say)). **Key reference:** G G Presting, O P Smith and C R Brown. 1995. Resistance to potato leafroll virus in potato plants transformed with the coat protein gene or with vector control constructs, *Phytopath.*, 85, 436–42.

COMMERCIALISATION: Sold as a component of potatoes transformed to show resistance to Colorado potato beetle and PLRV. **Tradenames:** NewLeaf Plus – NatureMark.

APPLICATION: NewLeaf Plus potatoes show resistance to PLRV and to Colorado potato beetle (*Leptinotarsa decemlineata*). For this reason less insecticide is used to control aphids and leaf-feeding beetles.

COMPATIBILITY: Compatible with all compounds registered for use in potatoes.

MAMMALIAN TOXICITY: NewLeaf Plus potatoes are considered to be substantially identical to conventionally-bred potatoes and, as such, are not considered to be hazardous to mammals. There are no records of allergic or other adverse toxicological effects from researchers, breeders or growers of the transgenic varieties. Considered to be non-toxic.

ENVIRONMENTAL IMPACT AND NON-TARGET TOXICITY: As the transgenic crop is considered not to be substantially different from conventionally-grown crops, it is not considered that it will have any adverse effects on non-target organisms or on the environment.

5:186 potato virus Y coat protein gene

Introduces resistance to potato virus Y potyvirus

NOMENCLATURE: **Approved name:** potato virus Y potyvirus coat protein gene; PVY coat protein gene. **Promoter:** cauliflower mosaic virus 35S (CaMV 35S).

SOURCE: The coat protein gene from potato virus Y potyvirus was isolated from potato virus Y potyvirus and was multiplied in *E. coli*. It is driven by the promoter isolated from cauliflower mosaic virus.

PRODUCTION: The gene is transferred into a breeding line of potatoes and this is used as a parent in the development of virus-resistant strains of potato.

TARGET PESTS: Potato virus Y potyvirus.

TARGET CROPS: Potatoes.

BIOLOGICAL ACTIVITY: **Biological activity:** It has been demonstrated that the presence of the coat protein from viruses reduces or eliminates the symptoms of the virus.
Mode of action: Two of the most important viruses of potatoes are potato virus Y potyvirus (PVY), aphid-transmitted and potato virus X potexvirus (PVX), mechanically-transmitted. Mixed populations of these viruses occur frequently in cultivated potato crops and together they produce a synergistic increase in disease severity. The control of PVY, therefore, is effective in reducing the damage that results from the single virus and the combination.
Efficacy: It has been shown that crops transformed with the coat protein gene of PVY are protected from many strains of the virus and suffer reduced symptoms when exposed to PVY and PVX. **Key reference:** R N Beachy, S Loesch-Fries and N E Turner. 1990. Coat protein-mediated resistance against virus infection, *Ann. Rev. Phytopath.*, **28**, 451–74.

COMMERCIALISATION: Transgenic potatoes expressing the PVY coat protein gene and the endotoxin gene from *Btt*, have been commercialised. **Tradenames:** NewLeaf Y – NatureMark.

APPLICATION: NewLeaf Y potatoes show resistance to PVY and to Colorado potato beetle (*Leptinotarsa decemlineata* (Say)). For this reason less insecticide is used to control aphids and leaf-feeding beetles.

COMPATIBILITY: Compatible with all crop protection agents that are registered for use on potatoes.

MAMMALIAN TOXICITY: NewLeaf Y potatoes are considered to be substantially identical to conventionally-bred potatoes and, as such, are not considered to be hazardous to mammals. There are no records of allergic or other adverse toxicological effects from researchers, breeders or growers of the transgenic varieties. Considered to be non-toxic.

ENVIRONMENTAL IMPACT AND NON-TARGET TOXICITY: As the transgenic crop is considered not to be substantially different from conventionally-grown crops, it is not considered that it will have any adverse effects on non-target organisms or on the environment.

5. Genes

5:187 sethoxydim-tolerance gene

Introduces tolerance to sethoxydim

NOMENCLATURE: **Approved name:** sethoxydim-tolerance gene; SR-tolerance; **Promoter:** not relevant – selected trait not transgenic.

SOURCE: A collaborative programme between BASF and DEKALB Genetics was established to identify maize plants that showed resistance to post-emergence applications of sethoxydim. The collaboration identified several plants that were used in conventional breeding programmes to produce "SR" hybrids that combined tolerance to sethoxydim with the quality traits of elite maize varieties.

PRODUCTION: Maize plants showing the tolerance were used in classical breeding programmes.

TARGET PESTS: Grass weeds.

TARGET CROPS: Maize.

BIOLOGICAL ACTIVITY: **Biological activity:** The cyclohexanedione herbicides show herbicidal effects against all grasses and this includes graminaceous crops such as maize. The selected maize tolerant of sethoxydim can be treated with over-the-top applications of the herbicide without damage. **Mode of action:** The basis of the tolerance is not certain but it may be associated with a change in the structure of the ACCase enzyme, the target of this herbicide.

COMMERCIALISATION: BASF has been working with DEKALB Genetics with a view to launching sethoxydim-tolerant maize into the US market. A number of seed companies are selling hybrids in the USA. **Tradenames:** Poast Protected Corn – Asgrow Seed, Cargill Hybrid Seeds, Countrymark Cooperative, Croplan Genetics, DEKALB Genetics and Growmark.

COMPATIBILITY: The sethoxydim-tolerant maize hybrids can be sprayed with full field rates of sethoxydim as Poast and are compatible with normal treatments used on maize.

MAMMALIAN TOXICITY: Sethoxydim-tolerant maize is considered to be substantially identical to conventional varieties and is not considered to pose any mammalian risks. There have been no reports of allergic or other adverse toxicological effects from research workers, breeders or field staff.

ENVIRONMENTAL IMPACT AND NON-TARGET TOXICITY: The breeding lines for these hybrids were selected from conventionally-bred maize and are not considered to show any adverse effects on non-target organisms or on the environment.

5:188   squash virus coat protein genes

Introduces resistance to viruses

NOMENCLATURE: **Approved name:** squash virus coat protein genes; cucumber mosaic virus cucumovirus plus zucchini yellows mosaic potyvirus plus water melon mosaic virus 2 potyvirus coat proteins; CMV plus ZYMV plus WMV2 coat protein genes.
Promoter: cauliflower mosaic virus 35S (CaMV 35S).

SOURCE: The coat protein genes were isolated from the three viruses that are important in the culture of cucurbits and were replicated in *E. coli*. These genes were then used to transform squash plants. The promoter was isolated from the cucumber mosaic virus and has been found to be very effective at enhancing transcription levels of foreign genes in plants.

PRODUCTION: The transformants were used as parents in classical squash breeding programmes.

TARGET PESTS: Cucumber mosaic virus cucumovirus (CMV), zucchini yellows mosaic potyvirus (ZYMV) and water melon mosaic virus 2 potyvirus (WMV2).

TARGET CROPS: Squash.

BIOLOGICAL ACTIVITY: **Biological activity:** It has been demonstrated that the presence of the coat protein from viruses reduces or eliminates the symptoms of the virus.
Mode of action: The search for a virus-resistant transformant examined the incorporation of genes coding for the coat proteins of CMV, ZYMV and/or WMV2. One of the resulting squash lines was coded ZW-20 and it showed good resistance to mixed infections of ZYMV and WMV2. a transgenic squash hybrid was developed from ZW-20 and this became the first virus-resistant genetically engineered crop to be deregulated by USDA-ARS. **Efficacy:** The transgenic varieties have been shown to be resistant to attack from the three major cucurbit viruses and also produced excellent quality fruit. **Key references:** 1) J P Arce-Ochoa, F Dainello, L M Pike and D Drews. 1995. Field performance comparison of two transgenic summer squash hybrids to their parental hybrid line, *Hort. Science*, **30**, 492–3. 2) G H Clough and P B Hamm. 1995. Coat protein transgenic resistance to watermelon mosaic and zucchini yellows mosaic virus in squash and canteloupe, *Plant Disease*, **29**, 1107–9.

COMMERCIALISATION: Commercialised by Asgrow Seeds following development work at Cornell University. **Tradenames:** Freedom II Squash – Asgrow Seeds.

COMPATIBILITY: Compatible with all compounds recommended for use in squash.

MAMMALIAN TOXICITY: Freedom II squash is considered to be substantially identical to conventionally-bred squash and, as such, is not considered to be hazardous to mammals. There are no records of allergic or other adverse toxicological effects from researchers, breeders or growers of the transgenic varieties. Considered to be non-toxic.

ENVIRONMENTAL IMPACT AND NON-TARGET TOXICITY: As the transgenic crop is considered not to be substantially different from conventionally-grown crops, it is not considered that they will show any adverse effects on non-target organisms or on the environment.

5. Genes

Glossary

Names include species referred to in the Main Entries and other agriculturally important organisms some of which are not specifically mentioned within a main entry. For each name which is identified in the first column at the Genus level (i.e. names in italics), the third column gives: for fungi, bacteria, insects and vertebrates, the Order then Family; for plants, the Family. The first column also includes some Families and Orders, with a corresponding higher level indicated in the third column. Where-ever possible the authorities for these Latin names are also given.

Latin	English	Order and/or Family
Abutilon theophrasti Medic.	Velvetleaf	Malvaceae
Acari	Mites	
Acaridae	Acarid mites	Acari
Acarina (see Acari)		
Acrididae	Grasshoppers & locusts	Saltatoria
Actinomycetales	Filamentous bacteria	
Aculops spp.	Mites	Acari: Eriophyidae
Aculus schlechtendali (Nalepa)	Rust mite, apple	Acari: Eriophyidae
Aculus spp.	Rust mites	Acari: Eriophyidae
Acyrthosiphon pisum (Harris)	Pea aphid	Homoptera: Aphididae
Adoxophyes spp.	Tortrix moths and leaf rollers	Lepidoptera: Tortricidae
Adoxophyes orana Fischer von Roeslerstamm	Summer fruit tortrix moth	Lepidoptera: Tortricidae
Aedes aegypti (Linnaeus)	Yellow fever mosquito	Diptera: Culicidae
Aeschynomene spp.	Joint vetches	Leguminosae
Aeschynomene virginica L.	Northern joint vetch	Leguminosae
Agaricales	Mushrooms, etc.	
Agriotes spp.	Wireworms	Coleoptera: Elateridae
Agromyza spp.	Leaf miners	Diptera: Agromyzidae
Agrobacterium radiobacter (Beijerink and van Delden)	Beneficial bacterium	Eubacteriales: Rhizobiaceae
Agrobacterium tumefasciens Conn.	Crown gall	Eubacteriales: Rhizobiaceae
Agropyron repens Beauv. (see *Elymus repens*)		
Agrostis gigantea Roth	Black bent	Gramineae
Agrostis stolonifera L.	Creeping bent	Gramineae
Agrotis spp.	Cutworms	Lepidoptera: Noctuidae
Agrotis segetum (Schiffermüller)	Turnip moth	Lepidoptera: Noctuidae
Alabama argillacea (Hübner)	Cotton leaf worm	Lepidoptera: Noctuidae
Albugo candida Kuntze	White blister	Oomycetes: Peronosporales
Aleurothrixus floccosus (Mask.)	Whitefly	Homoptera: Aleyrodidae

Latin	English	Family and/or Order
Aleyrodidae	Whiteflies	Homoptera
Alopecurus myosuroides Huds.	Black-grass	Gramineae
Alphitobius spp.	Mealworms	Coleoptera: Tenebrionidae
Alternaria spp.	Leaf spots, various	Deuteromycetes: Moniliales
Alternaria alternata	Leaf spot	Deuteromycetes: Moniliales
Alternaria brassicae Sacc.	Dark leaf spot, brassicas	Deuteromycetes: Moniliales
Alternaria brassicicola Wiltsh.	Dark leaf spot, brassicas	Deuteromycetes: Moniliales
Alternaria dauci Groves and Skolko	Carrot leaf blight	Deuteromycetes: Moniliales
Amaranthus spp.	Amaranths	Amaranthaceae
Amaranthus retroflexus L.	Redroot pigweed; common amaranth	Amaranthaceae
Amblyseius barkeri (Hughes)	Predatory mite	Mesostigmata: Phytoseiidae
Amblyseius californicus (McGregor)	Predatory mite	Mesostigmata: Phytoseiidae
Amblyseius cucumeris (Oudemans)	Predatory mite	Mesostigmata: Phytoseiidae
Amblyseius degenerans (Berlese)	Fruit tree red spider mite predator	Mesostigmata: Phytoseiidae
Amblyseius fallacis (Garman)	Spider mite predator	Mesostigmata: Phytoseiidae
Ambrosia artemisifolia L.	Ragweed, common	Compositae
Ampelomyces quisqualis	Hyperparasite of fungi	Deuteromycetes: Sphaeropsidales
Anagrapha falcifera (Kirby)	Celery looper	Lepidoptera: Noctuidae
Anagrus atomus (Linnaeus)	Leafhopper egg parasitoid	Hymenoptera: Mymaridae
Anarsia lineatella Zeller	Peach tree borer	Lepidoptera: Gelechiidae
Anthomyiidae, *Delia* spp. (=some *Hylemya* spp.) and others	Root flies or maggots	Diptera: Anthomyiidae
Anthonomus grandis Boheman	Cotton boll weevil	Coleoptera: Curculionidae
Anticarsia gemmatalis Hübner	Soybean looper, velvet bean caterpillar	Lepidoptera: Noctuidae
Aonidiella aurantii (Maskell)	Californian red scale	Homoptera: Diaspididae
Aonidiella orientalis (Newstead)	Oriental red scale	Homoptera: Diaspididae
Apera spica-venti Beauv.	Loose silky-bent	Gramineae
Aphanomyces spp.	Foot rot, root rot, various hosts	Oomycetes Saprolegniales
Aphanomyces cochlioides Drechs.	Blackleg, beet	Oomycetes Saprolegniales
Aphelinus spp.	Aphid parasitoid wasps	Hymenoptera Aphelinidae
Aphididae	Aphids	Homoptera
Aphidius spp.	Aphid parasitoid wasps	Hymenoptera: Aphelinidae
Aphidoletes aphidimyza Rondani	Aphid gall midge	Diptera: Cecidomyiidae
Aphis citricida (Kirkaldy)	Black citrus aphid	Homoptera: Aphididae
Aphis fabae Scopoli	Black bean aphid	Homoptera: Aphididae
Aphis gossypii Glover	Melon and cotton aphid	Homoptera: Aphididae
Aphyllophorales		Basidiomycotina
Aphytis lignanensis Compère	Red scale parasite	Hymenoptera: Aphelinidae
Aphytis melinus DeBach	Golden chalcid	Hymenoptera: Aphelinidae
Archips podanus (Scopoli)	Leaf roller	Lepidoptera: Tortricidae
Armillaria mellea Kumm.	Honey fungus	Basidiomycetes: Agaricales
Arrhenatherum elatius Beauv.	False oat-grass	Gramineae
Arrhenatherum elatius var. *bulbosum* Spenn.	Onion couch	Gramineae
Artemisia vulgaris L.	Mugwort; wormwood	Compositae
Ascochyta spp.	Leaf spots, various hosts	Deuteromycetes: Sphaeropsidales

Latin	English	Family and/or Order
Ascochyta chrysanthemi Stevens (see *Didymella ligulicola*)		
Ascochyta fabae Speg.	Leaf spot, beans	Deuteromycetes: Sphaeropsidales
Ascochyta pinodes Jones	Leaf and pod spot, peas	Deuteromycetes: Sphaeropsidales
Ascochyta pisi Lib.	Leaf and pod spot, peas	Deuteromycetes: Sphaeropsidales
Ascomycotina	Fungi, sexually produced spores in sacs	
Aspergillus spp.	Storage fungi	Deuteromycetes: Moniliales
Aspidiotus nerii (Bouché)	Red scale	Homoptera: Diaspididae
Athous spp.	Garden wireworms	Coleoptera: Elateridae
Atomaria linearis Stephens	Pygmy mangold beetle	Coleoptera: Cryptophagidae
Atriplex patula L.	Common orache	Chenopodiaceae
Aulacorthum solani (Kaltenbach)	Glasshouse potato aphid	Homoptera: Aphididae
Autographa californica (Speyer)	Alfalfa looper	Lepidoptera: Noctuidae
Avena spp.	Oats (wild and cultivated)	Gramineae
Avena barbata Brot.	Bearded oat	Gramineae
Avena fatua L.	Wild oat	Gramineae
Avena sterilis L.	Oat, sterile	Gramineae
Avena sterilis L. ssp. *ludoviciana* (= *A. ludoviciana* Durieu)	Wild oat, winter	Gramineae
Azadirachta indica A. Juss.	Neem tree	Meliaceae
Basidiomycotina	Fungi, spores produced exogenously in basidia	
Bacillus sphaericus Meyer and Neide		Schizomycetes: Eubacteriales
Bacillus subtilis Cohn.	Hay bacillus	Schizomycetes: Eubacteriales
Bacillus thuringiensis Berliner	Bt	Schizomycetes: Eubacteriales
Bactrocera oleae Gml. (= *Dacus oleae*)	Olive fruit fly	Diptera: Tephritidae
Beauvaria bassiana Balsamo	White muscardine	Deuteromycetes: Moniliales
Begonia elatior Hort.	Begonia	Begoniaceae
Belonolaimus longicausatus Rau	Sting nematode	Nematoda
Bemisia spp.	Whiteflies	Homoptera: Aleyrodidae
Bemisia tabaci (Gennadius)	Tobacco whitefly	Homoptera: Aleyrodidae
Betula lutea Michx.	Yellow birch	Betulaceae
Bilderdykia convolvulus Dum. (see *Fallopia convolvulus*)		
Bipolaris stenospila Shoemaker	Brown stripe, sugar cane	Ascomycetes: Sphaeriales
Blissus leucopterus (Say)	Chinch bug	Hemiptera: Lygaeidae
Blumeriella jaapii Arx	Coccomycosis, Cherry leaf spot	Ascomycetes: Helotiales
Botryosphaeria obtusa Shoemaker (= *Physalospora obtusa*)	Leaf spot and black rot, apple	Ascomycetes: Sphaeriales
Botrytis allii Munn	Neck rot, onions	Deuteromycetes: Moniliales
Botrytis cinerea Pers.	Fruit rot, various hosts	Deuteromycetes: Moniliales
Bradysia spp.	Sciarid flies	Diptera: Sciaridae
Brassica napus L.	Rape	Cruciferae
Bremia lactucae Regel	Downy mildew, lettuce	Oomycetes: Peronosporales
Brevipalpus phoenicis (Geijskes)	Red crevice tea mite	Acari: Tenuipalpidae

Reference

Latin	English	Family and/or Order
Bromus sterilis L.	Barren brome	Gramineae
Bryobia praetiosa Koch	Clover bryobia mite	Acari: Tetranychidae
Bryobia ribis Thom.	Gooseberry bryobia mite	Acari: Tetranychidae
Bryophyta	Mosses and liverworts	Bryophyta
Bucculatrix thurberiella Busck	Cotton leaf perforator	Lepidoptera: Lyonetiidae
Butomus umbellatus L.	Rush, flowering	Butomaceae
Caloptilia theivora (Wlsm.)	Tea leaf roller	Lepidoptera: Gracillariidae
Calepitrimerus spp.	Mite	Acari: Eriophyidae
Calystegia sepium R. Br. ssp. *sepium*	Bindweed, large	Convolvulaceae
Camponotus spp.	Carpenter ants	Hymenoptera: Formicidae
Candida spp.	Parasitic yeasts	Endomycetales
Capsella bursa-pastoris Medic.	Shepherd's purse	Cruciferae
Carduus spp.	Thistles	Compositae
Carex spp.	Sedges	Cyperaceae
Carposina niponensis Walsingham	Oriental fruit tree moth	Lepidoptera: Tortricidae
Cassia obtusifolia L.	Sickle pod	Leguminosae (Fabaceae)
Cecidomyiidae	Gall midges and predacious midges	Diptera
Cecidophyopsis ribis (Westwood)	Blackcurrant gall-mite	Acari: Eriophyidae
Centaurea spp.	Knapweeds	Compositae
Ceratitis capitata Linnaeus	Mediterranean fruit fly	Diptera: Tephritidae
Ceratobasidium cereale	Sharp eyespot, cereals	Basidiomycetes: Tulasnellales
Ceratocystis ulmi Moreau	Dutch-elm disease	Ascomycetes: Sphaeriales
Ceratodon purpureus Brid.	Moss	Bryophyta
Ceratophyllum demersum L.	Hornweed, common	Ceratophyllaceae
Cercospora spp.	Leaf spots, various	Deuteromycetes: Moniliales
Cercospora beticola Sacc.	Leaf spot, beet	Deuteromycetes: Moniliales
Cercospora zonata	Cercospora leaf spot, beans	Deuteromycetes: Moniliales
Cercosporella herpotrichoides Fron. (see *Pseudocercosporella herpotrichoides* Deighton)		
Cercosporidium spp. (includes *C. sojinum* = *Cercospora sojina*)	Frog eye, leaf spot, soybean	Deuteromycetes: Moniliales
Ceutorhynchus spp.	Brassica gall and stem weevils	Coleoptera: Curculionidae
Ceutorhynchus assimilis (Paykull)	Cabbage seed weevil	Coleoptera: Curculionidae
Ceutorhynchus pleurostigmata (Marsh.)	Turnip gall weevil	Coleoptera: Curculionidae
Ceutorhynchus quadridens (Panz.)	Cabbage stem weevil	Coleoptera: Curculionidae
Chaetocnema spp.	Flea beetles	Coleoptera: Chrysomelidae
Chaetocnema concinna (Marsh.)	Mangold flea beetle	Coleoptera: Chrysomelidae
Chamomilla spp.	Mayweeds (some)	Compositae
Chenopodium album L.	Fat hen	Chenopodiaceae
Chilo spp.	Stem borers	Lepidoptera: Pyralidae
Chilo plejadellus Zk.	Rice stem-borer	Lepidoptera: Pyralidae
Chilo suppressalis (Walker)	Rice stalk borer, rice stem borer	Lepidoptera: Pyralidae
Chondrostereum purpureum Pouzar	Silver leaf	Agaricales: Agaricaceae
Chorioptes spp.	Mange mites	Acari: Psoroptidae

Latin	English	Family and/or Order
Chromatomyia syngenesiae (see *Phytomyza syngenesiae*)		
Chromolaena odorata King and Rob.	Siam weed	Compositae
Chrysanthemum segetum L.	Corn marigold	Compositae
Chrysomelidae	Chrysomelid beetles	Coleoptera
Chrysopa carnea Stephens (see *Chrysoperla carnea*)		
Chrysoperla carnea (Stephens)	Pearly green lacewing	Neuroptera: Chrysopidae
Chrysoteuchia caliginosellus (= *Crambus caliginosellus*)	Grass moth	Lepidoptera: Pyralidae
Cicadellidae	Leafhoppers	Homoptera
Cirsium arvense Scop.	Thistle, creeping	Compositae
Cladosporium spp.	Black mould; sooty mould	Deuteromycetes: Moniliales
Cladosporium carpophilum Lev. (see *Stigmina carpophila*)		
Cladosporium fulvum Cke. (see *Fulvia fulva*)		
Clasterosporium carpophilum Aderh. (see *Stigmina carpophila*)		
Clavibacter michiganensis	Tomato canker	Eubacteriales
Cnaphalocrocis medinalis Gn.	Rice leaf roller	Lepidoptera: Pyralidae
Cnemidocoptes spp.	Bird skin mites	Acari: Sarcoptidae
Coccidae	Scale insects	Homoptera
Coccomyces hiemalis Higgins (see *Blumeriella jaapii*)		
Coccus hesperidum Linnaeus	Brown soft scale	Homoptera: Coccidae
Coccus spp.	Scale insects	Homoptera: Coccidae
Cochliobolus miyabeanus Drechs.	Brown spot, rice	Ascomycetes: Sphaeriales
Cochliobolus sativus Drechs.	Foot rot, root rot, cereals, grasses	Ascomycetes: Sphaeriales
Coleoptera	Beetles	Insecta
Colletotrichum spp.	Anthracnose, various root rot and leaf curl diseases	Ascomycetes: Melanconiales
Colletotrichum atramentarium Taub. (see *C. coccodes*)		
Colletotrichum coccodes Hughes	Root rot, tomato	Ascomycetes: Melanconiales
Colletotrichum coffeanum Noack (see *Glomerella cingulata*)		
Colletotrichum gloeosporoides Penz. (see *Glomerella cingulata*)		
Colletotrichum lindemuthianum Briosi and Cavara	Anthracnose, french beans	Ascomycetes: Melanconiales
Commelina spp.	Dayflower; Wandering Jew	Commelinaceae
Comstockaspis perniciosus Comstock (see *Quadraspidiotus perniciosus*)		
Convolvulus arvensis L.	Field bindweed	Convolvulaceae
Coptotermes formosanus Shiraki	Formosan termite	Isoptera: Rhinotermitidae
Coptotermes spp.	Termites	Isoptera: Rhinotermitidae
Corticium cerealis (see *Ceratobasidium cereale*)		

Reference

Latin	English	Family and/or Order
Corticium fuciforme Wakef. (see *Laetisaria fuciformis*)		
Corticium sasakii Matsu. (see *Pellicularia sasakii*)		
Corynebacterium michiganense Jens. (see *Clavibacter michiganensis*)		
Corynespora melonis Lindau	Leaf spot, melon	Deuteromycetes: Moniliales
Cosmopolites sordidus (Germ.)	Banana root borer; banana weevil	Coleoptera: Curculionidae
Costelytra zealandrica (White)	New Zealand grass grub	Coleoptera: Scarabaeidae
Cotesia spp.	Lepidopteran parasitic wasp	Hymenoptera: Aphidiidae
Crambus caliginosellus	Grass moth	Lepidoptera: Pyralidae
Cricetus spp.	Crickets	Saltatoria: Gryllidae
Cronartium ribicola Fisch.	Blackcurrant rust	Basidiomycetes: Uredinales
Cryptolaemus montrouzieri Mulsant	Mealybug predator	Coleoptera: Coccinelidae
Cryptolestes spp.	Grain beetles	Coleoptera: Cucujidae
Cryptophlebia ombrodelta (Lower)	Macadamia nut borer	Lepidoptera: Tortricidae
Crytophlebia illepida (Butler)	Koa seed worm	Lepidoptera: Tortricidae
Cucujidae	Flour beetles	Coleoptera
Culex spp.	Mosquitoes	Diptera: Culicidae
Culex fatigans (= *C. quinquefasciatus*)	House mosquito	Diptera: Culicidae
Culex quinquefasciatus (see *C. fatigans*)		
Culicidae	Mosquitoes	Diptera
Curculionidae	Weevils	Coleoptera
Curvularia spp.	Leaf spot	Moniliales: Dematiaceae
Cydia caryana Fitch	Hickory shuckworm	Lepidoptera: Tortricidae
Cydia molesta (see *Grapholitha molesta*)		
Cydia nigicana Fabricius	Pea moth	Lepidoptera: Tortricidae
Cydia pomonella Linnaeus	Codling moth	Lepidoptera: Tortricidae
Cynodon spp.	Bermuda grass, star grasses	Gramineae
Cynodon dactylon Pers.	Bermuda grass	Gramineae
Cyperus spp.	Nutsedges	Cyperaceae
Cyperus brevifolius Hassk.	Kyllinga, green	Cyperaceae
Cyperus difformis L.	Umbrella plant	Cyperaceae
Cyperus esculentus L.	Yellow nutsedge	Cyperaceae
Cyperus rotundus L.	Nutgrass	Cyperaceae
Cyperus serotinus	Late flowering cyperus	Cyperaceae
Dacnusa sibirica Telenga	Chrysanthemum leaf miner parasitoid	Hymenoptera: Braconidae
Dacus spp.	Fruit flies	Diptera: Tephritidae
Dacus cucurbitae Coquillet	Melon fly	Diptera: Tephritidae
Dacus oleae (Gmelin.) (see *Bactrocera oleae*)		
Datura stramonium L.	Jimson weed, thorn apple	Solanaceae
Decoceras spp.	e.g. field slug	Mollusca: Gastropoda

Latin	English	Family and/or Order
Delia spp. (=some *Hylemya* spp.)	Root flies	Diptera: Anthomyiidae
Delia brassicae (see *D. radicum*)		
Delia coarctata (Fallen)	Wheat bulb fly	Diptera: Anthomyiidae
Delia radicum (Linnaeus)	Cabbage root fly	Diptera: Anthomyiidae
Delphasus pusillus Leconte	Whitefly predatory beetle	Coleoptera: Coccinellidae
Dendroctonus frontalis Zimmerman	Southern pine beetle	Coleoptera: Scolytidae
Dendroctonus ponderosae Hopkins	Mountain pine beetle	Coleoptera: Scolytidae
Dendroctonus pseudotsuga Hopkins	Douglas fir beetle	Coleoptera: Scolytidae
Dendroctonus rufipennis (Kirby)	Spruce beetle	Coleoptera: Scolytidae
Deuteromycetes (= Fungi Imperfecti; mitosporitic fungi)	Fungi with no known sexual stage, or asexual stages of other fungi	
Diabrotica spp.	Corn rootworms	Coleoptera: Chrysomelidae
Diabrotica undecimpunctata Barber	Corn rootworm	Coleoptera: Chrysomelidae
Diaporthales		Ascomycetes
Diaprepes abbreviatus (Linnaeus)	Sugar cane rootstalk borer	
Diaporthe spp.	Includes stem canker fungi, various hosts	Ascomycetes: Sphaeriales
Diaporthe citri Wolf	Melanosis, citrus	Ascomycetes: Sphaeriales
Diaporthe helianthi	Leaf spot and stem canker, sunflowers	Ascomycetes: Sphaeriales
Diaspidae (and others)	Scale insects	Homoptera
Diatraea saccharalis (Fabricius)	Maize stalk borer; sugar cane borer	Lepidoptera: Pyralidae
Didesmococcus brevipes	Scale insect	Homoptera: Coccidae
Didymella applanata Sacc.	Spur blight, cane fruit	Ascomycetes: Sphaeriales
Didymella chrysanthemi (see *Didymella ligulicola*)		
Didymella ligulicola Arx	Ray blight, chrysanthemum	Ascomycetes: Sphaeriales
Digitaria spp.	Crabgrasses	Gramineae
Digitaria adscendens Henr. (= *D. ciliaris*)	Crabgrass, tropical	Gramineae
Digitaria ciliaris Koeler (see *Digitaria adscendens*)		
Digitaria sanguinalis Scop.	Crabgrass	Gramineae
Diplocarpon earliana Wolf	Leaf scorch, strawberry	Ascomycetes: Helotiales
Diplocarpon rosae Wolf	Blackspot, roses	Ascomycetes: Helotiales
Diplodia spp.	Stalk rots, various hosts	Deuteromycetes: Sphaeropsidales
Diplodia pseudodiplodia Fckl. (perfect stage of *Nectria galligena*)	Apple and pear canker	Deuteromycetes: Sphaeropsidales
Diplopoda	Millepedes	Myriapoda
Diprion spp.	Sawflies	Hymenoptera: Diprionidae
Diptera	Flies	Insecta
Distantiella theobroma (Dist.)	Cocoa capsid	Heteroptera: Miridae
Ditylenchus dipsaci (Kuehn)	Stem nematode	Nematoda: Tylenchidae
Dothidiales		Ascomycetes
Drechslera graminea (see *Pyrenophora graminea*)		

Latin	English	Family and/or Order
Drepanopeziza ribis Hoehn. (see *Pseudopeziza ribis*)		
Drosophila spp.	Fruit flies	Diptera: Drosophilidae
Drosophilidae	Fruit flies	Diptera
Dryocoetes confusus Swaine	Western balsam bark beetle	Coleoptera: Scolytidae
Earias spp.	Spiny bollworms	Lepidoptera: Noctuidae
Echinochloa colonum Link	Barnyard grass, awnless	Gramineae
Echinochloa crus-galli Beauv.	Barnyard grass	Gramineae
Echinochloa oryzicola (= *E. oryzoides*)	Cockspur, rice	Gramineae
Echinochloa spp.	Barnyard grasses	Gramineae
Eichhornia crassipes Solms	Water hyacinth	Pontederiaceae
Elateridae	Click beetles; wireworms	Coleoptera
Eleocharis acicularis Roem. And Schult.	Spike rush	Cyperaceae
Eleusine indica Gaertn.	Goosegrass	Gramineae
Elodea canadensis Michx.	Water weed; Canadian pondweed	Hydrocharitaceae
Elsinoe fawcettii Bitanc. and Jenkins	Scab, citrus	Ascomycetes: Myriangiales
Elymus repens	Common couch; quackgrass	Gramineae
Empoasca spp.	Cotton leafhoppers	Homoptera: Cicadellidae
Empoasca decipiens Poali	Leafhopper	Homoptera: Cicadellidae
Empoasca fabae (Harris)	Green leafhopper	Homoptera: Cicadellidae
Encarsia formosa Gahan	Glasshouse whitefly parasitoid	Hymenoptera: Aphelinidae
Endomycetales	Yeasts	Ascomycetes
Endothia parasitica Anders. and Anders.	Chestnut blight	Sphaeriales: Diaporthaceae
Eotetranychus spp.	Tetranychid mites	Acari: Tetranychidae
Ephestia elutella (Hübner)	Warehouse moth	Lepidoptera: Pyralidae
Epilachna spp.	Bean beetles	Coleoptera: Coccinellidae
Epilachna varivestis (Muls.)	Mexican bean beetle	Coleoptera: Coccinellidae
Epitrimerus pyri Nalepa	Pear rust mite	Acari: Eriophyidae
Epitrix hirtipennis (Marsh)	Tobacco flea beetle	Coleoptera: Chrysomelidae
Eretmocerus sp. nr. *californicus* Howard	Whitefly parasite	Hymenoptera: Aphelinidae
Eriophyes spp.	Mite	Acari: Eriophyidae
Eriophyidae	Eriophyid mites	Acari
Eriosoma lanigerum (Hausmann)	Woolly aphid	Homoptera: Pemphigidae
Erwinia amylovora Winsl.	Fire blight of pome fruit	Eubacteriales: Enterobacteriaceae
Erwinia carotovora Holl.	Bacterial rot, celery; basal stem rot, cucurbits; blackleg, potatoes	Eubacteriales: Enterobacteriaceae
Erysiphaceae		Erysiphales
Erysiphales	Powdery mildews	Ascomycetes
Erysiphe spp.	Powdery mildew, various hosts	Ascomycetes: Erysiphales
Erysiphe betae	Powdery mildew, beet	Ascomycetes: Erysiphales
Erysiphe cichoracearum DC.	Powdery mildew, cucurbits	Ascomycetes: Erysiphales
Erysiphe graminis DC.	Powdery mildew, cereals, grasses	Ascomycetes: Erysiphales
Eubacteriales	Cellular bacteria	

Latin	English	Family and/or Order
Eupatorium odoratum L. (= *Chromolaena odorata*)	Siam weed	Compositae
Euphorbia maculata L.	Spotted spurge	Euphorbiaceae
Eupoecilia ambiguella (Hübner)	Grape berry moth	Lepidoptera: Cochylidae
Eupterycyba jucunda	Potato leafhopper	Homoptera: Cicadellidae
Eutetranychus spp.	Tetranychid mites	Acari: Tetranychidae
Eutetranychus banksi (McGregor)	Texas citrus mite	Acari: Tetranychidae
Euxoa spp.	Cutworms; dart moths	Lepidoptera: Noctuidae
Exobasidium vexans Mass.	Blister blight, tea	Basidiomycetes: Exobasidiales
Fallopia convolvulus Adans.	Black bindweed	Polygonaceae
Feltiella acarisuga (Vallot)	Mite predator	Diptera: Cecidomyiidae
Fimbristylis spp.	Fringe rushes	Cyperaceae
Fomes annosus Cke.	Butt rot, conifers	Basidiomycetes: Agaricales
Formicidae	Ants	Hymenoptera
Frankliniella occidentalis (Pergande)	Western flower thrips	Thysanoptera: Thripidae
Frankliniella intonsa (Trybom)	Flower thrips	Thysanoptera: Thripidae
Fuchsia hybrida Voss	Fuchsia	Onagraceae
Fulvia spp.	Leaf moulds	Deuteromycetes: Hyphales
Fulvia fulva Cif.	Leaf mould, tomato	Deuteromycetes: Hyphales
Fusarium spp.	Rots, ear blights and wilts, various hosts (Imperfect fungi with perfect stages in various genera).	Deuteromycetes: Moniliales
Fusarium coeruleum Sacc.	Dry rot, post- harvest rot	Deuteromycetes: Moniliales
Fusarium culmorum Sacc.	Fusarium foot and root rots, various hosts	Deuteromycetes: Moniliales
Fusarium graminearum Schwabe (see *Gibberella zeae*)		Deuteromycetes: Moniliales
Fusarium moniliforme Sheldon (see *Gibberella fujikuroi* Wr.)		Deuteromycetes: Moniliales
Fusarium nivale Ces. (see *Microdochium nivalis*)		Deuteromycetes: Moniliales
Fusarium oxysporum Schlect.	Fusarium wilt, various hosts	Deuteromycetes: Moniliales
Galendromus occidentalis	Mite predator	Acarina: Phytoseiidae
Galium aparine L.	Cleavers	Rubiaceae
Ganoderma spp.	White rot, timber	Basidiomycetes: Agaricales
Gastropoda	Slugs and snails	Mollusca
Geotrichum candidum Ferr.	Rubbery rot, potatoes	Deuteromycetes: Moniliales
Geranium spp.	Crane's bills	Geraniaceae
Gibberella spp. (=various *Fusarium* spp.)	Scab, cereals; brown foot rot and ear blight and other cereal diseases	Deuteromycetes: Hypocreales
Gibberella fujikuroi Wr.	Banana black heart, cotton boll rot, maize stalk rot	Deuteromycetes: Hypocreales
Gibberella zeae Petch	Scab, cereals	Deuteromycetes: Hypocreales
Globodera spp.	Potato cyst nematodes	Nematoda: Heteroderidae
Gloeodes pomigena Colby	Sooty blotch, apple pear and citrus	Deuteromycetes: Sphaeropsidales

Latin	English	Family and/or Order
Gloeosporium spp.	Gloeosporium rot, apples	Deuteromycetes: Sphaeriales
Gloeosporium fructigenum Berk. (see *Glomerella cingulata*)		
Glomerella cingulata Spauld. and Schrenk	Gloeosporium rot, apples	Deuteromycetes: Sphaeriales
Gnathotricus retusus (LeConte)	Ambrosia beetle	Coleoptera: Scolytidae
Gnachotrichus sulcatus (LeConte)	Ambrosia beetle	Coleoptera: Scolytidae
Grapholitha molesta (Busck)	Oriental fruit moth	Lepidoptera: Tortricidae
Gryllidae	True crickets	Orthoptera: Gryllotalpidae
Gryllotalpa spp.	Mole crickets	Orthoptera: Gryllotalpidae
Gryllotalpa gryllotalpa (Linnaeus)	Mole cricket	Orthoptera: Gryllotalpidae
Guignardia bidwellii Viala and Rivas	Black rot, grapevines	Ascomycetes: Sphaeriales
Gymnosporangium spp.	Leaf scorch, apples; rust, various hosts	Basidiomycetes: Uredinales
Gymnosporangium fuscum DC.	Pear rust	Basidiomycetes: Uredinales
Harmonia axyridis Pallas	Ladybird; ladybug	Coleoptera: Coccinellidae
Hedera helix L.	Ivy	Araliaceae
Helianthus annuus L.	Sunflower	Compositae
Helicotylenchus spp.	Spiral nematodes	Nematoda: Tylenchidae
Helicoverpa armigera (Hübner)	Old World bollworm	Lepidoptera: Noctuidae
Helicoverpa assulta (Guen.)	Oriental tobacco budworm	Lepidoptera: Noctuidae
Helicoverpa zea Boddie	American bollworm	Lepidoptera: Noctuidae
Heliothis armigera (see *Helicoverpa armigera*)		
Heliothis assulta (see *Helicoverpa assulta*)		
Heliothis virescens (Fabricius)	Tobacco budworm	Lepidoptera: Noctuidae
Heliothis zea (see *Helicoverpa zea*)		
Helminthosporium oryzae B.de Haan	Helminthosporium blight, rice	Deuteromycetes: Moniliales
Helminthosporium solani Dur. And Mont.	Silver scurf, potatoes	Deuteromycetes: Moniliales
Helminthosporium turcicum Pass.	Northern leaf blight, maize	Deuteromycetes: Moniliales
Helotiales		Ascomycotina
Hemileia vastatrix Berk. And Br.	Coffee rust	Basidiomycetes: Uredinales
Hemitarsonemus latus (see *Polyphagotarsonemus latus*)		
Heterobasidion annosum Bref. (see *Fomes annosus*)		
Heterodera spp.	Lemon-shaped cyst nematodes	Nematoda: Heteroderidae
Heterodera cruciferae Fran.	Brassica cyst nematode	Nematoda: Heteroderidae
Heterodera goettingiana Liebs.	Pea cyst nematode	Nematoda: Heteroderidae
Heterodera schachtii Schm.	Beet cyst nematode	Nematoda: Heteroderidae
Heteroderidae	Cyst nematodes	Nematoda
Heteropeza pygmaea Winn.	Mushroom cecid	Diptera: Cecidomyiidae
Heteroptera	Bugs	Hemiptera
Hippodamia convergens Guerin	Ladybird; ladybug	Coleoptera: Coccinellidae
Homona spp.	Tortrix moths and leaf rollers	Lepidoptera: Tortricidae

Latin	English	Family and/or Order
Homona magnanima Diakonoff	Tea tortrix	Lepidoptera: Tortricidae
Homoptera	Aphids, hoppers, etc.	Hemiptera
Hoplochelis marginalis (Fairmaire)	White grub	Coleoptera: Scarabaeidae
Hydrilla verticillata Presl.	Elodea, Florida	Hydrocharitaceae
Hylemya spp. (see *Delia* spp.)		
Hymenoptera	Ants; bees; wasps; sawflies	Insecta
Hyphales		Deuteromycotina
Hypoaspis aculeifer (Canestrini)	Fungus gnat predator	Mesostigmata: Laelapidae
Hypoaspis miles (Berlese)	Sciarid fly predator	Mesostigmata: Laelapidae
Hypocreales		Ascomycotina
Ipomoea hederacea Jacq.	Morning glory, ivyleaf	Convolvulaceae
Ipomoea purpurea Roth	Morning glory, tall	Convolvulaceae
Ips sexdentatus (Borner)	Six-spined ips	Coleoptera: Ipidae
Ips typographus (Linnaeus)	Douglas fir beetle	Coleoptera: Ipidae
Ischaemum rugosum Salisb.	Saramatta grass	Gramineae
Juncus maritimus Lam.	Sea-rush	Juncaceae
Jussiaea spp.	Water primroses	Onagraceae
Jussiaea diffusa (see *Ludwigia peploides*)		
Keiferia lycopersicella (Walsingham)	Tomato pinworm	Lepidoptera: Gelechiidae
Kochia scoparia Roth.	Mock cypress	Chenopodiaceae
Lamium purpureum L.	Red dead-nettle	Labiatae
Laodelphax striatella (Fallen)	Small brown planthopper	Homoptera: Delphacidae
Lapsana communis L.	Nipplewort	Compositae
Laspeyresia nigricana (see *Cydia nigricana*)		
Lepidoptera	Butterflies; moths	Insecta
Leptinotarsa decemlineata (Say)	Colorado beetle	Coleoptera: Chrysomelidae
Leptochloa spp.	Sprangletop grasses	Gramineae
Leptochloa chinensis Nees	Sprangletop, red	Gramineae
Leptochloa fascicularis Gray (= *Diplachne fascicularis*)	Sprangletop, bearded	Gramineae
Leptomastix dactylopii Howard	Mealybug parasite	Hymenoptera: Encrytidae
Leptosphaeria nodorum Muell. (= *Septoria nodorum*)	Glume blotch, wheat	Ascomycetes: Sphaeriales
Leucoptera spp.	Leaf-mining moths	Lepidoptera: Lyonetiidae
Leucoptera malifoliella (Costa)	Pear leaf blister moth	Lepidoptera: Lyonetiidae
Leucoptera scitella (see *L. malifoliella*)		
Leveillula spp.	Powdery mildew, (includes *L. taurica* Arn., peppers)	Ascomycetes: Erysiphales
Lindernia procumbens Philcox	Pimpernel, false	Scrophulariaceae

Latin	English	Family and/or Order
Liriomyza spp.	Leaf miners	Diptera: Agromyzidae
Liriomyza bryoniae (Kalt.)	Tomato leaf miner	Diptera: Agromyzidae
Liriomyza huidobrensis (Blan.)	South American leaf miner	Diptera: Agromyzidae
Liriomyza trifolii (Burgess)	American serpentine leaf miner	Diptera: Agromyzidae
Lissorhoptrus oryzophilus Kusch	Rice water weevil	Coleoptera: Curculionidae
Lithocolletis spp. (see *Phyllonorycter* spp.)		
Lobesia botrana (Denis and Schiffermueller)	European grapevine moth	Lepidoptera: Tortricidae
Lolium spp.	Ryegrasses	Gramineae
Lolium multiflorum Lam.	Ryegrass, italian	Gramineae
Lolium perenne L.	Ryegrass, perennial	Gramineae
Lolium rigidum Gaud.	Wimmera ryegrass; annual ryegrass	Gramineae
Longidorus spp.	Needle nematodes	Nematoda
Ludwigia palustris Ell.	Water purslane	Onagraceae
Lycoriella auripila	Mushroom sciarid	Diptera: Sciaridae
Lymantria dispar (Linnaeus)	Gypsy moth	Lepidoptera: Lymantriidae
Lyonetia clerkella (Linnaeus)	Apple leaf miner	Lepidoptera: Lyonetiidae
Macrosiphum euphorbiae (Thomas)	Potato aphid	Homoptera: Aphididae
Macrosiphum rosae (Linnaeus)	Rose aphid	Homoptera: Aphididae
Magnaporthe grisea (see also *Pyricularia oryzae*)	Rice blast (perfect stage)	
Mamestra brassicae (Linnaeus)	Cabbage moth	Lepidoptera: Noctuidae
Marasmius oreades and other species	Fairy rings	Agaricales
Margarodidae	Scale insects	Homoptera
Marsilea spp.	Four-leaved water clover	Marsileaceae
Marssonina spp.	Leaf blotches etc., various hosts	Melanconiales
Marssonina potentillae ssp. *Fragariae* (see *Diplocarpon earliana*)		
Mastigomycotina	Primitive fungi (Phycomycetes) producing motile spores	
Matricaria spp.	Mayweeds (some)	Compositae
Matricaria perforata (= *M. inodora* L.)	Scentless mayweed	Compositae
Megaselia spp.	Scuttle flies	Diptera: Phoridae
Melanconiales		Deuteromycotina
Meligethes spp.	Blossom or pollen beetles	Coleoptera: Nitidulidae
Meligethes aeneus (Fabricius)	Pollen beetle	Coleoptera: Nitidulidae
Meloidogyne spp.	Root-knot nematodes	Nematoda
Meloidogyne incognita (K. and W.)	Southern root-knot nematode	Nematoda
Melolontha spp.	Cockchafers	Coleoptera: Scarabaeidae
Melolontha melolontha (Linnaeus)	Cockchafer	Coleoptera: Scarabaeidae
Metaphycus bartletti Annecke and Mynhardt	Scale insect parasite	Hymenoptera: Encrytidae
Metaphycus helvolus (Compère)	Scale insect parasite	Hymenoptera: Encrytidae
Microdochium nivalis	Snow mould, grasses, cereals	Deuteromycetes: Moniliales

Latin	English	Family and/or Order
Microthyriella rubi Petr. (see *Schizothyrium pomi*)		
Miridae	Capsid bugs	Heteroptera
Mollusca	Slugs and snails	
Monilia spp.	Various rots	Deuteromycetes: Moniliales
Monilia laxa Sacc. (see *Sclerotinia fructigena*)		
Monilia roreri Cif.	Pod rot, cocoa	Deuteromycetes: Moniliales
Monilinia spp. (see *Sclerotinia* spp.)		
Monilinia laxa Honey (see *Sclerotinia fructigena*)		
Monilinia mali	Monilinia leaf blight, apple	Deuteromycetes: Moniliales
Monochoria vaginalis Presl.	Pickerel weed	Pontederiaceae
Monographella nivalis	Rice leaf scald	Ascomycetes: Sphaeriales
Monomorium spp.	Seed-eating ants	Hymenoptera: Formicidae
Monomorium pharaonis (Linnaeus)	Pharaoh's ant	Hymenoptera: Formicidae
Morrenia odorata Lindl.	Strangler vine; milkweed vine	Asclepiadaceae
Mucor spp.	Fruit rot, strawberries	Mucorales
Mucorales		Zygomycotina
Mycogone perniciosa Magn.	White mould, mushrooms	Deuteromycetes: Moniliales
Mycosphaerella spp.	Leaf spot diseases, various hosts	Ascomycetes: Sphaeridales
Mycosphaerella arachidis Deighton	Brown spot, peanut	Ascomycetes: Sphaeridales
Mycosphaerella brassicicola Dud.	Ring-spot, brassicas	Ascomycetes: Sphaeridales
Mycosphaerella fijiensis Deighton	Black leaf streak, banana	Ascomycetes: Sphaeridales
Mycosphaerella fragariae Lindau	White leaf spot, strawberry	Ascomycetes: Sphaeridales
Mycosphaerella graminicola	Septoria leaf spot, wheat	Ascomycetes: Sphaeridales
Mycosphaerella musicola Leach	Banana leaf spot, sigatoka	Ascomycetes: Sphaeridales
Mycosphaerella pinodes Stone (see *Ascochyta pinodes*)		
Mycosphaerella pomi Lindau	Brooks spot, apple	Ascomycetes: Sphaeridales
Myzus nicotianae Blackman	Aphid	Homoptera: Aphididae
Myzus persicae (Sulzer)	Peach-potato aphid	Homoptera: Aphididae
Nectria galligena Bres. (imperfect stage of *Diplodia pseudodiplodia*)	Canker, apple, pear	Hypocreales
Nematoda	Nematodes	
Neodiprion lecontei Fitch	Pine sawfly	Hymenoptera: Diprionidae
Neodiprion sertifer Geoffrey	European pine sawfly	Hymenoptera: Diprionidae
Nephotettix spp.	Green leafhoppers	Homoptera: Cicadellidae
Nephotettix cincticeps (Uhl.)	Green rice leafhopper	Homoptera: Cicadellidae
Nephotettix nigropictus (Stål.)	Tropical green rice leafhopper	Homoptera: Cicadellidae
Nicotiana spp.	Tobacco	Solanaceae
Nicotiana rustica L.	Tobacco	Solanaceae
Nilaparvata spp.	Planthoppers	Homoptera: Delphacidae
Nilaparvata lugens (Stal.)	Rice brown planthopper	Homoptera: Delphacidae

Latin	English	Family and/or Order
Nitrosomonas spp.	N-fixing bacteria	Bacteria
Noctua spp.	Cutworms	Lepidoptera: Noctuidae
Noctua pronuba (Linnaeus)	Yellow underwing moth; cutworm	Lepidoptera: Noctuidae
Noctuidae	Noctuid moths	Lepidoptera
Oidium hevea Steinm.	Powdery mildew	Ascomycetes: Erysiphales
Oomycetes		Mastigomycotina
Oospora lactis Sacc. (see *Geotrichum candidum*)		
Oospora pustulans Owen and Wakef. (see *Polyscytalum pustulans*)		
Opomyza spp.	Grass and cereal flies	Diptera: Opomyzidae
Opomyza florum (Fabricius)	Yellow cereal fly	Diptera: Opomyzidae
Orius spp.	Minute pirate bugs	Hemiptera: Anthocoridae
Oryctes rhinoceros (Linnaeus)	Coconut rhinoceros beetle	Coleoptera: Scarabaeidae
Oscinella frit (Linnaeus)	Frit fly	Diptera: Chloropidae
Ostrinia furnacalis Guenee	Asiatic corn borer	Lepidoptera: Pyralidae
Ostrinia nubilalis (Hübner)	European corn borer	Lepidoptera: Pyralidae
Otiorhynchus sulcatus (Fabricius)	Black vine weevil	Coleoptera: Curculionidae
Oulema melanopus (Linnaeus)	Cereal leaf beetle	Coleoptera: Chrysomelidae
Oulema oryzae (Kuway.)	Rice leaf beetle	Coleoptera: Chrysomelidae
Pachnaeus litus Germar	Citrus weevil	Coleoptera: Curculionidae
Paecilomyces spp.	Saprophytic fungi	Hyphales
Pandemis heparana (Denis and Schiffermueller)	Leaf roller	Lepidoptera: Totricidae
Panicum spp.	Panic grasses	Gramineae
Panicum dichotomiflorum Michx.	Fall panicum; smooth witchgrass	Gramineae
Panicum purpurascens Raddi (see *Brachiaria mutica*)		
Panicum texanum Buckl.	Millet, Texas	Gramineae
Panonychus spp.	Red spider mites	Acari: Tetranychidae
Panonychus citri (McGregor)	Citrus red mite	Acari: Tetranychidae
Panonychus ulmi (Koch)	Fruit tree red spider mite	Acari: Tetranychidae
Papaver spp.	Poppies	Papaveraceae
Parthenothrips dracaenae (Hegeer)	Palm thrips	Thysanoptera: Thripidae
Pectinophora gossypiella (Saunders)	Pink bollworm	Lepidoptera: Gelechiidae
Pegomya betae (see *P. hyoscamni*)		
Pegomya hyoscamni (Panzer)	Beet leaf-miner; mangold fly	Diptera: Anthomyiidae
Pellicularia spp.	Rots, damping off, etc. various hosts	Basidiomycetes: Agaricales
Pellicularia sasakii Ito	Rice sheath blight	Basidiomycetes: Agaricales
Penicillium spp.	Penicillium rots	Deuteromycetes: Moniliales
Penicillium digitatum Sacc.	Green mould, citrus	Deuteromycetes: Moniliales
Penicillium expansum Link	Blue mold; blue rot, apples and pears	Deuteromycetes: Moniliales
Penicillium italicum Wehm.	Blue mould, citrus	Deuteromycetes: Moniliales
Periplaneta americana (Linnaeus)	American cockroach	Dictyoptera: Blattidae

Latin	English	Family and/or Order
Peronosclerospora spp.	Downy mildew, sorghum	Oomycetes: Peronosporales
Peronospora spp.	Downy mildews	Oomycetes: Peronosporales
Peronospora parasitica Fr.	Downy mildew, brassicae	Oomycetes: Peronosporales
Peronospora tabacina Adam (= *Plasmopara tabacina*)	Blue mould, tobacco	Oomycetes: Peronosporales
Peronosporales	Downy mildews, etc.	Oomycetes
Petunia spp.	Petunia	Solanaceae
Phakopsora pachyrhizi Syd.	Rust, soybean	Basidiomycetes: Uredinales
Phalaris paradoxa L.	Canary grass, awned	Gramineae
Phalaris spp.	Canary grasses	Gramineae
Phoma spp.	Root and stem rots, various	Deuteromycotina: Sphaeropsidales
Phoma exigua Desh. var. *foveata*	Gangrene, potatoes	Deuteromycetes: Sphaeropsidales
Phomopsis spp. (see *Diaporthe* spp.)		
Phomopsis citri Fawc. (see *Diaporthe citri*)		
Phomopsis helianthi (see *Diaporthe helianthi*)		
Phomopsis viticola Sacc.	Dead arm, grape vines	Deuteromycetes: Sphaeropsidales
Phoridae	Scuttle flies	Diptera
Phorodon humuli (Schrank)	Damson-hop aphid	Homoptera: Aphididae
Phragmidium mucronatum Schlect.	Rust, roses	Basidiomycetes: Uredinales
Phthorimaea operculella Zeller	Potato moth	Lepidoptera: Gelechiidae
Phycomycetes	Primitive fungi with coenocytic mycelium; includes the Divisions Mastigomycotina and Zygomycotina.	
Phyllactinia spp.	Powdery mildew, various hosts	Erysiphales
Phyllocoptes spp.	Mites	Acari: Eriophyidae
Phyllocoptruta spp.	Rust mites	Acari: Eriophyidae
Phyllocoptruta oleivora (Ashm.)	Citrus rust mite	Acari: Eriophyidae
Phyllonorycter spp.	Leaf mining moths	Lepidoptera: Gracillariidae
Phyllonorycter blancardella (Fabricius)	Apple leaf miner	Lepidoptera: Gracillariidae
Phyllotreta spp.	Flea beetles	Coleoptera: Chrysomelidae
Phyllotreta striolata (Fabricius)	Flea beetle	Coleoptera: Chrysomelidae
Physalospora obtusa Cke. (see *Botryosphaeria obtusa*)		
Phytomyza spp.	Leaf miners	Diptera: Agromyzidae
Phytomyza syngenesiae (Hardy)	Chrysanthemum leaf miner	Diptera: Agromyzidae
Phytophthora spp.	Blight, damping off, foot-rot, various hosts	Oomycetes: Peronosporales
Phytophthora cactorum Schroet.	Collar rot, crown rot, apple	Oomycetes: Peronosporales
Phytophthora capsici Leonian	Blight, capsicums	Oomycetes: Peronosporales
Phytophthora fragariae Hickman	Red core, strawberry	Oomycetes: Peronosporales
Phytophthora infestans De Bary	Late blight, potato, tomato	Oomycetes: Peronosporales
Phytophthora megasperma Drechs.	Root rot, brassicas	Oomycetes: Peronosporales
Phytophthora palmivora (Butl.) Butl.	Rot, various crops	Oomycetes: Peronosporales
Phytoseiulus persimilis Anthios-Henriot	Two-spotted spider mite predator	Mesostigmata: Phytoseiidae
Pieris spp.	Cabbage white butterflies	Lepidoptera: Pieridae

271

Latin	English	Family and/or Order
Pieris brassicae (Linnaeus)	Large white butterfly	Lepidoptera: Pieridae
Pieris rapae (Linnaeus)	Small white butterfly	Lepidoptera: Pieridae
Pistia stratiotes L.	Water duckweed	Araceae
Pityogenes chalcographus (Linnaeus)	Six-toothed spruce bark beetle	Coleoptera: Scolytidae
Planococcus citri (Risso)	Citrus mealybug	Homoptera: Pseudococcidae
Plantago spp.	Plantains	Plantaginaceae
Plasmodiophora brassicae Woron.	Clubroot, brassicas	Phycomycetes: Plasmodiophorales
Plasmodiophoromycetes	Parasitic members of the Myxomycota - a group with affinities with both primitive fungi and primitive animals.	
Plasmopara spp.	Downy mildews, various hosts	Oomycetes: Peronosporales
Plasmopara tabacina (see *Peronospora tabacina*)		
Plasmopara viticola Berl. and de T.	Downy mildew, grapevine	Oomycetes: Peronosporales
Platynota idaeusalis (Walker)	Tufted apple moth	Lepidoptera: Tortricidae
Platynota stultana (Walsingham)	Leaf roller	Lepidoptera: Tortricidae
Platyptilia carduidactyla (Riley)	Artichoke plume moth	Lepidoptera: Pterophoridae
Plusia spp.	e.g. silvery moth	Lepidoptera: Noctuidae
Plutella xylostella (Linnaeus)	Diamond-back moth	Lepidoptera: Yponomeutidae
Poa spp.	Meadow grasses	Gramineae
Poa annua L.	Meadow grass, annual	Gramineae
Poa trivialis L.	Meadow-grass, rough	Gramineae
Podisus maculiventris (Say)	Caterpillar predator	Heteroptera: Pentatomidae
Podosphaera spp.	Powdery mildew, various hosts	Ascomycetes: Erysiphales
Podosphaera leucotricha	Powdery mildew, apple	Ascomycetes: Erysiphales
Polychrosis botrana (see *Lobesia botrana* (Denis and Schiffermueller))		
Polygonum spp.	Knotweeds	Polygonaceae
Polygonum aviculare L.	Knot grass	Polygonaceae
Polygonum convolvulus L. (see *Fallopia convolvulus* Adans.)		
Polygonum cuspidatum Sieb. and Zucc. (see *Reynoutria japonica*)		
Polygonum lapathifolium L.	Pale persicaria	Polygonaceae
Polygonum persicaria L.	Redshank; persicaria; smartweed	Polygonaceae
Polygonum sachalinense (see *Reynoutria sachalinensis*)		
Polymyxa betae	Fungal vector or rhizomania virus	Phycomycetes: Plasmodiophorales
Polyphagotarsonemus latus (Banks)	Broad mite	Acari: Tarsonemidae
Polyscytalum pustulans	Skin spot, potatoes	Deuteromycetes: Hyphales
Polystigmatales		Ascomycetales
Popillia japonica Newman	Japanese beetle	Coleoptera: Scarabaeidae
Populus spp.	Poplars	Salicaceae
Portulaca spp.	Purslanes	Portulacaceae
Portulaca oleracea L.	Purslane	Portulacaceae
Potamogeton spp.	Pondweeds	Potamogetonaceae
Potamogeton distinctus Benn.	Pondweed, American	Potamogetonaceae

Latin	English	Family and/or Order
Pratylenchus spp.	Root-lesion nematodes	Nematoda: Hoplolaimidae
Prays oleae (Bernard)	Olive moth	Lepidoptera: Yponomeutidae
Prunus serotina Ehrh.	American black cherry	Rosaceae
Pseudocercosporella capsellae	White leaf spot, oilseed rape	Deuteromycetes: Hyphales
Pseudocercosporella herpotrichoides Deighton	Eye-spot, cereals	Deuteromycetes: Moniliales
Pseudococcidae	Mealybugs	Homoptera
Pseudococcus spp.	Mealybugs	Homoptera: Pseudococcidae
Pseudomonas spp.	Bacterial blights and leaf spots, various hosts	Pseudomonadales: Pseudomonadaceae
Pseudomonas glumae	Bacterial grain rot, rice	Pseudomonadales: Pseudomonadaceae
Pseudomonas lachrymans Carsner	Angular leaf spot, cucurbits	Pseudomonadales: Pseudomonadaceae
Pseudomonas mors-prunorum Wormold	Bacterial canker, prunus	Pseudomonadales: Pseudomonadaceae
Pseudomonas phaseolicola Dows	Halo blight, beans	Pseudomonadales: Pseaudomonadaceae
Pseudomonas syringae Van Hall pv. *lachrymans* (see *P. lachrymans*)		Pseudomonadales: Pseudomonadaceae
Pseudomonas syringae Van Hall pv. *mors prunorum* (see *P. mors-prunorum*)		Pseudomonadales: Pseudomonadaceae
Pseudomonas tabaci Stevens	Wild fire of tobacco and soybean	Pseudomonadales: Pseudomonadaceae
Pseudoperonospora cubensis Rostow	Downy mildew, cucurbits	Oomycetes: Peronosporaceae
Pseudoperonospora humuli Wils.	Downy mildew, hops	Oomycetes: Peronosporaceae
Pseudopeziza ribis Kleb.	Leaf spot, currants, gooseberry	Ascomycetes: Helotiales
Pseudotsuga menziesii Franco	Douglas fir	Pinaceae
Psila rosae (Fabricius)	Carrot fly	Diptera: Psilidae
Psylla spp.	Psyllids	Homoptera: Psyllidae
Psyllidae	Psyllids	Homoptera
Pteridium aquilinum Kuhn	Bracken	Filicales
Puccinia spp.	Rust, various hosts	Basidiomycetes: Uredinales
Puccinia chrysanthemi Roze	Brown rust, chrysanthemum	Basidiomycetes: Uredinales
Puccinia graminis Pers.	Black stem rust, grasses	Basidiomycetes: Uredinales
Puccinia hordei Otth	Brown rust, barley	Basidiomycetes: Uredinales
Puccinia recondita Rob.	Brown rust, wheat	Basidiomycetes: Uredinales
Puccinia striiformis West	Yellow rust, cereals	Basidiomycetes: Uredinales
Pyralidae	Pyralid moths	Lepidoptera
Pyrenopeziza brassicae	Light leaf spot, brassicas	Ascomycetes: Helotiales
Pyrenophora graminea Ito and Kuribay	Leaf stripe, barley	Ascomycetes: Sphaeriales
Pyrenophora teres Drechs.	Net blotch, barley	Ascomycetes: Sphaeriales
Pyrenophora tritici-vulgaris Dicks	Tan spot, wheat	Ascomycetes: Sphaeriales
Pyricularia oryzae Cavara (see also *Magnaporthe grisea*)	Rice blast (imperfect stage)	Deuteromycetes: Moniliales
Pythium spp.	Root rots, various	Oomycetes: Peronosporales
Quadraspidiotus perniciosus (Comstock)	San José scale	Homoptera: Coccidae

Latin	English	Family and/or Order
Radopholus similis	Burrowing nematode	Nematoda: Tylenchidae
Ramularia spp.	Leaf spots, various	Deuteromycetes: Moniliales
Ramularia beticola Fautr. And Lambotte	Leaf spot, beet	Deuteromycetes: Moniliales
Ranunculus spp.	Buttercups	Ranunculaceae
Raphanus raphanistrum L.	Wild radish; runch	Cruciferae
Reynoutria japonica Houtt. (= *Polygonum cuspidatum* Sieb. and Zucc.)	Japanese knotweed	Polygonaceae
Reynoutria sachalinensis (= *Polygonum sachalinense*)	Giant knotweed	Polygonaceae
Rhinotermitidae	Termites	Isoptera
Rhizoctonia spp.	Foot rot, root rot, various hosts	Deuteromycetes: Agonomycetiales
Rhizoctonia solani Kuehn (= *Thanetophorus cucumeris*)	Damping off; root rots, various	Deuteromycetes: Agonomycetiales
Rhizoglyphus callae, R. robini	Bulb mites	Acari: Acaridae
Rhizoglyphus echinopus (see *R. callae, R. robini*)		
Rhizopertha dominica (Fabricius) (see *Rhyzopertha dominica*)		
Rhizopus spp.	Post-harvest rots	Phycomycetes: Mucorales
Rhododendron ponticum L.	Rhododendron	Ericaceae
Rhyacionia buoliana (Denis and Schiffermueller)	European pine shoot moth	Lepidoptera: Tortricidae
Rhyncophorus palmatum (Linnaeus)	American palm beetle	Coleoptera: Curculionidae
Rhynchosporium spp.	Leaf spots, grasses	Deuteromycetes: Moniliales
Rhynchosporium secalis Davis	Leaf blotch, barley and rye	Deuteromycetes: Moniliales
Rhyzopertha dominica	Lesser grain borer	Coleoptora: Bostrichidae
Rubus spp.	Brambles	Rosaceae
Rumex spp.	Docks and sorrels	Polygonaceae
Sagittaria sagittifolia L.	Arrowhead	Alismataceae
Sahlbergella singularis Hagl.	Cocoa capsid	Heteroptera: Miridae
Saissetia coffeae (Walker)	Hemispherical scale; helmet scale	Homoptera: Coccidae
Saissetia oleae (Bernard)	Mediterranean black scale; black olive scale	Homoptera: Coccidae
Salsola kali L.	Russian thistle	Chenopodiaceae
Saltatoria	Crickets, grasshoppers, etc.	Insecta
Sanninoidea exitiosa (Say.)	Peach tree borer	Lepidoptera: Aegeriidae
Saprolegniales		Oomycetes
Scapteriscus vicinus Scudder	Mole cricket	Orthoptera: Gryllotapidae
Scerophthora spp.	Downy mildew, wheat	Oomycetes: Peronosporales
Scerophthora macrospora	Downy mildew, cereals	Oomycetes: Peronosporales
Sciaridae	Fungus gnats, sciarid flies	Diptera
Sciara spp.	Sciariad flies	Diptera: Sciaridae
Scirpus spp.	Club-rushes	Cyperaceae
Scirpus juncoides	Japanese bullrush	Cyperaceae
Scirpus maritimus L.	Sea club-rush	Cyperaceae
Scirpus mucronatus	Roughseed bullrush	Cyperaceae

Latin	English	Family and/or Order
Schizothyrium pomi Arx	Fly speck disease, apple	Ascomycetes: Hemisphaeriales
Sclerospora spp.	Downy mildews, e.g. on pearl millet	Oomycetes: Peronosporales
Sclerotinia spp.	Sclerotinia rots, various hosts	Ascomycetes: Helotiales
Sclerotinia fructicola Rehm	Brown rot, top fruit	Ascomycetes: Helotiales
Sclerotinia fructigena Anderh. and Ruhl.	Brown rot, apple, pear, plum	Ascomycetes: Helotiales
Sclerotinia homeocarpa Bennett	Dollar spot, turf	Ascomycetes: Helotiales
Sclerotinia laxa Anderh. and Ruhl.	Blossom wilt, apple, plum	Ascomycetes: Helotiales
Sclerotinia sclerotiorum De Bary	Rots of stems, storage organs, etc., various crops	Ascomycetes: Helotiales
Sclerotium spp.	Post-harvest rots, various hosts	Deuteromycetes: Agonomycetales
Sclerotium cepivorum Berk.	White rot, onion	Deuteromycetes: Agonomycetales
Sclerotium rolfsii Sacc.	Rots, various hosts	Deuteromycetes: Agonomycetales
Scolytus multistratus (Marsham)	Smaller European elm bark beetle	Coleoptera: Scolytidae
Septoria spp.	Leaf and glume spots, various hosts	Ascomycetes: Sphaeriales
Septoria nodorum Berk. (see *Leptosphaeria nodorum*)		
Septoria tritici Rob. (see *Mycosphaerella graminicola*)		
Sesamia cretica	Pink corn borer	Lepidoptera Pyralidae
Sesbania exaltata Cory	Hemp sesbania	Leguminosae
Setaria spp.	Foxtail grasses	Gramineae
Setaria faberi Herrm.	Foxtail, giant	Gramineae
Setaria glauca Beauv. (= *S. lutescens* Hurb.)	Foxtail, yellow	Gramineae
Setaria viridis Beav.	Foxtail, green	Gramineae
Sida spinosa L.	Spiny sida; prickly sida	Malvaceae
Simuliidae	Blackflies	Diptera
Simulium spp.	Blackflies	Diptera: Simuliidae
Sinapis alba L.	White mustard	Cruciferae
Sinapis arvensis L.	Charlock	Cruciferae
Sitobium avenae (Fabricius)	Grain aphid	Homoptera: Aphididae
Sitona spp.	Pea and bean weevils	Coleoptera: Curculionidae
Sitophilus oryzae (Linnaeus)	Rice weevil	Coleoptera: Curculionidae
Sitophilus zeamais Mutsch.	Maize weevil; rice weevil	Coleoptera: Curculionidae
Sitotroga cerealella (Oliver)	Angoumois grain moth	Lepidoptera: Gelechiidae
Sogatella furcifera (Howorth)	White-backed planthopper	Homoptera: Delphacidae
Solanum nigrum L.	Black nightshade	Solanaceae
Solenopsis spp.	Fire ants	Hymenoptera: Formicidae
Sonchus oleraceus L.	Smooth sowthistle	Compositae
Sorghum spp.	Sorghum grasses	Gramineae
Sorghum almum Parodi	Columbus grass	Gramineae
Sorghum bicolor Moench	Shattercane	Gramineae
Sorghum halepense Pers.	Johnson grass	Gramineae
Sparganium erectum L.	Branched bur-reed	Sparganiaceae
Spergula arvensis L.	Corn spurrey	Caryophyllaceae
Sphacelotheca reiliana Clint.	Head smut, maize	Basidiomycetes: Ustilaginales
Sphaeriales		Ascomycotina

Latin	English	Family and/or Order
Sphaeropsidales		Deuteromycotina
Sphaerotheca spp.	Powdery mildew, various hosts	Ascomycetes: Erysiphales
Sphaerotheca fuliginea Poll.	Powdery mildew, cucurbits	Ascomycetes: Erysiphales
Sphaerotheca pannosa Lev.	Powdery mildew, rose	Ascomycetes: Erysiphales
Spodoptera spp.	Army worms	Lepidoptera: Noctuidae
Spodoptera exigua (Hübner)	Beet armyworm; lesser armyworm	Lepidoptera: Noctuidae
Spodoptera frugiperda (J. E. Smith)	Fall armyworm	Lepidoptera: Noctuidae
Spodoptera littoralis (Boisch.)	Egyptian cotton leafworm	Lepidoptera: Noctuidae
Stellaria media Vill.	Common chickweed	Caryophyllaceae
Steneotarsonemus laticeps (Halb.)	Bulb scale mite	Acari: Tarsonemidae
Stethorus punctillum	Minute black ladybird	Coleoptera: Coccinellidae
Stigmina carpophila Ell.	Shothole, prunus	Deuteromycetes: Moniliales
Streptomyces scabies Walk.	Common scab of crops such as potato and beet	Schizomycetes: Actinomycetales
Symphyla spp.	Symphilids	Myriapoda
Syngrapha falcifera	Celery looper	Lepidoptera; Noctuidae
Synanthedon hector (Butler)	Cherry tree borer	Lepidoptera: Aegeriidae
Synanthedon myopaeformis (Borkhausen)	Apple clearwing moth	Lepidoptera: Aegeriidae
Synanthedon pictipes (Grote and Robinson)	Lesser peach tree borer	Lepidoptera: Aegeriidae
Synanthedon tipuliformis (Clerck)	Currant clearwing moth	Lepidoptera: Aegeriidae
Tanacetum cinerariaefolium	Pyrethrum daisy	Compositeae
Tanymecus palliatus Fabricius	Beet leaf weevil	Coleoptera: Curculionidae
Taphrina deformans Tul.	Peach leaf-curl	Ascomycetes: Taphrinales
Tarsonemus spp. (= *Phytonemus*, in part)	Tarsonemid mites	Acari: Tarsonemidae
Taxus baccata L.	Yew	Taxaceae
Tephritidae	Large fruit flies	Diptera
Tetanops myopaeformis (Roeder)	Sugar beet root maggot	Diptera: Otitidae
Tetranychidae	Spider mites	Acari
Tetranychus spp.	Spider mites	Acari: Tetranychidae
Tetranychus cinnabarinus (Boisduval)	Carmine spider mite	Acari: Tetranychidae
Tetranychus mcdanieli McG.	McDaniel's spider mite	Acari: Tetranychidae
Tetranychus urticae Koch	Two-spotted spider mite	Acari: Tetranychidae
Thanetophorus cucumeris Donk. (= *Rhizoctonia solani* Kuehn)	Damping-off disease	Basidiomycetes: Stereales
Thaumetopoea pityocampa (Denis and Schiffermueller)	Pine processionary caterpillar	Lepidoptera: Thaumetopoeidae
Thielaviopsis basicola Ferr.	Black root rot, tobacco	Deuteromycetes: Moniliales
Thripidae	Thrips	Thysanoptera
Thrips spp.	Thrips	Thysanoptera: Thripidae
Thrips fuscipennis Haliday	Rose thrips	Thysanoptera: Thripidae
Thrips obscuratus Crawford	New Zealand flower thrips	Thysanoptera: Thripidae
Thrips palmi Karny	Thrips	Thysanoptera: Thripidae
Thrips tabaci Lindeman	Onion thrips	Thysanoptera: Thripidae

Latin	English	Family and/or Order
Thysanoptera	Thrips	Insecta
Tilletia spp.	Smut, various hosts	Basidiomycetes: Ustilaginales
Tilletia caries Tul.	Bunt, stinking smut	Basidiomycetes: Ustilaginales
Tipula spp.	Crane flies; leatherjackets	Diptera: Tipulidae
Tortricidae	Tortrix moths	Lepidoptera
Tortrix spp.	Tortrix moths	Lepidoptera: Tortricidae
Tranzschelia discolor Tranz. and Litw. (see *Tranzchelia pruni-spinosae*)		
Tranzchelia pruni-spinosae Diet.	Plum rust	Basidiomycetes: Uredinales
Trialeurodes vaporariorum (Westwood)	Glasshouse whitefly	Homoptera: Aleyrodidae
Trichodorus spp.	Stubby-root nematodes	Nematoda
Trichogramma spp.	Lepidopteran egg parasites	Hymenoptera: Trichogrammatidae
Trichoplusia ni (Hübner)	Cabbage looper	Lepidoptera: Noctuidae
Tripleurospermum maritimum Koch (= *Matricaria inodora* L.)	Mayweed, scentless	Compositae
Trypodendron lineatum (Olivier)	Ambrosia beetle	Coleoptera: Scolytidae
Tulasnellales		Basidiomycotina
Typha spp.	Bullrushes	Typhaceae
Typhula incarnata Lasch	Snow rot, cereals	Basidiomycetes: Agaricales
Typhlodromus occidentalis Nesbitt (synonymous with *Galendromus occidentalis* and *Metaseiulus occidentalis*)	Predatory mite	Mesostigmata: Phytoseiidae
Typhlodromus pyri Scheuten	Fruit tree red spider mite predator	Mesostigmata: Phytoseiidae
Uncinula necator Burr	Powdery mildew, grapevines	Erysiphales: Erysiphaceae
Uredinales	Rust fungi	Basidiomycetes
Urocystis spp.	Leaf smuts, various hosts	Basidiomycetes: Ustilaginales
Uromyces spp.	Rusts, various crops	Basidiomycetes: Uredinales
Uromyces betae Lev.	Rust, beet crops	Basidiomycetes: Uredinales
Urtica spp.	Nettles	Urticaceae
Urtica dioica L.	Nettle, common	Urticaceae
Urtica urens L.	Nettle, small	Urticaceae
Ustilaginales	Smut fungi	Basidiomycetes
Ustilago spp.	Smut diseases, various hosts	Ustilaginales
Ustilago nuda Rostr.	Loose smut, barley, wheat	Basidiomycetes: Ustilaginales
Valsa ceratosperma	Valsa canker of apple	Ascomycetes: Sphaeriales
Vasates spp.	Mites	Acari: Eriophyidae
Venturia inaequalis Wint.	Scab, apples	Ascomycetes: Sphaeriales
Venturia pirina Aderh.	Scab, pears	Ascomycetes: Sphaeriales
Veronica spp.	Speedwells	Scrophulariaceae
Veronica filiformis Sm.	Speedwell, slender	Scrophulariaceae
Veronica hederifolia L.	Speedwell, ivy-leaved	Scrophulariaceae
Veronica persica Poir.	Speedwell, common field	Scrophulariaceae

Latin	English	Family and/or Order
Verticillium spp.	Verticillium wilt, various hosts	Deuteromycetes: Moniliales
Verticillium fungicola	Dry bubble, mushrooms	Deuteromycetes: Moniliales
Viola spp.	Wild pansies	Violaceae
Viola arvensis Murr.	Field pansy	Violaceae
Xanthium pennsylvanicum Wallr.	Cocklebur	Compositae
Xanthium strumarium L.	Rough Cocklebur	Compositae
Xanthomonas spp.	Bacterial leaf spots, various hosts	Pseudomonadales: Pseudomonadaceae
Xanthomonas campestris Dows. pv. *citri* (see *X. citri*)		Pseudomonadales: Pseudomonadaceae
Xanthomonas campestris Dows. pv. *malvacearum* (see *X. malvacearum*)		Pseudomonadales: Pseudomonadaceae
Xanthomonas campestris Dows. pv. *oryzae* (see *X. oryzae*)		Pseudomonadales: Pseudomonadaceae
Xanthomonas citri Dows.	Citrus canker	Pseudomonadales: Pseudomonadaceae
Xanthomonas malvacearum Dows.	Bacteriosis, cotton	Pseudomonadales: Pseudomonadaceae
Xanthomonas oryzae Dows.	Leaf blight, rice	Pseudomonadales: Pseudomonadaceae
Zygomycotina	Primitive fungi (Phycomycetes) which do not produce motile spores. Sexually produced spores are non-motile zygospores.	
Zygophiala jamaicensis Mason	Greasy blotch, carnation	Deuteromycetes: Moniliales

Glossary

English – Latin

This glossary is intended to help the reader to identify the Latin name in cases where the English name may be unfamiliar. The Latin name is presented as either genus and species or, if the English name is represented by a genus the specific name is excluded. For example, the causal organisms for anthracnose diseases are fungal pathogens from the genus *Colletotrichum* but the peach/potato aphid is *Myzus persicae*.

This glossary has been produced simply by inverting the Latin-English glossary, with limited subsequent editing. The reader should recognise that English-name and Latin-name groups of species are not congruent. For example, all *Peronospora* are downy mildews, but not all downy mildews are *Peronospora*; consequently, there are entries for various downy mildews, giving different Latin names.

In searching for English names, alternative forms of the name should be considered, especially with names containing an adjectival component.

Where these two problems occur together, this glossary needs to be used with particular care.

English	Latin	Order and/or Family
Alfalfa looper	*Autographa californica*	Lepidoptera: Noctuidae
Amaranths	*Amaranthus*	Amaranthaceae
Ambrosia beetle	*Gnathotricus retusus*	Coleoptera: Scolytidae
Ambrosia beetle	*Gnachotrichus sulcatus*	Coleoptera: Scolytidae
Ambrosia beetle	*Trypodendron lineatum*	Coleoptera: Scolytidae
American black cherry	*Prunus serotina*	Rosaceae
American bollworm	*Helicoverpa zea*	Lepidoptera: Noctuidae
American cockroach	*Periplaneta americana*	Dictyoptera: Blattidae
American palm beetle	*Rhyncophorus palmatum*	Coleoptera: Curculionidae
American serpentine leaf miner	*Liriomyza trifolii*	Diptera: Agromyzidae
Angoumois grain moth	*Sitotroga cerealella*	Lepidoptera: Gelechiidae
Angular leaf spot, cucurbits	*Pseudomonas lachrymans*	Pseudomonadales: Pseudomonadaceae
Annual ryegrass	*Lolium rigidum*	Gramineae
Anthracnose, french beans	*Colletotrichum lindemuthianum*	Ascomycetes: Melanconiales
Anthracnose, various root rot and leaf curl diseases	*Colletotrichum*	Ascomycetes: Melanconiales
Aphid	*Myzus nicotianae*	Homoptera: Aphididae
Aphid gall midge	*Aphidoletes aphidimyza*	Diptera: Cecidomyiidae
Aphid parasitoid wasps	*Aphelinus*	Hymenoptera Aphelinidae
Aphid parasitoid wasps	*Aphidius*	Hymenoptera: Aphelinidae
Apple and pear canker	*Diplodia pseudodiplodia*	Deuteromycetes: Sphaeropsidales
Apple clearwing moth	*Synanthedon myopaeformis*	Lepidoptera: Aegeriidae
Apple leaf miner	*Phyllonorycter blancardella*	Lepidoptera: Gracillariidae

English	Latin	Family and/or Order
Apple leaf miner	*Lyonetia clerkella*	Lepidoptera: Lyonetiidae
Army worms	*Spodoptera*	Lepidoptera: Noctuidae
Arrowhead	*Sagittaria sagittifolia*	Alismataceae
Artichoke plume moth	*Platyptilia carduidactyla*	Lepidoptera
Asiatic corn borer	*Ostrinia furnacalis*	Lepidoptera: Pyralidae
Bacterial blights and leaf spots, various hosts	*Pseudomonas*	Pseudomonadales: Pseudomonadaceae
Bacterial canker, prunus	*Pseudomonas mors-prunorum*	Pseudomonadales: Pseudomonadaceae
Bacterial grain rot, rice	*Pseudomonas glumae*	Pseudomonadales: Pseudomonadaceae
Bacterial leaf spots, various hosts	*Xanthomonas*	Pseudomonadales: Pseudomonadaceae
Bacterial rot, celery	*Erwinia carotovora*	Eubacteriales: Enterobacteriaceae
Bacteriosis, cotton	*Xanthomonas malvacearum*	Pseudomonadales: Pseudomonadaceae
Banana black heart	*Gibberella fujikuroi*	Deuteromycetes: Hypocreales
Banana leaf spot	*Mycosphaerella musicola*	Ascomycetes: Sphaeridales
Banana root borer	*Cosmopolites sordidus*	Coleoptera: Curculionidae
Banana weevil	*Cosmopolites sordidus*	Coleoptera: Curculionidae
Barnyard grass	*Echinochloa crus-galli*	Gramineae
Barnyard grass, awnless	*Echinochloa colonum*	Gramineae
Barnyard grasses	*Echinochloa*	Gramineae
Barren brome	*Bromus sterilis*	Gramineae
Basal stem rot, cucurbits	*Erwinia carotovora*	Eubacteriales: Enterobacteriaceae
Bean beetles	*Epilachna*	Coleoptera: Coccinellidae
Bearded oat	*Avena barbata*	Gramineae
Beet armyworm; lesser armyworm	*Spodoptera exigua*	Lepidoptera: Noctuidae
Beet cyst nematode	*Heterodera schachtii*	Nematoda: Heteroderidae
Beet leaf-miner	*Pegomya hyoscamni*	Diptera: Anthomyiidae
Beet leaf weevil	*Tanymecus pallidus*	Coleoptera: Curculionidae
Begonia	*Begonia elatior*	Begoniaceae
Beneficial bacterium	*Agrobacterium radiobacter*	Eubacteriales: Rhizobiaceae
Bermuda grass	*Cynodon*	Gramineae
Bermuda grass	*Cynodon dactylon*	Gramineae
Bindweed, large	*Calystegia sepium*	Convolvulaceae
Black-grass	*Alopecurus myosuroides*	Gramineae
Black bean aphid	*Aphis fabae*	Homoptera: Aphididae
Black bent	*Agrostis gigantea*	Gramineae
Black bindweed	*Fallopia convolvulus*	Polygonaceae
Blackflies	*Simulium*	Diptera: Simuliidae
Black leaf streak, banana	*Mycosphaerella fijiensis*	Ascomycetes: Sphaeridales
Black mould; sooty mould	*Cladosporium*	Deuteromycetes: Moniliales
Black nightshade	*Solanum nigrum*	Solanaceae
Black root rot, tobacco	*Thielaviopsis basicola*	Deuteromycetes: Moniliales
Black rot, grapevines	*Guignardia bidwellii*	Ascomycetes: Sphaeriales
Black stem rust, grasses	*Puccinia graminis*	Basidiomycetes: Uredinales
Black vine weevil	*Otiorhynchus sulcatus*	Coleoptera: Curculionidae
Blackcurrant gall-mite	*Cecidophyopsis ribis*	Acari: Eriophyidae
Blackcurrant rust	*Cronartium ribicola*	Basidiomycetes: Uredinales

English	Latin	Family and/or Order
Blackleg, beet crops	*Aphanomyces cochlioides*	Saprolegniales: Saprolegniacea
Blackleg, potatoes	*Erwinia carotvora*	Eubacteriales: Enterobacteriaceae
Blackspot, roses	*Diplocarpon rosae*	Ascomycetes: Helotiales
Blight, capsicums	*Phytophthora capsici*	Oomycetes: Peronosporales
Blight, damping off, foot-rot, various hosts	*Phytophthora*	Oomycetes: Peronosporales
Blister blight, tea	*Exobasidium vexans*	Basidiomycetes: Exobasidiales
Blossom or pollen beetles	*Meligethes spp.*	Coleoptera: Nitidulidae
Blossom wilt, apple, plum	*Sclerotinia laxa*	Ascomycetes: Helotiales
Blue mold; blue rot, apples and pears	*Penicillium expansum*	Deuteromycetes: Moniliales
Blue mould, citrus	*Penicillium italicum*	Deuteromycetes: Moniliales
Blue mould, tobacco	*Peronospora tabacina* (= *Plasmopara tabacina*)	Oomycetes: Peronosporales
Bollworms, spiny	*Earias*	Lepidoptera: Noctuidae
Bracken	*Pteridium aquilinum*	Filicales
Brambles	*Rubus*	Rosaceae
Branched bur-reed	*Sparganium erectum*	Sparganiaceae
Brassica cyst nematode	*Heterodera cruciferae*	Nematoda: Heteroderidae
Brassica gall and stem weevils	*Ceutorhynchus*	Coleoptera: Curculionidae
Broad mite	*Polyphagotarsonemus latus*	Acari: Tarsonemidae
Brooks spot, apple	*Mycosphaerella pomi*	Ascomycetes: Sphaeridales
Brown rot, apple, pear, plum	*Sclerotinia fructigena*	Ascomycetes: Helotiales
Brown rot, top fruit	*Sclerotinia fructicola*	Ascomycetes: Helotiales
Brown rust, barley	*Puccinia hordei*	Basidiomycetes: Uredinales
Brown rust, chrysanthemum	*Puccinia chrysanthemi*	Basidiomycetes: Uredinales
Brown rust, wheat	*Puccinia recondita*	Basidiomycetes: Uredinales
Brown soft scale	*Coccus hesperidum*	Homoptera: Coccidae
Brown spot, peanut	*Mycosphaerella arachidis*	Ascomycetes: Sphaeridales
Brown spot, rice	*Cochliobolus miyabeanus*	Ascomycetes: Sphaeriales
Brown stripe, sugar cane	*Bipolaris stenospila*	Ascomycetes: Sphaeriales
Bt	*Bacillus thuringiensis*	Schizomycetes: Eubacteriales
Bulb mites	*Rhizoglyphus callae, R. robini*	Acari: Acaridae
Bulb scale mite	*Steneotarsonemus laticeps*	Acari: Tarsonemidae
Bullrushes	*Typha*	Typhaceae
Bunt, stinking smut	*Tilletia caries*	Basidiomycetes: Ustilaginales
Burrowing nematode	*Radopholus similis*	Nematoda: Tylenchidae
Butt rot, conifers	*Fomes annosus*	Basidiomycetes: Agaricales
Buttercups	*Ranunculus*	Ranunculaceae
Cabbage looper	*Trichoplusia ni*	Lepidoptera: Noctuidae
Cabbage moth	*Mamestra brassicae*	Lepidoptera: Noctuidae
Cabbage root fly	*Delia radicum*	Diptera: Anthomyiidae
Cabbage seed weevil	*Ceutorhynchus assimilis*	Coleoptera: Curculionidae
Cabbage stem weevil	*Ceutorhynchus quadridens*	Coleoptera: Curculionidae
Cabbage white butterflies	*Pieris*	Lepidoptera: Pieridae
Californian red scale	*Aonidiella aurantii*	Homoptera: Diaspididae
Canadian pondweed	*Elodea canadensis*	Hydrocharitaceae

English	Latin	Family and/or Order
Canary grass, awned	*Phalaris paradoxa*	Gramineae
Canary grasses	*Phalaris*	Gramineae
Canker, apple, pear	*Nectria galligena*	Hypocreales
Carmine spider mite	*Tetranychus cinnabarinus*	Acari: Tetranychidae
Carpenter ants	*Camponotus*	Hymenoptera: Formicidae
Carrot fly	*Psila rosae*	Diptera: Psilidae
Carrot leaf blight	*Alternaria dauci*	Deuteromycetes: Moniliales
Caterpillar predator	*Podisus maculiventris*	Heteroptera: Pentatomidae
Celery looper	*Syngrapha falcifera*	Lepidoptera: Noctuidae
Cercospora leaf spot, beans	*Cercospora zonata*	Deuteromycetes: Moniliales
Cereal leaf beetle	*Oulema melanopus*	Coleoptera: Chrysomelidae
Charlock	*Sinapis arvensis*	Cruciferae
Cherry tree borer	*Synanthedon hector*	Lepidoptera: Aegeriidae
Chestnut blight	*Endothia parasitica*	Sphaeriales: Diaporthaceae
Chinch bug	*Blissus leucopterus*	Lygaeidae
Chrysanthemum leaf miner	*Phytomyza syngenesiae*	Diptera: Agromyzidae
Chrysanthemum leaf miner parasitoid	*Dacnusa sibirica*	Hymenoptera: Braconidae
Chrysomelid beetles	*Chrysomelidae*	Coleoptera
Citrus aphid	*Aphis citricida*	Homoptera: Aphididae
Citrus canker	*Xanthomonas citri*	Pseudomonadales: Pseudomonadaceae
Citrus mealybug	*Planococcus citri*	Homoptera: Pseudococcidae
Citrus red mite	*Panonychus citri*	Acari: Tetranychidae
Citrus rust mite	*Phyllocoptruta oleivora*	Acari: Eriophyidae
Citrus weevil	*Pachnaeus litus*	Coleoptera: Curculionidae
Cleavers	*Galium aparine*	Rubiaceae
Clover bryobia mite	*Bryobia praetiosa*	Acari: Tetranychidae
Club-rushes	*Scirpus*	Cyperaceae
Clubroot, brassicas	*Plasmodiophora brassicae*	Oomycetes: Plasmodiophorales
Coccomycosis, Cherry leaf spot	*Blumeriella jaapii*	Ascomycetes: Helotiales
Cockchafer	*Melolontha melolontha*	Coleoptera: Scarabaeidae
Cockchafers	*Melolontha*	Coleoptera: Scarabaeidae
Cocklebur	*Xanthium pennsylvanicum*	Compositae
Cockspur, rice	*Echinochloa oryzicola* (= *E. oryzoides*)	Gramineae
Cocoa capsid	*Sahlbergella singularis*	Heteroptera: Miridae
Cocoa capsid	*Distantiella theobroma*	Heteroptera: Miridae
Coconut rhinoceros beetle	*Oryctes rhinoceros*	Coleoptera: Scarabaeidae
Codling moth	*Cydia pomonella*	Lepidoptera: Tortricidae
Coffee rust	*Hemileia vastatrix*	Basidiomycetes: Uredinales
Collar rot, apple	*Phytophthora cactorum*	Oomycetes: Peronosporales
Colorado beetle	*Leptinotarsa decemlineata*	Coleoptera: Chrysomelidae
Columbus grass	*Sorghum almum*	Gramineae
Common amaranth	*Amaranthus retroflexus*	Amaranthaceae
Common chickweed	*Stellaria media*	Caryophyllaceae
Common couch	*Elymus repens*	Gramineae
Common orache	*Atriplex patula*	Chenopodiaceae

English	Latin	Family and/or Order
Common scab of crops such as potato and beet	*Streptomyces scabies Walk.*	Schizomycetes: Actinomycetales
Corn marigold	*Chrysanthemum segetum*	Compositae
Corn rootworm	*Diabrotica undecimpunctata*	Coleoptera: Chrysomelidae
Corn rootworms	*Diabrotica*	Coleoptera: Chrysomelidae
Corn spurrey	*Spergula arvensis*	Caryophyllaceae
Cotton boll rot	*Gibberella fujikuroi*	Deuteromycetes: Hypocreales
Cotton boll weevil	*Anthonomus grandis*	Coleoptera: Curculionidae
Cotton leaf perforator	*Bucculatrix thurberiella*	Lepidoptera: Lyonetiidae
Cotton leaf worm	*Alabama argillacea*	Lepidoptera: Noctuidae
Cotton leafhoppers	*Empoasca*	Homoptera: Cicadellidae
Crabgrass	*Digitaria sanguinalis*	Gramineae
Crabgrass, tropical	*Digitaria adscendens* (= D. *ciliaris*)	Gramineae
Crabgrasses	*Digitaria*	Gramineae
Crane flies	*Tipula*	Diptera: Tipulidae
Crane's bills	*Geranium*	Geraniaceae
Creeping bent	*Agrostis stolonifera*	Gramineae
Crickets	*Cricetus*	Saltatoria: Gryllidae
Crickets, grasshoppers, etc.	*Saltatoria*	Insecta
Crown gall	*Agrobacterium tumefasciens*	Eubacteriales: Rhizobiaceae
Crown rot, apple	*Phytophthora cactorum*	Oomycetes: Peronsporales
Currant clearwing moth	*Synanthedon tipuliformis*	Lepidoptera: Aegeriidae
Cutworm	*Noctua pronuba*	Lepidoptera: Noctuidae
Cutworms	*Agrotis*	Lepidoptera: Noctuidae
Cutworms	*Noctua*	Lepidoptera: Noctuidae
Cutworms; dart moths	*Euxoa*	Lepidoptera: Noctuidae
Cyst nematodes	*Heteroderidae*	Nematoda
Damping-off disease	*Thanetophorus cucumeris* (= *Rhizoctonia solani*)	Basidiomycetes: Stereales
Damping off	*Rhizoctonia solani* (= *Thanetophorus cucumeris*)	Deuteromycetes: Agonomycetiales
Damson-hop aphid	*Phorodon humuli*	Homoptera: Aphididae
Dark leaf spot, brassicas	*Alternaria brassicae*	Deuteromycetes: Moniliales
Dark leaf spot, brassicas	*Alternaria brassicicola*	Deuteromycetes: Moniliales
Dayflower	*Commelina*	Commelinaceae
Dead arm, grape vines	*Phomopsis viticola*	Deuteromycetes: Sphaeropsidales
Diamond-back moth	*Plutella xylostella*	Lepidoptera: Yponomeutidae
Docks and sorrels	*Rumex*	Polygonaceae
Dollar spot, turf	*Sclerotinia homeocarpa*	Ascomycetes: Helotiales
Douglas fir	*Pseudotsuga menziesii*	Pinaceae
Douglas fir beetle	*Dendroctonus pseudotsuga*	Coleoptera: Scolytidae
Douglas fir beetle	*Ips typographus*	Coleoptera: Ipidae
Downy mildew, brassicae	*Peronospora parasitica*	Oomycetes: Peronosporales
Downy mildew, cereals	*Scerophthora macrospora*	Oomycetes: Peronosporales
Downy mildew, cucurbits	*Pseudoperonospora cubensis*	Oomycetes: Peronosporales

English	Latin	Family and/or Order
Downy mildew, grapevine	*Plasmopara viticola*	Oomycetes: Peronosporales
Downy mildew, hops	*Pseudoperonospora humuli*	Oomycetes: Peronosporales
Downy mildew, lettuce	*Bremia lactucae*	Oomycetes: Peronosporales
Downy mildew, sorghum	*Peronosclerospora*	Oomycetes: Peronosporales
Downy mildew, wheat	*Scerophthora*	Oomycetes: Peronosporales
Downy mildews	*Peronospora*	Oomycetes: Peronosporales
Downy mildews, e.g. on pearl millet	*Sclerospora*	Oomycetes: Peronosporales
Downy mildews, various hosts	*Plasmopara*	Oomycetes: Peronosporales
Dry bubble, mushrooms	*Verticillium fungicola*	Deuteromycetes: Moniliales
Dry rot, post- harvest rot	*Fusarium coeruleum*	Deuteromycetes: Moniliales
Dutch-elm disease	*Ceratocystis ulmi*	Ascomycetes: Sphaeriales
Egyptian cotton leafworm	*Spodoptera littoralis*	Lepidoptera: Noctuidae
Elodea, Florida	*Hydrilla verticillata*	Hydrocharitaceae
European corn borer	*Ostrinia nubilalis*	Lepidoptera: Pyralidae
European grapevine moth	*Lobesia botrana*	Lepidoptera: Tortricidae
European pine sawfly	*Neodiprion sertifer*	Hymenoptera: Diprionidae
European pine shoot moth	*Rhyacionia buoliana*	Lepidoptera: Tortricidae
Eye-spot, cereals	*Pseudocercosporella herpotrichoides*	Deuteromycetes: Moniliales
Fairy rings	*Marasmius oreades*	Agaricales
Fall armyworm	*Spodoptera frugiperda*	Lepidoptera: Noctuidae
Fall panicum	*Panicum dichotomiflorum*	Gramineae
False oat-grass	*Arrhenatherum elatius*	Gramineae
Fat hen	*Chenopodium album*	Chenopodiaceae
Field bindweed	*Convolvulus arvensis*	Convolvulaceae
Field pansy	*Viola arvensis*	Violaceae
Field slug	*Decoceras*	Mollusca: Gastropoda
Fire ants	*Solenopsis*	Hymenoptera: Formicidae
Fire blight of pome fruit	*Erwinia amylovora*	Eubacteriales: Enterobacteriaceae
Flea beetle	*Phyllotreta striolata*	Coleoptera: Chrysomelidae
Flea beetles	*Chaetocnema*	Coleoptera: Chrysomelidae
Flea beetles	*Phyllotreta*	Coleoptera: Chrysomelidae
Fly speck disease, apple	*Schizothyrium pomi*	Ascomycetes: Hemisphaeriales
Foot rot, root rot, cereals, grasses	*Cochliobolus sativus*	Ascomycetes: Sphaeriales
Foot rot, root rot, various hosts	*Aphanomyces*	Oomycetes: Saprolegniales
Foot rot, root rot, various hosts	*Rhizoctonia*	Deuteromycetes: Agonomycetiales
Formosan termite	*Coptotermes formosanus*	Isoptera: Rhinotermitidae
Four-leaved water clover	*Marsilea*	Marsileaceae
Foxtail grasses	*Setaria*	Gramineae
Foxtail, giant	*Setaria faberi*	Gramineae
Foxtail, green	*Setaria viridis*	Gramineae
Foxtail, yellow	*Setaria glauca* (= *S. lutescens*)	Gramineae
Fringe rushes	*Fimbristylis*	Cyperaceae
Frit fly	*Oscinella frit*	Diptera: Chloropidae

English	Latin	Family and/or Order
Frog eye, leaf spot, soya	*Cercosporidium (C. sojinum = Cercospora sojina)*	Deuteromycetes: Moniliales
Fruit flies	*Drosophilidae*	Diptera
Fruit flies	*Dacus*	Diptera: Tephritidae
Fruit flies	*Drosophila*	Diptera: Drosophilidae
Fruit rot, strawberries	*Mucor*	Mucorales
Fruit rot, various hosts	*Botrytis cinerea*	Deuteromycetes: Moniliales
Fruit tree red spider mite	*Panonychus ulmi*	Acari: Tetranychidae
Fruit tree red spider mite predator	*Amblyseius degenerans*	Mesostigmata: Phytoseiidae
Fruit tree red spider mite predator	*Typhlodromus pyri*	Mesostigmata: Phytoseiidae
Fuchsia	*Fuchsia hybrida*	Onagraceae
Fungal vector of rhizomania virus	*Polymyxa betae*	Oomycetes: Plasmodiophorales
Fungus gnat predator	*Hypoaspis aculeifer*	Mesostigmata: Laelapidae
Fusarium foot and root rots, various hosts	*Fusarium culmorum*	Deuteromycetes: Moniliales
Fusarium wilt, various hosts	*Fusarium oxysporum*	Deuteromycetes: Moniliales
Gangrene, potatoes	*Phoma exigua*	Deuteromycetes: Sphaeropsidales
Garden wireworms	*Athous*	Coleoptera: Elateridae
Giant knotweed	*Reynoutria sachalinensis (= Polygonum sachalinense)*	Polygonaceae
Glasshouse potato aphid	*Aulacorthum solani*	Homoptera: Aphididae
Glasshouse whitefly	*Trialeurodes vaporariorum*	Homoptera: Aleyrodidae
Glasshouse whitefly parasitoid	*Encarsia formosa*	Hymenoptera: Aphelinidae
Gloeosporium rot, apples	*Glomerella cingulata*	Deuteromycetes: Sphaeriales
Gloeosporium rot, apples	*Gloeosporium*	Deuteromycetes: Sphaeriales
Glume blotch, wheat	*Leptosphaeria nodorum (= Septoria nodorum)*	Ascomycetes: Sphaeriales
Golden chalcid	*Aphytis melinus*	Hymenoptera: Aphelinidae
Gooseberry bryobia mite	*Bryobia ribis*	Acari: Tetranychidae
Goosegrass	*Eleusine indica*	Gramineae
Grain aphid	*Sitobium avenae*	Homoptera: Aphididae
Grain beetles	*Cryptolestes*	Coleoptera: Cucujidae
Grape berry moth	*Eupoecilia ambiguella*	Lepidoptera:
Grass and cereal flies	*Opomyza*	Diptera: Opomyzidae
Grass moth	*Chrysoteuchia caliginosellus (= Crambus caliginosellus)*	Lepidoptera: Pyralidae
Grass moth	*Crambus caliginosellus*	Lepidoptera: Pyralidae
Green leafhopper	*Empoasca fabae*	Homoptera: Cicadellidae
Green leafhoppers	*Nephotettix*	Homoptera: Cicadellidae
Green mould, citrus	*Penicillium digitatum*	Deuteromycetes: Moniliales
Green rice leafhopper	*Nephotettix impicticepts*	Homoptera: Cicadellidae
Green rice leafhopper	*Nephotettix cincticeps*	Homoptera: Cicadellidae
Gypsy moth	*Lymantria dispar*	Lepidoptera: Lymantriidae
Halo blight, beans	*Pseudomonas phaseolicola*	Pseudomonadales: Pseudomonadaceae
Hay bacillus	*Bacillus subtilis*	Schizomycetes: Eubacteriales

English	Latin	Family and/or Order
Head smut, maize	*Sphacelotheca reiliana*	Basidiomycetes: Ustilaginales
Helmet scale	*Saissetia coffeae*	Homoptera: Coccidae
Helminthosporium blight, rice	*Helminthosporium oryzae*	Deuteromycetes: Moniliales
Hemispherical scale	*Saissetia coffeae*	Homoptera: Coccidae
Hemp sesbania	*Sesbania exaltata*	Leguminosae
Hickory shuckworm	*Cydia caryana*	Lepidoptera: Tortricidae
Honey fungus	*Armillaria mellea*	Basidiomycetes: Agaricales
Hornweed, common	*Ceratophyllum demersum*	Ceratophyllaceae
House mosquito	*Culex fatigans* (= *C. quinquefasciatus*)	Diptera
Hyperparasite of fungi	*Ampelomyces quisqualis*	Deuteromycetes: Sphaeropsidales
Ivy	*Hedera helix*	Araliaceae
Japanese beetle	*Popillia japonicus*	Coleoptera: Scarabaeidae
Japanese bullrush	*Scirpus juncoides*	Cyperaceae
Japanese knotweed	*Reynoutria japonica* (= *Polygonum cuspidatum*)	Polygonaceae
Jimson weed	*Datura stramonium*	Solanaceae
Johnson grass	*Sorghum halepense*	Gramineae
Joint vetches	*Aeschynomene*	Leguminosae
Knapweeds	*Centaurea*	Compositae
Knot grass	*Polygonum aviculare*	Polygonaceae
Knotweeds	*Polygonum*	Polygonaceae
Koa seed worm	*Crytophlebia illepida*	Lepidoptera: Tortricidae
Kyllinga, green	*Cyperus brevifolius*	Cyperaceae
Ladybird; ladybug	*Harmonia axyridis*	Coleoptera: Coccinellidae
Ladybird; ladybug	*Hippodamia convergens*	Coleoptera: Coccinellidae
Large white butterfly	*Pieris brassicae*	Lepidoptera: Pieridae
Late blight, potato, tomato	*Phytophthora infestans*	Oomycetes: Peronosporales
Late flowering cyperus	*Cyperus serotinus*	Cyperaceae
Leaf-mining moths	*Leucoptera*	Lepidoptera: Lyonetiidae
Leaf and glume spots, various hosts	*Septoria*	Sphaeropsidales
Leaf and pod spot, peas	*Ascochyta pinodes*	Deuteromycetes: Sphaeropsidales
Leaf and pod spot, peas	*Ascochyta pisi*	Deuteromycetes: Sphaeropsidales
Leaf blight, rice	*Xanthomonas oryzae*	Pseudomonadales: Pseudomonadaceae
Leaf blotch, barley and rye	*Rhynchosporium secalis*	Deuteromycetes: Moniliales
Leaf blotches etc., various hosts	*Marssonina*	Melanconiales
Leaf miners	*Agromyza*	Diptera: Agromyzidae
Leaf miners	*Liriomyza*	Diptera: Agromyzidae
Leaf miners	*Phytomyza*	Diptera: Agromyzidae
Leaf mining moths	*Phyllonorycter*	Lepidoptera: Gracillariidae
Leaf mould, tomato	*Fulvia fulva*	Deuteromycetes: Hyphales
Leaf moulds	*Fulvia*	Deuteromycetes: Hyphales
Leaf roller	*Archips podanus*	Lepidoptera: Tortricidae

English	Latin	Family and/or Order
Leaf roller	*Pandemis heparana*	Lepidoptera: Totricidae
Leaf roller	*Platynota stultana*	Lepidoptera: Totricidae
Leaf scorch, apples; rust, various hosts	*Gymnosporangium*	Basidiomycetes: Uredinales
Leaf scorch, strawberry	*Diplocarpon earliana*	Ascomycetes: Helotiales
Leaf smuts, various hosts	*Urocystis*	Basidiomycetes: Ustilaginales
Leaf spot	*Alternaria alternata*	Deuteromycetes: Moniliales
Leaf spot	*Curvularia.*	Moniliales; Dematiaceae
Leaf spot and black rot, apple	*Botryosphaeria obtusa* (=*Physalospora obtusa*)	Ascomycetes: Sphaeriales
Leaf spot and stem canker, sunflowers	*Diaporthe helianthi*	Ascomycetes: Sphaeriales
Leaf spot diseases, various hosts	*Mycosphaerella*	Ascomycetes: Sphaeridales
Leaf spot, beans	*Ascochyta fabae*	Deuteromycetes: Sphaeropsidales
Leaf spot, beet crops	*Cercospora beticola*	Deuteromycetes: Moniliales
Leaf spot, beet crops	*Ramularia beticola*	Deuteromycetes: Moniliales
Leaf spot, currants, gooseberry	*Pseudopeziza ribis*	Ascomycetes: Helotiales
Leaf spot, melon	*Corynespora melonis*	Deuteromycetes: Moniliales
Leaf spots, grasses	*Rhynchosporium*	Hyphales
Leaf spots, various	*Alternaria*	Deuteromycetes: Moniliales
Leaf spots, various	*Cercospora*	Deuteromycetes: Moniliales
Leaf spots, various	*Ramularia*	Deuteromycetes: Moniliales
Leaf spots, various hosts	*Ascochyta*	Deuteromycetes: Sphaeropsidales
Leaf stripe, barley	*Pyrenophora graminea*	Ascomycetes: Sphaeriales
Leafhopper	*Empoasca decipiens*	Homoptera: Cicadellidae
Leafhopper egg parasitoid	*Anagrus atomus*	Hymenoptera: Mymaridae
Leatherjackets	*Tipula*	Diptera: Tipulidae
Lemon-shaped cyst nematodes	*Heterodera*	Nematoda: Heteroderidae
Lepidopteran egg parasites	*Trichogramma*	Hymenoptera: Trichogrammatidae
Lepidopteran parasitic wasp	*Cotesia*	Hymenoptera: Aphidiidae
Lesser grain borer	*Rhyzopertha dominica*	Coleoptora: Bostrichidae
Lesser peach tree borer	*Synanthedon pictipes*	Lepidoptera: Aegeriidae
Light leaf spot, brassicas	*Pyrenopeziza brassicae*	Ascomycetes: Helotiales
Loose silky-bent	*Apera spica-venti*	Gramineae
Loose smut, barley, wheat	*Ustilago nuda*	Basidiomycetes: Ustilaginales
Macadamia nut borer	*Cryptophlebia ombrodelta*	Lepidoptera: Tortricidae
Maggots	*Delia* and *Hylemya*	Diptera: Anthomyiidae
Maize stalk borer; sugar cane borer	*Diatraea saccharalis*	Lepidoptera: Pyralidae
Maize stalk rot	*Gibberella fujikuroi*	Deuteromycetes: Hypocreales
Maize weevil; rice weevil	*Sitophilus zeamais*	Coleoptera: Curculionidae
Mangold flea beetle	*Chaetocnema concinna*	Coleoptera: Chrysomelidae
Mangold fly	*Pegomya hyoscamni*	Diptera: Anthomyiidae
Mayweed, scentless	*Tripleurospermum maritimum* (=*Matricaria inodora*)	Compositae
Mayweeds (some)	*Chamomilla*	Compositae
Mayweeds (some)	*Matricaria*	Compositae
McDaniel's spider mite	*Tetranychus mcdanieli*	Acari: Tetranychidae
Meadow-grass, rough	*Poa trivialis*	Gramineae

English	Latin	Family and/or Order
Meadow grass, annual	*Poa annua*	Gramineae
Meadow grasses	*Poa*	Gramineae
Mealworms	*Alphitobius*	Coleoptera: Tenebrionidae
Mealybug parasite	*Leptomastix dactylopii*	Hymenoptera: Encrytidae
Mealybug predator	*Cryptolaemus montrouzieri*	Coleoptera: Coccinelidae
Mealybugs	*Pseudococcus*	Homoptera: Pseudococcidae
Mediterranean black scale; black olive scale	*Saissetia oleae*	Homoptera: Coccidae
Mediterranean fruit fly	*Ceratitis capitata*	Diptera: Tephritidae
Melanosis, citrus	*Diaporthe citri*	Ascomycetes: Sphaeriales
Melon and cotton aphid	*Aphis gossypii*	Homoptera: Aphididae
Melon fly	*Dacus cucurbitae*	Diptera: Tephritidae
Mexican bean beetle	*Epilachna varivestis*	Coleoptera: Coccinellidae
Milkweed vine	*Morrenia odorata*	Asclepiadaceae
Millet, Texas	*Panicum texanum*	Gramineae
Minute black ladybird	*Stethorus punctum*	Coleoptera: Coccinellidae
Minute pirate bugs	*Orius*	Hemiptera: Anthocoridae
Mite	*Calepitrimerus*	Acari: Eriophyidae
Mite	*Eriophyes*	Acari: Eriophyidae
Mites	*Aculops*	Acari: Eriophyidae
Mites	*Phyllocoptes*	Acari: Eriophyidae
Mites	*Vasates*	Acari: Eriophyidae
Mite predator	*Feltiella acarisuga*	Diptera: Cecidomyiidae
Mite predator	*Galendromus occidentalis*	Acarina: Phytoseiidae
Mock cypress	*Kochia scoparia*	Chenopodiaceae
Mole cricket	*Gryllotalpa gryllotalpa*	Orthoptera: Gryllotalpidae
Mole cricket	*Scapteriscus vicinus*	Orthoptera: Gryllotalpidae
Mole crickets	*Gryllotalpa*	Orthoptera: Gryllotalpidae
Monilinia leaf blight, apple	*Monilinia mali*	Deuteromycetes: Moniliales
Morning glory, ivyleaf	*Ipomoea hederacea*	Convolvulaceae
Morning glory, tall	*Ipomoea purpurea*	Convolvulaceae
Mosquitoes	*Culex*	Diptera
Moss	*Ceratodon purpureus*	Bryophyta
Mountain pine beetle	*Dendroctonus ponderosae*	Coleoptera: Scolytidae
Mugwort; wormwood	*Artemisia vulgaris*	Compositae
Mushroom cecid	*Heteropeza pygmaea*	Diptera: Cecidomyiidae
Mushroom sciarid	*Lycoriella auripila*	Diptera: Sciaridae
N-fixing bacteria	*Nitrosomonas*	Bacteria
Neck rot, onions	*Botrytis allii Munn*	Deuteromycetes: Moniliales
Needle nematodes	*Longidorus*	Nematoda
Neem tree	*Azadirachta indica*	Meliaceae
Net blotch, barley	*Pyrenophora teres*	Ascomycetes: Sphaeriales
Nettle, common	*Urtica dioica*	Urticaceae
Nettle, small	*Urtica urens*	Urticaceae
Nettles	*Urtica*	Urticaceae
New Zealand grass grub	*Costelytra zealandrica*	Coleoptera: Scarabaeidae

English	Latin	Family and/or Order
Nipplewort	*Lapsana communis*	Compositae
Northern joint vetch	*Aeschynomene virginica*	Leguminosae
Northern leaf blight, maize	*Helminthosporium turcicum*	Deuteromycetes: Moniliales
Nutgrass	*Cyperus rotundus*	Cyperaceae
Nutsedges	*Cyperus*	Cyperaceae
Oat, sterile	*Avena sterilis*	Gramineae
Oats (wild and cultivated)	*Avena*	Gramineae
Old World bollworm	*Helicoverpa armigera*	Lepidoptera: Noctuidae
Olive fruit fly	*Bactrocera oleae* (=*Dacus oleae*)	Diptera: Tephritidae
Olive moth	*Prays oleae*	Lepidoptera: Yponomeutidae
Onion couch	*Arrhenatherum elatius*	Gramineae
Onion thrips	*Thrips tabaci*	Thysanoptera: Thripidae
Oriental fruit moth	*Grapholitha molesta*	Lepidoptera: Tortricidae
Oriental fruit tree moth	*Carposina niponensis*	Lepidoptera: Tortricidae
Oriental red scale	*Aonidiella orientalis*	Homoptera: Diaspididae
Oriental tobacco budworm	*Helicoverpa assulta*	Lepidoptera: Noctuidae
Pale persicaria	*Polygonum lapathifolium*	Polygonaceae
Panic grasses	*Panicum spp.*	Gramineae
Parasitic yeasts	*Candida*	Ascomycetes: Endomycetales
Pea and bean weevils	*Sitona*	Coleoptera: Curculionidae
Pea aphid	*Acyrthosiphon pisum*	Homoptera: Aphididae
Pea cyst nematode	*Heterodera goettingiana*	Nematoda: Heteroderidae
Pea moth	*Cydia nigicana*	Lepidoptera: Tortricidae
Peach-potato aphid	*Myzus persicae*	Homoptera: Aphididae
Peach leaf-curl	*Taphrina deformans*	Ascomycetes: Taphrinales
Peach tree borer	*Anarsia lineatella*	Lepidoptera: Gelechiidae
Peach tree borer	*Sanninoidea exitiosa*	Lepidoptera: Aegeriidae
Pear leaf blister moth	*Leucoptera malifoliella*	Lepidoptera: Lyonetiidae
Pear rust	*Gymnosporangium fuscum*	Basidiomycetes: Uredinales
Pear rust mite	*Epitrimerus pyri*	Acari: Eriophyidae
Pearly green lacewing	*Chrysoperla carnea*	Neuroptera: Chrysopidae
Penicillium rots	*Penicillium*	Deuteromycetes: Moniliales
Persicaria	*Polygonum persicaria*	Polygonaceae
Petunia	*Petunia*	Solanaceae
Pharaoh's ant	*Monomorium pharaonis*	Hymenoptera: Formicidae
Pickerel weed	*Monochoria vaginalis*	Pontederiaceae
Pimpernel, false	*Lindernia procumbens*	Scrophulariaceae
Pine processionary caterpillar	*Thaumetopoea pityocampa*	Lepidoptera: Thaumetopoeidae
Pine sawfly	*Neodiprion lecontei*	Hymenoptera: Diprionidae
Pink bollworm	*Pectinophora gossypiella*	Lepidoptera: Gelechiidae
Plantains	*Plantago*	Plantaginaceae
Planthoppers	*Nilaparvata*	Homoptera: Delphacidae
Plum rust	*Tranzchelia pruni-spinosae*	Basidiomycetes: Uredinales
Pod rot, cocoa	*Monilia roreri*	Deuteromycetes: Moniliales

English	Latin	Family and/or Order
Pollen beetle	*Meligethes aeneus*	Coleoptera: Nitidulidae
Pondweed, American	*Potamogeton distinctus*	Potamogetonaceae
Pondweeds	*Potamogeton*	Potamogetonaceae
Poplars	*Populus*	Salicaceae
Poppies	*Papaver*	Papaveraceae
Post-harvest rots	*Rhizopus*	Mucorales
Post-harvest rots, various hosts	*Sclerotium*	Deuteromycetes: Agonomycetales
Potato aphid	*Macrosiphum euphorbiae*	Homoptera: Aphididae
Potato cyst nematodes	*Globodera*	Nematoda: Heteroderidae
Potato leafhopper	*Eupterycyba jucunda*	Homoptera: Cicadellidae
Potato moth	*Phthorimaea operculella*	Lepidoptera: Gelechiidae
Powdery mildew, apple	*Podosphaera leucotricha*	Ascomycetes: Erysiphales
Powdery mildew, beet crops	*Erysiphe betae*	Ascomycetes: Erysiphales
Powdery mildew, cereals, grasses	*Erysiphe graminis*	Ascomycetes: Erysiphales
Powdery mildew, cucurbits	*Erysiphe cichoracearum*	Ascomycetes: Erysiphales
Powdery mildew, cucurbits	*Sphaerotheca fuliginea*	Ascomycetes: Erysiphales
Powdery mildew, grapevines	*Uncinula necator*	Ascomycetes: Erysiphales
Powdery mildew, peppers	*Leveillula*	Ascomycetes: Erysiphales
Powdery mildew, rose	*Sphaerotheca pannosa*	Ascomycetes: Erysiphales
Powdery mildew, various hosts	*Erysiphe*	Ascomycetes: Erysiphales
Powdery mildew, various hosts	*Phyllactinia*	Ascomycetes: Erysiphales
Powdery mildew, various hosts	*Podosphaera*	Ascomycetes: Erysiphales
Powdery mildew, various hosts	*Sphaerotheca*	Ascomycetes: Erysiphales
Predatory mite	*Amblyseius barkeri*	Mesostigmata: Phytoseiidae
Predatory mite	*Amblyseius californicus*	Mesostigmata: Phytoseiidae
Predatory mite	*Typhlodromus occidentalis*	Mesostigmata: Phytoseiidae
Predatory mite	*Amblyseius cucumeris*	Mesostigmata: Phytoseiidae
Psyllids	*Psylla*	Homoptera: Psyllidae
Purslane	*Portulaca oleracea*	Portulacaceae
Purslane	*Portulaca*	Portulacaceae
Pygmy mangold beetle	*Atomaria linearis*	Coleoptera: Cryptophagidae
Pyrethrum daisy	*Tanacetum cinerariaefolium*	Compositeae
Quackgrass	*Elymus repens*	Gramineae
Ragweed, common	*Ambrosia artemisifolia*	Compositae
Rape	*Brassica napus*	Cruciferae
Ray blight, chrysanthemum	*Didymella ligulicola*	Ascomycetes: Sphaeriales
Red core, strawberry	*Phytophthora fragariae*	Phycomycetes: Peronosporales
Red crevice tea mite	*Brevipalpus phoenicis*	Acari: Tenuipalpidae
Red dead-nettle	*Lamium purpureum*	Labiatae
Red scale	*Aspidiotus nerii*	Homoptera: Diaspididae
Red scale parasite	*Aphytis lignanensis*	Hymenoptera: Aphelinidae
Red spider mites	*Panonychus*	Acari: Tetranychidae
Redroot pigweed	*Amaranthus retroflexus*	Amaranthaceae
Redshank	*Polygonum persicaria*	Polygonaceae

English	Latin	Family and/or Order
Rhododendron	*Rhododendron ponticum*	Ericaceae
Rice blast (imperfect stage)	*Pyricularia oryzae*	Deuteromycetes: Moniliales
Rice blast (perfect stage)	*Magnaporthe grisea*	
Rice brown planthopper	*Nilaparvata lugens*	Homoptera: Delphacidae
Rice leaf beetle	*Oulema oryzae*	Coleoptera: Chrysomelidae
Rice leaf roller	*Cnaphalocrocis medinalis*	Lepidoptera: Pyralidae
Rice leaf scald	*Monographella nivalis*	Ascomycetes: Sphaeriales
Rice sheath blight	*Pellicularia sasakii*	Basidiomycetes: Agaricales
Rice stalk borer	*Chilo suppressalis*	Lepidoptera: Pyralidae
Rice stem-borer	*Chilo plejadellus*	Lepidoptera: Pyralidae
Rice stem borer	*Chilo suppressalis*	Lepidoptera: Pyralidae
Rice water weevil	*Lissorhoptrus oryzophilus*	Coleoptera: Curculionidae
Rice weevil	*Sitophilus oryzae*	Coleoptera: Curculionidae
Ring-spot, brassicas	*Mycosphaerella brassicicola*	Ascomycetes: Sphaeridales
Root-knot nematodes	*Meloidogyne*	Nematoda
Root-lesion nematodes	*Pratylenchus*	Nematoda: Hoplolaimidae
Root and stem rots, various	*Phoma*	Deuteromycotina
Root flies	*Delia* (=*Hylemya*)	Diptera: Anthomyiidae
Root rot, brassicas	*Phytophthora megasperma*	Oomycetes: Peronosporales
Root rot, tomato	*Colletotrichum coccodes*	Ascomycetes: Melanconiales
Root rots, various	*Pythium*	Oomycetes: Peronosporales
Rose aphid	*Macrosiphum rosae*	Homoptera: Aphididae
Rose thrips	*Thrips fuscipennis*	Thysanoptera: Thripidae
Rot, various crops	*Phytophthora palmivora*	Oomycetes: Peronosporales
Rots of stems, storage organs, etc., various crops	*Sclerotinia sclerotiorum*	Ascomycetes: Helotiales
Rots, damping off, etc. various hosts	*Pellicularia*	Basidiomycetes: Agaricales
Rots, ear blights and wilts, various hosts (Imperfect fungi with perfect stages in various genera).	*Fusarium*	Deuteromycetes: Moniliales
Rots, various hosts	*Sclerotium rolfsii*	Deuteromycetes: Agonomycetales
Rough Cocklebur	*Xanthium strumarium*	Compositae
Roughseed bullrush	*Scirpus mucronatus*	Cyperaceae
Rubbery rot, potatoes	*Geotrichum candidum*	Deuteromycetes: Moniliales
Runch	*Raphanus raphanistrum*	Cruciferae
Rush, flowering	*Butomus umbellatus*	Butomaceae
Russian thistle	*Salsola kali*	Chenopodiaceae
Rust mite, apple	*Aculus schlechtendali*	Acari: Eriophyidae
Rust mites	*Aculus*	Acari: Eriophyidae
Rust mites	*Phyllocoptruta*	Acari: Eriophyidae
Rust, beet crops	*Uromyces betae*	Basidiomycetes: Uredinales
Rust, roses	*Phragmidium mucronatum*	Basidiomycetes: Uredinales
Rust, soybean	*Phakopsora pachyrhizi*	Basidiomycetes: Uredinales
Rust, various hosts	*Puccinia*	Basidiomycetes: Uredinales
Rusts, various crops	*Uromyces*	Basidiomycetes: Uredinales
Ryegrass, italian	*Lolium multiflorum*	Gramineae

Reference

English	Latin	Family and/or Order
Ryegrass, perennial	*Lolium perenne*	Gramineae
Ryegrasses	*Lolium*	Gramineae
San José scale	*Quadraspidiotus perniciosus*	Homoptera: Coccidae
Saramatta grass	*Ischaemum rugosum*	Gramineae
Sawflies	*Diprion*	Hymenoptera: Diprionidae
Scab, apples	*Venturia inaequalis*	Ascomycetes: Sphaeriales
Scab, cereals	*Gibberella zeae*	Deuteromycetes: Hypocreales
Scab, cereals; brown foot rot and ear blight and other cereal diseases	*Gibberella* (=*Fusarium*)	Deuteromycetes: Hypocreales
Scab, citrus	*Elsinoe fawcettii*	Ascomycetes: Myriangiales
Scab, pears	*Venturia pirina*	Ascomycetes: Sphaeriales
Scale insect	*Didesmococcus brevipes*	Homoptera: Coccidae
Scale insect parasite	*Metaphycus bartletti*	Hymenoptera: Encrytidae
Scale insect parasite	*Metaphycus helvolus*	Hymenoptera: Encrytidae
Scale insects	*Coccus spp.*	Homoptera: Coccidae
Scentless mayweed	*Matricaria perforata* (=*M. inodora*)	Compositae
Sciariad flies	*Sciara*	Diptera: Sciaridae
Sciarid flies	*Bradysia*	Diptera: Sciaridae
Sciarid fly predator	*Hypoaspis miles*	Mesostigmata: Laelapidae
Sclerotinia rots, various hosts	*Sclerotinia*	Ascomycetes: Helotiales
Scuttle flies	*Phoridae*	Diptera
Scuttle flies	*Megaselia*	Diptera: Phoridae
Sea-rush	*Juncus maritimus*	Juncaceae
Sea club-rush	*Scirpus maritimus*	Cyperaceae
Sedges	*Carex*	Cyperaceae
Seed-eating ants	*Monomorium*	Hymenoptera: Formicidae
Septoria leaf spot, wheat	*Mycosphaerella graminicola*	Ascomycetes: Sphaeridales
Sharp eyespot, cereals	*Ceratobasidium cereale*	Basidiomycetes: Tulasnellales
Shattercane	*Sorghum bicolor*	Gramineae
Shepherd's purse	*Capsella bursa-pastoris*	Cruciferae
Shothole, prunus	*Stigmina carpophila*	Hyphales
Siam weed	*Chromolaena odorata*	Compositae
Siam weed	*Eupatorium odoratum* (=*Chromolaena odorata*)	Compositae
Sickle pod	*Cassia obtusifolia*	Leguminosae (Fabaceae)
Sigatoka	*Mycosphaerella musicola*	Ascomycetes: Sphaeridales
Silver leaf	*Chondrostereum purpureum*	Agaricales: Agaricaceae
Silver scurf, potatoes	*Helminthosporium solani*	Deuteromycetes: Moniliales
Silvery moth	*Plusia*	Lepidoptera: Noctuidae
Six-spined ips	*Ips sexdentatus*	Coleoptera: Ipidae
Six-toothed spruce bark beetle	*Pityogenes chalcographus*	Coleoptera: Scolytidae
Skin spot, potatoes	*Polyscytalum pustulans*	Hyphales
Slugs and snails	*Gastropoda*	Mollusca
Small brown planthopper	*Laodelphax striatella*	Homoptera: Delphacidae
Small white butterfly	*Pieris rapae*	Lepidoptera: Pieridae

English	Latin	Family and/or Order
Smaller European elm bark beetle	*Scolytus multistratus*	Coleoptera: Scolytidae
Smartweed	*Polygonum persicaria*	Polygonaceae
Smooth sowthistle	*Sonchus oleraceus*	Compositae
Smooth witchgrass	*Panicum dichotomiflorum*	Gramineae
Smut diseases, various hosts	*Ustilago*	Ustilaginales
Smut, various hosts	*Tilletia*	Basidiomycetes: Ustilaginales
Snow mould, grasses, cereals	*Microdochium nivalis*	Deuteromycetes: Moniliales
Snow rot, cereals	*Typhula incarnata*	Basidiomycetes: Agaricales
Sooty blotch, apple pear and citrus	*Gloeodes pomigena*	Deuteromycetes: Sphaeropsidales
Sorghum grasses	*Sorghum*	Gramineae
South American leaf miner	*Liriomyza huidobrensis*	Diptera: Agromyzidae
Southern pine beetle	*Dendroctonus frontalis*	Coleoptera: Scolytidae
Southern root-knot nematode	*Meloidogyne incognita*	Nematoda
Soybean looper	*Anticarsia gemmatalis*	Lepidoptera: Noctuidae
Speedwell, common field	*Veronica persica*	Scrophulariaceae
Speedwell, ivy-leaved	*Veronica hederifolia*	Scrophulariaceae
Speedwell, slender	*Veronica filiformis*	Scrophulariaceae
Speedwells	*Veronica*	Scrophulariaceae
Spider mite predator	*Amblyseius fallacis*	Mesostigmata: Phytoseiidae
Spider mites	*Tetranychus*	Acari: Tetranychidae
Spike rush	*Eleocharis acicularis*	Cyperaceae
Spiny sida	*Sida spinosa*	Malvaceae
Spiral nematodes	*Helicotylenchus*	Nematoda: Tylenchidae
Spotted spurge	*Euphorbia maculata*	Euphorbiaceae
Sprangletop grasses	*Leptochloa*	Gramineae
Sprangletop, bearded	*Leptochloa fascicularis* *(=Diplachne fascicularis)*	Gramineae
Sprangletop, red	*Leptochloa chinensis*	Gramineae
Spruce beetle	*Dendroctonus rufipennis*	Coleoptera: Scolytidae
Spur blight, cane fruit	*Didymella applanata*	Ascomycetes: Sphaeriales
Stalk rots, various hosts	*Diplodia*	Deuteromycetes: Sphaeropsidales
Star grasses	*Cynodon*	Gramineae
Stem borers	*Chilo*	Lepidoptera: Pyralidae
Stem canker fungi, various hosts	*Diaporthe*	Ascomycetes: Sphaeriales
Stem nematode	*Ditylenchus dipsaci*	Nematoda: Tylenchidae
Sting nematode	*Belonolaimus longicausatus*	Nematoda
Storage fungi	*Aspergillus*	Deuteromycetes: Moniliales
Strangler vine	*Morrenia odorata*	Asclepiadaceae
Stubby-root nematodes	*Trichodorus*	Nematoda
Sugar beet root maggot	*Tetanops myopaeformis*	Diptera: Otitidae
Sugar cane rootstalk borer	*Diaprepes abbreviatus*	
Summer fruit tortrix moth	*Adoxophyes orana*	Lepidoptera: Tortricidae
Sunflower	*Helianthus annuus*	Compositae
Symphilids	*Symphyla*	Myriapoda
Tan spot, wheat	*Pyrenophora tritici-vulgaris*	Ascomycetes: Sphaeriales

English	Latin	Family and/or Order
Tarsonemid mites	Tarsonemus (=Phytonemus)	Acari: Tarsonemidae
Tea leaf roller	Caloptilia theivora	Lepidoptera: Gracillariidae
Tea tortrix	Homona magnanima	Lepidoptera: Tortricidae
Tetranychid mites	Eutetranychus	Acari: Tetranychidae
Texas citrus mite	Eutetranychus banksi	Acari: Tetranychidae
Thistle, creeping	Cirsium arvense	Compositae
Thistles	Carduus	Compositae
Thorn apple	Datura stramonium	Solanaceae
Thrips, flower	Frankliniella intonsa	Thysanoptera: Thripidae
Thrips, Western flower	Frankliniella occidentalis	Thysanoptera: Thripidae
Thrips, palm	Parthenothrips dracaenae	Thysanoptera: Thripidae
Thrips, New Zealand flower	Thrips obscuratus	Thysanoptera: Thripidae
Thrips	Thrips palmi	Thysanoptera: Thripidae
Thrips	Thrips	Thysanoptera: Thripidae
Tobacco	Nicotiana rustica	Solanaceae
Tobacco budworm	Heliothis virescens	Lepidoptera: Noctuidae
Tobacco flea beetle	Epitrix hirtipennis	Coleoptera: Chrysomelidae
Tobacco whitefly	Bemisia tabaci	Homoptera: Aleyrodidae
Tomato canker	Clavibacter michiganensis	Eubacteriales
Tomato leaf miner	Liriomyza bryoniae	Diptera: Agromyzidae
Tomato pinworm	Keiferia lycopersicella	Lepidoptera: Gelechiidae
Tortrix moths	Tortrix	Lepidoptera: Tortricidae
Tortrix moths and leaf rollers	Adoxophyes	Lepidoptera: Tortricidae
Tortrix moths and leaf rollers	Homona	Lepidoptera: Tortricidae
Tropical green rice leafhopper	Nephotettix nigropictus	Homoptera: Cicadellidae
Tufted apple moth	Platynota idaeusalis	Lepidoptera: Tortricidae
Turnip gall weevil	Ceutorhynchus pleurostigmata	Coleoptera: Curculionidae
Turnip moth	Agrotis segetum	Lepidoptera: Noctuidae
Two-spotted spider mite	Tetranychus urticae	Acari: Tetranychidae
Two-spotted spider mite predator	Phytoseiulus persimilis	Mesostigmata: Phytoseiidae
Umbrella plant	Cyperus difformis	Cyperaceae
Valsa canker of apple	Valsa ceratosperma	Ascomycetes: Sphaeriales
Various rots	Monilia	Deuteromycetes: Moniliales
Velvet bean caterpillar	Anticarsia gemmatalis	Lepidoptera: Noctuidae
Velvetleaf	Abutilon theophrasti	Malvaceae
Verticillium wilt, various hosts	Verticillium	Deuteromycetes: Moniliales
Wandering Jew	Commelina	Commelinaceae
Warehouse moth	Ephestia elutella	Lepidoptera: Pyralidae
Water duckweed	Pistia stratiotes	Araceae
Water hyacinth	Eichhornia crassipes	Pontederiaceae
Water primroses	Jussiaea	Onagraceae
Water purslane	Ludwigia peploides	Onagraceae
Western balsam bark beetle	Dryocoetes confusus	Coleoptera: Scolytidae

English	Latin	Family and/or Order
Western flower thrips	*Frankliniella occidentalis*	Thysanoptera: Thripidae
Wheat bulb fly	*Delia coarctata*	Diptera: Anthomyiidae
White-backed planthopper	*Sogatella furcifera*	Homoptera: Delphacidae
White blister	*Albugo candida*	Oomycetes: Peronosporales
White grubs	*Hoplochelis marginalis*	
White leaf spot, oilseed rape	*Pseudocercosporella capsellae*	Deuteromycetes: Hyphales
White leaf spot, strawberry	*Mycosphaerella fragariae*	Ascomycetes: Sphaeridales
White mould, mushrooms	*Mycogone perniciosa*	Deuteromycetes: Moniliales
White muscardine	*Beauvaria bassiana*	Deuteromycetes; Moniliales
White mustard	*Sinapis alba*	Cruciferae
White rot, onion	*Sclerotium cepivorum*	Deuteromycetes: Agonomycetales
White rot, timber	*Ganoderma*	Basidiomycetes: Agaricales
Whiteflies	*Bemisia*	Homoptera: Aleyrodidae
Whitefly	*Aleurothrixus floccosus*	Homoptera: Aleyrodidae
Whitefly parasite	*Eretmocerus sp. nr. Californicus*	Hymenoptera: Aphelinidae
Whitefly predatory beetle	*Delphasus pusillus*	Coleoptera: Coccinellidae
Wild fire of tobacco and soybean	*Pseudomonas tabaci*	Pseudomonadales: Pseudomonadaceae
Wild oat	*Avena fatua*	Gramineae
Wild oat, winter	*Avena ludoviciana*	Gramineae
Wild pansies	*Viola*	Violaceae
Wild radish	*Raphanus raphanistrum*	Cruciferae
Wimmera ryegrass	*Lolium rigidum*	Gramineae
Wireworms	*Agriotes*	Coleoptera: Elateridae
Woolly aphid	*Eriosoma lanigerum*	Homoptera: Pemphigidae
Yellow birch	*Betula lutea*	Betulaceae
Yellow cereal fly	*Opomyza florum*	Diptera: Opomyzidae
Yellow fever mosquito	*Aedes aegypti*	Diptera: Culicidae
Yellow nutsedge	*Cyperus esculentus*	Cyperaceae
Yellow rust, cereals	*Puccinia striiformis*	Basidiomycetes: Uredinales
Yellow underwing moth	*Noctua pronuba*	Lepidoptera: Noctuidae
Yew	*Taxus baccata*	Taxaceae

Directory of Companies

Parts of names given in bold represent the short form of the company name which is used in the text of Main Entries.

Abbott Laboratories
Chemical & Agricultural Products Division,
1401 Sheridan Road, North Chicago,
IL 60064, USA
Tel: 1 800 323 9597
Fax: 1 847 937 3679

AgBioChem Inc.
3 Fleetwood Court, Orinda, CA 94563,
USA
Tel: 1 510 254 0789
Fax: 1 916 527 6288

AGC MicroBio Ltd, see MicroBio

Ago Biocontol
Transversal 84A No. 138–95,
or Krr 80A No. 74–93, Bogata, COLOMBIA
Tel: 57 1 68 15134
Fax: 57 1 68 32691

Agralan Ltd
The Old Brickyard,
Ashton Keymes, Swindon,
Wilts SN6 6QR, UK
Tel: 44 1285 860015
Fax: 44 1285 860056

AgraTech Seeds Inc
5559 North 500 West, McCordsville,
IN 46055-9998, USA
Tel: 1 317 335 333
Fax: 1 317 335 9260

AgrEvo, see Hoechst Schering AgrEvo

AgrEvo UK Ltd **Environmental Health**
Hauxton, Cambridge CB2 5HU, UK
Tel: 44 1223 252638
Fax: 44 1223 252639

AgrEvo Environmental Health Inc.
95 Chestnut Ridge Rd., Montvale,
NJ 07645, USA
Tel: 1 201 307 3281
Fax: 1 201 307 3281

AgrEvo USA Co.
Little Falls Centre One, 2711 Centerville Rd.,
Wilmington, DE 19808, USA
Tel: 1 302 892 3000
Fax: 1 302 892 3013

Agrichem BV
4900 AG Oosterhout, NETHERLANDS

Agricultural Sciences Inc.
3601 Garden Brook, Dallas, TX 75234, USA
Tel: 1 972 243 8930
Fax: 1 972 406 1125

Agridyne Technologies Inc., see Thermo
Trilogy

Agrimm Biologicals Ltd
231 Fitzgerald Avenue, PO Box 13-245,
Christchurch, NEW ZEALAND
Tel: 64 03 366 8671
Fax: 64 03 365 1859

Agripro Seeds Inc.
PO Box 2962, 6700 Antioch,
Shawnee Mission, KS 66201-1362, USA
Tel: 1 913 384 4940
Fax: 1 913 384 0208

AgriSense-BCS Ltd
Treforest Industrial Estate,
Pontypridd, CF37 5SU, UK
Tel: 44 1443 841155
Fax: 44 1443 841152

AgriSystems International
125 West Seventh Street, Wind Gap,
PA 18091, USA
Tel: 1 610 863 6700
Fax: 1 610 863 4622

Agro-Kanesho Co. Ltd
Akasaka Shasta-East 7th Fl., 4-2-19 Akasaka,
Minato-Ku, Tokyo, JAPAN
Tel: 81 3 5570 4711
Fax: 81 3 5570 4708

Agropharm Ltd
Buckingham House, Church Road, Penn,
High Wycombe, Bucks, HP10 8LN, UK
Tel: 44 1494 816575
Fax: 44 1494 816578

AGSCI, see Agricultural Sciences Inc.

Agtrol Chemical Products
7322 Southwest Freeway, Suite 1400,
Houston, TX 77074, USA
Tel: 1 713 995 0111
Fax: 1 713 995 9505

AgVenture Inc.
PO Box 29, Kentland, IN 47951-0029, USA
Tel: 1 218 474 5557
Fax: 1 219 474 5533

Aimco Pesticides Ltd
Akhand Jyoti, Blocks 1 & 3, 8th Road,
Santacruz (East), P.O. Box 6822,
Mumbai 400 055, INDIA
Tel: 91 22 618 3042
Fax: 91 22 611 6736

Akzo Nobel B.V., see Nufarm B.V.

American **Cyanamid** Co.
Agricultural Research Division, P.O. Box
400, Princeton, NJ 08543 0400, USA
Tel: 1 609 716 2000

Andermatt Biocontrol AG
Unterdorf, CH-6146 Grossdietwil,
SWITZERLAND
Tel: 41 62 927 2840
Fax: 41 62 927 2123

Applied Bio-Nomics Ltd
11074 W. Saanich Rd, Sidney, BC V8L 5P5,
CANADA
Tel: 1 604 656 2123
Fax: 1 604 656 3844

Applied Chemicals (Thailand) Co. Ltd
1575/15 Phaholyothin Road,
Samsennai Nai Phrayathai, Bangkok 10400,
THAILAND
Tel: 66 2 279 2615
Fax: 66 2 278 1343

Aragonesas Agro, S.A.
Po Recoletos 27, 28004 Madrid, SPAIN
Tel: 34 91 5853800
Fax: 34 91 5852310

Arbico Inc.
P.O. Box 4247, Tucson, AZ 85738-1247,
USA
Tel: 1 520 825 9785
Fax: 1 520 825 2038

Aries Agro-Vet Industries Ltd
Aries House, 24 Deonar, Govandi E,
Mumbai Mah, 400 043, INDIA
Tel: 91 22 556 4052
Fax: 91 22 556 4054

Asahi Chemical Mnfg. Co. Ltd
500 Takayasu, Ikaruga-cho, Ikoma-gun,
Nara Pref., JAPAN
Tel: 81 7457 4 1131
Fax: 81 7457 4 1961

Asgrow Seed Co.
3000 Westown Parkway, West Des Moines,
IA 50266, USA
Tel: 1 515 224 4200 Fax; 1 515 224 4262

Atlantic and Pacific Research Inc.
PO Box 1336, Hendersonville, NC 28793,
USA
Fax: 1 704 693 0071

BASF AG
Postfach 120, D-67114 Limburgerhof,
GERMANY
Tel: 49 621 60 27084
Fax: 49 621 60 27123

Bayer AG
D-51368 Leverkusen, GERMANY
Tel: 49 2173 38 3188
Fax: 49 2173 38 3156

Bayer Corp. Agriculture Div.
8400 Hawthorn Rd., P.O. Box 4913,
Kansas City, MO 64120-0013, USA
Tel: 1 816 242 2000
Fax: 1 816 242 2738

BCP, see Biological Crop Protection

BCS, see Biosystemes France

Becker Microbial Products Inc.
9464 NW 11th St., Plantation, FL 33322,
USA
Tel: 1 954 474 7590
Fax: 1 954 474 2463

Becks Superior **Hybrids** Inc.
6767 East 276 Street, Atlanta, IN 47096,
USA
Tel: 1 317 984 2325
Fax: 1 317 984 3508

Beneficial Insectary
14751 Oak Run Rd., Oak Run, CA 96069,
USA
Tel: 1 916 472 3715
Fax: 1 916 472 3523

Bioagro Ninos Heroes
No. 105, Rio Bravo Tamaulipas, MEXICO
Tel: 52 893 45556

Biobest Ilse Velden
18, B-2260 Westerlo, BELGIUM
Tel: 32 14 231701
Fax: 32 14 231831

Bio Collect
5841 Crittenden St., Oakland, CA 94601,
USA
Tel: 1 510 436 8052
Fax: 1 510 532 0288

Biocontrol Ltd
PO Box 515, Warwick, Queensland 4370,
AUSTRALIA
Tel: 61 76 61 4488
Fax: 61 76 61 7211

Biofac Inc.
PO Box 87, Mathis, TX 78368, USA
Tel: 1 512 547 3259
Fax: 1 512 547 9660

BioLogic
Springtown Rd, PO Box 177, Willow Hill,
PA 17271, USA
Tel: 1 717 349 2789
Fax: 1 717 349 2922

Biological Crop Protection
Occupation Rd., Wye, Ashford,
Kent TN25 5AH, UK
Tel: 44 1233 813240
Fax: 44 1233 813383

Biological Services
PO Box 501, Loxton, South Australia 5333,
AUSTRALIA
Tel: 61 085 846 977
Fax: 61 085 845 057

Bio Protection Pty. Ltd
P.O. Box 35, Warwick, Queensland 4370,
AUSTRALIA
Tel: 61 76 661590
Fax: 61 76 661639

BioSafer
99/220 Tessabansongkraoh Rd., Ladyao,
Jatujak, Bangkok 10900, THAILAND
Tel: 66 2 9543120 6
Fax: 66 2 9543128 (& 5802178)

Biosys, see Thermo Trilogy

Biosystemes France
Parc d'Activites des Bellevues, BP 227,
95614 Cergy-Pontoise CEDEX, FRANCE
Tel: 33 34 48 99 26
Fax: 33 34 48 99 27

Boehringer Inc.
2621 North Belt Highway, St Joseph,
MO 64506-2002, USA
Tel: 1 816 390 0625
Fax: 1 816 390 0451

Brinkman, see Royal Brinkman BV

Buckman Laboratories Inc.
1256 N. McLean Blvd., Memphis, TN 38108,
USA
Tel: 1 901 278 0330
Fax: 1 901 276 5970

Bugs for Bugs
28 Orton St., Mundubbera 4626,
AUSTRALIA
Tel: 61 71 654576
Fax: 61 71 654626

Burlington Bio-Medical & Scientific Corp.
222 Sherwood Avenue, Farmingdale,
NY 11735, USA
Tel: 1 516 694 9000
Fax: 1 516 694 9177

Caffaro S.p.A.
Via Friuli 55, 20031 Cesano Maderno,
Milano, ITALY
Tel: 39 362 51 4266
Fax: 39 362 51 4454

Callahan Seeds
1122 East 169th Street, Westfield,
IN 46074, USA
Tel: 1 317 896 5551
Fax: 1 317 896 9209

Calliope S.A.
Route d'Artix, BP 80, 64150 Nogueres,
FRANCE
Tel: 33 59 60 92 92
Fax: 33 59 60 92 99

Caltec Agri Marketing Services
PO Box 576 155, Modesto, CA 95357, USA
Tel: 1 209 575 1295
Fax: 1 209 575 0366

Campbell Seeds Inc.
1375 North 800 West, Tipton, IN 46072,
USA
Fax: 1 765 963 2047

Cargill Hybrid Seeds
PO Box 5645, Minneapolis,
MN 55440-2399, USA
Tel: 1 612 337 9100
Fax: 1 612 742 7233

CCT Corp.
5115 Avenida Encinas, Suite A, Carlsbad,
CA 92008, USA
Tel: 1 760 929 9228
Fax: 1 760 929 9522

Cequisa Muntaner
322 1°, 08021 Barcelona, SPAIN
Tel: 34 93 200 0322
Fax: 34 93 200 5648

CFPI
28 Boulevard Camelinat, BP 75,
92233 Gennevilliers, FRANCE
Tel: 33 1 40 85 5050
Fax: 33 1 47 92 2545

Chemgro Seeds Co.
PO Box 218, East Petersburg, PA 17520,
USA
Tel: 1 717 569 3296
Fax: 1 717 560 0117

Cheminova Agro A/S
PO Box 9, 7620 Lemvig, DENMARK
Tel: 45 97 83 4100
Fax: 45 97 83 4555

ChemTica Internacional Apdo.
159-2150 San Jose, COSTA RICA
Tel: 506 261 2424
Fax: 506 261 5397

Ciba Bunting, see Novartis BCM

Ciba-Geigy, see Novartis

Ciech SA Agro-Sulphur Group
PO Box 271, Powazkowska St. 46/50,
00-950 Warsaw, POLAND
Tel: 48 22 639 1580
Fax: 48 22 639 1598

Coated Seed Ltd
2a O'Briens Road, Sockburn, Christchurch,
NEW ZEALAND

Consep Inc.
213 SW Columbia Street, Bend, OR 97703,
USA
Tel: 1 503 388 3688
Fax: 1 503 388 3705

Countrymark Cooperative Inc.
PO Box 2500, Bloomington, IL 61702-2500,
USA
Tel: 1 309 557 6399
Fax: 1 309 557 6860

Crop Genetics International, see Thermo
Trilogy

Croplan Genetics
PO Box 64089, MS 690 St Paul,
MN 55164-0089, USA
Tel: 1 612 451 5458

Cyanamid, see American Cyanamid

Cyclo International S. A. de C. V.
Calle Laurel, Rosarita #10, Baja California,
MEXICO 22710
Tel: 52 66 123 209
Fax: 52 66 121 976

Dainippon Ink & Chemicals Inc.
7-20 Nihonbashi 3-chome, Chuo-ku,
Tokyo 103, JAPAN
Tel: 81 3 3272 4511
Fax: 81 3 3281 8589

Dairyland Seed Co. Inc.
PO Box 958, West Bend, WI 53095-0958,
USA
Fax: 1 414 626 2281

Defensa S.A.
Industria de Defensivos Agricolas S,
Rua Padra Chagas, 79 - 7th Fl.,
90570-080 Porto Alegre RS, BRAZIL
Tel: 55 51 346 2121
Fax: 55 51 346 1844

DEKALB Genetics Corp.
3100 Sycamore Road, Dekalb, IL 60115,
USA
Tel: 1 815 758 9273
Fax: 1 815 756 2672

Delicia GmbH
Delitzsch Duebener Str. 137,
04509 Delitzsch, GERMANY
Tel: 49 34202 65 300
Fax: 49 34202 65 309

Deltapine Seed
Box 157, Scott, MS 38732, USA
Tel: 1 601 742 4000
Fax: 1 601 742 4055

Dow AgroSciences
9330 Zionsville Rd., Indianapolis,
IN 46268-1054, USA
Tel: 1 317 337 4974
Fax: 1 317 337 7344

DowElanco, see Dow AgroSciences

Dunhill Chemical Co
3026 Muscatel Avenue, Rosmead,
CA 91770, USA
Tel: 1 818 288 1271
Fax: 1 818 288 3930

Du Pont, see E. I. du Pont de Nemours

Ecogen Inc.
2005 Cabot Boulevard West,
P.O. Box 3023, Langhorne, PA 19047-1810,
USA
Tel: 1 215 757 1590
Fax: 1 215 757 2956

EcoScience Corp.
10 Alvin Court, East Brunswick, NJ 08816,
USA

E. I. **du Pont** de Nemours
Du Pont Agricultural Products, Walker's Mill,
Barley Mill Plaza, Wilmington, DE 19880,
USA
Tel: 1 800 441 7515
Fax: 1 302 992 6470

Eikou Kasei Co., Ltd
Agrochemicals Division,
Violet Akihabara Bldg.,
18-1 Kanda Matsunaga-cho, Chiyoda-ku,
Tokyo 101, JAPAN
Tel: 81 3 5256 3861/2
Fax: 81 3 5256 3864

e-nema GmbH
Klausdorfer Str., 28–36, 24223 Raisdorf,
GERMANY
Tel: 49 4307 838813
Fax: 49 4307 838314

English Woodlands Biocontrol
Hoyle Depot, Graffham, Petworth,
West Sussex, GU28 0LR, UK
Tel: 44 1798 867574
Fax: 44 1798 867574

Fargro Ltd
Toddington Lane, Littlehampton,
West Sussex, BN17 7PP, UK
Tel: 44 1903 721591
Fax: 44 1903 730737

Reference

Farmers Cooperative Co.
PO Box 208, 109 Railroad Street, Bayard,
IA 50029, USA
Tel: 1 712 651 2091

Fine Agrochemicals Ltd
3 The Bull Ring, Worcester, WR2 5AA, UK
Tel: 44 1905 748444
Fax: 44 1905 748440

FMC Corp.
Agricultural Products Group,
1735 Market St., Philadelphia, PA 19103,
USA
Tel: 1 215 299 6661
Fax: 1 215 299 6256

Fortune Bio-Tech Ltd
14 Ishaq Colony, 1208 Bazar Road,
Secunderabad 500 015, INDIA
Tel: 91 40 841 519
Fax: 91 40 843 945

Forward International Ltd
PO Box 81-249, 5/F No. 112,
Tun Hua Road, Tiapei, TAIWAN
Tel: 886 2 545 1592
Fax: 886 2 718 2614 (& 2094)

Fujisawa Pharmaceutical Chemicals Group
3-4-6 Nihonbashi Honcho, Chuo-ku,
Tokyo 103, JAPAN
Tel: 81 3 3279 0882
Fax: 81 3 3241 5805

Garst Seed Co.
PO Box 300, Coon Rapids, IA 50058, USA
Tel: 1 712 684 3243
Fax: 1 712 684 3300

Gharda Chemicals Ltd
B-27-29, MIDC, Dombivli (E), 421 203,
Dist. Thane, INDIA
Tel: 91 251 471215
Fax: 91 251 472777

Gist-Brocades B.V.
Wateringseweg 1, Postbus 1,
2600 MA Delft, NETHERLANDS
Tel: 31 15 2799111
Fax: 31 15 2793200

Golden Harvest Seeds Inc.
220 Eldorado Road, Suite E, Bloomington,
IL 61704-3544, USA
Tel: 1 309 664 0558
Fax: 1 309 664 0984

Grace, see Thermo Trilogy

Greenfire Inc.
347 Nord Avenue #1, Chico, CA 95926,
USA
Tel: 1 916 895 8301
Fax: 1 916 895 8317

Griffin Corp.
P.O. Box 1847, Rocky Ford Road, Valdosta,
GA 31603, USA
Tel: 1 912 249 5203
Fax: 1 912 244 5978

Growmark Inc.
PO Box 2500, Bloomington, IL 61702-2500,
USA
Tel: 1 309 557 6399
Fax: 1 309 557 6860

Gustafson Inc.
P.O. Box 660065, Dallas, TX 75266-0065,
USA
Tel: 1 214 985 8877
Fax: 1 214 867 0816

Gutwein Seeds
RR 1 Box 40, Francesville, IN 47945, USA
Tel: 1 219 567 9141
Fax: 1 219 567 2645

Hawkesbury Integrated Pest Management
Service
PO Box 436, Richmond, NSW 2753,
AUSTRALIA
Tel: 61 45 701331
Fax: 61 45 701314

Hercon Environmental Corp.
PO Box 467, Aberdeen Road, Emigsville,
PA 17318-0467, USA
Tel: 1 717 764 1191
Fax: 1 717 767 1016

Hodogaya Chemical Co., Ltd
66-2 Horikawa-cho, Saiwai-ku, Kawasaki,
Kanagawa 210, JAPAN
Tel: 81 44 549 6600
Fax: 81 44 549 6630

Hoechst Schering **AgrEvo** GmbH
D-65926, Frankfurt am Main, GERMANY
Tel: 49 69 305 2735
Fax: 49 69 395 16352

Hoegemeyer Hybrids
1755 Hoegemeyer Road, Hooper,
NE 68031, USA
Tel: 1 402 654 3399
Fax: 1 402 654 3342

Hoffman Seeds Inc.
144 Main Street, Landisville, PA 17538-1297,
USA
Tel: 1 717 898 2261
Fax: 1 717 898 9458

Hokko Chemical Industry Co. Ltd
Central Research Laboratories, 2165 Toda,
Atsugi, Kanagawa 243, JAPAN
Tel: 81 462 28 5881
Fax: 81 462 28 0164

Hortichem Ltd
14 Edison Rd., Churchfields Industrial Estate,
Salisbury, Wilts, SP2 7NU, UK
Tel: 44 1722 320133
Fax: 44 1722 326799

Hubei **Sanonda** Co. Ltd
1 East Beijing Road, Shashi, Hubei 434001,
CHINA
Tel: 86 716 8316975
Fax: 86 716 8315265

Hydro-Gardens Inc.
PO Box 25845, Colorado Springs,
CO 80936, USA
Tel: 1 719 495 2266

Integrated Pest Management p/l, see Bugs
for Bugs

International Institute of Biological Control
(IIBC)
Silwood Park, Ascot, Berks, SL5 7PY, UK
Tel: 44 1344 872999
Fax: 44 1344 872901

International Specialty Products
1361 Alps Road, Wayne, NJ 07470, USA
Tel: 1 201 628 4000
Fax: 1 201 628 4117

Interstate Seed Co.
PO Box 338, West Fargo, ND 58078, USA
Tel: 1 701 282 7338
Fax: 1 701 282 8218

Intrachem (International) S.A.
34 Quai de Cologny, Cologny,
CH-1223 Geneva, SWITZERLAND
Tel: 41 22 736 78 87
Fax: 41 22 736 24 10

IPM Laboratories Inc.
Main St, Locke, NY 13092-0300, USA
Tel: 1 315 497 2063
Fax: 1 315 497 3129

IPM Technologies Inc.
4134 North Vancouver Avenue, Suite 305,
Portland, OR 97217, USA
Tel: 1 503 288 2493
Fax: 1 503 288 1887

Isagro S.p.A.
Centro Direzionale Milano Oltre,
Palazzo Raffaello, Via Cassanese, 224,
20090 Milano, ITALY
Tel: 39 2 26996 425
Fax: 39 2 26996 287

Ishihara Sangyo Kaisha, Ltd
3-1, Nishi-Shibukawa 2-chome, Kusatsu,
Shiga 525, JAPAN
Tel: 81 775 62 8338
Fax: 81 775 62 9506

Japan Tobacco Inc.
Agribusiness Division,
4-12-62 Higashi-Shinagawa, Shinagawa-ku,
Tokyo 140, JAPAN
Tel: 81 3 3474 3111
Fax: 81 3 5479 0360

Reference

J. J. **Mauget** Co.
2810 North Figueroa St., Los Angeles,
CA 90065, USA

Kaken Pharmaceutical Co. Ltd
4-18-4 Nihonbashi-honcho, Chuo-ku,
Tokyo 103, JAPAN
Tel: 81 3 3231 1223
Fax: 81 3 3270 5360

Kemira Agro Oy
P.O. Box 330, FIN-00101 Helsinki 10,
FINLAND
Tel: 358 9 132 1564
Fax: 358 9 132 1384

Koppert BV
Veilingweg 17, PO Box 155,
2650 AD Berkel en Rodenrijs,
NETHERLANDS
Tel: 31 10 5140444
Fax: 31 10 5115203

Krishi Rasayan (Bihar)
FMC Fortuna, Block No. A11, 4th Fl.,
234/3A Acharya Jagadish Chandra Bose Rd.,
Calcutta 700 020, INDIA
Tel: 91 33 247 5719/37
Fax: 91 33 247 1436

Kubota Corp.
1-2-47 Shikitsuhigashi, Naniwa-ku,
Osaka 556-91, JAPAN
Tel: 81 6 648 2111
Fax: 81 6 648 3826

Kumiai Chemical Industry Co. Ltd
4-26 Ikenohata 1-chome, Taitoh-ku,
Tokyo 110, JAPAN
Tel: 81 3 3822 5165
Fax: 81 3 3822 5005

Kunafin
Route 1, Box 39, Quemado, TX 78877,
USA
Tel: 1 800 832 1113
Fax: 1 512 757 1468

Kureha Chemical Industry Co. Ltd
Nishiki Research Laboratories, 16 Ochiai,
Nishiki, Iwaki 974, JAPAN
Tel: 81 246 63 5111
Fax: 81 246 63 7356

Ladda Co. Ltd
GPO Box 2562,
99/220 Tessabarnsongkroah Road, Ladyao,
Jatujak, Bangkok 10900, THAILAND
Tel: 66 2 954 3120 6
Fax: 66 2 580 2178 (& 954 3128)

Latham Seeds
131 180th Street, Alexander, IA 50420, USA
Tel: 1 515 692 3258
Fax: 1 515 692 3250

M&R Durango Inc.
PO Box 886, Bayfield, CO 81122, USA
Tel: 1 303 259 3521
Fax: 1 303 259 3857

Makhteshim-Agan, see Makhteshim

Makhteshim Chemical Works Ltd
P.O. Box 60, 84100 Beer-Sheva, ISRAEL
Tel: 972 7 6296611
Fax: 972 7 6280304

Mauget, see J. J. Mauget

McLaughlin Gormley King Co.
8810 Tenth Avenue North, Minneapolis,
MN 55427, USA
Tel: 1 612 544 0341
Fax: 1 612 544 6437

Meiji Seika Kaisha Ltd
Agrochemical Department, 2-4-16 Kyobashi,
2-chome, Chuo-ku, Tokyo 104, JAPAN
Tel: 81 3 3272 6511
Fax: 81 3 3281 4058

Merck & Co., Inc., see Novartis

Merschman Seeds
103 Avenue D, West Point, IA 52656, USA
Tel: 1 319 837 6111
Fax: 1 319 837 6104

MicroBio Ltd
Dales Manor Business Park, Babraham Road,
Sawston, Cambridge, CB2 4LJ, UK
Tel: 44 1223 8308608
Fax: 44 1223 830861

Midwest Seed Genetics
PO Box 518, Carroll, IA 51401, USA
Tel: 1 712 792 6691
Fax: 1 712 792 6725

Mitsubishi Chemical Corp.
Mitsubishi Building, 5-2 Marunouchi 2-
chome, Chiyoda-ku, Tokyo 100, JAPAN

MGK, see McLaughlin Gormley King Co.

Monsanto Co.
Crop Protection, 800 N. Lindbergh Blvd.,
St. Louis, MO 63167, USA
Tel: 1 314 694 3540
Fax: 1 314 694 2306

Monterey Chemical Company
PO Box 5317, Fresno, CA 93755, USA
Tel: 1 209 499 2100
Fax: 1 209 499 1015

Mycogen Crop Protection
5501 Oberlin Drive, San Diego, CA 92121,
USA
Tel: 1 619 453 8030
Fax: 1 619 453 9089

Mycogen Seeds
1340 Corporate Center Curve, St Paul,
MN 55121-1428, USA
Tel: 1 612 405 5954
Fax: 1 612 405 5957

Mycotech Corp.
630 Utah Avenue, Butte, MT 59701, USA
Tel: 1 406 782 2386

Nagarjuna Agrichem Ltd
Auto Plaza, First floor, Road No. 3,
Banjara Hills, Hyderabad 500 034, INDIA
Tel: 91 40 318217
Fax: 91 40 319234

Natural Plant Protection, see NPP

NatureMark Potatoes
300 East Mallard Drive, Suite 220, Boise,
ID 83706, USA
Tel: 1 208 389 2236
Fax: 1 208 309 2280

Nature's Alternative Insectary Ltd
Box 19, Dawson Rd., Nanoose Bay,
BC V0R 2R0, CANADA
Tel: 1 604 468 7912
Fax: 1 604 468 7912

NC+ Hybrids
PO Box 4408, Lincoln, NE 68504, USA
Tel: 1 402 467 2517
Fax: 1 402 467 4217

Neudorff, see W. Neudorff

Nicobrand, see The Nicobrand Company

Nihon Nohyaku Co. Ltd
8th Floor Eitaro Building,
2-5 Nihonbashi, 1-chome, Chuo-ku, Tokyo
103, JAPAN
Tel: 81 3 3278 0461
Fax: 81 3 3281 2443

Nippon Kayaku Co. Ltd
Agrochemicals Division, 11-2 Fujimi 1-
chome, Chiyoda-ku, Tokyo, JAPAN
Tel: 81 3 3237 5221
Fax: 81 3 3237 5089

Nippon Soda Co. Ltd
Agrochemicals Division, 2-1 Ohtemachi,
2-chome, Chiyoda-ku, Tokyo 100, JAPAN
Tel: 81 3 3245 6266
Fax: 81 3 3245 6289

Nissan Chemical Industries Ltd
Kowa-Hitotsubashi Building, 7-1, 3-chome,
Kanda-nishiki-cho, Chiyoda-ku, Tokyo 101,
JAPAN
Tel: 81 3 3296 8151
Fax: 81 3 3296 8016

NOR-AM, see AgrEvo USA

Novartis BCM
Aldham Business Centre, New Road,
Aldham, Colchester, CO6 3PN, UK
Tel: 44 1206 243200
Fax: 44 1206 243209

Novartis Crop Protection AG
CH-4002, Basel, SWITZERLAND
Tel: 41 61 697 1111
Fax: 41 61 324 8001

Novartis Seeds Inc.
7500 Olson Memorial Highway,
Golden Valley, MN 55427, USA
Tel: 1 612 593 7189
Fax: 1 612 593 7203

NPP
Route d'Artix, B.P. 80, 64150 Nogueres,
FRANCE
Tel: 33 559 60 92 92
Fax: 33 559 60 92 19

Nufarm B.V.
Welplaatweg 12, Rotterdam Botlek 3197,
NETHERLANDS
Tel: 31 10 438 9545
Fax: 31 10 472 2826

Nufarm Ltd
102-105 Pipe Rd., Laverton North,
Victoria 3026, AUSTRALIA
Tel: 61 39 282 1000
Fax: 61 39 282 1001

Pacific Biocontrol Corp.
400 E. Evergreen Blvd., #306, Vancouver,
WA 98660, USA
Tel: 1 206 693 2866
Fax: 1 206 693 3088

Patriot Seeds Inc.
208 South Worrell, PO Box 97, Bowen,
IL 62316-0097, USA
Fax: 1 217 842 5209

Paushak Ltd
Alembic Road, Baroda 390 003, Gujarat,
INDIA
Tel: 91 265 380 371
Fax: 91 265 380 371

Paymaster Cottonseed
1301 East 50th Street, Lubbock, TX 79404,
USA
Tel: 1 806 740 1600
Fax: 1 870 673 6319

Perifleur Products Ltd
Hangleton Lane, Ferring, Worthing,
West Sussex, BN12 6PP, UK

PGS, see Plant Genetic Systems

Pioneer Hi-Bred International Inc.
7100 NW 62nd Avenue, PO Box 1150,
Johnston, IA 50131, USA
Tel: 1 515 334 6908
Fax: 1 515 334 6886

Plant Genetic Systems
Josef Plateaustraat 22, B-9000 Ghent,
BELGIUM
Tel: 32 9 235 8411
Fax: 32 9 224 0694

Plant Health Technologies
PO Box 15057, Boise, ID 83715, USA
Tel: 1 208 345 1021
Fax: 1 208 345 1032

Point Enterprises
P O Box 48, 12 rue des Marchandises,
CH-1260 Nyon, SWITZERLAND
Tel: 41 22 362 5535
Fax: 41 22 362 5557

Praxis
2723 116th Avenue, Allegan, MI 49010,
USA
Tel: 1 616 673 2793
Fax: 1 616 673 2793

Prentiss Inc.
21 Vernon St. CB 2000, Floral Park,
NY 11001, USA
Tel: 1 516 326 1919
Fax: 1 516 326 2312

Productos OSA
Avenida de Mayo 1161 - 1° Piso,
1085 Buenos Aires, ARGENTINA
Tel: 54 1 325 6481
Fax: 54 1 383 8139

Pyrethrum Board of Kenya
P.O. Box 591, Nakuru, KENYA
Tel: 254 9037211 567
Fax: 254 903745 274

Rallis India Ltd
Agrochemical Res. Station,
21/22 Peenya Industrial Area, P.O. Box
5813, Bangalore 560 058, Karnataka, INDIA
Tel: 91 80 8394959
Fax: 91 80 8394015

Remeslo ssro
Tylisovska 1/722, Prague 6, 16000,
CZECH REPUBLIC

Rhône-Poulenc
Secteur Agro, 14/20 Rue Pierre Baizet,
B.P. 9163, F-69263 Lyon Cedex 09,
FRANCE
Tel: 33 472 29 25 25
Fax: 33 472 29 27 99

Rincon-Vitova Insectaries Inc.
P.O. Box 1555, Ventura, CA 93002, USA
Tel: 1 805 643 5407
Fax: 1 805 643 6267

Rohm & Haas Co.
100 Independence Mall West, Philadelphia,
PA 19106, USA
Tel: 1 215 592 3000
Fax: 1 215 592 2797

Rotam Group
7/F Cheung Tat Centre,
18 Cheung Lee Street, Chai Wan,
HONG KONG
Tel: 852 2896 5608
Fax: 852 2558 6577

Royal **Brinkman** BV
PO Box 2, 2690 AA 's-Gravenzande,
NETHERLANDS
Tel: 31 174 411 333
Fax: 31 174 414 301

Rupp Seeds Inc.
17919 County Road B, Wauseon,
OH 43567, USA
Tel: 1 419 337 1841

Russell Fine Chemicals Ltd
111 Garden Lane, Chester, CH1 4EY, UK
Tel: 44 1244 371 821
Fax: 44 1244 372 048

Sandoz Agro Ltd, see Novartis

Sands of Iowa
PO Box 468, Marcus, IA 51035-0648, USA
Tel: 1 712 376 4135
Fax: 1 712 376 4140

Sanex Inc.
5300 Harvester Rd., Burlington,
Ontario, L7L 5N5, CANADA
Tel: 1 905 639 7535
Fax: 1 905 639 3488

Sankyo Co. Ltd
Agrochemicals Division, 7-12 Ginza 2-
chome, Chuo-ku, Tokyo 104, JAPAN
Tel: 81 3 3562 7524
Fax: 81 3 3562 7525

Sanonda, see Hubei Sanonda

Sautter & Stepper GmbH
Rosenstr. 19, D-72119 Ammerbuch 5,
Altingen, GERMANY
Tel: 49 7032 75501
Fax: 49 7032 74199

Scentry Inc., see Ecogen Inc.

Scotts Quality Seeds
1701 North Broadway, Mt. Pleasant,
IA 52641-0110, USA
Tel: 1 319 385 8518

Searle (India) Ltd
21 D. Sukhadvala Marg, P.O. Box 233,
Mubai 400 001, INDIA
Tel: 91 22 207 7731
Fax: 91 22 207 7009

SEDQ, see Sociedad Espanola de
Desarrolos Quimicos, S.A.

Shin-Etsu Chemical Co. Ltd
Fine Chemicals Dept., 2-6-1 Ohtemachi,
Chiyoda-ku, Tokyo 100, JAPAN
Tel: 81 3 3246 5280
Fax: 81 3 3246 5371

Reference

Siebens Hybrids Inc.
633 North College Avenue, Geneseo, IL
61254, USA
Tel: 1 309 944 5131
Fax: 1 309 944 6090

Sociedad Espanola de Desarrolos Quimicos
S.A. (**SEDQ**)
Avda. Diagonal 352 entlo, 08013 Barcelona,
SPAIN
Tel: 34 93 458 85 00
Fax: 34 93 458 40 07

Soil Technologies Corp.
2103 185th Street, Fairfield, IA 52556, USA
Tel: 1 515 472 3963
Fax: 1 515 472 6189

Source Technology Biologicals Inc.
3355 Hiawatha Ave., Suite 222, Minneapolis,
MN 55406, USA
Tel: 1 612 724 7102
Fax: 1 612 724 1642

Stine Microbial Products and Stine Seed
2225 Laredo Trail, Adel, IA 50003, USA
Fax: 1 515 677 2716

Stoneville Pedigreed Seed Co.
6625 Lennox Park Drive, Suite 117,
Memphis, TN 38115, USA
Tel: 1 901 375 5800
Fax: 1 901 375 5860

Sumitomo Chemical Company Ltd
5-33 Kitahama 4-chome, Chuo-ku,
Osaka 541, JAPAN
Tel: 81 6 220 3683
Fax: 81 6 220 3342

Svenska Predator AB
Box 14017, 250 14 Helsingborg, SWEDEN
Tel: 46 42 20 11 30
Fax: 46 42 20 09 05

Synexus
Avenue deTervuren 270 272, 1150 Brussels,
BELGIUM
Tel: 32 2 776 4111
Fax: 32 2 776 4385

Takeda Chemical Industries Ltd
Agro Company, 12-10 Nihonbashi 2-chome,
Chuo-ku, Tokyo 103, JAPAN
Tel: 81 3 3278 2111
Fax: 81 3 3278 2000

Tecomag Srl
via Quattro Passi 108,
41043 Formigine (Modena), ITALY
Tel: 39 59 57 37 45
Fax: 39 59 57 21 70

Terra Industries Inc.
PO Box 6000, Sioux City, IA 51102-6000,
USA
Tel: 1 712 277 1340
Fax: 1 712 233 3648

The **Nicobrand** Company
189 Castleroe Rd., Coleraine,
Northern Ireland, BT51 3RP, UK
Tel: 44 1265 868733
Fax: 44 1265 868735

Thermo Trilogy Corp.
7500 Grace Dr., Columbia, MD 21044, USA
Tel: 1 410 531 4711
Fax: 1 410 531 4780

Tide International Co. Ltd
486-26 Jian Guo Bei Road, Hangzhou,
CHINA 310004
Tel: 86 571 5181421
Fax: 86 571 5181422

Tifa (C.I.) Ltd
Tifa Square, Millington, NJ 07946, USA
Tel: 1 908 647 2517
Fax: 1 908 647 7338

Tomono Agrica Co., Ltd
2-12-25 Kasuga, Shizuoka City 420, JAPAN
Tel: 81 54 254 6261
Fax: 81 54 254 6263

Trece Inc.
PO Box 6278, 1143 Madison Lane, Salinas,
CA 93912, USA
Tel: 1 408 758 0204
Fax: 1 408 758 2625

Trisler Seed Farms Inc.
3274 East 800 North Road, Fairmont,
IL 61841-6139, USA
Tel: 1 217 288 9301
Fax: 1 217 288 9301

Troy Biosciences Inc.
2620 N. 37th Drive, Phoenix, AZ 85009,
USA
Tel: 1 602 233 9047
Fax: 1 602 254 7989

T Stanes & Co. Ltd
8/23-24 Race Course Road, PO Box 3709,
Coimbatore 641 018, INDIA
Tel: 91 422 211 514
Fax: 91 422 217 857

Ube Industries Ltd
Ube Research Laboratory, 1978-5 Kogushi,
Ube City, Yamaguchi Pref 755, JAPAN
Tel: 81 836 31 6438
Fax: 81 836 31 6282

Uniroyal Chemical Ltd
Benson Road, Middlebury, CT 06749, USA
Tel: 1 203 573 2000
Fax: 1 203 573 3394

United Phosphorus Ltd
Readymoney Terrace, 167 Dr. Annie Besant
Rd., Worli, Bombay Maharashtra 400 018,
INDIA
Tel: 91 22 493 0681/49
Fax: 91 22 493 7331

Vietnam Pesticide Co.
102 Nguyen Dinh Chieu Street, District 1,
Ho Chi Minh City, VIETNAM
Tel: 84 8 8230751
Fax: 84 8 8230752

Vitax Ltd
Owen St, Coalville, Leics, LE6 2DE, UK
Tel: 44 1530 510060
Fax: 44 1530 510299

Wilbur-Ellis Co.
191 West Shaw Avenue, Suite 107, Fresno,
CA 93704-2876, USA
Tel: 1 209 226 1934
Fax: 1 209 226 7630

Wilson Seeds Inc.
PO Box 391, Harlan, IA 51537, USA
Tel: 1 712 755 3841
Fax: 1 712 755 5261

W. **Neudorff** GmbH
KG Abt. Nutzorgardsmen, An der Muhle 3,
Postfach 1209, D-31857 Emmerthal,
GERMANY
Tel: 49 5155 62460
Fax: 49 5155 62457

Zeneca Agrochemicals
Fernhurst, Haslemere, Surrey, GU27 3JE,
UK
Tel: 44 1428 644061
Fax: 44 1428 652922

Abbreviations and Codes

Throughout the Main Entries of *The BioPesticide Manual* many standard abbreviations and codes have been used. For those unfamiliar with these abbreviations and codes, they are listed in the following pages under three headings:

1. GCPF (Global Crop Protection Federation) (formerly GIFAP) formulation codes
2. WHO (World Health Organisation) and EPA (Environmental Protection Agency) Toxicity Classification
3. General abbreviations

1. GCPF (formerly GIFAP) formulation codes

The following standard codes are used. For further details, see *Catalogue of Pesticide Formulation Types and International Coding System,* Technical Monograph No. 2, February 1989, ref. MT02E, (and addendum dated 20 November 1994), GCPF, Brussels.

CODE	TERM	CODE	TERM
AB	Grain bait	FS	Flowable concentrate for seed treatment
AE	Aerosol dispenser		
AI	Active ingredient	FT	Smoke tablet
AL	Other liquids to be applied undiluted	FU	Smoke generator
		FW	Smoke pellet
AP	Other powder	GA	Gas
BB	Block bait	GB	Granular bait
BR	Briquette	GE	Gas generating product
CB	Bait concentrate	GC	Macrogranule
CG	Encapsulated granule	GL	Emulsifiable gel
CS	Capsule suspension	GP	Flo-dust
DC	Dispersible concentrate	GR	Granule
DP	Dispersible powder	GS	Grease
DS	Powder for dry seed treatment	GW	Water soluble gel
EC	Emulsifiable concentrate	HN	Hot fogging concentrate
ED	Electrochargeable liquid	KK	Combi-pack solid/liquid
EG*	Emulsifiable granule	KL	Combi-pack liquid/liquid
EO	Emulsion, water in oil	KN	Cold fogging concentrate
ES	Emulsion for seed treatment	KP	Combi-pack solid/solid
EW	Emulsion, oil in water	LA	Lacquer
FD	Smoke tin	LS	Solution for seed treatment
FG	Fine granule	MG	Microgranule
FK	Smoke candle	OF	Oil miscible flowable concentrate (oil miscible suspension)
FP	Smoke cartridge		
FR	Smoke rodlet	OL	Oil miscible liquid

CODE	TERM	CODE	TERM
OP	Oil dispersible powder	SS	Water soluble powder for seed treatment
PA	Paste		
PB	Plate bait	SU	Ultra-low volume (ULV) suspension
PC	Gel or paste concentrate	TB	Tablet
PO	Pour-on	TC	Technical material
PR	Plant rodlet	TK	Technical concentrate
PS	Seed coated with a pesticide	TP	Tracking powder
RB	Bait (ready for use)	UL	Ultra-low volume (ULV) liquid
SA	Spot-on	VP	Vapour releasing product
SB	Scrap bait	WG	Water dispersible granules
SC	Suspension concentrate (= flowable concentrate)	WP	Wettable powder
		WS	Water dispersible powder for slurry treatment
SE	Suspo-emulsion	XX	Others
SG	Water soluble granules		
SL	Soluble concentrate		
SO	Spreading oil		
SP	Water soluble powder		* Proposed code, not adopted by GCPF.

2. WHO and EPA Toxicity Classification

WHO toxicity classification

The World Health Organisation classification for estimating the acute toxicity of pesticides.

		LD_{50} for the rat (mg/kg b.w.)			
	Class	Oral		Dermal	
		Solids	Liquids	Solids	Liquids
Extremely hazardous	Ia	≤5	≤20	≤10	≤40
Highly hazardous	Ib	5–50	20–200	10–100	40–400
Moderately hazardous	II	50–500	200–2000	100–1000	400–4000
Slightly hazardous	III	≥501	≥2001	≥1001	≥4001
Product unlikely to present acute hazard in normal use	Table 5	≥2000	≥3000	–	–
Not classified; believed obsolete	Table 6				
Fumigants not classified under WHO	Table 7				

EPA toxicity classification

Class	Acute toxicity to rat			Eye effects	Skin effects
	Oral LD$_{50}$ (mg/kg)	Dermal LD$_{50}$ (mg/kg)	Inhalation LC$_{50}$ (mg/l)		
I	≤50	≤200	≤0.2	Corrosive; corneal opacity not reversible within 7 days.	Corrosive
II	50–500	200–2000	0.2–2.0	Corneal opacity reversible within 7 days; irritation persisting for 7 days.	Severe Irritation at 72 hours.
III	500–5000	2000–20 000	2.0–20	No corneal opacity; irritation reversible within 7 days.	Moderate irritation at 72 hours.
IV	≥5000	≥20 000	≥20	No irritation.	Mild or slight irritation at 72 hours.

3. General abbreviations

The following abbreviations have been used, some being SI units

a	acre
ACS	American Chemical Society
ADI	acceptable daily intake
a.e.	acid equivalent (active ingredient expressed in terms of parent acid)
AG	Aktiengesellschaft (Company)
a.i.	active ingredient
ALC_{50}	approximate concentration required to kill 50% of test organisms
als	acetolactate synthase
ANPP	Association Nationale pour la Protection des Plantes
ANSI	American National Standards Institute
AOAC	Association of Official Analytical Chemists
AOAC Methods	Official Methods of Analysis of The Association of Official Analytical Chemists
BAN	British Approved Name (by British Pharmacopoeia Commission)
BBA	Biologische Bundesanstalt Abteilung
BCPC	British Crop Protection Council
BIOS	British Intelligence Objective Sub-Committee
BS	British Standard
BSI	British Standards Institution
B.V.	Beperkt Vennootschap (Limited)
b.w.	body weight
c.	circa (about)
C.A.	Chemical Abstracts
CAS RN	Chemical Abstracts Services Registry Number
CBI	carotenoid biosynthesis inhibitor
cf	compare
cfu	colony forming units
CIPAC	Collaborative International Pesticides Analytical Council Limited
Co.	Company
COLUMA	Comite de Lutte Contre les Mauvaises Herbes
concn.	concentration
Corp.	Corporation
d	day(s)
DT_{50}	time for 50% loss; half-life
EC_{50}	median effective concentration
ed.	editor
Ed.	edition
e.g.	for example
E-ISO	ISO name (English spelling)

EPA	Environmental Protection Agency (of USA)
EPPO	European and Mediterranean Plant Protection Organisation
ESA	Entomological Society of America
est.	estimated
et al.	and others (authors)
EU	European Union
EWRC	European Weed Research Council (pre-1975)
EWRS	European Weed Research Society (since 1975)
FAO	Food and Agricultural Organisation (of the United Nations)
F-ISO	ISO name (French spelling)
GABA	γ-aminobutyric acid
g	gram (hence also ng, mg, mg, kg, *etc.*)
gc	gas chromatography
gc-ms	combined gas chromatography-mass spectrometry
GCPF	Global Crop Protection Federation (formerly GIFAP)
GIFAP	Groupement International des Associations Nationales de Fabricants de Products Agrochimiques (now known as GCPF)
glc	gas-liquid chromatography
GV	granulovirus (formerly granulosis virus)
h	hour(s)
ha	hectare(s) (10^4 m^2)
hl	hectalitre (100 l)
HMSO	Her Majesty's Stationary Office (UK)
hplc	high performance liquid chromatography
IARC	International Agency for Research on Cancer
ibid.	in the journal last mentioned
ICM	integrated crop management
idem	by the author(s) last mentioned
i.e.	that is
Inc.	Incorporated
INRA	Institut National de la Recherche Agronomique
IOBC	International Organisation for Biological Control
i.p.	intraperitoneal
IPM	integrated pest management
i.r.	infrared
ISO	International Organisation for Standardisation
i.u.	international unit (measure of activity of micro-organisms)
i.v.	intravenous
IUPAC	International Union of Pure and Applied Chemistry
JMAF	Japanese Ministry for Agriculture, Forestry and Fisheries (*formerly* Japanese Ministry for Agriculture and Forestry)
JMPR	Joint meeting of the FAO Panel of Experts on Pesticide Residues and the Environment and the WHO Expert Group on Pesticide Residues

j.v.	joint venture
k	kilo, multiplier (1000) for SI units
kg	kilogram(s)
l	litre (hence also ml, etc.)
lb/a	pounds per acre
lc	liquid chromatography
LC_{50}	concentration required to kill 50% of test organisms
LD_{50}	dose required to kill 50% of test organisms
LOEC	lowest observed effect concentration
Ltd	Limited
m	metre (hence also nm, mm, etc.)
m	milli, multiplier (10^{-3}) for SI units
M	mega, multiplier (10^6) for SI units
MAFF	Ministry of Agriculture Fisheries and Food (England and Wales)
mg	milligram(s), (0.001 g)
mm	millimetre(s), (0.001 m)
m/m	proportion by mass
m.p.	melting point
n	nano, multiplier (10^{-9}) for SI units
N	Newtons (hence also mN, etc.)
ng	nanogram, (10^{-9} g)
nm	nanometre, (10^{-9} m)
mmr	nuclear magnetic resonance
NOAEL	no observed adverse effect level
NOEL	no observed effect level
nPa	nanopascal, (10^{-9} Pa)
NPV	nucleopolyhedrovirus (formerly nuclear polyhedrosis virus)
NRDC	National Research and Development Corporation (former, of UK)
N.V.	Naamloze Vennootschap (Limited)
p	pico, multiplier (10^{-12}) for SI units
pH	-log10 hydrogen ion concentration
PIB	polyhedral inclusion body
plc	Public Limited Company
post-em.	after emergence
ppb	parts per billion
ppi	pre-plant incorporated
ppm	parts per million
pre-em.	before emergence
q.v.	quod vide (which see)
r.h.	relative humidity
rp-tlc	reversed phase thin layer chromatography
rplc	reversed phase chromatography

s	second(s)
S.A.	Société Anonyme (Company)
SI	International System of Units
sp.	species (singular)
S.p.A.	Societe par Actions (Company)
spp.	species (plural)
t	tonne, 1000 kg
tech.	technical grade
tlc	thin-layer chromatography
UK	United Kingdom
UNEP	United Nations Environment Programme
USDA	United States Department of Agriculture
u.v.	ultraviolet
v.p.	vapour pressure
w	week(s)
WHO	World Health Organisation (of the United Nations)
WIPO	World Intellectual Property Organisation
WSSA	Weed Science Society of America
wt.	weight
y	year(s)
μ	micro, multiplier (10^{-6}) for SI units
>	greater than
$\geq$	greater than or equal to
<	less than
$\leq$	less than or equal to

Reference

Index 1

Chemical Abstract Service (CAS) Registry Numbers

CAS RN	Entry no.	CAS RN	Entry no.
[54-11-5]	1:15	[19396-06-6]	1:20
[57-92-1]	1:28	[19408-46-9]	1:11
[77-06-5]	1:07	[20261-85-2]	1:19
[79-57-2]	1:16	[20711-10-8]	2:71
[80-56-8]	2:47	[20711-10-8]	2:73
[80-56-8]	2:48	[22083-74-5]	1:15
[80-56-8]	2:61	[22976-86-9]	1:21
[83-79-4]	1:25	[26532-22-9]	2:50
[87-51-4]	1:09	[28079-04-1]	2:40
[112-05-0]	1:17	[29804-22-6]	2:35
[112-79-1]	1:06	[31654-77-0]	2:67
[112-80-1]	1:06	[33189-72-9]	2:73
[121-20-0]	1:24	[33596-61-5]	1:19
[121-21-1]	1:23	[33956-49-9]	2:31
[121-29-9]	1:24	[34010-21-4]	2:54
[468-44-0]	1:08	[35597-43-4]	1:04
[510-75-8]	1:08	[35900-26-6]	2:45
[1172-63-0]	1:24	[37248-47-8]	1:29
[1214-39-7]	1:03	[38363-29-0]	2:40
[1569-60-4]	2:61	[40642-40-8]	2:40
[1637-39-4]	1:30	[40716-66-3]	2:44
[1845-30-3]	2:43	[50933-33-0]	2:49
[2027-47-6]	1:06	[51596-10-2]	1:12
[2058-46-0]	1:16	[51596-11-3]	1:12
[2079-00-7]	1:05	[51606-94-4]	2:49
[2540-06-6]	1:23	[52207-99-5]	2:49
[3572-06-3]	2:56	[53042-79-8]	2:49
[3790-78-1]	2:44	[53939-28-9]	2:51
[3810-74-0]	1:28	[53939-28-9]	2:52
[4466-14-2]	1:23	[53939-28-9]	2:53
[4602-84-0]	2:44	[53939-28-9]	2:54
[6980-18-3]	1:10	[54364-63-5]	2:37
[7212-44-4]	2:44	[55774-32-8]	2:37
[7561-71-9]	1:19	[56196-53-3]	2:65
[7681-93-8]	1:14	[60018-04-4]	2:42
[8003-34-7]	1:22	[60018-04-4]	2:43
[11002-92-9]	1:05	[60478-96-8]	2:46
[11113-80-7]	1:20	[60478-96-8]	2:47
[11113-80-7]	1:21	[60478-96-8]	2:48
[11141-17-6]	1:02	[62532-53-0]	2:42
[12767-55-4]	1:05	[62532-53-0]	2:47
[15662-33-6]	1:26	[65195-55-3]	1:01
[16725-53-4]	2:67	[65195-56-4]	1:01
[16725-53-4]	2:72	[65954-19-0]	2:74
[16974-10-0]	2:72	[68038-70-0]	3:90

Index 1 – CAS RN

Index 2

Approved Names, Common Names, Code Numbers and Tradenames

This index lists alphabetically all approved names, common names, code numbers, tradenames and chemical names by which the Main Entries are known. They are referred to by entry number.

Name	Entry no.	Name	Entry no.
(E)-5-10Ac	2:32	Ambly-line cu 25000	4:138
(E)-5-10OH	2:32	Ambly-line d	4:139
(Z)-9-12Ac	2:39	Amblyseius-C	4:138
(Z)-11-14Ac	2:71	*Amblyseius barkeri*	4:136
(3Z,13Z)-18Ac	2:63	*Amblyseius barkeri*	
		(plus *Amblyseius cucumeris*)	4:138
A.q.	3:78	Amblyseius Breeding System (ABS 5)	4:138
AAP 2539	4:143	*Amblyseius californicus*	4:137
Abacide	1:01	*Amblyseius cucumeris*	4:138
abamectin	1:01	Amblyseius cucumeris	
abamectine	1:01	(non-diapause strain)	4:138
ABG-8007	3:133	Amblyseius cucumeris Mite	4:138
Able	3:82	*Amblyseius degenerans*	4:139
Accel	1:03	*Amblyseius fallacis*	4:140
acide gibbérellique	1:07	Amblyseius fallacis	4:140
AcMNPV	3:81	Amblyseius System	4:138
AcNPV	3:81	Amblyseius Thrips Predators	4:138
Acrobe	3:84	ambrosia beetle aggregation	
Adoxophyes orana granulosis virus	3:76	pheromone	2:60
Adult Aphidius	4:143	ambrosia beetle aggregation pheromone	
AfMNPV	3:79	and host kairomones	2:61
AfNPV	3:79	Ambrosia Beetle Trap Lures	2:61
AgMNPV	3:80	Ambsure (abs)	4:138
AgNPV	3:80	Ambsure (c)	4:138
Ago Biocontrol Bassiana 50	3:91	Ambsure (cal)	4:137
Ago Biocontrol Metarhizium 50	3:109	American palm weevil aggregation	
Ago Biocontrol Trichoderma 50	3:133	pheromone	2:66
Ago Biocontrol Vorticillium 50	3:135	*Ampelomyces quisqualis*	3:78
Agree	3:83	*Anagrapha falcifera* NPV	3:79
Agri-Mek	1:01	*Anagrapha falcifera* nucleopolyhedrovirus	
Agrimycin 17	1:28		3:79
Agrispon	1:18	*Anagrus atomus*	4:141
Agrobac	3:82	Anagrus atomus Native Species	4:141
Agrobacterium radiobacter	3:77	Anagsure	4:141
AIA	1:09	Antibiotic B-98891	1:13
aker-tuba	1:25	*Anticarsia gemmatalis* nucleopolyhedrovirus	
Alfadex	1:22		3:80
Align	1:02	AoGV	3:76
als 1 gene	5:176	Aphel-line ab	4:142
AM 301	3:121	Aphelinus-System	4:142
amber disease	3:124	Aphelinus	4:142
Ambly-line cal 2000	4:137	*Aphelinus abdominalis*	4:142

Index 2 – Approved names, common names, code numbers and tradenames

Index 2 – Approved names, common names, code numbers and tradenames

Reference

Reference

333